# FIRST BLITZ

## The Secret German Plan to Raze London to the Ground in 1918

# NEIL HANSON

## Doubleday

LONDON · TORONTO · SYDNEY · AUCKLAND · JOHANNESBURG

TRANSWORLD PUBLISHERS
61–63 Uxbridge Road, London W5 5SA
A Random House Group Company
www.rbooks.co.uk

First published in Great Britain
in 2008 by Doubleday
an imprint of Transworld Publishers

A CIP catalogue record for this book
is available from the British Library.

ISBNs 9780385611701 (cased)
9780385611718 (tpb)

Addresses for Random House Group Ltd companies outside the UK
can be found at: www.randomhouse.co.uk
The Random House Group Ltd Reg. No. 954009

The Random House Group Limited supports The Forest Stewardship
Council (FSC), the leading international forest-certification organization. All our
titles that are printed on Greenpeace-approved FSC-certified paper carry the FSC logo.
Our paper procurement policy can be found at
www.rbooks.co.uk/environment

Typeset in 11/15pt Minion by
Falcon Oast Graphic Art Ltd.

Printed and bound in Great Britain by
Clays Ltd, Bungay, Suffolk

2 4 6 8 10 9 7 5 3

**Mixed Sources**
Product group from well-managed
forests and other controlled sources
www.fsc.org  Cert no. TT-COC-2139
© 1996 Forest Stewardship Council
FSC

For Lynn, Jack and Drew, who make everything worthwhile

*Fliege nach England,*
*England wird abgebrannt.*

Fly to England,
England shall be burned down.

German children's song

'In comparison, the fire of Rome would have seemed a minuscule, match-box affair.'

Diary of Major Wilhelm Siegert, 1918

# CONTENTS

# ACKNOWLEDGEMENTS

My sincere thanks to the staff of the Bodleian Library in Oxford; the British Library in London and its outstation at Boston Spa; the Guildhall Library; the Imperial War Museum; the Trustees of the Liddell Hart Centre for Military Archives, King's College London; the Liddle Collection, Brotherton Library, University of Leeds; the London Library; the London Metropolitan Archives; the National Archives; the Royal Air Force Museum, Hendon; Bayerisches Hauptstaatsarchiv, Munich; Deutsche Bucherei, Leipzig; Generallandesarchiv, Stuttgart; Bundesarchiv-Militärarchiv, Kriegsgeschichtliche Forschungsanstalt des Heeres, Freiburg.

My gratitude also to the individuals who have provided help in all manner of ways, including Frau Ursula Schäfer-Simbolon of the Deutsches Technikmuseum, Berlin; Frau R. Jansen of the Bundesarchiv-Militärarchiv, Freiburg; Herr Dr Wolf Siegert, Berlin; Frau Anne Huhn; Herr Henning Heyne; Patrizia Nava, whose translations from the German were of invaluable assistance to me, and her colleagues Carole Thomas and Thomas Allen at the University of Texas at Dallas; Steph and Andy Burgess for their translation of a vital French document; and Christian Kuhrt, whose research on my behalf in German archives and translation of German documents has added immeasurably to the book.

My thanks as ever to my agent Mark Lucas and his assistant Alice Saunders, in New York to Kim Witherspoon and David Forrer, and to the magnificent team at Transworld including, among many others, Bill Scott-Kerr, Marianne Velmans, Sophie Holmes, Sheila Lee, Helen Edwards, Dan Balado-Lopez, Richard Shailer, Madeline Toy and Deborah Adams.

# CHAPTER 1
# THE FIRST BLOWS

ON CHRISTMAS EVE 1914, whatever might have been taking place across the Channel, Britons continued to enjoy a sense of domestic security, based on the inviolability of their island, that had been undisturbed for centuries. All that was about to change for ever.

At 10.45 that morning, local auctioneer and valuer Tommy Terson was in his garden in the shadow of one of the symbols of that inviolability, Dover Castle. As he was stooping to pick the sprouts for his Christmas dinner, he heard a loud droning sound. Looking up, he saw a dark shape emerging from the clouds drifting over the Channel. A German seaplane had dropped two bombs into the sea near the Admiralty Pier in Dover three days earlier, but this was the first aircraft that Tommy had ever seen.

He watched in amazement as it approached at an almost incomprehensible speed – fifty miles an hour – and passed directly overhead. He was still staring upwards, open-mouthed, when his garden erupted in a cloud of dust, smoke and flying metal. When he picked himself up, unhurt but for a few cuts and bruises, he saw a still-smoking crater, ten feet by four, where his vegetable patch had been. The windows of the surrounding houses had been shattered and Terson's neighbour had been blown out of the tree where he had been cutting holly for Christmas decorations. He also suffered only minor injuries, but the damage to the national psyche was rather more substantial. For the first time ever, the mainland of Britain had been subjected to an attack from the skies, its civilian population deliberately targeted.

Aircraft technology was in its infancy: it was only eleven years since the Wright Brothers' first flight and just five since Louis Blériot had made the first airborne crossing of the Channel. The German Friedrichshafen FF 29 seaplane that carried out the raid on Dover was a canvas-and-wire biplane so crude it 'might almost be compared to the archaeopteryx of prehistoric days'. It was operating at the absolute limit of its fifty-mile range, and so tight were the weight limits to get it airborne at all, even the four 2kg bombs it carried were a serious strain on its capacity. The pilot, Leutnant Karl Caspar, had nothing with which to defend himself other than the Mauser pistol he wore at his belt; but that would have caused him few concerns, for virtually every serviceable British military aircraft was with the British Expeditionary Force in France. Untroubled by any fighter or anti-aircraft gun, Caspar swung his aircraft around and disappeared back into the clouds drifting up the Channel.

The next day, Christmas Day, as most Britons were settling down to their festive meal, there was another, even more sinister attack. At 12.20 that afternoon the gun-crew of the Barton's Point anti-aircraft battery near Sheerness in Kent heard an aircraft approaching from the east. Five minutes later a German seaplane was spotted, flying at an altitude of 7,000 feet. Barton's Point and several other gun-batteries opened fire, but they recorded no hits. The gunners at Beacon Hill, Sheppey, were so overexcited by this first opportunity to engage an enemy that all they contrived to shoot down were their own telephone wires.

Oberleutnant Stephan Prondzynski flew on, following the Thames past Gravesend, Tilbury, Dartford and Erith, before spotting a Vickers 'Gunbus' aircraft rising to intercept him. He could count himself very unfortunate to have happened upon the sole Home Defence aircraft in Britain at the time that could be described as a fighter, and he was forced to turn and fly back towards the coast as the Gunbus began firing bursts at him from its Maxim machine-gun.

As he climbed to escape the ponderous Gunbus, Prondzynski dumped his bombs on the thirteenth-century ragstone-and-flint village church of Cliffe, on the low chalk bluff of the Hoo peninsula, where a Christmas wedding was in progress. 'We heard a noise like someone banging carpets against the walls of the church . . . The happy couple and the guests made an undignified rush for the carriages and home. Bombs had been dropping; we could not partake of the wedding breakfast because some of the guests fainted.' Their discomfiture would have been of far less concern to the Government than the knowledge that when he turned back the German raider had been within five miles of Woolwich Arsenal and the start of London's sprawling docklands. The implication was clear: the nation's vital industries and the capital itself were now within range of German bombs.

The French authorities were already aware that Paris, only sixty miles from the front lines, was a target for German bombers. On 13 August 1914, just ten days after Germany's declaration of war with France, a Taube aeroplane had dropped two or three small bombs on the Quai de Valmy in

Paris – the first ever attack on a capital city by an aircraft. It also dropped a leaflet that read 'Parisians, attention! This is the greeting of a German aircraft.' In a second raid on 30 August, five bombs fell on Paris, killing three civilians, and in a further attack a few days later another German pilot, Hauptmann Keller, dropped six 10kg bombs on the Gare de l'Est. 'Undisturbed by defensive fire and aircraft, I could let myself go and be enchanted completely by the sight of the capital in the autumn sun' – a strangely poetic description of the city he was doing his best to destroy. Afternoon raids became such a regular event during the following months that Parisians would 'assemble along the River Seine or another good viewing place to watch for the arrival of the German plane, which became known as *les cinq heures du Taube*.'

The civilized world's attitude to the bombing of cities far removed from the front lines of a conflict had been expressed in resolutions passed by Peace Conferences held at The Hague in 1899 and 1907, and was reiterated at a further conference after the First World War was over. 'Aerial bombardment is legitimate only when it is directed against a military objective, i.e. an objective whereof the total or partial destruction would constitute an obvious military advantage for the belligerent ... Aerial bombardment for the purpose of terrorising the civilian population, of destroying or damaging private property not of a military character, or of injuring non-combatants, is prohibited.'

Military commanders were often less concerned with niceties of legitimacy and morality than their political masters, and one of the first significant theorists of air power, the Italian General Giulio Douhet, took a more pragmatic stance on the question of bombing cities. 'The complete destruction of the objective has moral and material effects ... we need only envision what would go on among the civilian population of congested cities once the enemy announced that he would bomb such centres relentlessly, making no distinction between military and non-military objectives.'

The bombing of cities and civilian populations was also entirely in keeping with the German General Staff's belief in unlimited warfare and *Schrecklichkeit* – acts of 'frightfulness', what might now be called 'shock and awe' – that would sap an enemy's will to resist, an attitude encapsulated in a document published in 1902, *Kriegsbrauche im Landkriege* (The Custom of War in Land Warfare). It stated that 'The conduct of war allows any belligerent state to employ any means which will facilitate the accomplishment of the aim of war . . . A war waged with energy cannot be directed solely against the combatants of the hostile state and the positions which they defend, but will and *should* equally endeavour to destroy the collective intellectual and material resources of the enemy. Humanitarian considerations, such as would protect individuals or their property, can only be regarded in so far as the nature and the object of war will allow.' Not only the 'fortresses, but also every town and village which may be an impediment to military progress . . . may be besieged, bombarded, stormed and destroyed if the enemy defends them, and in some cases if he only occupies them'.

When war was declared, the German Minister in Stockholm, Franz von Reichenau, expressed the hope 'with all his heart' that German airships and aircraft would drop bombs on England until the 'vulgar huckster souls' and 'cowardly assassins' had forgotten 'even how to do sums'. Admiral Paul Behncke, the Deputy Chief of the Naval Staff, was equally bellicose and sent a memo to his superior, Admiral Hugo von Pohl, urging the bombing of London. The target was uniquely vulnerable. One of the most densely populated cities in the world, London was not merely the political and administrative hub of Britain and the Empire, and the headquarters of its military establishment, it was the nation's principal manufacturing and warehousing site, its prime seaport, the nexus of its railway system, and the home of a banking and insurance system that covered the world.

The celebrated German air ace Max Boelcke might complain that the main result of bombing a city was likely to be 'the death of an old woman', but the commander of the Zeppelin fleet, Korvettenkapitän Peter Strasser, probably spoke for the majority of German pilots when he remarked, 'if what we do is frightful, then may frightfulness be Germany's salvation'. Admiral von Tirpitz claimed that he was 'not in favour of the evil policy . . . of "frightfulness"' and called 'the indiscriminate dropping of bombs . . . repulsive when they kill and maim children and old women', but he then added that 'if one could set fire to London in thirty places, then what in a small way is odious would retire before something fine and powerful. All that flies and creeps should be concentrated on that city.' It was the first expression of a secret strategy that was to be employed to bring Britain to its knees: *Der Feuerplan* (The Fire Plan) – 'England shall be destroyed by fire'. Air-dropped incendiary bombs would create firestorms engulfing entire districts of London, creating mass panic and popular unrest that would 'render it doubtful that the war can continue' and force the British Government to sue for peace.

It was ironic that the target of this first airborne 'blitz' was to be Britain, the only country at the 1899 Peace Conference at The Hague whose representative had refused to sign an agreement prohibiting 'the dropping of projectiles or explosives from balloons or other airships'. Britain's Lord Wolseley had argued that dropping bombs would 'confer an enormous advantage on a power like Britain that possessed only a small army' and that British prowess in science and industry should not be undermined by prohibitions imposed by less successful nations. Although Britain did sign the amended declaration produced eight years later, at The Hague Peace Conference in 1907, Germany did not, and German scientific and industrial prowess would now be used to put Britain to the test.

In the face of this new and potentially overwhelming threat, Britain's air defences were almost non-existent. As early as 1908, a group of British aircraft manufacturers had been rebuffed by the War Office when they attempted to promote the military virtues of aircraft. Colonel J. E. B. Seely, Parliamentary Private Secretary to Minister for War Viscount Haldane, explained, 'we do not consider that aeroplanes will be of any possible use for war purposes'. Although Lord Montagu of Beaulieu warned in 1911 that air-raids would be 'more nerve-shattering and would do more to shake the confidence of a people than a definite threat on sea or land' and called for 'an adequate air force' to be constructed, his words went unheeded.

The reluctance of the War Office and the Admiralty to embrace military aviation was heightened by a fear that by so doing they would undermine the Navy, Britain's traditional defensive system and the under-pinning of her imperial power. 'We stood to gain nothing by forcing a means of warfare which tended to reduce the value of our insular position and the protection of our sea power.' Lest anyone still be in any doubt, Sir William Nicholson, Chief of the General Staff from 1908 to 1912, spelled it out in even more explicit terms: aviation was a 'useless and expensive fad advocated by a few individuals whose ideas are unworthy of attention'.

Pre-war literature had predicted the combat role of aircraft and airships, and the targeting of civilian populations through bombing raids, and fears of air attack were fanned by the 1911 release of a film showing a city viewed from the control car of a Zeppelin. 'What strikes the viewer even today is the massive and menacing shadow of the airship cast upon the defenceless buildings below.' Widely seen in Britain, the film provoked an 'airship panic' and was probably one of the prime causes of the rash of bogus 'sightings' of Zeppelins hovering over ports, cities and military installations that continued throughout the pre-war years.

In the event of war, it was widely assumed that 'terror-raids' would cause mass panic and a collapse of civilian morale. British forces could already testify to the efficacy of terror bombardment, albeit using ships' guns rather than bombs, having shelled Alexandria 'from sunrise to sunset' in 1882. During the night, the city was 'transformed into a sea of fire' and reduced to 'rubble and ash', though perfidious Albion claimed that the Egyptians had burned their own city to cover their retreat.

Of all the First World War combatants, only Italy, France and Bulgaria (which, allying itself with Germany, declared war on Serbia on 12 October 1915) had any prior experience of the military use of aircraft. From the very start the use of air-dropped bombs was indiscriminate, attacking civilian as well as military targets. 'The floodgates of blood and lust' were thrown open and what followed 'was not war. It was butchery.' The first man to drop a bomb from an aeroplane was an Italian, Lieutenant Giulio Cavotti, during the colonial war in Libya, when on 1 November 1911 he released the first of four 2kg projectiles on the oasis of Tagiura, near Tripoli. Another Italian pilot became the first to use an incendiary bomb during the same conflict.

The following year, 1912, France sent six aircraft on 'police actions' in Morocco. Knowing the inaccuracy of their bomb-aiming, the pilots deliberately chose 'large targets – villages, markets, grazing herds'. In 1913, Spain, which was to remain neutral in the First World War, also bombed its colonial possessions in Spanish Morocco, using German 'cartouche bombs' packed with ball bearings to spread their destructive impact to 'as many living targets as possible'. And during the war with Turkey in 1912–13 a small Bulgarian air force using mercenary pilots dropped leaflets on Adrianople (modern Edirne) ordering the city to surrender or 'be set on fire by aerial bombardment'; it was then attacked with 10kg bombs.

France and Germany were also pressing ahead with the development of their fledgling air forces. As early as 1910, General Roques, France's first Director of Aviation, had proposed arming aircraft with machine-guns, and using *fléchettes* (steel darts), shells or bombs to attack and demoralize enemy troops – a plan adopted by Belgian forces after war broke out, when their aeroplanes bombed the advancing German troops with 'iron arrows'. The Germans described the attacks as 'aerial terrorism ... these crude weapons having the reputation to pass through a horse and his rider to kill both', a complaint that might have been justified had not German air-crews on the Eastern Front also been dropping steel *Fliegerpfeilen* (flyer's arrows).

Senior French officers had openly discussed carrying out bombing raids on German cities to terrify the civilian population. The French Army fitted aircraft with machine-guns and incendiary shells but tests of their effectiveness were inconclusive, and, like many of his British counterparts, the future Allied Supreme Commander General Ferdinand Foch was reported to have dismissed the whole idea of using aircraft as offensive weapons, describing their value thus: 'as an instrument of war, *c'est zéro*'. He may also have been influenced by their safety record: two hundred French 'aviation deaths' were recorded in 1913 alone. Another French officer said that arming aircraft smacked 'more of Jules Verne than of real-ity' and could only distract pilots from their primary task.

In Germany there were visionary officers, such as Major Wilhelm Siegert, who foresaw aircraft being used in aerial combat, strategic and tactical bombing and ground-attack roles, and the first Chief of the German Air Staff, General Max von Wever, who proposed the construction of a heavy bomber fleet; but he died in an air crash soon afterwards, and others who saw the role of aircraft as primarily tactical took his place. By early 1914 the German General Staff had not advanced beyond considering arming some planes with machine-guns.

However, with the development of the Zeppelin – its inventor, Count Ferdinand von Zeppelin, had been hailed by the Kaiser as 'the greatest German of the twentieth century' before its first decade was even over – Germany had a clear lead in airship technology. Many in the military, including Helmuth von Moltke, Chief of the German General Staff, believed that it could help them launch a devastating and potentially decisive strike against the Allies. Speaking in 1912, von Moltke claimed that the Zeppelin was a weapon 'far superior to all similar ones of our opponents and cannot be imitated in the foreseeable future if we work energetically to perfect it. Its speediest development as a weapon is required to enable us at the beginning of a war to strike a first and telling blow whose practical and moral effect could be quite extraordinary.'

By 1912, the pace of development overseas, particularly in France and Germany, could no longer be ignored in Britain. The military potential of aircraft was being nightly demonstrated in 'aerial war-games' at Hendon featuring 'bombing, aerial flights and even night-flying with the aid of huge searchlights', and in April of that year Colonel Seely, by now promoted to Under-Secretary of State for War, announced the creation of the Royal Flying Corps.

The planning of the new corps was meticulous in every aspect except one crucial area. The RFC would include a pilot training establishment: the Central Flying School; a production and development facility: the Royal Aircraft Factory at Farnborough; a reserve section and two active service units: the Military and Naval Wings. However, there was to be no unified command structure; the Military Wing of the new Royal Flying Corps would be controlled by the War Office, and the Naval Wing by the Admiralty. Since the two perpetually feuding bodies could not even agree on the types of aircraft they should build nor the roles that they would fulfil, it was a flaw that would hamper the RFC throughout its brief existence.

The unfortunate Colonel Seely was deputed to chair the Air Committee, set up in July 1912 to coordinate the activities of the two wings of the RFC, but Prime Minister Asquith gave him no effective executive power and the refusal of the Admiralty in particular to collaborate with its rival ensured the committee's perpetual impotence. It met with less and less regularity, and though never formally abolished, eventually it ceased to meet at all.

Brigadier General David Henderson, commander of the Military Wing, was one of Britain's earliest and oldest military pilots, having learned to fly in 1911 at the age of forty-nine, but his failure to comprehend the aerial threat that now faced his country was revealed by his comment that Germany would not bomb 'undefended towns . . . no enemy would risk the odium such action would involve'. The War Office insisted that the vast majority of the RFC's aircraft would be required only for aerial reconnaissance and target-spotting for the ground troops of the British Expeditionary Force, and even that role was dismissed by the future British Commander-in-Chief General Douglas Haig, who told an audience of officers in 1914, 'I hope none of you gentlemen is so foolish as to think that aeroplanes will be able to be usefully employed for reconnaissance purposes in the air. There is only one way for a commander to get information by reconnaissance, and that is by the use of cavalry.' Given that Haig's forces had been thrashed at the 1912 Army manoeuvres by General Grierson's troops who had 'made full use of aerial reconnaissance' to defeat him, it was an extraordinarily blinkered statement.

The slow BE two-seater aircraft produced by the Royal Aircraft Factory were adequate – just – for reconnaissance, indeed a lack of speed was held to be essential for it; in 1913 Henderson had ordered the Royal Aircraft Factory not to produce any engines exceeding 100 horsepower. One 'air expert' made the even more bizarre claim that aircraft would be useless for bombing until machines capable of travelling even more slowly were developed. His view was shared by many others at the time, and as a result the RFC went to war 'equipped with machines that were too slow to catch the enemy (and would have been unable to hurt them even if they could have caught them), that could not attack Zeppelins, and that were incapable of manoeuvring out of trouble if attacked by enemy machines or ground fire'.

Unofficial attempts by pilots to improve their or their aircraft's fighting capacity were also likely to fall foul of the prejudices of hidebound senior officers. In August 1914, as the country went to war, Louis Strange of the RFC's 5 Squadron was ordered to remove the Lewis gun he had mounted on his biplane, and pilots were actively discouraged from aerobatics such as rolls, loops, dives and spins – the very essence of fighter tactics that might bring victory in combat or save their lives when targeted themselves, but which were dismissed by the commander of the Military Wing as 'merely cheap selfishness' bringing 'discredit'.

While insisting on the primacy of the reconnaissance role, the War Office was also simultaneously claiming sole responsibility for the air defence of the United Kingdom, for which BE two-seaters were virtually useless. As Winston Churchill, First Lord of the Admiralty, acerbically noted, 'When asked how they proposed to discharge this duty, they admitted that they had not got the machines and could not get the money.' Nor did they have any engines: partly as a result of Henderson's strictures, not a single British aero engine of suitable quality was being produced and the RFC was dependent on France for supplies. The shortage of pilots was even more critical. As Seely revealed with masterly British understatement, the Army 'had about eleven actual flying men' and the Navy 'about eight ... France has about 263, so we are what you might call behind'. They remained that way for some time; the pre-war restriction of pilots to 'gentlemen flyers' who could afford the £75 bill for the only recognized qualification, the Aero Club Certificate of Competence, was unofficially maintained by the snobbery and social exclusion of the RFC.

It was widely assumed that a gentleman who could ride could also fly an aircraft. One officer stressed the need for 'sensitive hands', as if an aircraft was fitted with a bridle and bit, and as late as January 1917 the Deputy Director General of Military Aeronautics remarked that 'flying is perhaps a little easier than riding a horse because you sit in a comfortable armchair instead of a slippery saddle on a lively horse'. The gentlemen also tended to treat their aircraft as their own private runabouts; the official historian of the RFC recorded a number of cases in which pilot officers went missing for up to a week, and then reappeared claiming that they had been the victims of mechanical failure when in fact they had been guests at a house party in some stately home.

Such fossilized attitudes underwent a slow erosion as the rate of losses on the Western Front forced the recruitment as pilots of a class of men who had never ridden to hounds. Among them was James McCudden, a former boy-soldier in the Royal Engineers, who transferred to the RFC and became an aircraft fitter, then an observer, and finally one of the few NCO pilots. He proved so brave and skilful in air combat that he became one of Britain's greatest fighter aces and was awarded the Victoria Cross.

While the RFC maintained its gentlemanly pursuits, it was left to the rival Naval Wing – where the ambitious plans of Murray Sueter, Director of the Air Department at the Admiralty, received Churchill's wholehearted backing – to carry out pre-war tests on airborne machine-guns, bombs and torpedoes. They produced 'a crude but workable' bomb-release gear, and carried out development work on a bombsight and a reliable aerial compass. In their efforts to find a counter to the potential threat posed by Zeppelins, the Naval Wing also experimented with shotguns firing chain-shot, shells attached to grappling hooks, and even fitted a Vickers semi-automatic cannon to an aircraft. The experiment was not a complete success: the recoil from the gun was so powerful that each time it was fired it stopped the aircraft dead in mid-air and caused it to plummet 500 feet. Even more eccentric was the plan for an 'aerial minefield' of mines dangling from balloons on a cable. It was rejected out of hand by Churchill, who commented, 'since Damocles, there has been no such experiment', though, without the mines, screens of barrage balloons would later form a vital component of British air defences.

After the declaration of war in August 1914, the Admiralty announced that it was forming the Naval Wing into the Royal Naval Air Service, the death-knell to any hope of unifying the Royal Flying Corps. Britain was now effectively saddled with two rival air forces, each with its own distinct training methods, aircraft and equipment, and temperamentally dis-inclined to cross-service cooperation.

Virtually the entire strength of the RFC – and that was feeble enough – was sent to France with the British Expeditionary Force. Germany had put 180 aircraft into service on the Western Front alone; in response, the RFC could put only four squadrons of twelve aircraft in the field and they were of such varied makes, vintages and conditions that their fitness for the task at hand was dubious in the extreme. Meanwhile, the air defence of

Britain was dependent on the solitary Vickers Gunbus and the handful of geriatric or decrepit aircraft that had been deemed unfit for frontline service overseas. Anti-aircraft guns were equally sparse, and the barrels of virtually none of the existing artillery pieces could be elevated far enough to fire at aircraft.

Churchill and the First Sea Lord, Lord Fisher, had made Admiralty funds available by 'various shifts and devices' and were able to 'scrape and smuggle together' seventy-one aircraft. Divided among a number of air stations along the south and south-east coasts, they constituted virtually the only defence against an airborne attack on Britain.

The assault on Antwerp on 26 August 1914, during which 800kg of bombs were dropped on the city by German Zeppelins, reawakened the fears and apprehensions among British civilians about air attacks, and concentrated British military minds. Realizing that the RFC was unable to play any worthwhile role at that stage, on 3 September the War Minister, Lord Kitchener, asked the Admiralty to assume full responsibility for Britain's air defence. Churchill, who earlier that year had made the hollow claim that any hostile aircraft attacking England would be 'promptly attacked, and in superior force, by a swarm of formidable hornets', now had to try to justify his words by undertaking 'very reluctantly ... the thankless and – as it seemed then – the almost hopeless task' of doing 'what was possible with the wholly inadequate resources which were available'.

He wasted little time. On 5 September he circulated a detailed memo setting out his priorities for the air defence of Britain which, given the importance of the capital's ports, munitions factories and military and political infrastructure, effectively meant London. With characteristic energy and enthusiasm, and an equally characteristic distaste for red tape and any opinions other than his own, Churchill threw himself into the task of improving Britain's feeble air defences. In a series of brusque memoranda he dealt with the deployment of aircraft to defend the coast and the capital, the siting of anti-aircraft guns and searchlights, and the provision and lighting of airfields and temporary landing strips. Instructions were also issued for 'the guidance of the police, Fire Brigade and civil population under bombardment. This will have to be sustained with composure.'

Churchill ordered flights of RNAS aircraft to be stationed at Calshot, Eastchurch and Hendon. Their first priority was to defend the ports and naval facilities; they would only operate inland when enemy aircraft or Zeppelins had actually crossed the coastline. The handful of RFC aircraft were based at Hounslow and Joyce Green, near Dartford, and floodlit landing strips were also established in London parks so that aircraft could operate by day or night. In a bizarre reversal, the anti-aircraft batteries around the ports were manned by Army crews, while naval guns, crewed by naval ratings, were set up around London to act as anti-aircraft guns, though a shortage of suitable gunners for London's defence then had to be alleviated by recruiting part-time volunteers.

A limited blackout system was also introduced. On 1 October 1914, the Home Secretary, Reginald McKenna, prohibited illuminated signs and ordered shop and street lighting to be partially obscured. At first street-lamps were merely fitted with hoods to screen their light from the sky, but the pools of light they cast on the ground were just as visible from the air, and in December further controls were introduced. Since the vast majority of street-lamps were gaslights that had to be lit and extinguished in-dividually, it was impossible to turn them off within five minutes of receiving a warning of an impending air-raid, as required by order of General Headquarters, Home Forces, and many thousands of street-lamps were permanently extinguished. The glass panes of the remainder were obscured by dark blue or black paint so that they cast only a dim, un-certain light. Whitewashing the kerbstones did not compensate for the lack of light from overhead, and on dark nights pedestrians had to grope their way along the unlit streets.

Shop lights were further dimmed, and buses and trams were 'lit only enough to collect fares. Street markets closed at dusk. Black curtains became the rule.' Panic about air-raids 'ran rampant ... little Minnie O'Brien, with her bent little legs and pinched face showing childhood's rickets' came crying to Sylvia Pankhurst 'to tell me her father had smacked her face when she sat playing the piano after dusk, the gas lit and the dark curtains not drawn'.

Other British cities were even darker than the capital. In Sheffield no more than forty-five out of a total of twelve thousand street lights were in use, and even those were extinguished at 7.30 in the evening. After that the only light was provided by the headlights of passing trams, and they ceased to run at eleven o'clock. Houses were also blacked out with thick curtains, screens or blankets, a 'complete exclusion of light from all houses and windows, and later from trains, churches and road lamps; oh, how dreary the winter world looked'. The fear of attracting air-raids was so great that there were prosecutions, and convictions, for striking matches in the open; even 'a lighted cigarette-end was enough at times to gain a man a blow'. The darkness was welcomed by criminals. Burglaries and street crimes showed sharp increases and there were appeals for street lighting to be improved, but many people found the pitch darkness of the night streets reassuring, on the semi-superstitious grounds that if the German raiders couldn't see them, they couldn't attack them.

While the city itself was blacked out, fake lighting was installed in open areas such as parks and commons to confuse German pilots and navigators trying to fix the position of their targets by reference to known landmarks; but little or nothing could be done to conceal the dome of St Paul's, Big Ben or the bridges over the Thames. The lake in St James's Park had been drained to prevent its moonlit reflection being used by German raiders to orient themselves, but the Lea Valley reservoir that supplied much of the capital's water supply could not be drained, and in any event, the Thames provided an unmistakable marker by day and on any cloudless night.

Despite the defensive measures he had ordered, Churchill had no intention of merely waiting for German raiders to appear in British skies. He had informed the House of Commons on 17 March 1914 that 'passive defence against aircraft is perfectly hopeless and endless. You would have to roof in the world to be quite sure', and he would wholeheartedly have endorsed the view of the German air pioneer Major Wilhelm Siegert that 'an air blockade as an end in itself is nothing but an admission of one's own weakness. Is there nothing better against burglary than a passive closing of the door?' The Admiralty's purchases of bomber aircraft had already signalled Churchill's aggressive intentions, and they were confirmed as early as 5 September by his assertion that 'the great defence against aerial menace is to attack the enemy's aircraft as near as possible to their point of departure'.

A key part of this doctrine was that the RNAS should set up a forward base in Dunkirk to bomb the bases in Belgium from which German air attacks on Britain would be launched. Murray Sueter, commander of the RNAS, shared Churchill's enthusiasm for attacks on Zeppelin 'sheds', targets 'bigger than a battleship and more vulnerable than the Crystal Palace', and on 22 September 1914, Captain E. L. Gerrard and Lieutenant Charles Collett, flying Sopwith Tabloids from the Eastchurch RNAS squadron, took off from Antwerp to attack the Zeppelin base at Dusseldorf, while Commander D. A. Spencer-Grey and Flight Lieutenant Reggie Marix targeted the Cologne base.

The raid was not a success. Although they achieved complete surprise, fog was shrouding the targets; Collett compared his task to 'going into a dark room to look for a black cat'. Only one pilot located his target, and of the three bombs he dropped one missed completely and the other two failed to explode. On 8 October they tried again. Spencer-Grey once more failed to find his target because of mist and bombed the Cologne railway station instead, but Marix found the Zeppelin sheds and two direct hits on a hangar ignited the airship inside, sending a pillar of flame hundreds of feet into the air. It was the first successful British bombing attack on Germany.

The following month, four new aircraft were shipped, still crated, straight from the Avro factory in Manchester to Belfort in eastern France. There they were assembled, fuelled and armed, and on 21 November they were launched against the Zeppelin works at Friedrichshafen on Lake Constance, a site the Germans had considered invulnerable to air attack. The raid was planned by Lieutenant Noel Pemberton-Billing, who carried out a reconnaissance of the target by dressing in peasant costume, travelling across neutral Switzerland and crossing Lake Constance by rowing boat, then hiding out on the German shore for a day and a night.

Of the four British aircraft, one failed to get airborne because of engine problems, but the other three dropped a total of nine bombs on the Zeppelin sheds and the neighbouring hydrogen plant. The aircraft piloted by Commander E. F. Briggs was shot down by ground fire, but the other two pilots, Flight Commander Babington and Flight Lieutenant Sippe, returned to base to a hero's welcome and the award of the Légion d'Honneur from their delighted French allies. The German leadership protested that bombs had been dropped 'in a barbaric manner upon innocent civilians' and, under pressure from Berlin, the neutral Swiss Government complained that its airspace had been violated and one of its nationals killed in the raid. In response, Churchill reportedly told them to 'go and milk their cows'.

The RFC did not share his enthusiasm for strategic bombing, after the dismal failure of early attempts on the Western Front, including raids launched on railheads and stations well behind the lines to impede the movement of German troops during the battles of Neuve Chapelle and Loos. Of 141 targets attacked, only three were hit, and the RFC's aircraft were henceforth confined to ground support and 'contact patrols' over the front line.

Despite the RNAS's early successes, Churchill's policy of pre-emptive attack did not survive his tenure as First Lord of the Admiralty. In May 1915 the disastrous failure of the campaign at Gallipoli that Churchill had championed forced him to resign. His successor, Arthur J. Balfour, was a man cut from entirely different cloth, a prognosticator and prevaricator whose preferred method of action was always inaction, or, if pressed, to form a committee. Balfour ordered the immediate cessation of attacks on Zeppelin bases and later signalled a major shift in the Admiralty's aviation policy by commissioning a series of rigid airships like the German Zeppelins. Millions of pounds – Churchill later claimed that £40 million had been spent – that could have bought faster and more powerful fighter and bomber aircraft were instead diverted to the airship project, and not a single one of these airships ever rendered any useful war service.

# CHAPTER 2
# ZEPPELINS OVERHEAD

THE VICKERS GUNBUS THAT HAD PURSUED the Christmas Day raider down the Thames may have deterred further aircraft attacks on London by giving the Germans an entirely false impression of the efficiency of the capital's air defences, and the sporadic coastal raids by German aircraft over the months following those first attacks on England had little more than nuisance value. Bombs were small and inaccurate, dropped by hand without aiming mechanisms, and aircraft remained fragile, unstable and mechanically temperamental death-traps for their pilots. London was also at the outer limits of range from the nearest German-occupied territory, and any attempt to use more than a token bombload put the city beyond reach of aircraft altogether – but not of Zeppelins, which posed a far more significant and immediate threat. Although unwieldy and vulnerable to high winds, they could carry a much heavier bombload than the existing aircraft and were becoming an increasingly ominous presence in British skies.

The air offensive had initially been hampered by the reluctance of the Kaiser and his Chancellor, Theobald von Bethmann-Hollweg, to countenance attacks on London. The Kaiser feared for the safety of the capital's monuments, cathedrals and palaces if air attacks were mounted and, much as he resented his English cousins, he had no wish to preside over their murder. The Chancellor, a dapper figure with a manicured goatee, was similarly reluctant. Although he had justified the German invasion of neutral Belgium with the comment 'necessity knows no law', he was also a confirmed Anglophile who had served at the German Embassy in London before the war and lived in suburban Walton-on-Thames.

Zeppelin attacks on England had been proposed as early as 2 October 1914, but in the face of opposition from the Kaiser and the Chancellor, the elderly and ailing Admiral Pohl at first resisted the clamour for an all-out air assault from his subordinates. However, by the end of the year, with stalemate setting in along the Western Front and his junior officers chafing at the restrictions, he persuaded the Kaiser to give his grudging approval to limited bombing raids on areas outside London, while 'historic buildings and private property will be spared as much as possible'. On the night of 19/20 January 1915, two German Zeppelins dropped a series of 50kg high-explosive bombs and 3kg incendiaries on Great Yarmouth, King's

Lynn and several small villages in Norfolk, though one pilot claimed he had bombed 'fortified places' between the Rivers Tyne and Humber.

News of the raid was greeted with wild acclaim in Germany, where *'Gott strafe England'* was already a national rallying cry, daubed on walls, fences and lamp-posts and recited by German schoolchildren in their daily morning assemblies. Germany's rulers were less delighted: the Chancellor complained that bombing 'apparently undefended places makes a very unfavourable impression on foreign neutrals, particularly in America', and the Kaiser once more reiterated his implacable opposition to bombing attacks on 'residential areas of London and, above all, on royal palaces', though for the first time he did concede that the London docks were legitimate targets. His commanders chose to interpret that as permission to bomb anything east of Charing Cross station, forcing the Kaiser to issue a warning that they were 'going beyond his wishes and desires'; but his resolve continued to erode under relentless pressure from his officers, aided and abetted by the new Chief of the Naval Staff, Admiral Gustav Bachmann, who had replaced the dying Admiral Pohl in February.

On 30 May 1915, after procrastinating for three weeks, the Kaiser was persuaded to sign an edict legitimizing air-raids on all of London east of the Tower. The following night, 31 May, the first attempt to initiate the Fire Plan was made as London was bombed for the very first time. It had been a bright spring day, though unseasonably cold, and smoke from thousands of domestic fires was rising into the still air as dusk fell. Crossing the Belgian coast at sunset, Hauptmann Erich Linnarz, piloting Zeppelin L38, arrived over England under cover of darkness, though a bright moon was shining. He crossed the coast near Margate at 9.40 p.m. and overflew London at around eleven o'clock on that beautiful night. The city was clearly visible, illuminated by the street lights that, although dimmed, were still left burning, and Linnarz had dropped his bombs – eighty-seven incendiaries and twenty-five high-explosive projectiles – and was on his way back to base before dawn broke.

Heralded by the deep throb of its powerful engines, the dark, menacing Zeppelin – a blacker shape, barely visible against the night sky – instilled terror in London's population. The fear was heightened when, as sometimes happened, the throb of the engines was apparently stilled and the Zeppelin drifted, silent, on the wind over the City. Like their children under the V-bombs a generation later, Londoners endured agonies of fear and uncertainty in that long silence before the first explosion shook the streets. Only the roar and thunder of detonating bombs marked the track of the airship as it flew on. In fact, no Zeppelin commander would have cut his engines deliberately – they could have frozen at the altitudes at which they were flying – but the sound of the engines was sometimes carried away on the wind, giving listeners below the illusion of a 'silent raid'.

Stoke Newington, Dalston, Stepney and Shoreditch, north-east and east of Central London, suffered the worst damage and casualties in the raid, and the Fire Brigade was almost overwhelmed by calls – seven in the space of four minutes at the height of the raid. Some were minor blazes, but others 'burned furiously for over an hour, casting a lurid glow' into a night sky 'red with the reflection of many fires'. Three serious fires required a number of engines, and one necessitated 'a district call', pulling in all the available engines from that area, but all were eventually extinguished without merging into a more general conflagration. Had more of the incendiaries ignited rather than falling as 'duds', the problems might have been far worse.

Two young children, May and Elsie Leggatt, received fatal burns when one of the incendiaries struck a house in Cowper Road, Stoke Newington, and Mr and Mrs Good died in a fire that gutted a large house in Balls Pond Road, Dalston. Their charred bodies were found the next morning, kneeling together at the side of their bed, Mr Good's arm still around the waist of his wife. Two other children, Lily Lehrmann and Samuel Reuben, on their way home from the cinema, were also killed by shrapnel as they tried to shelter from the bombs in a shop doorway in Commercial Road, Stepney.

The communiqué hurriedly issued by the Admiralty in the aftermath of that first raid on London was a masterpiece of obfuscation: 'Zeppelins are reported to have been seen near Ramsgate and Brentford, and in certain outlying parts of London. Many fires are reported but these cannot absolutely be connected with the visit of airships.' The idea that 'many fires' would have broken out simultaneously without the ominous presence of Zeppelins overhead was so laughable to Londoners that it made them regard future official announcements about air-raids, including the more accurate one issued late the following day, with great scepticism.

A Leipzig newspaper, with considerable hyperbole, proclaimed that 'The City of London, the heart which pumps the lifeblood into the arteries of the brutal huckster nation, has been sown with bombs', but German elation at the success of the raid was muted in some quarters, for inter-service rivalries were as intense in Berlin as they were in London. Aircraft manufacturer Anthony Fokker revealed how, on the very day that war was declared, 'an army telegram reached me confiscating all planes for its use. The next day an excited naval commander, frothing at the mouth . . . ordered that all my planes must be turned over to the navy. Price was no object . . . It seemed to make no difference whether the airplanes would be of any use to the navy once they got them . . . My mood was to say yes to everyone and sell to the first buyer who plonked down his money on the barrel-head.'

To the undisguised fury of the Imperial Admirals, not only had this first raid on the enemy capital been made by an Army airship, but virtually all the targets 'of direct service to the [British] war effort' that the Navy's spies and reconnaissance had identified – the main railway stations, the Stock Exchange, the Bank of England, the Admiralty, the War Office and the rest of the commercial, legislative and administrative infrastructure – remained out of bounds to German airships and aircraft.

Admiral Bachmann was a fervent advocate of unrestricted warfare on all fronts – he was soon to resign over the Kaiser's refusal to endorse an all-out U-boat campaign against merchant shipping – and a French air-raid on Karlsruhe on 15 June, an 'open town, far from the theatre of operations, and not in any way fortified', that killed twenty-nine civilians and wounded fifty-eight gave him the pretext to lobby the Kaiser once more. Bachmann first persuaded Bethmann-Hollweg that the time had come to remove the restrictions on bombing London, though the Chancellor continued to argue that raids should take place only at weekends when the City was largely empty of people. Bachmann then pointed out that this also applied every night, and on 20 July he at last won the agreement of the

Chancellor and the Kaiser to unrestricted air-raids on London, saving only the royal palaces and 'national shrines' such as St Paul's, Westminster Abbey and the Tower of London.

Bachmann was happy to agree to this restriction, though, given the imprecision of the bombsights then in use, his pledge was really little more than a pious hope. As a British air force commander later remarked, the techniques of bombing at the time were 'much more of a spray than a hypodermic. Under peace conditions . . . it is estimated that eighteen per cent of bombs would be effective against an isolated target such as a battleship or building, dropped from ceiling height. But the generality of pilots, or of bombing crews, especially in the unsteadying condition of active service flight, would lower this average exceedingly and that is why a city target, nearly all bull's-eye, offers the fairest measure of success . . . but the rain of bombs would still descend on the just and the unjust alike.'

The first attack on London was followed by a succession of other raids on the south-east and eastern counties. As the Zeppelin crews made concerted attempts to activate the Fire Plan, up to three-quarters of the bombloads they carried were incendiaries. One hundred and ninety-eight of the 278 bombs dropped on London in four Zeppelin raids on 31 May, 7 and 8 September, and 13 October 1915 were incendiaries, but they proved inadequate in every respect. Unreliable at detonation – over half failed to ignite – inefficient at combustion and easy to extinguish, they nonetheless registered one considerable success.

During the 8 September raid, a single airship, Zeppelin L13, under the command of the thirty-two-year-old Leutnant Heinrich Mathy, targeted the Cripplegate garment manufacturing district, bounded by Aldersgate Street, London Wall, Moorgate and Cheapside, where German Intelligence had reported that a fire in 1897 had 'raged out of control' and become the most serious conflagration in London since the Great Fire of 1666. 'Several large blocks of business premises were set on fire, many completely gutted, and all seriously damaged.' Fifty-one of the fifty-nine fire engines available to the London Fire Brigade had been required to bring that blaze under control.

Mathy dropped forty-five incendiaries and thirteen high-explosive bombs on this district, and at the height of the ensuing fires, twenty-two motor-pumps were fighting blazes around Wood Street alone. Warehouse after warehouse was engulfed and gutted, killing twenty-two people and causing half a million pounds' worth of property damage, a third of the total inflicted on Britain during the entire Zeppelin campaign. Had even one more fire of similar intensity broken out elsewhere in London at the same time, the fire services would have been stretched to breaking point, 'and of course, the whole point of the German plan was that such outbreaks should occur, practically simultaneously at a dozen different points'.

Struggling to combat the Zeppelin threat, the Admiralty was put under further strain by the growing U-boat menace. By mid-1915 most of its aircraft were engaged on anti-submarine patrols, and it was urging the Army to take over the role of mainland air defence, but the War Office successfully argued that it would need some time to build up capacity for its expanded role. It was not until 10 February 1916 that the Asquith Government's War Committee finally rubber-stamped the change, and the only immediate result was that additional anti-aircraft guns were sited around the capital, most of which were concentrated around the great arsenal at Woolwich. 'Having regard to the great importance of the munitions work concentrated in the Woolwich district, the Anti-Aircraft Defence of this area should take precedence over the rest of London.'

The War Committee had still failed to eliminate the rivalry between the RNAS and the RFC. The RNAS would continue 'to undertake to deal with all hostile aircraft attempting to reach this country' by engaging Zeppelins and German aircraft over the Channel and the North Sea, while the RFC would 'undertake to deal with all such aircraft that reach these shores'. Although the committee required 'the two services to co-operate so as to prevent unnecessary duplication', without a unified command structure that was never more than wishful thinking. The Admiralty refused to allow RFC pilots to use radio communications with the ground, for example, because of fears that it might interfere with naval signals traffic. As a result, once airborne, RFC aircraft were effectively on their own.

On 15 February, Prime Minister Asquith set up a further committee to control and coordinate the design and production of aircraft for the two rival air services. Its terms of reference were deceptively simple:

1) To prevent overlapping demands by the two services on the manufacturing resources available;
2) To prevent the two services bidding against one another for contractors;
3) To co-ordinate designs;
4) To endeavour, by all means, to extend the output of aircraft.

Lord Derby, then Secretary of State for War, was persuaded to chair the committee. It was a duty he initially thought 'of a very minor character', but within six weeks he had reversed his opinion and resigned, frustrated by the sheer impossibility of persuading the warring rivals at the Admiralty and the War Office to compromise on any but the most trivial points. 'On no point therefore can a decision on any large question be arrived at without reference to these bodies, and the Committee simply becomes the fifth wheel on the coach.' He found it 'quite impossible to bring the two wings closer together ... unless and until they are amalgamated into one service'. The situation was made even more intractable by the Byzantine complexity of the Admiralty's internal systems, with a number of rival departments responsible for different aspects of the RNAS.

Noel Pemberton-Billing, the architect of the air-raid on Friedrichshafen, who had resigned his commission and been elected as an Independent MP for East Hertfordshire, styling himself 'The First Air Member', launched a furious assault in the Commons on the Government's aviation policy. The monocle-wearing sometime actor, salesman and inventor was a political maverick, still nursing a grievance over the refusal of the War Office and the Admiralty to commission the fighter aircraft he had designed on the eve of the war. He now claimed that RFC pilots were being 'rather murdered than killed' because the obsolete products of the Royal Aircraft Factory – 'Fokker fodder' as he termed them – were no match for the sophisticated German aircraft. However, despite his expert knowledge and his own war record, his criticisms tended to be dismissed because of the choleric and intemperate 'abuse of language' with which they were presented.

Asquith commissioned another committee to investigate the charge; it took eight months to report that it was 'unjustifiable'. Meanwhile yet another air committee was established to replace Lord Derby's, albeit this time graced with the title of 'Air Board', with Lord Curzon as its president. Its remit was wide-ranging, but its chances of success, in Churchill's view, were nil. 'The members of the Board may advise the President, but he need not take their advice, and the President may advise the Admiralty and the War Office, but they need not take his advice.'

The resignation of David Lloyd George as War Minister on 5 December 1916 triggered a political crisis that forced Asquith to resign later the same day; Lloyd George then formed a coalition government with Conservative support. A reconstituted Air Board was established in February 1917 under the presidency of an industrialist, Viscount Cowdray, and given offices in the requisitioned Hotel Cecil in the Strand. The board was given sufficient powers to effect dramatic improvements in aircraft design and in production rates, but it lacked the ability to make a similar impact on operational efficiency. The rival services continued jealously to operate rigid demarcation lines between their respective areas of responsibility and failed to pool intelligence, expertise and experience, to the continuing detriment of the UK's air defence. The Hotel Cecil became such a hornets' nest of duplicity, intrigue and back-stabbing that it was given the cynical nickname 'Hotel Bolo', after a notorious enemy agent, 'Bolo Pasha', who had done great harm to the Allied cause.

The air-raids on London continued unabated. Throughout 1915 and the early part of 1916, Zeppelins were effectively invulnerable to the British air defences. They flew at 10,000 feet, out of range of artillery and near the 'ceiling' of most Home Defence fighters at the time; the ponderous rate of climb of the British aircraft also ensured that by the time they reached the airships' operating height the Zeppelins had already dropped their bombs and were long gone on their return flight. Any that did manage to get within range immediately came under fire from the airships' banks of machine-guns. Not a single Zeppelin was lost to enemy fire during the whole of 1915, though a number were destroyed in accidents, the majority arising from the highly combustible hydrogen that kept them airborne.

However, the balance of air power shifted in 1916 with the British development of aircraft capable of operating at greater altitude and speed, and the introduction of incendiary and explosive bullets loaded with phosphorus – 'an invention of the devil' according to the disgruntled Germans. 'Had we caught the man who invented that bullet, we should gladly have burned him in a stream of burning hydrogen.' The incendiary bullet was manufactured with a soft nose that flattened on impact, causing a larger hole in the target than standard ammunition. It was doubly pro-hibited under the existing rules of war: inflammable munitions had been outlawed in 1868, and soft-nosed 'Dum-Dum' bullets in 1899, because their effect on the human body was so devastating. The Government therefore permitted the use of incendiary bullets only for the purpose of shooting down Zeppelins raiding Britain, since it was believed that if German forces captured any British pilots equipped with them, they would 'murder them'. One officer noted that German forces 'had a habit of shooting you there and then' if they found soft-nosed ammunition on a crashed or captured aircraft, and pilots were sometimes issued with a letter stating that their ammunition was only for use against gas-filled balloons, in the hope of avoiding that fate. One pilot, shot down behind enemy lines, hid his incendiary rounds under the body of a German soldier in an open grave.

It was extraordinary that it had taken so long to devise such a blind-ingly obvious solution to the problem of shooting down a craft that was effectively a metal framework housing a series of bags filled with highly inflammable gas, but it had been erroneously assumed that the Zeppelins' hydrogen containers were protected by a layer of inert gas, probably collected from the exhausts of the engines. There was no intelligence to support this assumption and its basis appears to have been little more than incredulity that anyone would be foolhardy enough to go aloft in a hydrogen-filled airship that did not have such a protective layer, but the result was that British pilots were initially issued with high-explosive and incendiary bombs in the belief that the only way to halt Zeppelins was to drop bombs on them. None was ever destroyed in this way and the bombs merely proved an added hazard for unfortunate British civilians on the ground.

A cocktail of ammunition was eventually devised for British fighters: 'sparklet' or tracer bullets partly developed by Flight Lieutenant F. A. Brock, a scion of the firework family; explosive bullets devised by a New Zealand engineer, John Pomeroy, who was awarded £25,000 for his invention after the war; and incendiary bullets created by a Coventry engineer, James Buckingham. Fired in sequence, the tracer rounds indicated the path of fire, allowing the gunner to correct his aim, and the explosive rounds penetrated the hydrogen 'gas-bags' of the Zeppelin, which were then ignited by the incendiary rounds. The great Zeppelin ace Lieutenant Mathy was one of the many air-crew killed when his airship was shot down in flames by a British fighter during another raid on London on 1 October 1916.

The Germans tried to counter the threat with a new super-lightweight airship, the 'Height-Climber'. Fuel- and bombloads and defensive armaments were reduced, a lighter control car was installed, and the rear gondola housing three engines with separate propellers was replaced by two engines linked to a single propeller. The metal struts of the Zeppelin's rigid frame were also pared down to the minimum, and it was stripped of all other excess weight, including parachutes for the crew, which left the Height-Climber capable of reaching altitudes of over 20,000 feet, above the reach of even the newest British aircraft. The undersides of the airships were also painted black, making them harder to detect against the night sky. Despite this, they were not a success. British air defenders sometimes succeeded in jamming the Zeppelins' radios, preventing them from getting a fix on their positions, the extreme cold and the need for oxygen made conditions for the crews almost intolerable, and the lightweight construction was not always strong enough to withstand the severe atmospheric conditions, including jet-stream winds, that the airships encountered at high altitudes. Several simply broke up under the strains of high winds and bad weather, and without parachutes the crews plunged to their deaths. Those airships that did not break up were sometimes literally scattered all over Europe by the jet-stream.

Although the German Imperial Navy continued to operate them until 1918, the virtual extinction of the Zeppelin threat was signalled by the shooting down of two airships off Lowestoft and Hartlepool in the early hours of 28 November 1916, before either had even reached the British coastline. The German belief that they could use airships to launch the Fire Plan against Britain had proved to be a chimera.

# CHAPTER 3
# TURK'S CROSS

THE ZEPPELIN MENACE HAD ARISEN, peaked and then been extinguished in the space of just two years, but some perceptive Britons were already warning that the Zeppelin raids were only the beginning; the real threat to London would come from the heavy bombers that Germany was even now constructing.

What could be achieved, even with the existing German aircraft, had been demonstrated on the night of 20 July 1916 when four German raiders bombed the British ammunition dump at Audricq on the Calais–St Omer railway. A direct hit on one building ignited a fire that rapidly spread to others; twenty-three buildings and some 8,000 tons of ammunition were completely destroyed and a mile of railway track torn up. Although news of the raid was suppressed at the time, the official British historian of the air war admitted that 'it was a [German] success of the first importance'.

Unaware of such precedents, ordinary Britons did not at first feel that aircraft carried the same apocalyptic air of menace as the massive, brooding Zeppelins, but the potential for devastation and the threat to British cities and populations from bomber aircraft was to prove more dangerous and far more long-lasting.

On 28 November 1916, only a few hours after those Zeppelins had crashed into the sea off Lowestoft and Hartlepool with no survivors, the first harbinger of that change appeared in the skies over London. The morning was still and windless with a thin veil of night-mist slowly dispersing in the pale winter sunlight. Very few people stopped to stare in wonder at the silvery shape of an aircraft passing high overhead. Reporters could later find only two people who claimed to have witnessed it, and neither connected that extraordinary sight with the explosions that rumbled through the streets between Victoria and Knightsbridge a few minutes later. Although the aircraft was armed with six 10kg bombs, the primary task of its crew, Deck-Offizier Paul Brandt and Leutnant Walter Ilges, was reconnaissance. Taking off from Mariakerke in Belgium, they had flown their LVG biplane on a circuitous course over Essex and the Thames estuary, photographing potential targets – airfields, docks, oil storage tanks, munition factories and government buildings. They dropped their bombs on London just before noon. They were aiming at the Admiralty, but the inaccuracy of their bombsighting, exacerbated by the height – 13,000 feet – at which they were flying, meant that all six missed the target by at least a mile and instead struck a bakery, an office, some mews houses in Belgravia and a dressing room at the Palace of Varieties music hall near Victoria station.

Brandt and Ilges did not make it back to their base. As they flew back across the Channel they suffered an engine failure and, losing height, threw overboard almost everything, including their sophisticated and very expensive camera, to lighten the load. They managed to glide as far as the French coast, and crash-landed near Boulogne. Having torched their aircraft, they set off towards the German lines on foot, but almost at once were captured by French troops who found the large-scale map of London they were still carrying.

The damage from their raid was so modest that newspaper reports catalogued not only the dressing room demolished at the Palace of Varieties, a stable wrecked, the roof of one house smashed and the chimney of another, but also the scarcely earth-shattering news that 'one cobblestone was cracked in Eccleston Mews, opposite No. 23'. The official reports were equally dismissive: 'Between 11.50 and noon this morning six bombs were dropped on London by a hostile aeroplane flying at a great height above the haze.' Injuries were reported as no more than four wounded, later revised to ten, but they were all so minor that the fact that 'Henrietta Simonds (40) suffered a cut on her right hand' was faithfully reported. Rather less well publicized was the fact that the Admiralty Air Department had not been informed of the raid until after half-past twelve. It took a further ten minutes for the alert to be passed to the Home Defence Wing and yet another fifteen minutes before the first fighters were actually airborne, by which time the German raider was not even a speck on the far horizon.

While most newspapers and British citizens preferred to concentrate on the destruction of the Zeppelins, Lord Northcliffe's stable of papers reflected his own concerns. Northcliffe had greeted the news of the first heavier-than-air flight in Europe with the doom-laden remark that 'England is no longer an island . . . there will be no more sleeping safely behind the wooden walls of old England', and he now warned in a *Times* editorial that 'cheap and elusive' aeroplanes offered Germany 'far more dangerous possibilities than the large and costly Zeppelins . . . It is wise to regard it [the raid] as a prelude to further visits on an extended scale.' The magazine *The Aeroplane* echoed the warnings: 'When the aeroplane raids start and prove more damaging than the airship raids, the authorities cannot say that they have not had a fair warning of what to expect.' The 'London shopkeeper' was now aware that 'there is a serious chance of proper war being carried into the very heart of his sacred city'.

No further German aircraft appeared in the skies over London that winter, but, as Northcliffe had predicted, the raid proved to be the harbinger of a switch to daylight bombing raids by aircraft. As a *Times* leader writer, Lovat Fraser, noted the following summer, albeit with the benefit of hindsight, 'If I were asked what event of the last year has been of most significance to the future of humanity, I should reply that it is not the Russian Revolution, nor even the stern intervention of the United States in a sacred cause, but the appearance of a single German aeroplane flying at high noon over London last November.'

What those aircraft might be able to inflict on London was graphically demonstrated on the pitch-dark night of 9 January 1917, when 'the melt-pot room of the Danger Building' (where crude TNT was purified) in the Brunner-Mond chemical factory at Silvertown, east London, 'a sordid district of one-storied houses lying about the riverside and the docks', exploded in a huge fireball that engulfed the entire site. A 'tongue of crimson flame darted right across the river to the Woolwich side, setting a gasometer near the Royal Arsenal ablaze'. For a time it was even feared that the arsenal was also in danger of exploding.

One witness, sitting several miles away in a tramcar at Blackfriars Bridge, 'saw in the sky the most wonderful spectacle of beauty and terror combined that I have ever seen . . . Suddenly a golden glow lit up the eastern sky, making everything clear as day; and looking down the Thames I saw a high column of yellow flames rising, as I thought, from the river. This quickly died down and the sky immediately became overspread with the loveliest colours – violet, indigo, blue, green, yellow, orange and red – which eddied and swirled. Dazzled and awestruck, I saw that London, so dark a few moments before, was made glorious as if by a marvellous sunset the like of which had never been seen before. The phenomenon lasted,

I should think, several seconds. Its disappearance was accompanied by a terrific explosion, riving and shattering, and dying away with an angry growl. I had the sensation that at the same moment a vibrating tremor ran through London.'

The capital's 'tinted firmament' was seen for twenty-five miles around and the sound of the blast heard eighty miles away; the factory was still burning two days later. 'A huge crater marks the site . . . it is the centre of a square mile within which many hundreds of the little dwellings have been razed to the ground.' Seventy thousand houses were damaged to a greater or lesser extent. Official figures showed seventy-three people killed and over a thousand injured, 'but by common report they [the casualties] are really far greater. The locality is made a prohibited area, and is enclosed and guarded by military and police. Admittance is allowed only on an order issued by the Ministry of Munitions or War Office.'

The first thought of most Londoners was that the explosion had been the result of a bombing raid – 'it must be an air-raid, one of a new and more terrifying kind' – or sabotage: 'foul play is more than suspected. It is positively asserted that German spies are at the bottom of it.' In fact, unless the Government was more than usually successful at suppressing the facts, it appears to have been a genuine accident, but it was a salutary lesson – one absorbed in Germany as well as Britain – on the devastation that could be caused by a spark, let alone an incendiary or high-explosive bomb.

German engineers had been at work since 1914 on the design and pro-duction of large bomber aircraft with the range to reach London and the bomb-carrying capacity to enact the Fire Plan against the greatest city on earth. While the aircraft were still in development, an elite corps of flight crews was being assembled to fly them, under the direction of Major Wilhelm Siegert.

Aged forty-two when war broke out, Siegert was 'passionately devoted to the whole flying sector'. He appeared a caricature of a Junker officer, with close-cropped grey hair and neat moustache, a hawk nose and a faint facial scar, but he was a radical thinker and a great innovator in military aviation, his gaze seemingly always fixed on some distant horizon. He was one of the oldest and most experienced German pilots, firstly as a balloon pilot – he owned his own balloon, 'Baby' – and later as a 'peace flyer', learning his skills before the outbreak of war. However, his flying career had been curtailed by a crippled hand, the legacy of an incident at a pre-war air show when he had thrown himself at a runaway aeroplane in an attempt to stop it careering into a crowd of onlookers. Unable to fly, he threw his formidable energies into training other pilots, proclaiming that the German airman had to be 'a true revolutionary to rise to the stars'. Those who impressed him were awarded medals. Siegert had no authority to do so, such awards were the sole prerogative of the Kaiser, but if challenged, he claimed that he had merely lent the medals to their recipients.

In 1913 Siegert had initiated night-flying training for his unit, rapidly winning over the sceptics who thought the idea was impractical at best and mad at worst. As soon as war was declared, he approached the Oberste Heeresleitung (OHL), the Army High Command, and proposed a strategic air bombardment of London to force Britain's capitulation. The limited range and payloads of the available aircraft at that time made the Pas de Calais the only area from which such raids could be launched. It was French territory, but such was the apparently inexorable progress of Germany's armies that its capture seemed a foregone conclusion and Siegert's scheme was approved at once. On 19 October 1914 the then Chief of the General Staff of the Army, General von Falkenhayn, appointed Siegert commander of a new air corps – Der Fliegerkorps der OHL – to carry out the attacks. The importance attached to bombing was emphasized soon afterwards by the newly appointed commander of the Army Air Force, who ordered that 'all machines were to carry bombs on every war flight'.

Siegert assembled 'the best and most experienced pilots from every branch of the Air Force', all of whom were volunteers. At first they were based at a temporary airfield at Ghistelles in occupied Belgium, set in pastureland studded with orchards, ten miles south of the coastal sand-dunes of Ostend. Thirty-six single hangars were erected around the edge of the airfield, and the runway, of wooden planks laid over stout beams, was constructed from scratch in three or four days. The fruit trees around it were 'preserved as camouflage'.

To disguise its function, the Fliegerkorps was given the implausible code-name Breiftauben Abteilung (the Carrier Pigeon Squadron). It did have some basis in fact since, in the absence of radio equipment, air-crews were to be issued with homing pigeons before each air-raid on England. If an aircraft suffered mechanical failure or ran out of fuel, its pigeons would carry back to their lofts a message giving the last position and heading of the aircraft. German U-boats or motor torpedo boats would then be sent to rescue the crew. The time delays involved made it unlikely that any German would ever be saved from drowning or death from hypothermia in the frigid waters of the North Sea, but it was at least some faint reassurance to the air-crews as they contemplated the long, perilous missions that they would soon be flying.

The Carrier Pigeon Squadron was allocated thirty-six 100-horsepower two-seater aircraft of varying types. One, the 'Otto' biplane, was described by Siegert as 'an antediluvian machine. In daytime raids the [French] enemy thought it was one of their own Farmans and therefore left it alone; unfortunately our own anti-aircraft gunners thought the same and used it as a welcome target. In spite of this, the brave crew remained faithful to its archaeopteryx.'

To preserve the secrecy of the unit, the aircraft were brought to Ghistelles after dark and at once hidden in the hangars. Each one was equipped with four hand-dropped 10kg bombs, but the Army's water-cooled machine-guns were far too heavy to use in such underpowered aircraft and they lacked any defensive armaments other than 'a bracket next to the observer to mount a hand gun, an automatic pistol or rapid-fire rifles which Fritz von Falkenhayn had "organised" from the museum of the firearms testing commission'. Most air-crew used Mauser automatic pistols, 'one for the pilot and one for the observer', though one had 'a carbine as my only weapon . . . [and] nailed a gramophone horn on to the stock, so that in the event of meeting an enemy, I might at least dismay and terrify him with its illusory calibre'.

The men of the Carrier Pigeon Squadron were quartered in railway sleeping carriages 'to increase their mobility', and 'to avoid bombing' the train was moved to 'a small railway station some miles away' every night, returning after daybreak. The air-crews waited with some impatience for the capture of Calais, but in November 1914, the German Fourth Army's advance ground to a halt at Ypres and the 'war of movement' of the opening phase evolved into a war of attrition that was to ossify the front lines for over three years. With the aircraft then available London remained out of range, and Siegert's planned air offensive, the first strategic air campaign the world had ever seen, was postponed. The Carrier Pigeon Squadron was switched to tactical bombing on the Western Front and carried out its first raid on Dunkirk on 28 January 1915.

As they flew towards their target, the air-crews had time to take in the beauty of the scene as well as its menace. 'The moon illuminated the surf of the North Sea; flames blazed at a factory near Firmeny; the artillery firing on both sides looked like chains of glowing beads, hundreds of thousands of balls of light of all colours were like dancing pearls in black champagne. Between them our star shells to signal to our own artillery: "Good people, don't shoot" – and then the countless searchlights.'

The squadron bombed Dunkirk, leaving dozens of fires blazing in the city that was the principal supply port for the British Expeditionary Force at the time, though, as Major Siegert sardonically noted, the French and Belgian press preferred to claim that 'the only result of the "cowardly night raid of the flying Boches on the harmless spa of Dunkirk" ' had been 'the death of that standard trinity "women, children and old people"'.

'To train the crews and gain technical experience' the Carrier Pigeon Squadron also carried out 'raids on Furnes, La Panne and Nieuport'. Among the pilots who learned their trade with the squadron were a number who would go on to greater fame after switching to fighters, including Hermann Goering and Germany's greatest fighter ace, Manfred von Richthofen.

While awaiting delivery of the promised fleet of 'G-type' long-range twin-engined heavy bombers that would bring London within range of the existing German airbases in occupied Belgium, part of the Fliegerkorps was detached to Metz and renamed the Metz Carrier Pigeon Squadron, while the reduced Ostend squadron was briefly sent to the Eastern Front. After its return to Ghistelles in July 1915, 'its work being bombing, escort of returning Zeppelins, escort and line patrol duty', it was reorganized as the Kampfgeschwader (Battle Group) 1 der OHL – soon abbreviated to Kagohl 1 – comprising six *Staffeln* (flights) of six aircraft.

The prototype variants of the new Grossekampfflugzeug 'Gotha' bombers (named after the factories where they were made, the Gothaer Waggonfabrik AG, peacetime manufacturers of railway wagons and carriages), the G I, G II and G III, were all bedevilled with problems and changing specifications, and were not equal to the daunting task they had been set. By the end of 1915 fewer than twenty were in service at the Front, but the latest model Gotha G IVs at last appeared to match the formidable specification laid down for them, and in early 1916 the first production machines began to roll off the assembly lines. Meanwhile, development work was proceeding on an even larger and more ambitious aircraft: the Riesenflugzeugen R-type 'Giant' bomber.

In the spring and summer of 1916 all available aircraft were thrown into the furious battles of Verdun and the Somme, but by November of that year the battle of the Somme had at last ground to a bloody end in the winter mud. Allied losses were horrendous, but the German forces had fared little better and the High Command adopted a twin-pronged strategy to ease the burden on its ground troops and exert pressure on Britain to make peace or succumb.

Beginning in February 1917, simultaneous assaults would be launched on Britain by air and sea. While unrestricted U-boat attacks devastated Allied merchant shipping, German bombers would pound London with high-explosive and incendiary bombs. Irrespective of the material damage to factories, housing and infrastructure that such attacks might inflict – and it was intended to be massive – the German High Command believed they would also have a devastating impact on civilian morale, and a propaganda effect that would echo around the world.

Aiming to end inter-service rivalries and give the air forces a clear chain of command, the High Command had announced the previous autumn that 'The increasing significance of aerial warfare demands the entire aerial battle and aerial defence resources in the field and at home be united in a single department.' The German Air Force was formally established as a separate branch of the services: the Luftstreitkräfte (Combat Air Force) with its own Kommandierender General der Luftstreitskräfte, abbreviated to Kogenluft. Siegert did not have the rank to be given command; he was compensated with the post of Inspector General of the Flying Corps, while the job of Kogenluft – 'the coherent restructuring and allocation of these war resources' – was given to the fifty-eight-year-old Ernst Wilhelm von Höppner.

Slight of build with white hair and a dark grey moustache, von Höppner had a stern, almost haughty demeanour; even when relaxed he held his slim figure as if at attention. A lifetime career soldier, he had left his home on the Baltic island of Wollin at the age of twelve to join the military academy at Potsdam. To Siegert's barely concealed disgust, the new commander was a General of Cavalry with no previous experience of aviation, and when von Höppner was later awarded Germany's highest military honour, the Pour le Mérite, Siegert reportedly ceased wearing his own medals in protest. The award may also have been uppermost in his mind when he coined the joke 'What do an aerial bomb and a decoration have in common? Both come from high up, originate way behind the front line and land on innocents.' However, despite Siegert's criticisms, von Höppner proved to be a formidably effective administrator, with an energy and enthusiasm for the task that belied his years.

His first directive to his new service laid out his aims. 'Since an airship raid on London has become impossible, the Air Service is required to carry out a raid with aeroplanes as soon as possible. The undertaking will be carried out in accordance with two entirely separate schemes: 1. Bombing squadrons equipped with G-type aircraft. 2. Giant flights equipped with R-type aircraft. The G-type aircraft for this task is now ready and the R-type so far developed that its use will be practicable in the near future.' He proposed to set up Operation Turk's Cross (*Turkencreuz*) using a squadron of thirty G-type Gotha IV bombers that were to be ready to begin raids on London by 1 February 1917. The men of Siegert's Ostend Carrier Pigeon Squadron, Kagohl 1, would form half of the six flights of the new unit, now renumbered Kagohl 3, though it was soon better known as *Der Englandgeschwader* – the England Squadron. The air-crew were to be based at Ghistelles, pending the completion of new airfields around Ghent, 175 miles as the crow (or bomber) flew from London.

General Erich Ludendorff, second-in-command to General-feldmarschal Paul Ludwig Hans von Beneckendorf und von Hindenburg,

43

who had replaced von Falkenhayn as Chief of the General Staff on 29 August 1916, spelled out the aims of the bombing campaign. It was 'a matter of urgent necessity' to supplement the military campaign on the Western Front and the 'economic warfare' being waged by the U-boat campaign by 'making war on the morale of the enemy people and armies . . . to ensure the final victory by sowing dissension among the allies and taking from them their faith in ultimate victory'.

What the Zeppelin raids had begun, the England Squadron would now finish; 'war was, for the first time in military history, to be carried beyond the actual theatre of war to the capital of the enemy country, the nerve centre of the nation, the centre of resistance and the source of supplies'. The secondary objectives of Turk's Cross would be 'the crippling of the British war supplies industry, of communications between the coast and London, of the coastal depots and transport across the English Channel'; but the prime object, said Ludendorff, 'was the moral intimi-dation of the British nation and the crippling of the will to fight, thus preparing the ground for peace'. London would be seeded with incendiary and high-explosive bombs, paralysing the capital and scattering the population in panic. 'These ends attained, the British Government might fall, the "solidarity of the enemy nations" be shaken' and final victory achieved.

That the principal aim was propaganda and the destruction of British morale was emphasized by the targeting priorities given to the England Squadron: London was the main objective, but within the capital the prize targets were not, as might have been expected, the munitions factories, docks, warehouses and railway stations, but 'the Government buildings around Downing Street, the Admiralty, the Bank of England and the Press buildings in Fleet Street'.

Von Höppner reported to the German High Command that 'by dis-patching eighteen aeroplanes, each carrying a load of 300kg of bombs, 5,400kg could be dropped on London in a single raid', but the attack could only succeed if 'every detail is carefully prepared, the crews are practised in long-distance overseas flight and the squadron is made up of especially good aeroplane crews. Any negligence and undue haste will only entail heavy losses for us, and defeat our ends.'

Operation Turk's Cross was highly secret; even the air-crews selected for the squadron – 'only battle-proven officers with experience at the Front are transferred there' – were not told of their ultimate mission. Among them was Leutnant Walter Aschoff, a former infantry officer who had transferred to the Army Air Service in July 1916 after serving for almost two years in the trenches. In the rest periods between Aschoff's tours of duty in the mud and filth of the front lines – 'pretty soon one will have to swim through the trenches' – he often 'lay out in the sun for a long time and watched the airplanes. I always envy them.' At night, he heard 'the hum of approaching aircraft . . . then, right above us, suddenly machine-guns were chattering. One saw the gun flashes in the air, sparkling like minuscule fires. Then it was quiet and the German flew peacefully home.'

On 2 April 1916, sick of the trenches, and ambitious, impatient and more than a little in love with the mystique of flying, Aschoff submitted 'a request to be detached to the flying troops . . . Why did I enlist? 1) Because the monotony is too terrible. 2) Because I finally want to earn the EK1 [Iron Cross, First Class].' In July, after completing his basic flight training, he was sent to the Observers' Training School at Forgnier, near St Quentin, within earshot of the 'constant roaring of bombs from the Somme; it is supposed to be horrible there'. While there, he heard that a bomb had killed seven of his comrades from the Army unit he had just left.

He completed his training on 16 August and was posted to a bomber squadron where he began flying tactical missions over the front lines. 'At first, of course, it is an eerie feeling to fly in the shrapnel fire of the anti-aircraft guns, 800 to 3,000 metres [2,500 to 10,000 feet] above the British lines. Many aircraft are flying to and fro there, a wonderful picture, and below a giant battle is raging. There is fire everywhere, shells of all calibres hit the ground, gunsmoke lies over the pulverised earth, one can hardly see any trace of the villages; it must be horrible down there.'

Aschoff and his pilot, Vizefeldwebel D. R. Richter, were mentioned in dispatches for their 'daring and correct intelligence' on a low-altitude flight near Cléry, and on 16 December, after distinguishing himself on several other flights, he was recommended for a transfer that, as he wrote to his parents, 'can be considered as a special distinction. Where, why, everything strictly confidential . . . what I experience and see, not very many get to see.'

By 19 December he was at Wilhelmshaven with the rest of his new comrades, and two days later, the rumours about the true purpose of this secret unit hardened into certainty when they were sent to the drab naval stations on Heligoland and Westerland on the Isle of Sylt to begin two months' specialized training in flying over the grey reaches of the North Sea. There could be only one purpose to such training: to prepare the aircrews for bombing missions against England.

It was an environment in which Navy pilots already operated, but having invested its hopes and funds in the airship programme the Navy had no suitable aircraft and it fell to the Army Air Service's élite unit to take up the air war against England. Pilots and observers were given intensive training in navigation out of sight of land, using dead-reckoning, compass and star-sights, recognition of enemy ships, bomb-aiming and machine-gunning. They were also schooled in flying in close 'hedgehog' formation, bristling with machine-guns to provide mutual defence against fighters.

The German High Command's deadline of 1 February 1917 for thirty Gotha G IVs to be ready to launch a daylight raid on London came and went, as design and manufacturing difficulties and shortages of raw materials caused by the tightening British blockade on Germany's sea coast reduced the number of Gothas coming off the production lines to a trickle. Those that were produced were often poorly constructed. The scarcity of raw materials was forcing manufacturers to use substandard or substitute materials, with an inevitable impact on the quality of the end-product. A later British report on a captured German bomber revealed some of the problems. The workmanship and construction 'does not appear to attain a very high standard. The main spars were of hollow, square section and were not even screwed or pinned together, being merely glued', and, though the core of the 'roughly finished and clumsily designed' propeller was made of high-quality hardwood, it was laminated to cheaper softwoods. The Gotha engines were a particular area of concern. Although a large number were rejected as defective and returned to the factory, engine failures would continue to blight the England Squadron. Only on very rare occasions did all the aircraft setting out to attack England reach the Belgian coast, let alone the English one.

The design of the G IVs may also have been further refined and modified after a brand-new British Handley-Page 0/400 bomber, straight from the manufacturer and containing all its documentation, fell into German hands on 2 February 1917. A navigational error by the pilot of the Handley-Page led him to land at an airfield near Laon that he believed to be British, but which was in fact a German base. The five-man crew were captured and interrogated and the aircraft was handed to a specialized department devoted to evaluating such windfalls, which 'examined captured enemy aircraft minutely and distributed its findings to the German industry and aviation press'.

The first handful of G IVs finally arrived in March 1917, but 'owing to the unsatisfactory performance of the first aeroplanes, trial flights with full load could not be carried out until the beginning of May 1917', and the required strength of thirty aircraft was not reached until later that month. They were biplanes with a seventy-eight-foot wingspan that dwarfed any other German aircraft at the time, and were powered by two 260-horse-power Mercedes engines driving 'pusher' propellers three metres (ten feet) in diameter at the rear of the engine block. The G IVs were a major step forward from their predecessors, but the first batch of engines 'suffered from bad bearing metal and a whole series of these engines had to be scrapped'. Once that problem had been rectified, the new Gothas had a significantly improved rate of climb and a much-increased range – five hundred miles – and bomb-carrying capacity – 500kg – though the need to carry sufficient fuel for the return flight ensured that they rarely carried the maximum load on a raid over England, and it was even 'frequently impossible to utilise the full fuel capacity because the piping was badly designed'.

Despite these problems, London was now within range, and the G IV and its later replacement, the G V, were to become the workhorses of the England Squadron. With the first Gothas came the unit's new commander, Hauptmann Ernst Brandenburg, who had been personally hand-picked by von Höppner and received his orders direct from the OHL. He was also allocated a headquarters staff of seven, including specialist officers in intelligence, meteorology, aviation medicine, fire protection and air-photography.

Brandenburg was just thirty-four, young for such a command. Born in Sophienfeld in West Prussia, he was a tall figure with dark, fathomless eyes, a high forehead and thinning brown hair. A chess player and an intellectual with a keen interest in philosophy, he had a slightly forbidding demeanour – perhaps the product of his shy nature – but he commanded the complete respect and admiration of his men from the outset, and soon won their affection too. A former infantry officer, he had been so badly wounded in 1914 that he was barred from further service in the trenches. He had already done some flight training before the war, having attended the Institution for Aerial Training and Testing in March 1911; after suffering his wounds, he then transferred to the Army Air Service, serving as an observer in two-seater aircraft operating over the front lines.

Brandenburg ordered each new Gotha to be flown for at least twenty-five hours before it could be considered combat-ready, and many flaws were highlighted during this intensive testing. The England Squadron's personnel were also tested every bit as rigorously as their machines. All pilots trained at the Freiburg training school, and observers and gunners, and ground-crew and mechanics, also went through their own training courses. Brandenburg would accept no pilot as qualified until he had made twenty landings, half by day and half by night, the latter a reflection of the commander's belief that improvements in British air defences would soon make the level of losses on daytime raids unacceptable, forcing a switch to night bombing.

Landings were the most difficult and dangerous part of any flight, even one braving the anti-aircraft defences over England. Without the weight of their fuel- and bombloads, the Gothas were dangerously unstable, particularly in crosswinds, and the undercarriage was so fragile that it sometimes collapsed under the impact of a landing. Engineers had been unable to eradicate these twin problems despite two years of development and redesign, and they were never adequately resolved. The England Squadron's losses from crashes far exceeded those sustained as a result of air defence actions; in the course of the Fire Plan campaign, twenty-four were shot down, but thirty-seven were lost in landing accidents.

After test flights with full tanks and maximum bombloads, Brandenburg concluded that London, 175 miles distant by the shortest route, was at the absolute limit of the Gothas' range. Since the direct route was also likely to be the most heavily guarded by anti-aircraft guns and patrolling fighters, he ordered seventy-gallon auxiliary fuel-tanks to be fitted to the Gothas as soon as possible, giving them extra range even at the price of reducing the bombload to compensate for the extra weight of fuel. This allowed a flight-path due north from the Gotha bases, parallel to the front lines, until well out over the North Sea. A turn on to a westerly heading would then bring the Gothas in over the Thames estuary, leaving them the shortest possible distance to travel over enemy territory before reaching London. Even so, on the first daylight raids no aircraft carried more than seven 50kg bombs and many carried no more than a 150kg bombload, and, as a temporary expedient while waiting for the auxiliary fuel-tanks to be fitted, the Gothas would refuel at an airfield just short of the Belgian coast, giving them a precious additional range of forty miles. In adverse weather or headwinds, it might well be the difference between life and death for the crew.

Each Gotha had a three-man crew – observer, pilot and rear-gunner – and, unlike the RFC, the pilot was not the senior officer, nor always drawn from the upper classes. The observers were the aircraft commanders and were always officers; pilots were either officers or NCOs, and the rear-gunners were invariably NCOs or other ranks. As well as commanding the aircraft, the observer was responsible for navigation, bomb-aiming and manning an air-cooled 7.9mm machine-gun. The rear-gunner operated the other two machine-guns, one covering the centre and rear of the aircraft above the fuselage, and the other firing through the ventral 'firing tunnel' extending right down through the fuselage to cover the normally vulnerable blind area below the tail. Both gunners carried several two-hundred-round drums of armour-piercing Mauser ammunition, every fourth round a tracer bullet to help direct fire on to the target. Unlike the air-crew, all three machine-guns were electrically heated by a dynamo connected to the starboard engine, which prevented the lubricating oil from freezing at high altitude.

On the early flights each Gotha carried a mixture of 12.5kg *Splitterbomben* – fragmentation bombs filled with a mixture of TNT and phosphorus – and 50kg high-explosive bombs loaded with 60 per cent

TNT and 40 per cent hexanitrodiphenylamine. The 12.5kg bombs, stacked in a vertical row in the observer's compartment, were anti-personnel weapons designed to explode on impact and also threw up a clearly visible smoke cloud as they exploded, allowing them to be used as sighting shots before dropping the heavy bombs. The latter, painted pale blue, were cigar-shaped, five feet long and seven inches maximum in diameter with a triple-vaned tail and a sharp steel point to aid penetration of the roofs of buildings. After falling for several thousand feet, their momentum was enough to drive them down through several floors to the ground floor or cellar areas, where their detonation would reap the maximum number of casualties and damage.

Driven by the two powerful six-cylinder Mercedes engines, the Gotha had a maximum speed of eighty-seven miles an hour at sea-level, making it as fast as many of the ageing British fighters targeting it. However, if a strong headwind was blowing, the top speed would drop to as little as fifty miles an hour. Even at such slow speeds, the three ring-mounted Parabellum machine-guns it carried still made it a formidable adversary for fighters.

Although its climb rate was slow, freed of its bombload it could reach altitudes of 5,000 metres (16,500 feet) – close to the height-ceiling of British fighters at the time – but Gotha pilots normally aimed to fly at between 2,500 and 3,500 metres (8,000 to 11,500 feet), ensuring less dis-comfort for themselves and their crews while still affording a measure of protection from ground-fire and fighter attack.

All air-crew had to endure terrible discomfort when flying in open cockpits at such altitudes. Even on a balmy summer's day they could find the air temperature plummeting below −40°C at altitudes approaching 20,000 feet, wind chill lowering the apparent temperature still further. To counteract the extreme cold, crews were issued with thick gauntlets, fur-lined thigh-boots, fur coats to wear over their uniforms and fur hats, though many preferred their leather flying helmets, which they found both warmer and more comfortable. Despite layer upon layer of clothing, pilots were numbed to the core. Some even took hot baked potatoes into the cockpit with them, not to eat, but to act as primitive hot water bottles.

Air-crew were also subjected to the endless cacophony of the engines, the teeth-rattling vibrations and pounding headaches from the cold, the stink of aviation fuel and exhaust fumes, and the lack of oxygen in the air. Oxygen cylinders were provided, but the gas had to be inhaled by sucking on a rubber tube, rather than by breathing through a face-mask, and users invariably suffered severe sore throats as a result. There was also the stress of flying combat missions and the gnawing uncertainty whether, even if not attacked, their fragile aircraft would survive the mission without breaking down and crashing. In the end, 'the strain reduced all men by stages until it becomes as dangerous for the best pilots to fly a machine as a beginner'.

Brandenburg's brief for the men of the England Squadron who would soon be enduring those conditions over enemy territory was a broad one. The England Squadron's prime task remained the bruising and breaking of the morale of the British people and their will to fight by attacking London, the centre of British political and military power, but they were also tasked with targeting war industries and supply dumps, and disrupting ports and the rail and sea transport of war materials. At the least, it was intended that the raids would also force Britain to divert scarce resources – aircraft, pilots, guns, men – away from the Western Front to boost the air defences of London and the Channel ports.

After completing their training at Heligoland and Westerland, Walter Aschoff and his comrades were sent to the original base of the Carrier Pigeon Squadron at Ghistelles. On 18 March 1917 Aschoff drove to nearby Ostend, 'listened to the military concert on the square and took a stroll . . . It's wonderful there, fine, tall houses standing at the edge of the beach, which stretches a long, long way from the ocean. There is hardly a trace of the war to be seen, just soldiers and citizens strolling in the sunshine. How wonderful it must be in peacetime . . . I shall take my honeymoon here!'

The following month the England Squadron moved from Ghistelles, dangerously close to the front lines and within easy reach of British reconnaissance aircraft and bombers, to permanent airfields around Ghent, forty miles behind the lines. Staffeln 13 and 14 were assigned to St Denijs-Westrem, seven kilometres south-west of Ghent. Set in the endless Flanders plain, the airfield was fringed by a railway line and the Ringvaart canal, marked by a line of pollarded willows along its banks, with woodland to two sides. Staffeln 15 and 16 were based at Gontrode to the east of the city, where there was a hangar, previously used for Zeppelins, so vast that it dwarfed the aircraft housed there. Officers were billeted at the Chateau of Borluut, though some crews were given quarters in railway wagons drawn up in a siding by the airfield. After further Gothas were delivered, Staffeln 17 and 18 went to Mariakerke, in rich agricultural land just to the north-west of Ghent. Ghistelles remained the principal diversionary airfield and all four airfields were scrupulously graded and levelled to minimize wear and tear on the Gothas' vulnerable landing-gear.

Brandenburg's headquarters was in the Villa Drory, just outside Gontrode. His office, overlooking the gardens, was dominated by a giant map of London and the south-east of England, pinned to the wall next to his desk, so that every time he looked up he was confronted with a reminder of the target he had been assigned to destroy. The furnishings of the room were spartan: a large desk and hard wooden chair, a small side table and a pair of similarly uncomfortable chairs for visitors. The desktop carried a telephone, inkstand and blotter, neat piles of documents and a large magnifying glass resting on a sheaf of maps and reconnaissance photographs.

By mid-May, Brandenburg had completed his preparations and he contacted the German High Command to pronounce his squadron ready to take the war to London. On 24 May, over twenty glistening white Gothas were drawn up in a line on the grass of St Denijs-Westrem. They would have been an easy target for any marauding British aircraft, but none darkened the blue skies overhead, and in brilliant sunshine 'the squadron was inspected by General Ludendorff'. Under an awe-struck Walter Aschoff's gaze, Ludendorff 'inspected everything. The man does make a fantastic impression. I'm happy that I was able to meet him.' Brandenburg paced alongside, pointing out the Gothas' armaments, and offered him a cockpit inspection, though Ludendorff deputed another staff officer to scale the ladder propped against the fuselage of Brandenburg's own Gotha, while he extolled its virtues.

Ludendorff could not hide his pride and enthusiasm for his new secret weapon. Driven by the imperatives of total war, the astonishing pace of technological change in the combatant nations had already produced a series of inventions and radical developments in the machinery and materials of warfare, but more than any other innovation, more even than the British tanks that had appeared on the battlefields the previous year, the German heavy bombers held the promise of transforming the war and bringing victory. The Fire Plan would be renewed and reborn, and before long a black rain of high explosives and incendiaries would fall on London.

# CHAPTER 4
# THE GOTHA HUM

WHILE THE ENGLAND SQUADRON was making its preparations, London and the south-east had remained untroubled by bombers. The failure of the Zeppelin campaign had been signalled by the losses of October and November 1916, and for several months after that no German airship or aircraft had targeted the capital. Its air defences had been allowed to deteriorate, air-raid drills and precautions had virtually ceased, and the clamour for replacements for losses on the Western Front had seen more and more pilots and aircraft sent to France. Sir David Henderson, Director General of Military Aeronautics, informed the War Cabinet that 'from a Royal Flying Corps standpoint' the diminished risk from Zeppelin attack amply justified a reduction in the number of pilots on Home Defence duty. Thirty-six were transferred to the Western Front in February 1917 and many more were required each month as replacements for those killed in action. The additional anti-aircraft guns ordered for the protection of the capital were re-allocated to merchant ships as some defence against the U-boat menace, and the Government even eased restrictions on London's outdoor lighting. Controls were now about to be reimposed, but not through fear of air-raids, rather as a measure to save power-station coal. For the first time ever British Summer Time was also introduced as another power-saving measure.

Almost the only voice to oppose the weakening of the capital's air defences was that of Field Marshal Viscount Sir John French, who had been replaced as commander-in-chief of the BEF by Sir Douglas Haig on 19 December 1915. Florid of face, with white hair and drooping moustache, French was given a peerage and the title of Commander-in-Chief, Home Forces, as consolations, and though many of his duties were largely ceremonial, his responsibilities since early 1916 had included air defence. A Zeppelin raid in March 1917, though fruitless, prompted him to furious complaints about the way Home Defence fighter squadrons were being 'reduced to a dangerously low point and one which does not enable the general scheme of defence . . . to be carried out'. From 130 pilots at the height of the Zeppelin campaign, the Home Defence establishment had been reduced to just seventy-one by 17 March. French recommended that at least a hundred pilots trained in night-flying should be retained in England, but this was at once rejected by the War Office, since the existing shortages at home were 'not disproportionate' to those on the Western Front, where pilots were being killed in action and in training at such a terrifying rate that both the quantity and the quality of replacements fell well short of meeting the demand.

The men who arrived in France were lucky even to have got that far. In the spring of 1917, when the slaughter of 'Bloody April' saw over three hundred British air-crew killed or shot down and captured in that one month alone, the RFC computed that of six thousand pilots in training, a fifth – 1,200 men – would fail to complete their course, not because they had failed to qualify but because they had been killed in training accidents. Only 10 per cent of pilots survived a crash, a statistic improved neither by the design of aircraft, which often seated the air-crew directly above the fuel-tank, nor by the Air Board's refusal to issue parachutes. With frigid official logic it was argued that 'the presence of such apparatus might impair the fighting spirit of pilots and cause them to abandon machines which might otherwise be capable of returning to base for repair'.

Those who survived, young and barely trained, were merely being 'fattened for the Front', in the view of an officer who later rose to the rank of Air Commodore. 'Flying Corps headquarters in France was constantly demanding supplies of these youths, in fives, tens and twenties, according as the need arose, and sometimes there were enough ready and to spare. But at other times there was a scarcity, and the alternative of a confession, on the part of those responsible for home training, of failure to keep pace with the demand, was to send over the half-trained and hope for the best. The proceeding was almost mechanical and quite as inhuman . . . little short of murder.' As Philip Gibbs wrote, with even more biting contempt, 'our aviators had been trained in the school of General Trenchard [the commander of the RFC], who sent them out over the German trenches to learn how to fight'.

When James McCudden began his operational career as a fighter pilot, he 'had not even flown the type which I was to fly over the lines the next morning, let alone not having received any fighting instruction . . . I did not even appreciate the necessity of turning at once when an opponent got behind me, and I only just realised that I had to get directly behind him to get a shot at him without having to make allowances for his speed or mine.'

Given Lord French's concerns about Home Defence, the directive he issued after a meeting at the War Office on 6 March convened to discuss means of reducing still further the numbers of aircraft and pilots, guns, searchlights and the personnel manning them was nothing short of astonishing. The order issued in French's name the next day forbade all anti-aircraft batteries, other than those based along the sea coast, from firing at enemy aircraft under any circumstances: 'No aeroplanes or sea-planes, <u>even if recognised as hostile</u>, will be fired at either by day or night.' Since the guns were not to be fired, they no longer needed to be manned round the clock, and the personnel spared could be shipped to the Western Front; but, given the parallel reduction in defensive fighters and air-crew, if German raiders could evade the coastal defences, they had now been handed the virtual freedom of the skies over London and the south-east. The dumbfounded commander of the London anti-aircraft batteries, Colonel Simon, continued discreet preparations of a gun defence system so that it could rapidly be deployed whenever French had a change of heart.

The equanimity of French and the War Cabinet remained un-disturbed by a raid on Kent on 11 April, when the intruder 'ventured only a hundred yards inland, and the only damage he did was the breaking of seven panes of glass in a greenhouse. There were no casualties, but a cyclist on the cliff road had a narrow escape.' The ban on inland anti-aircraft fire also survived a raid on London by a single 'nocturnal Albatros' on 7 May, the first German aircraft to overfly the capital at night. It dropped five bombs across Hackney and Holloway, killing one man in his bed, but the total damage was estimated at 'under £100' and, despite intelligence suggesting that the Germans were developing a bomber larger than any-thing seen before, the raid was still seen as an isolated and rather futile incident rather than as the harbinger of a deadly new campaign.

War Office complacency and Britain's growing sense of domestic peace and security were rudely shattered on Friday, 25 May 1917, when the first squadron of the new Gotha bombers attacked England. The previous day, as the ground-crews of the England Squadron were preparing their aircraft on the grass at St Denijs-Westrem, warning sirens sounded and a flight of de Havilland DH4s from Dunkirk swooped down on the airfield, dropping sticks of bombs that bracketed the eight Gothas drawn up on the edge of the runway. No serious damage was done to the airfield or the aircraft, but it was a warning that German hopes of maintaining the secrecy of the England Squadron were doomed. Undeterred, the air-crews readied themselves for their first flight to England. London was the principal target, but Brandenburg had also identified a series of secondary objectives such as 'the war ports of Sheerness, Harwich and Dover and the coastal towns of Margate and Ramsgate' if weather precluded an attack on the capital.

At two o'clock on the afternoon of 25 May, the England Squadron's flight of twenty-three Gotha bombers took off in bright sunshine from St Denijs-Westrem and Gontrode, with the spires of the city of Ghent shimmering in the haze of a hot afternoon. 'It was a rarely beautiful sight to see the squadron take off and climb into the sky,' Major Siegert noted. Within thirty minutes they were landing again. 'Our aircraft weren't equipped with a reserve fuel tank ... and, to increase our range, we stopped to refuel at Nieumunster near Blankenberghe on the Flanders coast.' Less than forty miles from their starting point, it was a further reminder of how tight were the margins when attacking a target at or close to the limit of the Gothas' range.

After they took off again, the rates of climb of the individual aircraft varied considerably and the crews of the first Gothas were forced to idle their engines as they awaited the others, for the leader 'could not give the signal for departure until the last aeroplane had reached the height of its companions'. Finally they were together, in 'a V-formation like a flight of ducks', with aircraft positioned to the right and left in trail of the flight leader, and stepped by altitude, ensuring the most effective fields of defensive fire when under attack by fighters, though this advantage was vitiated to some degree by the close-packed formation offering 'a better target for the enemy A/A defences'. One aircraft had already developed engine problems and turned back before they had refuelled, and as they flew on, climbing to 12,000 feet over the empty expanses of the North Sea, a second Gotha – its white fuselage painted with writhing snakes which had earned it the nickname of 'The Serpent Machine' – began to struggle.

The crew could already make out the English coastline when the smooth engine-note suddenly changed. The pilot, Leutnant Erwin Kollberg, struggled to maintain control of the Gotha as its starboard engine spluttered and faded. He waved to his observer, Walter Aschoff, at his seat in the nose of the aircraft, and pointed at the right engine. When Aschoff wriggled through the narrow tunnel connecting his cockpit with the rest of the aircraft he 'saw at once that the rev-counter was swinging wildly and the engine was steadily losing power. All the weight of the fully-laden aircraft was now falling on the second engine.

'Would this one last, despite the strain, or would it also fail? Were we doomed not to see our homes again? We were powerless and at the mercy of the failing engines, preying on our nerves more even than combat with all its dangers. We fell ever further behind the squadron and were steadily losing altitude. We had to accept the inevitable and turn for home, and I fired red flares to signal that we were aborting the flight. It was a hard decision to make, but facing the enemy defences with only one engine would have been suicide.

'The squadron disappeared to the north-west, leaving us alone over the sea and, without the protection of the formation, exposed to the greatest risk of being shot down. The rear-gunner could hold off a single attacking aircraft, but he would be powerless against two or more enemies. We were still losing altitude and I jettisoned into the sea all the precious bombs that should have been destroying enemy targets.' Lacking a radio, Aschoff fixed a distress message to the leg of one of the two pigeons they carried and handed it back to the rear-gunner, Sergeant Mayer, who tossed it high into the slipstream safely behind the murderous discs of the Gotha's spinning propellers. It circled for a few seconds while it got its bearings and then sped away into the mist, heading south-east towards its loft at a coastal station. The alarm would be raised when it arrived, but that would almost certainly be too late to save Aschoff and his crew if they had to ditch in the sea.

They flew on, still losing altitude and speed, 'the passing minutes feeling like hours'. As they dropped lower, the grey-green waves beneath them came into ever sharper focus. Scarcely daring to breathe, his stomach muscles taut as he willed the aircraft onwards, Aschoff watched the waves slip by below them with agonizing slowness, while the starboard engine coughed black smoke and the vibrations from the straining port engine rattled the teeth in his head. Half an hour crawled by before he saw a grey, cylindrical shape, the hull of a submarine steering a north-westerly course towards them.

He stood upright, the slipstream tearing at him as he fired a flare as a recognition signal. There was a heart-stopping pause before the answering signal, a white circle, was unfurled on the submarine's deck. The recognition mark showed that it was a German craft, one of the U-boats stationed off the coast to aid bomber crews with failing engines, or who had run out of fuel. As the Gotha passed overhead, a smiling Aschoff waved to the sailors grouped on the U-boat's deck. 'Our hopes rose again; if we had to make an emergency landing on the sea, there was now at least a chance that we would be saved. The submarine tracked us all the way to the coast. We crossed it at near-minimum altitude at seven that evening, and made an immediate emergency landing on the airfield at Ghistelles where the navy flyers gave us a friendly welcome.'

Aschoff's Gotha landed not long before the return of the remainder of the squadron. Those twenty-one aircraft had flown on, passing over the Tongue lightship off the Thames estuary at about a quarter to five. The crew of the lightship radioed an immediate alert to the Admiralty, giving the estimated number of raiders and their heading, but for unexplained reasons the alert was not relayed to the London air-raid Warning Controller for another fifteen minutes. By then the raiders, 'big white machines, making a loud noise', were crossing the Essex coast just north of the River Crouch. As they did so, they formed themselves into two close formations, providing cross-protection against attack by fighters.

There was scant need of that precaution for, to the German air-crews' surprise, no aircraft rose to meet them and, in accordance with French's orders, no anti-aircraft fire speckled the skies with dark smoke-bursts as they flew on, save for a single shot fired at them them from a battery at Highland Farm, Burnham-on-Crouch. It was the only shell to be launched at them until they reached the south coast and were already turning for home. However, if the defences were inadequate – one Briton described them as 'absolutely puerile' – the weather came to London's aid. The forecast fine weather that had accompanied them all the way from Belgium gave way to thickening cloud streaming in from the west and mist was also spreading over the land below them, shrouding their sighting landmarks.

Brandenburg still hoped that his squadron could reach London before the weather closed in completely, and he would also have been aware of Zeppelin commanders' claims that 'the texture of the upper surface of the cloud belt was markedly distinct over the estuary and the broader reaches of the Thames, and that in such a way the river's course was roughly traceable towards London blanketed beneath'. He now swung his formation on to a south-westerly course, making for the Thames east of the capital.

The belated alert had now been received by the London Warning Controller and relayed to officials right across the south-east. Pilots scrambled from Manston, Westgate, Stow Maries and Rochford to intercept the raiders, but at the rate of climb of the ageing BE12s that most of them were flying it would be at least twenty minutes before they could hope to reach the German aircraft, and by that time they would be twenty-five miles away. Those British fighters had a 'ceiling' of 14,000 feet. At that height, not only would they climb no higher, but any manoeuvre, such as a sharp turn, caused them to lose five hundred feet. 'Another thing,' as one pilot laconically remarked, 'is the liability of the engine to catch fire in the air.'

Captain Cooke, Commander of C Flight at Rochford, had all those flaws demonstrated to him that May afternoon. He spotted the Gothas through a break in the clouds as he scrambled from Rochford but they were out of sight by the time his BE12 had laboured its way to 5,000 feet. Still climbing slowly, he tracked south-westwards, hoping to spot the formation again, but when he reached 13,000 feet his aircraft's engine suddenly burst into flames. He managed to extinguish the fire by executing a 'tail-slide' – dropping tail-first, using the reversed slipstream to blow the flames away from the fuselage and engine – but then noticed that the wings and centre-section were vibrating alarmingly 'owing to the inability of the machine to withstand rough usage such as it would undergo in an air fight' – an absurd state of affairs in what was supposed to be a fighter aircraft. Cooke returned to base without sighting the Gothas again.

As the raiders overflew Tilbury, dense cloud was filling the western skies and shrouding London, still twenty miles distant, from view. Cursing his luck, Brandenburg fired more signal flares: the lack of radio communications meant that once airborne he could only use hand-signals or prearranged sequences, combinations and numbers of red, green and white flares to order changes in direction, alterations to the squadron's flying formation and switches to different targets, or to abort the mission altogether. Uniquely among the aircraft of the squadron, the tail of Brandenburg's Gotha was painted blood-red to aid identification of the leader in the air.

In response to Brandenburg's signal, the formation turned south, switching the attack to the secondary targets along the Kent coast. Unaware of this change, British fighters continued to search along the Gothas' reported track towards London. For twenty-five minutes no one on the ground or in the air had the least idea where the raiders were; they had apparently disappeared without trace. Although 'observation of the enemy was greatly hampered by the clouds which were very thick over Essex', there were no such problems in Kent where the cloud cover was broken. Information from ground observers, unfamiliar with the undulating note of the Gothas' twin engines, merely added to the confusion. As the Gothas passed over Gravesend, a local naval unit reported 'a fleet of Zeppelins making a great noise, overhead a stink of paraffin'. Still, had anyone known the Gothas' new routeing, they would have struggled to communicate that information to the fighter pilots, because once they were airborne the direction of the threat could only be signalled by laying out large white arrows on the ground, or using a system devised by Lieutenant Ingram of the RNAS involving three eight-foot-diameter discs and a cloth T-shape forty feet long by twenty feet wide. The position of the discs relative to the 'T' could be used to convey up to forty different prearranged messages. In theory, both systems were visible from 14,000 feet to as much as 17,000 feet; in practice, in cloudy or misty conditions, such as the heat haze and overcast sky of 25 May 1917, they were invisible.

The Gothas were next spotted over Wrotham, heading south, but once more warnings were delayed or mislaid – one police constable was unable to get his warning through because 'the reply came they were engaged' – and the military bases and towns in their path remained unaware of the danger. A scattering of bombs was dropped on villages and railway lines in Kent – the first casualty of the raid was a sheep – and the railway works at

Ashford. The raiders also encountered the first British aircraft they had seen since they crossed the coastline, but it was airborne not because it had been scrambled to fight the raiders but because it was being delivered from the factory to the Western Front; even worse, the pilot, Lieutenant Baker, had not been issued with ammunition for his guns and was a sitting target. Hit repeatedly by machine-gun fire, he was forced to make an emergency landing at the RFC base at Lympne. He had barely touched down when the Gothas swept overhead and peppered the airfield with a score of bombs, damaging hangars and aircraft.

They reached the south coast at Hythe, home of the RFC's School of Aerial Gunnery. No aircraft had been scrambled from the base and no anti-aircraft gunners had been alerted. Air- and ground-crews scattered in panic as the Gothas unleashed another fusillade of bombs. The bomb-aiming was less accurate this time and more damage was done to the Church of England than the RFC: the verger of Hythe parish church and a member of the congregation were killed by a bomb, and the vicar and his wife injured. Local people, infuriated that none of the pilots had even tried to get airborne, later hurled abuse and stones at the cowering trainees.

The raiders now swung east, back towards home, but on an into-wind course that would take them directly over Folkestone. 'Bombs had to be dropped into the wind, to prevent tail- and crosswinds blowing them off course. Experienced observers used their small 12.5kg bombs for pre- or trial drops, before releasing the heavier bombs.' As they approached, each observer in the cockpit in the nose of his Gotha placed his right hand on the bomb-release levers to his right and hunched over his Goertz bomb-sight. It was effectively a long telescope marked with cross-hairs, but the best sight available to any air-crew at the time, though it was a double-edged weapon: 'anyone who spent any time at all looking down telescopes was likely to be shot dead; it was much wiser continually to scan the sky'.

The town they were approaching was a genuine military target. Folkestone was the primary transit point for British soldiers embarking for France, and for the returning wounded and those on leave. The town was surrounded by armed camps where departing troops spent their last nights on English soil, and the harbour, bristling with guns, was busy with transports and their escort vessels. However, it was the Whitsun holiday weekend and the spring sunshine had also drawn crowds of civilians on to the streets. In the warm late-afternoon sun, visitors and day-trippers mingled with housewives and children finishing their weekend shopping.

Tontine Street, in the poorer district near the harbour, was crowded with people. Gosnold's drapers was packed, and across the street a queue snaked out of Stokes's greengrocers, where there had just been a fresh delivery of potatoes. Food shortages were now commonplace; bread was adulterated with barley, while other staples such as maize, rice, beans, oatmeal, potatoes, butter, meat, sugar, jam and even the British standby, tea, were scarce, rationed or sometimes unobtainable. A new law forbade the traditional throwing of rice at weddings – it was now too precious a foodstuff to be wasted – and one peeress railed in the newspapers against 'the wasting of the food of the common people by the starching of men's collars and cuffs, rice and maize being used in the making of starch'.

Masters of foxhounds made their own contribution to food conservation by agreeing to the previously unthinkable practice of 'shooting foxes . . . in order to prevent destruction of poultry and vegetables. More than that, they are prepared to slaughter a very large proportion of their hounds' to allow the meat and offal that the hounds normally ate to be made available for human consumption. As one cynical observer remarked, 'What a recognition of the stern necessity of conserving food for human consumption! Who ever imagined they would hear of masters of foxhounds recommending the shooting of foxes – hitherto the unforgivable sin . . . Then think of the poor fox. He is to be slaughtered instead of hunted, which it is said he so much enjoys!'

People were so desperate to find a little extra food for their families that even the rumour of a delivery to a local shop was enough to cause a queue to form. 'Anyone who penetrated the poor neighbourhoods became familiar with the queues of women and children who waited outside the shabby shops common to the poor districts of all towns. They carried baskets, string-bags, fish-basses, bags made of American cloth and babies, and stood shifting their burdens from one arm to another to ease their aching backs.' In addition to Stokes's, such queues snaked from a number of shops in Tontine Street that afternoon. At a wine shop, the owner hailed a regular customer, offered him a tasting of a new shipment and went to the back of the shop to fetch some glasses, leaving his customer gazing upwards at a flight of aeroplanes that had appeared in the sky overhead, the sun glinting from their dazzling white wings.

The distinctive double-note drone of their engines – troops described it as 'the Gotha hum' – caused more and more people to look up at the sky. One described two aeroplanes 'emerging from the disc of the sun almost overhead. Then four more, or five, in a line, and others, all light, bright, silver insects hovering against the blue of the sky . . . There were about a score in all, and we were charmed with the beauty of the sight. I am sure few of us thought seriously of danger.' Other witnesses reflected the lack of alarm the Gothas provoked, in descriptions of them as 'like seagulls', 'white and golden', 'swan-shaped' and 'like snowflakes'. A woman strolling in the sunshine saw 'about twenty aeroplanes circling and pirouetting over my head. I stopped to watch their graceful antics and thought to myself, at last we are up and doing, fondly imagining that they were our own machines practising.'

The bombs already dropped on Hythe had been clearly audible in Folkestone but the inhabitants were used to the sound of heavy gunfire from Royal Navy ships and the coastal batteries, and dismissed it as more firing practice. There was no air-raid warning to alert the population – the town's Chief Constable, Harry Reeve, later said that neither the London air-raid Warning Controller nor the Army's Eastern Command had contacted him – and unsurprisingly, a flight of aircraft heading towards the coast from inland was taken by every onlooker to be British.

There was no reason for alarm; no sirens, no anti-aircraft fire, no shouts of 'Take cover!', no warning at all, just the warmth and peace of the afternoon, and the beauty of the aircraft overhead . . . and then a series of massive blasts. The small town of Sandgate and the Shorncliffe and Cheriton military camps just west of Folkestone were the first targets; a dozen large bombs and a score of 12.5kg bombs fell on and around them. One detonated in the midst of a group of Canadian infantry assembling for an evening exercise, killing seventeen men and wounding another ninety-three.

Twenty high-explosive and thirty anti-personnel bombs were then dropped on Folkestone itself, a dozen of which detonated prematurely or failed to explode at all. The remainder wreaked havoc in the town. The wine shop owner was still at the back of his shop when an explosion shook the building. He raced outside to find his customer lying on the ground, decapitated, and the people who had been queuing outside Stokes's greengrocers strewn around the rim of a still-smoking crater. Through the dense clouds of dust and smoke swirling through the streets, he could see other bloody, prone figures and others, alive but horribly mutilated by shrapnel and flying glass, staggering away. Three or four horses also lay dead in the shafts of the carts and cabs they had been pulling. Gosnold's drapers had collapsed, entombing its staff and customers, and the neighbouring buildings had caught fire.

Three girls had been walking down Tontine Street as the bomb fell. A man standing in the doorway of the Brewery Tap pub, next door to Stokes's shop, grabbed one of them by the arm and pulled her inside, saving her life; her two friends were blown to pieces. Another bomb detonated prematurely in the air above a narrow alleyway, and the force of the blast killed every person passing through it at the time. A butler, Edward Horn, was killed in the road while trying to stop a runaway horse, another man was blown across a road and impaled on the iron railings of a school, and a housemaid and two soldiers sauntering down the street together were all killed by shrapnel from the same bomb. A girl saw a man running 'towards the hospital with a baby in his arms, and the baby was covered in blood', and a nine-year-old boy was traumatized by an even more terrible sight: 'a man's head rolled across a path and into a gutter. I didn't stop running until I got home to my parents.'

A group of girls playing in a field behind their school had a miraculous escape when a bomb fell in the middle of them but failed to detonate. The area around Tontine Street had taken the brunt of the bombing, but two cabmen and their horses were killed on the cab-rank outside the station and broken glass covered many streets like 'a thin coating of ice on a winter's day, which crackled and broke under one's feet'.

Everywhere lay the dead and dying, while the moans and cries of the injured echoed through the ruined streets. A ruptured gas main sent a jet of flame fifty feet into the air and there were 'smoke and flames all over, but worst of all were the screams of the wounded and dying, and mothers looking frantically for their kids. A couple of minutes before, those of us who were on the street were like innocent kids ourselves, as we watched those swine in the sky.' Men put the dead 'on a brewer's dray'.

Later, queues of people formed outside the hospital 'trying to find or recognise their lost ones.' Every loss that day was a tragedy, but two multiple deaths seemed particularly bleak. Three members of one family – Florence Norris, her two-year-old baby daughter and her son, who was just ten months old – were killed in Tontine Street, leaving William Norris triply bereaved. Sisters Gertrude and Mabel Bowbrick, aged twelve and nine, were also killed outright in Tontine Street and their mother, who was with them at the time, was so physically and mentally scarred that she was never released from hospital during the remaining eight years of her life.

# CHAPTER 5
# FEVERISH WORK

HIGH ABOVE THE SHATTERED STREETS, Brandenburg and the other commanders checked that the series of small lamps in their cockpits had lit up, showing that the Gotha's large bombs – stowed, nose-forward, directly under the fuselage and on either side of the centre section – had successfully been released, then continued their homeward course. They passed within range of Dover at about six o'clock. They aimed their few remaining bombs at the naval base and met the only anti-aircraft fire they had encountered during their hour-long tour of the Home Counties. Dover residents 'were startled . . . by the siren sounding and a heavy fire opening simultaneously from every A.A. gun in the place, both from the shore batteries and the ships in harbour. Looking seawards in the direction of the exploding shrapnel, we could see a long line of enemy aeroplanes.' 'The nearest bomb fell and I saw it splash into the sea just below me. I could see little clouds, probably shrapnel, bursting round the aeroplanes, but they were really too high up to be in much danger. The heavy guns from Dover began to roar and went on for some time.'

None of the anti-aircraft barrage of over three hundred shells from the coastal batteries and the Royal Navy ships just offshore found its target, though the anti-aircraft fire may have deterred the raiders from making too close a pass over the town. An onlooker watched them 'passing in a south-easterly direction over the Straits, and long after I could no longer see them I observed little clouds shining in the air'.

Although a total of seventy-four British aircraft tried to intercept the raiders, they attacked singly rather than in formation, and only two even came within range. Taking off from Dover in a Sopwith Pup, RNAS pilot Flight Lieutenant Reginald Leslie saw one Gotha that was trailing the main formation and pursued it halfway across the Channel, firing bursts into it from less than a hundred yards' range. According to Leslie, the German aircraft went into a 'steep nose-dive, emitting smoke and steam', but two other Gothas then intervened, driving off Leslie with their guns. His claimed 'kill' remained unconfirmed, but as the first British pilot to put so much as a bullet into the new German raiders, he was later awarded the Distinguished Service Cross. Another pilot, Lieutenant G. W. Gatherwood, flying a DH5 from Lympne, found a Gotha – probably the same one – trailing the main formation with black smoke pouring from one of its engines but his guns jammed as he closed in for the kill. He steered with his knees as he cleared the jam, but by then the labouring Gotha was at extreme range and Gatherwood gave up the chase.

British fighters from 4 and 9 Squadrons, operating out of Dunkirk, intercepted the Gothas out at sea as they made for the Belgian coast and shot down one of them. It crashed into the sea, killing the three crewmen – Oberleutnant Manfred Messerschmidt, Leutnant Werner Scholz and Leutnant Willy Neumann – and a senior officer, General von Arnim, who had flown with them to see this first Gotha raid on England for himself. Claims of another victim were contradicted by German records that showed that, while one Gotha had indeed been lost over the Channel, only one other aircraft had gone down, at Beernem near Bruges, probably as a result of the pilot, Leutnant Hans Parschau, having had a heart attack, though a captured German rear-gunner later told his interrogators that the pilot had 'gone mad'. The other members of the crew, Oberleutnant Kurt Paul Kleeman and Unteroffizier Alfred Dickhaut, were also killed in the crash.

The raid on Folkestone had produced the worst domestic casualty figures of the war so far: ninety-five dead and 195 injured. That black day, 'never to be effaced from memory', had a long-lasting impact on Folkestone. 'There was a change in the local atmosphere. Gone was our complacency; gone was that feeling of security and immunity with which we had previously pursued the even tenure of our way.' Many families left the town, never to return. 'The husbands said it was their wives and children who insisted on their going, while the wives said they did not mind, but it was their husbands who became so worried.'

There were mass burials in the town, and the sight of the tiny coffins of babies and children, the endless lines of mourners, and the mounds of flowers heaped around the bomb craters and the graves of the dead, fuelled a popular outrage that was as much aroused by the lack of warning and the ineffectual air defences as by the Germans' 'wholesale murder of women and children'. 'The official description of raids as "visits" drew scorn and derision', and rumours and public fears were fanned by the decision to impose strict censorship on press reports of the attack. Even though 'all Fleet Street knew the facts that same evening', newspapers were forbidden to give specific details of the raid, including its location and the extent of the damage caused. All that they were allowed to say was that German aircraft had bombed 'a coastal town to the South-East'.

The official statement that was finally put out by the War Office in Sir John French's name at midday the following day read: 'A large squadron of enemy aircraft, about sixteen in number, attacked the South-East of England between 5.15 and 6.30 p.m. last night. Bombs were dropped at a number of places but nearly all the damage occurred in one town where some of the bombs fell into the streets causing considerable casualties among the civil population. The total casualties reported by the police from all districts are: killed men 26, women 27, children 23, total 76; injured men 112, women 43, children 19, total 174 [these figures were later revised upwards as more deaths and injuries came to light].'

The ostensible purpose of the news blackout was to deny German military planners knowledge of the success of the raid; the actual consequence was to cause maximum anxiety and distress to the friends and relatives of people living in every coastal town from Harwich to Southampton. The Government was pilloried in the press for the 'childish and dangerous' way in which it had tried to stifle the news. As Lord Montagu chided the War Minister, Lord Derby, 'The public have nearly ceased to believe in official statements on account of their ambiguous character. If the Government as a whole were franker . . . some confidence would be re-established in official statements.' German newspapers were running full reports of the raid, including the identity of its target, yet British papers, in full possession of the facts, were forbidden to communicate them. By the time the Government relented a few days later and allowed Folkestone to be identified, the damage had been done.

The ability to gag the press was only one of the powers the Government had taken upon itself through the Defence of the Realm Act passed by Parliament on 8 August 1914, after a debate lasting five minutes that effectively signed away the rights won by Magna Carta seven hundred years earlier and progressively enshrined and increased over the intervening centuries. Britain was now under martial law, with civil rights and individual freedoms suspended 'for the duration', though some were never to be restored.

The claim by the first German pilot to be captured that 'You would not find one officer in the German Army or Navy who would go to war to kill women and children; such things happen accidentally in war' did nothing to dampen the public outrage and the demands for revenge, and several inquest juries returned verdicts of 'wilful murder against the Kaiser and his son, the Crown Prince'. Some British propagandists painted the German air-crews as degenerates: 'a couple of hours before the Gothas started, their crews were summoned from the brothels in which they spent most of their time'. While some sections of the press joined the chorus of condemnation of German 'baby-killers', *The Times* conceded that the German objectives had been 'essentially of military importance and the plan for attaining them was most carefully conceived and carried out'. It was clear that London would soon be attacked – a captured German airman confirmed that the capital had been the primary target for the Folkestone raid until cloud intervened – and Lord Montagu acknowledged that 'it is absolute humbug in my opinion to talk about London being an undefended city. The Germans have a perfect right to raid London. It is defended by guns and squadrons of aeroplanes and it is the chief seat of energy for the war. We are only deluding ourselves when we talk about London being an undefended city, and of no military importance.' In an unguarded moment, Lloyd George later gave German propagandists all the ammunition they needed by describing London as a 'second Woolwich – one single arsenal'.

In the House of Commons, Noel Pemberton-Billing once more castigated the Government and Lord French for their failings. He went on to warn that during the coming summer, German bombers flying at 15,000 or 20,000 feet 'may drop their bombs and get back before we know where they are'. He advocated pre-emptive raids and reprisals; 'otherwise we shall have such a wail of indignation if we are raided day and night in the coming months that it may bring the Government down'. He had a surprising supporter in Lord Fisher, who had only narrowly been prevented from resigning as First Sea Lord after the Government declined to adopt his preferred remedy: for every civilian killed by German bombs, a hostage from the German population in British hands should be shot.

The furore prompted the Chief of the Imperial General Staff, Field

Marshal Sir William 'Wullie' Robertson, to call a conference to discuss means of improving 'the defence of the United Kingdom against attack by aeroplanes'. The Admiralty, still charged with the air defence of Britain's inshore waters and coastline, was lambasted for its failure to relay rapid early warnings of the raiders' approach, preventing the RFC aircraft responsible for inland airspace from getting airborne in time to engage the enemy. Changes were proposed and implemented, but they were modest in the extreme. Bombing raids were to be stepped up on the Gothas' home airfields in the hope of disrupting future attacks on England; two dozen anti-aircraft observers were recalled from France and stationed on light-ships along the east coast and in the Thames estuary to watch for German raiders; and some air-training squadrons were moved to airfields in the south-east, where attacks by German bombers were most likely to occur.

These moves fell far short of the sweeping changes that were needed, and French criticized the folly of basing London's air defence on 'such machines and pilots as happen to be at any given time available at Training Squadrons . . . the present policy may have disastrous results'. Excluding the RNAS aircraft under Admiralty control, a theoretical total of forty RFC aircraft was now available to defend London – only twenty-two had got airborne on the day of the Folkestone raid – but even this modest number included a number of outmoded SE5s that in speed and rate of climb were incapable of overhauling a Gotha, even when carrying a full bombload. Yet, despite his criticisms, French did not even revoke the order prohibiting gun-crews, other than those at coastal stations, from firing at enemy aircraft, and a further attempt by Sir David Henderson to install ground-to-air radio communications in fighter aircraft was again vetoed by the Admiralty on the grounds that it might interfere with communications with the Fleet.

The first retaliatory bombing raids on one of the England Squadron's home airfields, St Denijs-Westrem, on 28 May and 4 June 1917, damaged the runway but destroyed no further Gotha bombers, and after the success of the Folkestone raid von Höppner was now pressing for a swift attack on London. However, Brandenburg's elation at the previous raid was tempered by his displeasure at the unreliability of the Mercedes engines and the losses of aircraft and men, and he petitioned von Höppner to make fighter cover available to meet all future returning bombers.

The next raid was set for 5 June, but faced with a forecast of probable thunderstorms over the capital, Brandenburg designated the sprawling naval dockyards at Sheerness on the Isle of Sheppey as an alternative target. At five o'clock that afternoon, twenty-two Gothas of the England Squadron took off from St Denijs-Westrem and Gontrode. All were now fitted with reserve tanks and they overflew Nieumunster without needing to refuel. 'The visibility was particularly clear', and while still twenty-five kilometres from the English coast they were spotted by a patrol of four RNAS aircraft flying out of Dunkirk. They pursued the Gothas towards the coast without engaging them, and were then forced to land at Manston to refuel. The raiders had also been spotted by the Kentish Knock lightship at twenty to six that evening and they immediately alerted the Admiralty. By coincidence an air defence exercise had been in progress that afternoon, and when the alarm was raised thirty RFC aircraft had just landed after a two-hour patrol. Most were refuelled and airborne again within twenty minutes of that, but their rate of climb was too slow to intercept the Gothas, flying at 15,000 feet, and they passed overhead, well out of range.

They crossed the coast near Foulness Point, triggering a barrage of anti-aircraft fire from the shore batteries – which, unlike the inland batteries, were still permitted to fire at enemy aircraft – and then swung southwards, overflying the munitions works and the Army gunnery ranges at Shoeburyness on the north shore, where twenty-one high-explosive bombs and a handful of 12.5kg anti-personnel bombs were dropped to minimal effect, save the killing of two soldiers. Most of the bombs fell on the beach or on waste ground and others exploded prematurely or not at all. The raiders were met with concentrated anti-aircraft fire, and though it brought down none of them, Brandenburg formally gave up the attempt to reach London at that point and fired flares to signal the switch to the principal alternative target. He then led the formation southwards across the Thames to begin the attack run on Sheerness.

Land-based fighters were still rising to the defence, though the majority of the sixty-six that did get airborne failed even to get within firing range of the raiders. But one bomber – possibly suffering from the Gothas' perennial engine problems – fell behind the formation. It dropped four bombs on the anti-aircraft battery at Barton's Point but was then attacked 'by several one-seaters and went into a tailspin'. The commander of another Gotha 'watched as the spiralling turns became tighter and tighter, until it crashed into the waters of the Thames estuary far below us. I could see English coastal vessels setting out from the shore towards the crash-site and prayed that they would be in time to save the crew.'

Those watching from the shore took an understandably different view. It was a perfect summer's afternoon and the sea-front at Sheerness was packed with people. Some were convalescent wounded soldiers, but the majority were civilians, predominantly women and children. They watched spellbound as the raiders 'came across the water from Essex; one was seen to fall and the onlookers raised a great cheer, despite their own imminent danger'. The pilot of the Gotha, Vizefeldwebel Erich Kluk, drowned, and though the other two crewmen were rescued, one of them, Leutnant Hans Francke, died of his wounds. The gunner, Unteroffizier Georg Schumacher, nursing a broken leg, was the only survivor.

The rest of the Gothas flew on, 'despite the flak bursting all round us, and dropped 5,000kg of bombs on the target'. Several bombs exploded in and around the docks, sinking a number of small vessels and setting fire to the Grand Store. The arsenal was also hit, one bomb causing a huge explosion that sent debris flying several hundred feet into the air. It may have been one of the ones dropped by Walter Aschoff, who exulted that his bombs had fallen 'on a huge building/arsenal in the middle of the fortress, which soon started burning merrily . . . on the way back, one still saw two large fires'.

The damage and casualties could have been much worse: several bombs 'which hit important targets failed to explode'; a group of 'curious soldiers' kept prodding one of them with their canes and had to be begged to stop by alarmed onlookers. Local newspaper reports on the raid, identifying Sheerness only as 'a Kentish town', claimed that 'when the anti-aircraft guns were heard, most of the people in the streets took shelter, otherwise the casualties would have been heavier . . . but the local hospitals are dealing with a considerable number of serious cases'. In fact, thirteen people were killed and another thirty-four injured but, in marked contrast to the attack on Folkestone, only a quarter of the casualties were civilians.

The raiders turned for home at once, pursued by a handful of British fighters. More were lying in wait off Dunkirk but they were intercepted by the German fighters waiting to escort the Gothas back to base, as Brandenburg had requested. A running battle ensued along the Dutch coast and British pilots claimed to have shot down one Gotha and three fighters, though official German documents refuted those claims. In a letter to his parents the next day, Walter Aschoff, who 'came home safe, but tired, but can't hear yet' – the incessant thunder of the engines during his long flight had taken its toll – noted that 'all but one of my *Staffel* made it home'.

Whether by accident or design, British newspapers were misinformed about the results of the raid and splashed the claim that of twenty German bombers half had been destroyed. One paper sneered that 'England hopes such attacks will be repeated often'. In fact, only one Gotha had been shot down; its mangled wreckage was dredged from the murky waters of the Thames estuary so that British commanders could attempt to evaluate this new German secret weapon. Under interrogation, the captured rear-gunner of the doomed aircraft, Georg Schumacher, revealed for the first time the existence and aims of the England Squadron.

One immediate result was that Sir John French at last rescinded the order prohibiting inland anti-aircraft batteries from firing at enemy aircraft, and further attempts were also made to improve the response time of the RFC. On 9 June, more than thirty fighters were able to reach operational height within twenty minutes of a practice air-raid warning being received. Whether they could respond with such alacrity to the next genuine alert would soon be tested. On the same day a squadron of RNAS bombers from Dunkirk again pounded the airfield at St Denijs-Westrem, but once more the damage was rapidly repaired, the craters filled and levelled.

With varying degrees of patience, the commander and crews of the England Squadron awaited the favourable weather conditions that would trigger another attack on England. Everything had now been 'well planned and field-tested . . . but we have now encountered an enemy that we cannot evade – the weather'. Even with reserve fuel-tanks and a reduced bombload, London still represented the outer limits of the Gothas' range in any but the most favourable conditions. The prerequisite for a successful flight to London was 'a weather pattern that on average only occurs once every three weeks, and even when those conditions are in place, the weather, and above all the wind strength and direction in the Channel and across Flanders, must remain stable for six to seven hours'.

The squadron's weather officer, Leutnant Cloessner, a trained meteorologist recruited from an airship squadron, was hampered by two serious obstacles. The weather conditions ruling on one side of the Channel were often an imperfect guide to what was happening on the far side, and given the prevailing westerlies that dominated the British weather and the fact that Ghent was 150 miles east of London, Cloessner was effectively trying to predict the atmospheric conditions in London in several hours' time by the weather patterns that had been ruling several hours before. However, on 12 June he made a confident forecast of very favourable weather conditions for the following day and the members of the England Squadron at once began final preparations. 'All squadrons were working feverishly, with everyone wanting to contribute to the success of the first raid on London.'

Targets were selected the day before the raid, so that 'pilots and observers might have an opportunity of studying aerial photographs of the target, so as to imprint its appearance from the air upon their memories'. Walter Aschoff's maps and equipment had been prepared for a long time. 'We had envisaged every conceivable scenario and there was now nothing more to be done, but just the same, I subjected everything to yet another round of checks. I pored over the big map of London, memorising the twists and turns of the Thames, the lie of the streets and the location of our targets, and calculated the possible flight-paths one last time, then I headed for the airfield.

'The air was filled with the roar and rumble of the magnificent Mercedes engines and as I listened, I closed my eyes and let my thoughts carry me far away to England. Engineers hurried to and fro, aircraft rolled past, engines fired, as everyone strove to eliminate any last minor errors. Above me an aircraft on a test flight came in to land, and the black serpents painted on its side showed it was the one to which I and my crew would soon entrust our lives.'

While his pilot was speaking to the engineers and giving his last orders, Aschoff climbed into the observation turret, 'tested the bomb-release levers, flipped open the compass, looked into the panels where spare parts, flares and other pieces of equipment are stowed, and pulled on the signal devices, just to check them'. Then the crew of the Serpent Machine returned to their quarters.

It was a short night for air- and ground-crews alike. Before three in the morning of 13 June they were once more at Gontrode and St Denijs-Westrem, standing on the dew-sodden grass of the airfields as one after another the Gothas, gleaming an eerie white in the moonlight, were pushed out of the hangars and readied for take-off. While pilots, observers and gunners made final checks of their equipment, armourers in-stalled and activated their bombloads. Each crew member had his own superstitions before a flight, but all shared an aversion to letting their gaze dwell on the equipment stored in the centre of the fuselage, carried in case of an emergency landing.

To save weight, the crew were not issued with parachutes – they would have been little use anyway if forced to bail out over the North Sea – and being shot down or suffering a total engine failure was likely to be fatal for the entire crew. The Gothas had been fitted with air-bags, water-brakes and watertight vents in the fuselage, but the manufacturers' original claims that they would stay afloat for eight hours after ditching in the sea proved to be wildly optimistic, if not wilfully misleading. 'The Gotha "G" aero-planes could perhaps, under the most favourable circumstances, have kept afloat for half an hour', but in practice crewmen knew that their aircraft was likely to break up and sink almost at once and many did not even bother loading the air-bags on to their aircraft. Even if they did remain afloat, they carried no radio to alert rescuers to their position and were only permitted to fire flares once they had already sighted a rescuer.

A wire and wood cage containing two carrier pigeons was one of the last items to be installed – not mascots for the unit that had formerly borne the name of the Carrier Pigeon Squadron, of course, but the only means by which the commander of a damaged or failing aircraft far out over the North Sea could alert potential rescuers waiting on the Belgian shore. The most advanced technology of its age was dependent for survival on a system first used by the ancient Egyptians and Persians three thousand years earlier.

After taking further observations in the early hours of that morning, 13 June, Cloessner predicted a light easterly wind up to 4,000 metres (13,000 feet) and a light westerly above 4,500 metres (14,500 feet). If his prediction was correct, the squadron could use those tailwinds on both the outward and return flights. Hours passed, the day broke and the sun rose higher and higher in a clear blue sky, burning off the thick mist that had crept over the airfields before dawn. The air-crews breakfasted together on black bread, sausage and coffee. They ate better than most of their countrymen at home for whom meat, even sausage adulterated with grain and ersatz ingredients that were alleged to include sawdust, was becoming a great rarity.

Twenty-two aircraft would be taking off from the airfields of Gontrode and St Denijs-Westrem. Those left behind needed minor repairs and adjustments that would 'quickly have been remedied. I was only dissuaded from this,' Brandenburg later wrote, 'because Leutnant Cloessner warned me that there would be thunderstorms after 1500 hours.' Brandenburg dared delay no longer and gave orders to take off at ten o'clock.

As the disappointed flight crews stood down, the engineers and armourers carried out their final checks on the other aircraft, and Brandenburg briefed his men on the latest wind and weather data, their routeing and target allocation. Following the earlier raids, the British defences would be on alert, and Brandenburg had chosen two diversionary targets, Margate and Shoeburyness, hoping to draw off some of the capital's fighter defences. Squadrons of naval aircraft were again on standby to protect the raiders on the last stages of their return flight. Another Gotha, unburdened by bombs, was to carry out a photo-reconnaissance of the Thames, gathering information on future targets and the disposition of defensive gun batteries. With the stimulus of war, aerial photography had undergone a similar exponential development to the aircraft themselves: from blurred images to 'stereoscopic clarity', single exposures to 'cinematographical series of many hundred exposures', and dependence on sunlight to night-photography.

Brandenburg wished his men good luck, then strode away to his own aircraft as the ground-crew brought each crewman his fur coat, gloves and protective clothing. 'We dressed or were dressed. Swaddled like mummies, unrecognisable, but protected from the cold, we climbed into our aircraft.' Walter Aschoff squeezed himself through the narrow passageway past the cockpit of his pilot, Erwin Kollberg, to his own cramped, circular 'pulpit' in the nose of the aircraft, its rim marked by the geared Parabellum ring that allowed him to swivel his machine-gun. He settled himself into his seat and went through his final series of checks, practised so many times that they had become automatic.

A steel oxygen cylinder, fitted with a rubber breathing tube, occupied part of the limited space, but like many of his peers Aschoff rarely used it, preferring the discomforts of the thin air at high altitude to the sore throat that resulted from sucking the oxygen into his mouth. Directly in front of him was the rubber eyepiece of the one-metre, vertically mounted telescope projecting right through the fuselage – the Goertz bombsight he would use to target London. As he waited for the signal to move off, he let his hand rest for a moment on the bank of bomb-release levers, then reached down once more to touch his lucky charm, the scarred, thin iron rod he carried on every flight. His crewmates shared his superstition and each of them had asked him as they arrived at the airfield that morning, 'You haven't left the rod behind?'

At last all was ready. 'The propellers were started, the brake blocks taken away – all free. We gave a quick wave to the ground-crew, whose eyes sent the unspoken message, "Come back in one piece."' Groaning, shuddering and belching fumes from their exhausts, the massive aircraft lined up one behind another, waiting for the signal that would launch them into the air. At exactly ten o'clock, Brandenburg, seated in the pulpit in the nose of his distinctive red-tailed aircraft, raised his hand and let it fall, and his pilot, Leutnant Radke, at once gunned the engines and sent his aircraft roaring and rattling over the airfield. It climbed into the sky, followed by the other two flight leaders.

In metronomic succession the flight leaders' squadrons, comprising another nineteen Gothas, turned on to the runway of their airfields and, at the wave of the red flag from the Startoffizier, accelerated and took off.

Most carried a payload of 12.5kg and 50kg bombs, totalling no more than half the aircraft's theoretical capacity; the range and altitude at which they would be flying precluded a heavier bombload. Apart from the aircraft detailed to carry out the photo-reconnaissance mission, a few other Gothas also carried no bombs, the extra speed and manoeuvrability this allowed enabling them to take on or decoy away enemy fighters targeting the formation.

In the Serpent Machine, Aschoff 'gave a quick look back at Kollberg, answered by a nod – ready then – and off'. Kollberg was a nineteen-year-old who had begun his military career in an Uhlan regiment and still wore his cavalry uniform and spurs, as if his aircraft was an airborne steed. He had had ambitions to follow in the footsteps of Richthofen, who had served in the same Uhlan regiment before becoming Germany's greatest fighter ace, but Kollberg still found himself flying a lumbering white Gotha rather than a blood-red fighter from Richthofen's Flying Circus.

As he pushed the throttle lever forward, the engines thundered, sending shuddering vibrations through the aircraft and the bodies of its crew. Ponderously at first, but then accelerating as the white, tense faces of the watching ground-crew blurred and disappeared from view, the Gotha rumbled down the runway, the smell of crushed grass beneath its wheels lost in the stink of exhaust fumes. There was a bump and a rattle as it crossed the dirt track running diagonally across the airfield, then a groan and a thud as the nose wheels lifted clear, and for a second the rear landing-gear carried the full weight of the heavily laden aircraft. Then with a final bump and lurch the Gotha was airborne, climbing towards the heavens, trailing parallel streams of black smoke from its straining engines. 'We flew towards the sky and distant shores . . . and perhaps death. To the east, through the mist, I could see the silhouettes of the other squadrons.'

Once airborne, they throttled back, waiting as the last aircraft to take off joined them, then formed up, first in groups and then, as the flights from the two airfields came together, taking up the squadron's diamond formation. Headed by Brandenburg, they set a course towards the distant, invisible target, 'like a flock of migratory birds, on the way to unknown territories'.

Their course at first took them northwards. The sunlight shimmered on rivers and canals, though the meadows were still wreathed in thin mist. 'Old towns woke from their dreams, pretty Flanders villages appeared and then faded from our view again as new sights caught our eyes. As we drew closer to the coast, we could see in the distance the light catching the long white strand that marked the limit of the land. Beyond lay the North Sea.'

Signalling engine problems, two Gothas had dropped out of the formation almost at once and returned to base. Genuine engine trouble was a regular occurrence, but some pilots also turned tail through fear. A later German report reached the conclusion that 'it was always the same few crews that made it through to the heart of London and achieved the desired incisive effect. Not the quantity, but first and foremost the quality of the crews and of the technical material, were decisive.'

The remainder of the formation flew on to the north, climbing to 9,000 feet by the time they passed over Zeebrugge. The curving concrete mole extending out to sea from the harbour showed as a white arc against the grey-green waters. Far below the Gothas, torpedo boats stood ready to go to the aid of any air-crew forced to come down over the sea. The black plumes of smoke from their funnels drifted south-west with the breeze. The Gothas were now 'out over the open, eternal sea. Other aircraft of our formation danced within our sight, hovering above or below us, so close that we had to remain constantly alert to the danger of a collision that could send us plummeting into the depths before we had even reached the target. We were still climbing, now at 13,500 feet, high above the white-crested waves of the North Sea. In the clear air I could see an almost infinite distance, and far ahead I caught a first glimpse of a strip of land – English land. From then on our eyes and thoughts were directed only at what lay before us.'

Halfway between Zeebrugge and the English coast, Brandenburg fired a flare to signal the turn on to a south-westerly course to make landfall just north of the Thames estuary, and at around 10.30, just to the north of the Tongue lightship, a solitary Gotha peeled away from the main formation to make the diversionary attack on Margate.

As the rest flew on, the changing colour of the sea below them showed that they were nearing the coast, the muddy outflow of the Thames staining the sea for miles around. In near-perfect visibility with only a faint haze in the distance, they had little trouble in identifying their coastal marker-points. To the north they could see well beyond Harwich, and southward, past the broad estuary of the Thames, Margate and Ramsgate stood out on the distinctive peninsula of the North Foreland. Even further south, gleaming in the sunlight, the white cliffs rose sheer from the sea, broken by the ports of Dover and Folkestone.

As they neared the coast, ships of all sizes ploughed through the waves beneath them. South-east of Harwich, a convoy of over twenty merchant ships was sailing north, with an escort of torpedo boats and destroyers to guard against U-boat attack. As soon as the Gothas were sighted, fearing the bombs they carried, the warships began steering a zigzag course, churning the grey waters behind them to foam, but the German crews flew on without a backward glance; 'today our bombs are meant for a better target'.

As the land came into closer, sharper focus, the ships on picket duty offshore and then the air defence batteries lining the coast at Southend fired the first salvos at the raiders. 'Suddenly, small white puffs of smoke burst in the air around us. As they dissolved, others covered the sky, but they didn't distract or deter the experienced flyers who were well used to shell-bursts and blasts.' In any event, most of the anti-aircraft fire was aimed too high. 'German bomber squadrons were now flying over the hitherto unreachable and invulnerable island. The feeling that we were part of a unique and extraordinary experience lit up our eyes and made our hearts pound in our chests.'

The first Gotha had already reached Margate. Two defensive guns unleashed a barrage that left the enemy aircraft unscathed and it dropped its load of 50kg bombs on the town, causing minimal damage beyond broken window glass, though four people were injured. However, the diversion had its desired effect when a message that Margate was under attack by German bombers caused fighters from Manston and Westgate to scramble to repel the intruders. Almost simultaneously, a lighthouse radioed a warning that nineteen Gothas had crossed the coast on course for Foulness, but that failed to set alarm bells ringing in London. Three other Gothas split from the formation as they passed over the mouth of the River Crouch. One sped up the Thames on its reconnaissance mission, the others attacked Barling and Shoeburyness, where the bombs, missing the village, buried themselves in the deep mud and did little damage beyond injuring two people.

As the diversionary raiders turned for home, the remainder of the dwindling formation – seventeen Gothas – passed over their marker point of Foulness Island and held their course for London. They adopted the same route on almost all the London flights, using as way-points 'Ostend, Foulness Sands on the North side of the Thames Estuary, [and] a big wood [Epping Forest] just north of London'.

They flew on, parallel to the Thames and twenty kilometres to the north, as 'out of the green fields ahead of us a monstrous dark mass, black and grey, began to take shape. It grew broader and longer, increasing in size until it filled the horizon. Houses rose up, thousands upon thousands of them, streets, squares and open spaces, forming the unmistakable outline of the metropolis – London.' As they overflew the northern suburbs, Brandenburg's aircraft, leading the way, signalled by firing a red flare and the formation wheeled southward towards the city's heart.

Visibility over London was unusually clear and 'all details could be made out with ease'. 'We were flying 15,000 feet above the world's biggest city, an enthralling, indescribable experience. Stations, factories and warehouses looked like pieces in a game. Further to the east, on the many tributaries and canals leading to the Thames, large shipyards and docks unfurled. Out of the formless masses of stone and brick, the sinister fortress of the Tower, St Paul's Cathedral and the Bank of England were unmistakable landmarks. What panic and fear of death was now gripping those people in the sea of houses far below us, as they desperately searched for protection and cover? But though they were like us and of our blood, we could not think about the people who lived in this metropolis. We were at war after all, total war that demanded all our strength and resolve.'

The people in the streets three miles below them gazed up 'wonderstruck' at the sight of the pure white Gothas, silvered by the morning sunlight and hovering 'like hawks over a dovecot'. The sky was 'blue and gold and clear, enemy aeroplanes journeyed though the clouds like little silver birds and their passage was watched by thousands of men and women . . . It was not easy to believe that those little silver specks far up in the heavens had the power to bring death and destruction and unendurable suffering.'

The Gothas remained unchallenged by any British aircraft, but the guns defending the capital were pumping shells into the sky. They exploded with a sound one pilot likened to 'a gorilla cracking a nut'. 'Projectiles from hostile batteries were sputtering and exploding beneath and all around us, while below the earth seemed to be rocking.' 'The barrage of defensive fire from the gun-batteries encircling the city grew so intense that the smoke from shell-bursts clouded the otherwise clear sky. The blasts of the explosions were so loud in our ears that they sometimes drowned the roar of our engines, and forced our aircraft to weave and lose height to dodge them, beating them down at times, threatening to rip apart the squadron formation.'

The German navigators stood upright, crouched over their bomb-sights, peering down, searching for their marks, as the panorama of London unfolded beneath them with agonizing slowness. The first bomb was dropped on Barking around half past eleven that morning and seven fell on East Ham, killing four people and wounding another thirteen. In Stratford Broadway 'the sun was shining and everything looked at peace' when a commercial traveller, William Walker, suddenly saw 'everyone was jumping off buses, trams were left deserted. An inspector of police grabbed my shoulder, saying, "Look up there. And for God's sake take cover." The sight fascinated me. Over my head were a number of what looked like large white butterflies. Now puffs of white smoke were break-ing high in the air round them . . . Soon came the frequent dull boom, then a horrid crash. I ran across the road. Three people were laid out at my feet. The gutters were running red.'

In Stoke Newington on that bright June morning 'the drone overhead of an aeroplane caused hardly anyone to look upwards, for we had grown accustomed to the passing to and fro of our own machines. A peculiar intermittent feature of the droning, with a decided increase in its volume, however, aroused the curiosity of one soldier home on leave from France and, looking skywards, he shouted, "Blimey, take cover!" A policeman on point duty took up the cry and blew his whistle loudly . . . Simultaneously a shattering explosion rent the air, followed by others and then a rush. Pedestrians dashed madly for the nearest deep shelter [but] there was no friendly depth of Underground stations here in this district.'

One of the children in a nearby school recalled that their teacher told them to sing 'what we like and the louder the better', but it did not drown out the crash of bombs. 'Tongues of flame leapt in the air and these and the continued crashes told of targets found – houses, schools, factories. Across the road lay a horse writhing in its death-throes. Its driver was buried beneath the splintered debris of the cart. Screams of terrified children mingled with the moans of the wounded.'

Out of 'a shop with its front demolished . . . a limp form was being carried between two men – a young girl, whom they placed in the doubt-ful shelter of a doorway, putting a screen of flour sacks to hide from view the terrible wounds she had received. A shop shutter-board bore another victim; and then flames enveloped the whole shop. Further rescue was impossible and we heard the piteous cry of the friends of those two people claimed by death after all.'

The Royal Albert Docks were also hit, killing eight dockers, and in Bethnal Green a bootmaker, a Jewish refugee from pogroms in Russia, returned home to find his house destroyed by a bomb, and his wife and four of his seven children dead. Four children of a munitions worker were killed by another bomb, and yet another slaughtered Annie Stamford, three, and her baby sister Ivy. Their mother, whose husband was serving on the Western Front, 'had had four children and now had none'.

One of the Gotha formation's prime targets, Liverpool Street station, now lay ahead. 'With my telescope in one hand, I signal with the other to my pilot. Slowly long rows of streets pass the small orbit of the sight. At last it is time . . . I push the levers and anxiously follow the flight of the released bombs. With a tremendous crash they strike the heart of England. It is a magnificently terrific spectacle . . . the earth seems to be rocking and houses are disappearing in craters and conflagrations, in the light of the glaring sun.'

Between 11.40 and 11.42 that morning, seventy-two bombs rained down on and around Liverpool Street. Of those, only three hit the station itself and one of them failed to explode. The other two, bursting through the great arched glass roof, blew apart two trains and left the platforms 'knee-deep in broken glass, through which killed and wounded could only be removed with difficulty'. One train comprised a series of coaches in which railway employees eligible for military service were being examined by an Army Medical Board. Several men were killed or injured. The other bomb destroyed a passenger train that was about to leave for Hunstanton from the 'country' end of platform nine. The dining-car was destroyed and two other coaches set ablaze, as gas cylinders exploded, trapping several people and burning three to death.

Mrs W. Pawney had been sitting with three other people in one of the train's compartments when they heard 'an explosion in the distance. The men exchanged a scared look; they lived at Stratford and had had many sleepless nights due to raids; my friend and I lived at Hammersmith, so we laughed at them, saying, "Don't worry. We shall be all right." At that moment another bang, louder than the first, made them insist on our leaving the train to seek shelter. We condescendingly gave in. A porter was taking luggage down in a lift from the platform. We asked him to take us. "Of course," he said, and we stepped in. One of the men hung behind. "Wait for our friend," I said, but the liftman said, "No time to wait for anyone."

'Then two terrific bangs. We were all thrown up in the air and down in a heap. My friend and I were very badly injured and the man who had been left behind, we never saw again. The carriage we had just left was completely flattened to the rails.'

Siegfried Sassoon was on the station at the time, and while he 'stood wondering what to do, a luggage trolley was trundled past me; on it lay an elderly man, shabbily dressed and apparently dead . . . In a trench one was acclimatised to the notion of being exterminated and there was a sense of organised retaliation. But here one was helpless; an invisible enemy sent destruction spinning down from a fine weather sky; poor old men bought a railway ticket and were trundled away again dead on a barrow; wounded women lay about in the station groaning.'

The remaining bombs fell in the area around the station, wreaking havoc in the streets and close-packed buildings. One bomb made a direct hit on a bus and Hector Poole saw the driver 'standing in the road, gazing at his hand, from which several fingers were missing. He seemed unaware of what had happened and said, "I think I've run someone over, mate. Help me get him out." I looked under the bus and saw a man's head and shoulders; much of the body had been blown to pieces. The bomb had apparently entered the bus over the driver's head, travelled through the floor and burst beneath the platform of the conductor, who had been killed. The passengers were blown towards the front of the bus, shockingly injured and killed. The sole exception was a girl of about nine, who was seated on the remains of the floor and crying. The lower part of both her legs was missing.

'A fire engine drew up with an Army officer perched on the mudguard. "Come along to the fire. You can't do much more here." I jumped on to the other mudguard and off we went to a fire near Wood Street, caused by an incendiary bomb. I was given the business end of a hose and told to go up a fire-escape to the roof. On the roof were some soldiers. Feeling the roof give beneath my feet, I sat astride the parapet, calling to the others to join me. All but one did so. Suddenly the roof caved in and flame, clouds of smoke and showers of sparks arose from within the building. The soldier who failed to gain the parapet disappeared into the fire and lost his life. On my hands and knees, I proceeded along the wall, which seemed to sway, with the street fifty feet below to my left and the fire to my right. I reached earth by a fire-escape and felt a sudden attack off nausea. At my hotel the porter could scarcely recognise me, for my face was blackened and scorched by the fire.'

Thomas Summers threw himself flat as the first bomb went off. As he got to his feet, he saw that 'a pram with a baby in it that I noticed just before, near a shop, has vanished, and a hole marks the place where it stood. Panic prevails as a ring of crashes descends around us; fires start and numbers of women and children are rushing for a railway shelter where nearly eight hundred people have sought safety. A pair of maddened horses rush by. I attend to a boy who was lost. After getting him safely to shelter, I miss my wife. I call; I search; then race towards home, passing on my way horses lying dead with their drivers. At one corner I see a couple of men with police, searching debris for a man buried underneath. I reach home; my wife is not there, but three hours later, back at the railway shelter, I find her. All round in the street are the dead and dying.'

A woman was shopping with her two young children in Whitecross Street when 'everything changed. People started to run helter-skelter. I picked up my youngest kiddie and with the other one hanging on to my skirt and clutching my heavy basket, I ran blindly over the road to a big warehouse. The aeroplanes were almost on us, ominous booms could be heard, and suddenly with a terrific noise, a bomb fell at the top of the street. The horses in a carrier's yard near us reared with fright and shrapnel was raining on to the glass roof. Another and far worse crash almost deafened us; a bomb fell on an iron-foundry opposite [eight foundry workers were killed there]. A kindly porter snatched my basket and the youngest child and yelled to me to follow him to the basement. We stayed there in terror until the "All Clear". Never shall I forget the scene when we emerged. The greengrocer from whom I had shopped a short while before was blown to bits; the butcher's boy was killed by falling masonry. Horses were maimed and lay screaming in the road. Ambulances and Red Cross were taking the dead and dying to St Bartholomew's Hospital.'

Two more bombs struck a four-storey building in Fenchurch Street, and fifteen people died when it collapsed. Thomas Burke was working in the building when 'there came two deafening crashes. The building swayed and trembled. Two big plate glass windows came smashing through, deep fissures appeared in the walls and I was thrown almost to my knees. Nearly half our building had been torn down . . . Three girls employed in a translation bureau on the top floor had rushed out, but one returned for her handbag and the two others were blown to pieces.' The girl had 'snatched the bag from beside the typewriter I had just been using and had only run a few steps towards the door again when a bomb crashed through. I was swung round and dropped the bag in putting up my hands to cover my ears at the terrific explosion. I stood there terrified, surrounded by debris, calling for help and not daring to move.' She managed to retain her perilous foothold on 'a crag of brickwork', and as the pall of dust and smoke began to clear a little she 'saw heads peep cautiously round doors and windows, and then people began to emerge again. The fire escape came soon after and a fireman was going to carry me down but I thought I could manage it myself, so he guided my feet on to the rungs of the escape. I got the heel of my shoe caught at the top so he just wrenched it off. I looked down once when I was nearing the bottom but it was a sickening sight – several dead lying on the pavement.' As she reached the ground, she was greeted by 'the cheers of a crowd in the street'.

Thomas Burke and the other survivors were surrounded by 'safes burst open with their scattered contents, piles of books and papers and other debris in the road. A girl who had been standing in the doorway of a provision shop next door had now lost both her legs; a certified accountant who had offices near mine, lying dead beside his daughter who had tried to help him; a small cat mewing piteously with its fur blown away.'

A man repairing a flagpole on a neighbouring roof had a narrow escape when he saw 'something like a stick falling [and] never came off a roof quicker in my life'. Another man drinking tea in a nearby café was less fortunate: his arm was blown off 'as he was raising a cup of tea to his lips'; and a caretaker's wife in a nearby building was beheaded by flying glass after a 12.5kg bomb detonated on the roof as she was working in the attic.

Another bomb fell in Aldgate High Street, killing eleven passers-by. The whole glass frontage of the Albion Clothing Store was blown out and the apparent death toll was made even worse because among the dead, dying and injured were a dozen or more mutilated shop window dummies, blown into the street, where they mingled with the bodies lying there. A 'Number 25 bus stood silently by the kerb, every window shattered, a solitary figure of a man was hunched up in the seat immediately behind the driver . . . a piece of glass was said to have pierced his neck and we were told he was already dead'.

A man driving a horse and cart 'had just given the sign to a lad in a van to come out of Duke Street into Aldgate East. As soon as I turned, there was a terrific bang. I jumped down to put my horse at rest, in to the kerb, and then went to see the result. The little lad I had made way for came running back, half insane, with his leg black, saying, "They've killed my horse." I could not get him to stop; off he ran. The sight I saw in that busy street was a battlefield. A man of foreign appearance was on his back, moaning his last. Another man lay on his back, past hope, and a fine City policeman who had been standing "on point" was just being put into an ambulance. There must have been eight or ten horses with their teeth snarling as if in pain, lying dead and green with the powder from the bombs. I never felt so lonely in a City street; everyone had run to shelter.'

A woman at work in a factory in Islington 'all of a sudden felt the building shake. Someone came rushing in, shouting, "An air-raid! Quick!" I was the first to run down the stairs and into the street, when a constable, PC Alfred Smith of the Metropolitan Force, rushed up and pushed me and all the others back again; he had just shut the door when a bomb dropped and he was killed, with some passers-by. I was buried in the debris for hours but only suffered shock.' As a favour to a colleague, PC Smith had swapped his beat that morning. His sacrifice was later commemorated in a tiled plaque erected in 'Postmen's Park' in Aldersgate Street, and his widow's police pension of fifteen shillings and threepence a week was augmented by a collection among his fellow officers, private companies and members of the public that raised £471. The Carnegie Hero Fund also awarded her ten shillings a week.

The Tower of London escaped damage when a bomb embedded itself in the dry moat without exploding, and the children of the Cowper Street Foundation School had a miraculous escape when a 50kg bomb smashed down through all five floors of the building but again failed to detonate. Somewhere around the third floor it 'turned on its side and fell through the remaining floors in this position, thus putting the fuse out of action'.

In London Wall, the music-loving registrar at the National Debt Office had ushered about 150 employees to safety 'when a noise of bombs dropping sounded in the distance. Many doubted the need of the warning to get down in the basement as quickly as possible. Girls and women clung to me and screamed in their terror as I tried to get them to go before me down the very narrow staircase . . . The only way to describe the noise the raid made in the basement is a perfect crescendo of explosions, and then the intense relief of a grand diminuendo. This was followed by the thud, thud of women, one after another, falling in dead faints on the floor. In the wall in that basement was one tiny tap from which I and one or two who had managed to keep our heads a bit fetched water and did our best to revive those women lying helpless from terror . . . treading carefully in and out among their bodies. It was late afternoon before some revived.'

The pilots of two Bristol Fighters, scrambled from Northolt, had now glimpsed the Gothas, but were unable to engage them, and the formation then split in half, one group targeting railways north of the river while the other, including Walter Aschoff's Serpent Machine, flew over the river near Blackfriars Bridge, targeting docks, warehouses and railway yards along the south bank of the Thames. The neighbouring aircraft to Aschoff's dropped a stream of bombs, and then he too had his target in sight and 'directed my pilot over it with a quick wave of my hand. Vast warehouses and shipyards spread out beneath us, and I held the bomb release tightly, then squeezed the lever and one bomb after another dropped clear of the security ropes and plummeted into the depths. A lurch followed every air-drop and, freed of the weight, our aircraft shot upwards. I clung to the seat for dear life, but was pitched forwards and then back into my seat.'

Three men working on the roof of Pink's Jam Factory in Bermondsey were killed when a bomb 'blew a hole in twelve inches of very poor concrete' on the roof. Another bomb slaughtered three workers and seriously injured five others at the British and Bennington Tea Company in Southwark. When the air-raid began most of the employees had hurried to shelter in the strongroom, protected by its solid walls and thick concrete roof, but when the bomb struck, the concrete roof collapsed, entombing them under tons of rubble, cast-iron safes and steel shelving.

As the other Gotha flight made for the river to rejoin the rest of the formation, they unloaded the remainder of their bombs over Poplar. A canary in the kitchen of one bombed house was 'still alive though glass had stuck in the wall all round him; everything else was broken'. Several other houses were bombed, but the worst incident, at the Upper North Street School in the East India Dock Road, was a vivid demonstration of 'the peculiar aptitude of the aerial bomb . . . for the massacre of innocents'.

Six hundred children attended the school. The girls had lessons together on the top floor of the two-storey building, with the boys on the ground floor and the infant classes in the basement. It was a poor area; many of the children wore threadbare 'hand-me-down' clothes and only a minority had shoes on their feet. At 11.40 that morning, twenty minutes before the lunch-break, all the children were at their desks in their high-ceilinged classrooms, with coal fireplaces and unplastered brick walls painted a drab dark green and white, when a 50kg bomb struck the roof.

The bomb did not detonate immediately. Split in two by the impact with the roof, the larger part crashed down through the floors, killing thirteen-year-old Rose Martin and crippling another girl. It burst through the ceiling of the Boys Department, killing twelve-year-old Edwin Powell, injuring several of his classmates, and leaving 'the headmaster all covered with ink . . . there were two large holes where the bomb had come and gone'.

Sixty-four smaller children were in the basement, in two infants classes separated by a wooden partition. They had been making paper lanterns, but when the air-raid began the teachers tried to keep the children calm by 'getting us to sing together. Soon, however, the noise of the anti-aircraft guns and the detonations of the enemy's bombs became audible even above our shrill voices.' Seconds later the bomb smashed through the ceiling. There was a momentary pause, then a metallic click, and it exploded, leaving a six-foot crater in the concrete floor, in which the bloodied body of five-year-old Florence Wood was later found. One child later recalled that she was 'actually blasted across the room' and two of her classmates were 'driven like stakes into the earth' by the force of the blast. Another child, Ivy Major, was the only survivor of a dozen children in the row closest to the bomb when it detonated. 'The eleven other children in my row of twelve were all killed, while I myself, although I managed to run home somehow, was unconscious for six weeks.'

One of the older girls in the top-floor class remembered that a 'horrible vibration shook the whole building as the bomb exploded and I was flung down several stone steps . . . Looking back, I saw a teacher staggering out with the limp form of a girl in her arms. One of the girl's legs was practically hanging off . . . I ran as I have never run before or since, making a beeline for home. In the meantime my father had arrived at the school and, finding me missing, had given me up for dead.' He later found her sitting on their doorstep.

Few children lived more than a couple of streets away from the school and distraught parents were soon on the scene, fighting their way past police, firemen and ambulancemen, tearing at the rubble, crying and screaming their children's names. Not many received an answer. Another older girl at the school, 'thinking only of my little sister, aged five . . . forced my way along the corridor, which was filled with men and women frantically searching for their children, and all screaming and shouting . . . She could not be found anywhere in the school and it was two hours later that my father found her dead in the mortuary.' 'Some mothers were almost insane with grief and, when they couldn't find their own children, would rush through the bodies looking for them,' and the school caretaker, Mr Batt, had the devastating experience of finding the body of his own six-year-old son as he searched through the debris.

A soldier had stopped to talk to a policeman in the street outside the school just before the bomb exploded and the two men were among the first into the smoking ruins of the building. In the basement they found 'many of the little ones were lying across their desks, apparently dead, and with terrible wounds on heads and limbs, and scores of others were writhing with pain and moaning pitifully . . . Many of the bodies were mutilated, but our first thought was to get the injured . . . we packed the little souls on the lorries as gently as we could.' 'The pathetic little bodies, tainted with yellow deposits of TNT, were carried from the building to Poplar Hospital on horse-drawn carts.' The soldier and the police, fire crews and ambulancemen still at the school now faced 'the worst part of our task . . . picking up the mutilated fragments of humanity'.

Dazed and wounded survivors staggered around, deafened by the blast, their wounds matted by TNT powder and concrete and brick dust. A child covered from head to foot in yellow TNT powder and too traumatized to speak was taken to Chinatown by a well-meaning adult in the hope that someone there would recognize him. He was eventually reunited with his frantic family who had been scouring the bomb-site, the hospital and the mortuary in search of him.

Another survivor, Rose Symons, owed her life to the persistence of her brother Jimmy. He refused to leave the school, even when police and fire chiefs had given up all hope of finding further survivors. Convinced that his sister was still alive, he continued to search the debris under the area where she had been sitting when the bomb went off. His fierce determination persuaded some adults to help him dig through the rubble, and eventually, three days after the raid, Rose was found, unconscious but still alive.

When Queen Mary visited some of the injured survivors in Poplar Hospital, Rose, who had lost all her hair in the blast and looked 'none too attractive', was chosen to present her with a posy of flowers, but her main memory of the day was her disappointment at not being allowed to keep 'the pretty dress the Hospital had given her for the presentation, it being taken away as soon as Queen Mary had left the ward'. Seventy years later, with children and grandchildren of her own, she still bore 'many scars to testify to the injuries she sustained' that summer day in 1917.

Sixteen children at the school had died instantly, two more perished later from their wounds, and another thirty were grievously injured. Scores more suffered less serious injuries. Only two of the dead were more than five years old. The only feeble consolation was that if the bomb had not broken in two as it impacted with the building, leaving at least a third of its explosive material undetonated, the resultant explosion and the death toll would have been even worse.

Heartbroken parents now faced another ordeal: identifying the pathetic remains of their children, an almost impossible task in many cases as the bodies had been mangled beyond all recognition. One dead child could be identified only by an unusual button that his mother had sewn on his shirt-cuff the previous evening. One of the survivors, Jack Brown, harboured vivid memories of the headmaster of the school, a powerful, commanding figure, calling the roll the next morning as the children assembled at their bomb-blasted school. 'As he stood there, reading the register, he was crying.'

Another child whose school in East Ham escaped the bombing found that tragedy awaited her at home. At the height of the air-raid, she 'heard my mother calling to me, but teacher looked out, when I told her so, and said there was nobody there. Presently it was all over and those living near were allowed to go. I found our house damaged and when I got inside the passage there was a lot of blood. My mother and brother had been killed.'

The raiders had spent ninety minutes in British airspace and unloaded four tons of bombs on London, killing a total of 162 people and injuring 432. Unaware of the full extent of the horrors they had wrought, Walter Aschoff was still watching the results of his bombs among the warehouses on the south bank of the Thames when his aircraft came under fire. 'With the last bomb gone, as my pilot levelled the aircraft, I stood up again in the bow of my turret and watched the impacts. My target appeared to have been hit, as smoke and flames were rising from the warehouses and stores around the docks. I was still absorbed by this eerie sight when I heard a crackle like blazing sticks; enemy aircraft were attacking. The rattle of my machine-gun sounded simultaneously with that of the rear-gunner. The first magazine was used up in only a few seconds, and I tried to reload at lightning speed, despite the motion of our aircraft. I fired more bursts at the enemy and the phosphorus tracer bullets showed that my aim was good. He tried to dodge them and then his aircraft dived and did not reappear. Did he end the battle because he was hit or was he just escaping our fire? We had no way of confirming it.'

It is possible that the attacker was a Bristol Fighter flown by Captain Cole-Hamilton of 35 Squadron, who was attacking one of three Gothas trailing a little behind the main formation over Ilford, 'with its left wing very much down, as if injured' in Cole-Hamilton's anthropomorphic description, when his observer, Captain C. H. Keevil, was hit in the heart by German gunfire and killed instantly.

While they were fighting off the attacker, Kollberg maintained the Gotha's homeward course and they left 'the city's sea of houses behind us. Looking back I could see smoke still rising in thick, black clouds into the sky.' A number of other fighters had now reached, or almost reached, the Gothas' altitude, but they flew solo, uncoordinated attacks and, faced with the formidable array of machine-guns the Gotha formation could bring to bear, none of them 'dared to attack the squadron'. Anti-aircraft guns also continued to fire in vain as the raiders approached the coast but one of their only recorded hits was on a pursuing British fighter, flown by Captain T. Grant of 39 Squadron, who was forced to make an emergency landing at Rochford.

The Gothas flew on, 'over British airfields that sent up new aircraft to pursue us and on every side we could see the gun-batteries pumping shells into the sky. The whole South of England seemed to be in uproar, but we maintained our course for the coast and soon the grey swell of the North Sea lay below us once more.' The physical strain of the prolonged flight 'in rarefied air' was exacerbated by the stresses of bombing and combat and then the strain of keeping the formation together as, exhausted, the pilots made for home, with British-based fighters often in pursuit and others patrolling from Dunkirk to intercept the Gothas before they reached the safety of the Belgian seaboard. 'Aeroplanes which lagged behind had to be waited for, those engaged in air combat had to be supported, those flying low kept in sight.'

'At high altitude and maximum speed', Aschoff and his comrades made for home. 'Then the rear-gunner signalled me to look back and pointed to an enemy aircraft chasing us from Southend and closing very fast. It was one of the feared English "triple-deckers" [a Sopwith triplane with a top speed of 114mph at altitude and capable of climbing to 10,000 feet in just over ten minutes], but either the enemy pilot was not very brave or he didn't dare approach the squadron as a lone fighter. We heard him shooting desperately but unavailingly from out of range, and then gave him one in the eye by firing a few rounds at him.

'As he fell away behind us, every eye resumed the search of the horizon for the first glimpse of land. There! The white rows of houses of Ostend silhouetted by the sun. Far beyond, the sun glinted on the flooded, terrible battlefields of Flanders. Within a quarter of an hour we would be over the land and safe, with German fighters to greet us and escort us home. As I searched the sky for them, I saw a few black dots. Slowly, the dots grew into the outlines of aircraft, but as we closed on them I suddenly made out the cockade symbols of the enemy gleaming in the sunlight. Fast as lightning they launched themselves at us. I signalled "Achtung" to the rear-gunner, swung my own machine-gun to the right, pressed it to my shoulder and fired at an enemy swooping in front of us, but seconds later we were under attack from another on our tail. A Sopwith [Camel] one-seater had pounced on us like a hawk, showering us with rounds. Tracer bullets seared through the air, punching holes into our wings. Our rear-gunner's machine-guns hammered incessantly in reply, forcing the enemy to dive beneath us. As the gunner picked up the lower gun, I crawled to the back and threw him more ammunition – otherwise I would have been damned to idleness at this crucial moment, as my gun could not be brought to bear on an enemy behind us.

'Other German aircraft had now seen our danger and added their firepower, driving off the enemy fighters. As they fell back and turned to run for home, our engines coughed and faltered, and the pilot's hands shot to the levers for the fuel inlet pipes. The reserve tank was undamaged, but the other two tanks had been holed. Nursing the failing engines, Kollberg brought us to base on the last drops of fuel. We circled once, signalling the alarm to indicate an immediate, emergency landing. On the northern edge of the airfield, near a lonely farmhouse, we saw the ruins of a wrecked aircraft and on the airfield itself another was ablaze, perhaps having fallen foul of a bomb crater from an enemy air-raid while we were airborne.

'As we came in on our final approach, the aircraft, dangerously unstable without the weight of any bombs or fuel, reared like a wild horse. Kollberg had to use every ounce of skill and concentration to bring us safely to land, a task that would have been beyond many an inexperienced pilot. The engines fell silent, out of fuel, and we coasted lower and lower. The hangars and trees flanking the airfield suddenly grew bigger – we were over the grass runway – and Kollberg forced the aircraft down. The wheels hit the ground, with a thud, we bumped and rumbled over some hastily repaired craters and rolled to a halt.

'Still swaddled in our furs, the heat was so intense that we tore off our goggles and caps while we were taxiing towards the hangar. Our engineers recognised their Serpent Machine and rushed towards us, smiling and waving. They took hold of the ends of the wings and hauled us into the hangar. Two ground-crewmen were waiting for us, holding our wolfhounds Snake and Storm. Clumsy with tiredness and stiff from the long hours in the cramped space of the aircraft, we climbed down and were stripped of the suffocating flight clothing and furs. The ground-crew clustered around us, besieging us with questions – "How did it go?" "Did the engines work well?" – but we were so deafened by the noise of the engines that we could barely understand their words.

'We counted numerous bullet-holes as we checked the aircraft for damage. The main fuel-tanks had been holed, the wings and struts, and both propellers had been shot through in several places, and the tailplane bore the scorch marks of tracer impacts. We were lucky it had not burst into flames in mid-air. Each bullet-hole was marked with an "X" and the date, so that they would always remind us of this "lucky day".

Half an hour after landing, the predicted storm, with thunder and hailstones 'the size of pigeons' eggs', swept over the airfields. If it had broken a little earlier, 'the squadron might have come to grief'. Aschoff wrote his report on the flight and then 'went to our makeshift quarters, where we ate and quenched our thirst with a big bottle of wine, as we compared notes on this first London flight. Our pride at having achieved a great success was mixed with sadness and quiet mourning for those who did not return.'

Aschoff's comment must relate to crewmen killed in crash-landings, since official German records show that no aircraft were lost to enemy fire. The British pilot Cole-Hamilton had claimed that a Gotha had been hit and was in evident trouble, and it may have been one of the ones that crash-landed, but there is no other evidence that any German aircraft were shot down by aircraft or ground gunfire. The losses of the England Squadron that day were negligible; those sustained by the citizens of London, and of Poplar in particular, left a scar that the passing years never erased.

# CHAPTER 6
# A CITY IN TURMOIL

O N 20 JUNE 1917, the victims of the Upper North Street School bomb were laid to rest in a communal funeral. Rows of tiny coffins stood upon trestle tables in All Saints Church, Poplar, and six hundred wreaths almost filled the Town Hall across the road. The parents of three of the dead had insisted on private burials, but the other fifteen children were interred together in the east London cemetery. A sixteenth coffin was buried with them, containing remains that could not be identified as belonging to any particular one of the victims. Almost £1,500 was raised to build a memorial, the majority of it from door-to-door collections around the East End. The wording of the inscription was restrained, commemorating '18 children who were killed by a bomb dropped from a German aeroplane', but that calm and measured tone did not reflect the fury that the raid and its toll of innocent lives had provoked.

The Times editorialized 'If it were possible . . . to increase the utter and almost universal detestation with which he [the Kaiser] is held by the people of this country, he did it' with the bombing of the Upper North Street School. A public meeting at Newington Town Hall passed a resolution demanding that the Government recognize the necessity of 'a) Giving a PUBLIC WARNING on the occasion of enemy air-raids, and b) Taking immediate steps, if necessary, in the way of REPRISALS for air-raids on London.' Angry newspaper correspondents also queued up to demand retaliation in full measure. The Daily Mail printed a 'Reprisal Map' showing all German cities within 150 miles of the Allied front lines, and William Joynson-Hicks MP told a gathering on Tower Hill, 'amid great cheering', that in return for every raid on London British bombers should 'blot out' a German town. Even this was far too moderate for at least one of his audience, who demanded five raids on Berlin for every one on London.

East Enders also took to the streets, harassing and assaulting not only the persons and properties of people with Germanic or even foreign-sounding names, but also the ghoulish sightseers flocking to Poplar to gaze at the bomb-wrecked school and the other bomb-sites. 'Unaccustomed visitors came flocking to the East End – well-dressed people in motors, journalists, photographers, high military officials, Red Cross nurses, policewomen, travellers from all over the world . . . Today these mean streets were thronged and seething. Poor people in frowsy garments crowded the roadways and squeezed past each other in the narrow alleys. What sights for the pretty ladies in dainty dresses, craning their slender white throats from taxicab windows! What sights for the rather too generously fed business men and well-groomed officers: miserable dwellings, far from fit for human families, poorly-dressed women of working sort, with sad, worn faces; and others, sunk lower, just covered, no more, in horrid rags, hopeless, unhappy beings; half-clad, neglected little children . . . Crowds mostly made up of women gathered before each ruined home. One, where a child had been killed, was still inhabited. A soldier in khaki stood at the door, striving in vain to keep back the press of human bodies surging against it. The people who lived there were scarcely able to force a way to their own door.'

Amid the fury, recriminations and the clamour for reprisals against German cities, the War Minister, Lord Derby, bravely tried to uphold the moral principles of a vanishing age – 'it would be better to be defeated, retaining honour, chivalry and humanity, rather than obtain a victory by methods which have brought upon Germany universal execration' – but he was, as he must have known, profoundly out of step with the public mood. George Bernard Shaw's was one of the few other rational voices, warning that the wave of public outrage was sending the wrong message to Germany: 'We have been steadily impressing on the enemy, apparently without realising it ourselves, that the moral effect of killing a single baby is greater than that of annihilating a whole battalion in the field.'

Unswayed by such arguments, popular fury continued unabated, directed not only at the 'Hun baby-killers' who had perpetrated the crime, but also at the British authorities who were apparently powerless to prevent it. A claim in the *Berliner Morgenpost*, reprinted in *The Times*, that 'the English Government is seriously entertaining the intention of removing the seat of government from London' because of the threat of continued air-raids heightened the atmosphere of crisis.

*The Times* also complained that the German aircraft had been able to bomb the East End 'with comparative impunity . . . The aeroplanes were fired at by many anti-aircraft guns but apparently without visible results . . . We have constantly pointed out that aeroplane raids of this character will become larger and more frequent and that they are much more dangerous than attacks made with the cumbrous and more vulnerable Zeppelins ... Their repetition will assuredly lead to a constantly increasing demand for better defensive measures, for a more efficient system of warning and for prompter retaliation ... The ultimate remedy lies in hunting out the raiders in their lairs, but there is obviously an immense amount of leeway to be made up in the matter of rapid communication of the invaders' arrival on the coast, of engaging them in time and of warning the public.'

There was a heated debate in the House of Commons, during which Pemberton-Billing reminded MPs that he had 'prophesied what was going to occur'; he then lambasted the Government for its failings with such vehemence that he was eventually expelled from the chamber for his failure to respect 'the authority of the Chair'. Neither the Commons debate nor a more measured discussion in the Lords secured any assurances of an improved performance by the air defences in the inevitable event of a further raid. When questioned in the Lords about whether any of the raiders had been shot down, Lord Derby was forced to reply, 'I am afraid not. There are some doubts about one, but I would not like to say for certain.' He also made the smug assertion that 'not a single soldier' had been killed in the raid, which was not only false but also grievously offensive to the relatives mourning the civilian dead.

Their outrage would only have been compounded by remarks made in the Commons by the Member for the City of London, Sir Frederick Banbury, who showed a purblind loyalty to the financial interests of his constituents, if not their personal safety, by proposing that the bells of St Paul's be tolled as a warning of future raids. His suggestion was made not to allow defenceless civilians to take shelter, but so that bank tellers would have time to return cash to the vaults before abandoning the counter. The Chancellor, Andrew Bonar Law, retorted angrily that 'we are more interested in the lives of the people than the money in the banks'.

At a War Cabinet meeting on the day after the raid, Sir William Robertson pointed out to critics of the air defences that the raiders could fly from the coast to London in less time than most of the available British aircraft required to climb to the Gothas' cruising height. 'Before they can get up, the enemy has done his job and is on his way home.' However, he agreed that 'some special effort should be made to deal the raiders a nasty knock'. The Cabinet accordingly resolved to recall two squadrons equipped with faster, more modern aircraft from the Western Front to augment the Home Defence squadrons.

Robertson told Douglas Haig of the Cabinet's decision the next day, but tried to sugar the pill by assuring him that he would only have to give up the squadrons 'for a week or two . . . so as to give the enemy a warm reception, and the machines would then return to you'. Haig and the commander of the RFC, Major General Hugh Trenchard, were both fiercely opposed to any dilution of their forces on the Western Front, and would have sympathized with the view expressed by one newspaperman that the casualties of the raid were less than 'a before-breakfast skirmish almost any morning on the Somme', but the Cabinet would not budge.

The two commanders were summoned to London, Haig to a meeting of the War Cabinet on 17 June and Trenchard to a special Cabinet meeting three days later, where he was pressed on the means by which the air defences of Britain could be improved. Haig wanted no distractions from the ground offensive he was about to launch on the Western Front and Trenchard supported him, reiterating his belief that 'the capture by us of the Belgian coast would be the most effective step of all', forcing German bombers to overfly occupied territory bristling with Allied guns and fighter aircraft.

Trenchard argued against any transfer of fighter squadrons away from the Western Front. 'By bombing raids against London and in England, they [the German Air Service] have tried, trusting to their effect on public opinion and to the political agitation which was bound to follow, to make us dislocate our flying forces in the field.' Both men also forcibly stated their opposition to retaliatory air-raids on German cities. 'I have no reason to suppose,' Haig said, invoking high principle that happened to coincide with his personal wishes, 'that the bombing of open towns merely for the purpose of terrifying the civil population is a method of warfare which would be approved by His Majesty's Government, nor would I recommend its adoption.' Trenchard was equally dismissive. 'Reprisals on open towns are repugnant to British ideas but we may be forced to adopt them.

It would be worse than useless to do so, however, unless we are determined that, once adopted, they will be carried through to the end. The enemy would almost certainly reply in kind – and unless we are determined and prepared to go one better than the Germans, whatever they may do and whether their reply is in the air, or against our prisoners, or otherwise, it will be infinitely better not to attempt reprisals at all.' However, he stressed the importance both of inflicting 'the utmost damage on the enemy's sheds and machines behind the Western Front' and of increasing combat air patrols over the front lines, serving 'the double purpose of assisting the Allies in overcoming the enemy and at the same time reducing his power to send expeditions to England'. It was no coincidence that all of these proposals would keep all the available aircraft under Trenchard's and Haig's command on the Western Front, allowing them to redeploy them to ground-support roles when the great offensive began.

Haig also reiterated his opposition to retaliatory raids, including Lloyd George's suggestion of an attack on Mannheim, chosen because its chemical factories produced huge quantities of nitrates, an essential ingredient of explosives. Bombing them would damage the German war effort and, just as importantly, be justifiable to American public opinion, but Haig added the rider that 'there is always the danger ... [that the French may refuse the use of their airfields to stage the raids] owing to the fact that it will bring about retaliation'. Although Haig was fiercely opposed to any diversion of aircraft away from the Front, the Cabinet was equally insistent that Home Defence must be strengthened. After furious arguments, the demand that two squadrons of fighters be returned to England to augment London's defences was successfully diluted by Haig and Trenchard. Only one, 56 Squadron, would be sent back and based at Bekesbourne, and even this would be a purely temporary measure as Haig insisted on it being returned to his command by 5 July, to prepare for the launch of his great Flanders offensive. One other squadron, 66, would also be moved, but only to Calais, from where it would patrol the Channel. Like its sister squadron, it would also return to its base on the Western Front before the July offensive.

The news had 'twelve elated pilots of 56 Squadron packing a week's kit into our cockpits'. Among them was Cecil Lewis, who had joined the RFC straight from Oundle School at the age of sixteen and a half – one of many to lie about his age in order to enlist ('we walked off the playing fields into the lines'). Still only eighteen but now an experienced pilot, Lewis and his peers in 56 Squadron felt that 'to fight Hun bombers over London would have been a picnic after a month of gruelling Offensive Patrols' on the Western Front. 'Good old Jerry! Good old Lloyd George!'

A Cabinet committee, set up to plan a long-term strategy for defeating the bombing raids, rapidly came up with a proposal to almost double the size of the RFC from 108 to 200 squadrons, and divert resources into aircraft production even at the expense of tank and truck manufacture. There was also to be a 'progressive increase in the output of aero engines to 4,500 a month', though it was one thing to make such a pronouncement and quite another to deliver on it. The War Cabinet also discussed introducing an air-raid warning system, but its value was disputed, with claims that warnings fuelled public fears as much as they allayed them. Bonar Law suggested that 'the result of sounding warnings of danger from air-raids is to drive people into the street', and he could point to the aftermath of a Zeppelin raid on Hull in 1915 when the local MP reported that 'Citizens of all classes are in a state of great alarm; the night after the raid a further warning was given and tens of thousands of people trooped out of the city. The screams of the women were distressing to hear.' Fears were also voiced that warnings would merely increase the disruption to war production that was one of the German High Command's aims; as a result, no public warning system was introduced.

Responding with an alacrity that shamed the sluggish response of the authorities, one enterprising newspaper, while echoing the general condemnation of the raids in its editorial comments, also took the chance to boost its circulation with an unusual reader offer: 'Order the Daily News to be delivered daily and your HOME is insured for £250 against damage by bombs . . . The Daily News has already paid two £1,000 death claims as well as a number of minor claims.' Showing surprising business acumen, the Government then began its own air-raid insurance scheme; it 'charged one-sixth per cent and made a profit of £10,898,205'.

The quantity and quality of aircraft available to the permanent Home Defence squadrons had been slightly improved, but that did little to stifle calls for more vigorous defensive efforts and for reprisals against Germany. Some suggested that, to prevent further raids, caches of explosives should be air-dropped into enemy territory and used by Special Forces to destroy the hangars and aircraft of the Gotha squadrons. That plan was never realized, but day and night bombing raids were stepped up on the airfields at Gontrode, Ghistelles, Mariakerke and St Denijs-Westrem. At first the attacks were carried out in daylight, 'the attacking squadrons appearing at high altitude above the airfield, but they didn't achieve any significant results and before long the raids were moved to dusk and night. Hardly had it grown dark when the drone of approaching English aircraft could be heard. They hovered at very low altitude above the airfield and dropped their bombs.'

These first night raids took the England Squadron by surprise, and 'our defences were poorly organised, but within a few days, machine-guns were mounted and manned around the hangars and the perimeter of the airfield, and all the gunners were striving to be the first to shoot down an Englishman. On days when we were not flying, the air-crew also took part in this sport and our ferocious defensive fire forced the enemy planes to retreat to higher altitudes, with a corresponding reduction in the accuracy of their bombing.

'When we were night-flying ourselves, the English often arrived shortly before or during our take-off times, something that had the ground staff understandably worried. Explosive and incendiary bombs whistled down, gouging deep craters out of the turf, and more than once shrapnel and shell splinters ripped pieces out of the Gothas, but apart from the disruption to our take-off schedules and a few hits on planes and hangars, the enemy flyers didn't achieve any notable successes and were unable to weaken, let alone break, our will to continue the fight.'

An official communiqué had given the German public news of the success of the first daylight raid on 'fortress London'; as L. E. O. Charlton remarked, 'The Germans were always careful to refer to London as "a fortress" [it was also often described as *befestigt* – fortified] when reporting the results of the raids for home consumption, knowing well how indiscriminate the process was.' It could not be otherwise, given the inaccuracy of even the best bombsights then in use. The German official communiqués also always listed the military objectives that the raiders claimed to have bombed. Two days after the raid of 13 June 1917, for example, they reported that seventeen aircraft had reached London and dropped 4,000kg of bombs on 'the docks, wharves, railways, Government stores and warehouses situated in the centre of the town on the banks of the Thames'. As a French historian of the air war noted with biting sarcasm, 'in the war reports there are always passages which make one smile, such as the dropping of bombs from a height of 2,000 metres [6,500 feet] upon "military establishments"'.

The news was greeted with euphoria by the German press and public – 'As history had seen it in days of yore, "Hannibal at the gates"; now the English coin the slogan "Brandenburg over London"!' – but not everyone in Germany was so delighted. Chancellor Bethmann-Hollweg, never more than a very reluctant supporter of bombing London, now feared that any chance of a negotiated peace would be jeopardized by the air-raids. He wrote to Hindenburg, urging him to avoid 'anything which could impede England's decision to enter into peace negotiations ... no doubt the last aerial attack on London has had a disastrous effect in this respect ... No English government which was willing to treat with Germany after such an occurrence would be able to withstand the indignation of the nation for a day.' He declared himself 'unable to believe that such aerial attacks are absolutely necessary' and urged Hindenburg to order their immediate cessation.

However, undermined and outmanoeuvred by Germany's military leaders, the Chancellor's position was precarious, and Hindenburg's reply dripped sarcasm, urging Bethmann-Hollweg to 'acquaint me with the facts' demonstrating that the raid had 'aroused the passions of the English nation to a disastrous degree'. Under the pressure of the war and the shortages and even starvation produced by the Allied blockade, the German people, Hindenburg said, had become 'a hard race with an iron fist ... The hammer is in our hands and will fall mercilessly and shatter the places where England is forging weapons against us.' Within a month, Bethmann-Hollweg had been forced to resign as Chancellor; his successor was hand-picked by Hindenburg and Ludendorff. True power now rested entirely in their hands, with the Kaiser little more than a figurehead.

On 15 June, two days after the raid, Brandenburg was summoned to the German Supreme Headquarters in Kreuznach. There he made a personal report to Hindenburg, Ludendorff and the Kaiser. Ludendorff in particular questioned him closely about the raid and its impact, and Brandenburg replied that 'the effect must have been great'. Most of the bombs had fallen 'among the docks and the city warehouses . . . a station in the City and a Thames bridge, probably Tower Bridge, had been hit'.

At the end of Brandenburg's report, the Kaiser decorated him with the coveted Pour le Mérite medal, an eight-pointed blue enamelled Maltese cross that was nicknamed 'The Blue Max' in honour of Max Immelmann, the first pilot to be awarded the decoration. However, as the triumphant Brandenburg began the flight back to Gontrode on 19 June, his Albatros aircraft suffered an engine failure and crashed on take-off. The pilot, Oberleutnant Freiherr Hans-Ulrich von Trotha, was killed instantly and Brandenburg suffered such serious injuries that one of his legs had to be amputated. Von Trotha, a founder member of the Carrier Pigeon Squadron and one of the German Army Air Force's most experienced pilots, was buried at Kreuznach in a ceremony attended by the Kaiser.

The news 'shatters Ghent. Brandenburg seems irreplaceable.' With no prospect of his early return to duty, command of the England Squadron was handed to the thirty-year-old Hauptmann Rudolf Kleine. A narrow-shouldered man with a high forehead and the beginnings of a widow's peak, Kleine was the epitome of a haughty 'Junker', possessed of 'knightly refinement and the noble soldierly virtues'. Kleine's forbidding air made it difficult for his men to form an affectionate bond with him, and if his bravery earned him their respect, it was also tinged with fear that a reckless streak might lead them to disaster. A driven character, he was 'an officer distinguished for his rashness in undertaking risks in the most un-favourable weather conditions', who had already shown himself willing to gamble his own and his men's lives for the chance of glory.

He had already been awarded the Iron Cross Second Class and First Class, and the Knight Cross of the Royal Order of the House of the Hohenzollern, one of Germany's highest military decorations, and though some saw him as a true patriot, others regarded him as a 'gong-hunter' who would go to any lengths to win the coveted Pour le Mérite. Not every airman shared Kleine's eagerness to win the medal. 'For us fliers the Pour le Mérite was thought to be a bad luck award.' To the superstitious, Brandenburg's fate, within hours of receiving the medal, already offered ample proof of the bad luck associated with it, and he was not alone: 'almost all who received it were soon on the casualty list or the register of the dead'.

The son of an infantry officer and a career soldier himself, Kleine had transferred to the air force in 1913. After training as a pilot at the Herzog-Karl-Eduard Aviation School in Gotha, he achieved his pilot's badge a month before the outbreak of war, and was one of the first pilots in action, flying reconnaissance during the German attack on Liège. A stray bullet shattered the bone of his left upper arm in October 1914, but within two months he was back with his unit. He was decorated and promoted to captain, served as Flight Leader of Kagohl 1 of the Carrier Pigeon Division Ostend, and was then appointed Commander of Field Flight Division 53 at the end of August 1916. He was awarded another decoration after the German offensive in Champagne but was wounded in combat again in 1917 and was still recuperating from his wounds when he assumed command of the England Squadron.

By then, one of Brandenburg's last improvements, a dedicated weather station to continuously monitor conditions and provide more reliable forecasts, was already in place at Gontrode. It was headed by Leutnant Walter Georgii, Germany's most acclaimed meteorologist. Still only twenty-eight, he had made his reputation by successfully predicting the three-day period of clear skies and below-zero temperatures that the German High Command had required to launch an attack on Verdun. Although he could draw on a wide range of data to assist his forecasts for the England Squadron, he was still hampered by the total lack of German weather stations to the west and south-west of the British Isles – the Atlantic U-boat fleet could have provided invaluable reports, but was never used for this purpose – which reduced some of his forecasting to little more than educated guesswork.

On the night of 16/17 June, as Georgii scanned his charts for the conditions that would permit another attack on London, and the impetuous, impatient Kleine kicked his heels at Gontrode, two of the German Navy's Zeppelin 'height-climbers', L42 and L48, launched their own attack on England, targeting the Suffolk coast. Even though flying at 18,000 feet, L48 was soon spotted and engaged by British aircraft. Its bombs fell on Harwich without significant effect and, after being attacked by a succession of aircraft, L48 was finally shot down at around ten past three in the morning. Three aircraft had just engaged it and two of the pilots, Captain R. H. M. S. Saundby and Lieutenant L. P. Watkins, claimed the kill. It crashed in flames on farmland near Theberton and, unusually, three of its crew escaped the inferno, though one of them, badly burned, died later. L42 was also spotted off the coastline and failed to drop a single bomb on English soil. As one of their compatriots later scathingly remarked, 'Airships usually threw overboard their explosives directly searchlights and guns were turned on them.' L42 was chased by a number of fighters, but managed to evade them and return to its base.

Kleine's first raid at the head of the England Squadron finally went ahead on 4 July. In the early hours of that morning British bombers again attacked the airbases in occupied Belgium, but on this occasion they targeted Ghistelles and Nieumunster. The ground-crews preparing the Gothas at St Denijs-Westrem and Gontrode were undisturbed and twenty-five aircraft of the England Squadron took off, as planned, at 5.30 that morning; but over the next few minutes the pilots of no fewer than seven Gothas claimed engine problems and returned to their airfields, though in at least some cases mechanical trouble may have been less to blame than Kleine's reputation for reckless glory-hunting.

He led the remaining eighteen aircraft on a northerly course, keeping well away from the British squadrons patrolling from Dunkirk and the lightships in the Thames estuary that had given the Admiralty early warning of previous raids. There was a light easterly wind and 'a considerable amount of cloud', but that was not the prime reason why the England Squadron chose not to target London on this occasion: German Intelligence had discovered that 56 Squadron had been temporarily transferred to Bekesbourne and that probably led Kleine to avoid the capital. Flying at an altitude of 14,000 feet, the Gothas crossed the English coastline at Bawdsey, a few miles north of Felixstowe, and swung south to begin their attacks. As they did so the formation split in two, one group targeting Harwich while the other made for Felixstowe.

The raiders had been heard off the coast at five to seven but, in the belief that their target was London, not a single fighter was scrambled to intercept them until half an hour later. By then the raid was over and the Gothas were heading for home. Only one British aircraft was airborne as the raiders approached the coast, flown by Captain John Palethorpe and First Air Mechanic James Jessop, who were endurance-testing a DH4. Palethorpe spotted the Gothas and at once tried to engage them, but his gun jammed, and though Jessop fired one burst, he was then killed by a bullet through the heart as their aircraft was raked by fire from several Gothas. Palethorpe, who was later awarded the Military Cross for his bravery, landed only long enough for Jessop's body to be removed and then took off again with a hastily drafted replacement observer, but by then the England Squadron was already well out to sea and beyond his reach.

Eighty-three fighters eventually got airborne, none of which so much as sighted the enemy, and the RFC's 66 Squadron was not informed of the raid until forty-five minutes after the Gothas' bombs began dropping, probably because the duty officer forgot that there was a squadron on call on the other side of the Channel. By the time they reached the correct altitude and began patrolling their 'beat' between Dunkirk and the North Hinder lightship, the homeward-bound German raiders had already crossed the Belgian coast. However, twenty RNAS pilots from Dunkirk intercepted the Gothas thirty-five miles north-west of Ostend. Flight Commander Alexander Shook claimed to have hit one which 'began to smoulder' and then fell away from the formation, and was later awarded the DSC for this alleged victory. Another pilot, Flight Lieutenant S. E. Ellis, also claimed a 'kill', saying that a Gotha had gone down 'twisting and turning, with heavy smoke coming from the rear-gunner's cockpit' after he poured three hundred rounds into it, but German records, though noting that six air battles took place, showed no Gotha losses at all.

Despite the lack of airborne opposition during the raid, it was not a great success for the England Squadron. A third of the sixty-five bombs dropped fell harmlessly into the sea, and British estimates put the damage caused at only £2,000. Harwich escaped almost unscathed, but seventeen people were killed and thirty wounded when the raiders hit an RNAS base, an army camp near Felixstowe, and the Shotley balloon station. The only other casualties were among a flock of pedigree sheep grazing at Trimley Marshes, slaughtered by one of many misdirected bombs; newspapers reported that twenty-one sheep were killed and twenty-nine injured.

56 Squadron patrolled without effect, well to the south-west of the raiders, but, freed from the stress of combat patrols on the Western Front, where every flight carried the threat of being shot down and killed, the pilots were revelling in the freedom of the skies and the sheer exhilaration of flight. 'Sometimes, returning from patrols, we would break off and chase each other round about the clouds, zooming their summits, plunging down their white precipitous flanks, darting like fishes through their shadowy crevasses and their secret caves.'

Like their counterparts in the England Squadron, Cecil Lewis and his peers 'lived supremely in the moment. Our preoccupation was the next patrol, our horizon the next leave . . . We were trained with one object – to kill. We had one hope – to live', but if death had to come, then better to die as a lord of the air than scrabbling in the mud at the bottom of a trench. As Lewis wrote after the death in combat of his close friend from 56 Squadron Arthur Rhys-Davids, 'I hope the gunner of that Hun two-seater shot him clean, bullet to heart, and that his plane, on fire, fell like a meteor through the sky he loved. Since he had to end, I hope he ended so.'

The proximity of death lent an added zest to life, and, when not on patrol, the men of 56 Squadron maintained a hectic social calendar. 'The defence of London was quite a secondary affair. The things of real importance were squadron dances . . . A large marquee was run up as a Mess. The Major scrounged some planking, and very soon there was a regular Savoy dancing floor. Visits were paid to Canterbury to enrol the fair sex. Those lightning two- or three-day acquaintanceships began to ripen. The weather continued cloudless and perfect for bombing London but, whether the Hun had advice of the squadron's return or not . . . there were no signs of him. The squadron stood by, gloriously idle. It was a grand war.'

Lord French tried to prevent 56 Squadron's return to France, telling

Sir William Robertson that it would leave 'wholly inadequate forces . . . If London is again subjected to attack, the results may be disastrous'; but, despite his protests, and not without some reluctance, the men of 56 Squadron left Bekesbourne on the morning of 7 July to fly back to their base at Estree Blanche on the Western Front. 'Dawn came up, ghostly over the hopfields . . . The machines were standing out, engines running. The sun was up, the day glorious, cloud-free. We took off, wheeled, formed flights and turned south.' They had not fired a single shot in anger while they had been in England.

Whether by coincidence or not – and German Intelligence had shown itself to be very well informed about British deployments – while 56 Squadron was still airborne on its way back to France, the next Gotha raid on London took place. It was probably as well for the Government that the public remained unaware that the squadron had been removed from the capital's defence and sent back to its bases on the Western Front earlier that very morning.

Expecting stiffer resistance this time, Kleine had ordered a reduction in bombloads to increase the Gothas' speed and rate of climb. Twenty-four of them took off from Gontrode and St Denijs-Westrem that morning and this time only two of them returned to the airfield with engine trouble. At 9.14, the Kentish Knock lightship made the first sighting of the enemy formation, flying at a height of 10,000 to 12,000 feet, and within two minutes the Admiralty had relayed the alert to the RNAS at Chatham. The London Warning Centre was also notified and the first aircraft from the Home Defence squadrons were airborne by 9.24. As the Gothas passed over the mouth of the River Crouch about twenty minutes later, two aircraft peeled away from the main formation. One, whether by design or because of engine trouble, made the now customary diversionary raid, targeting Margate; the other was on a further reconnaissance mission, photographing targets and defences along the banks of the Thames.

In addition to the RNAS squadrons on and near the coast, around eighty aircraft from the Home Defence squadrons were now attempting to intercept the Gothas. Several fighters got into firing range but were bedevilled with jamming of their Vickers machine-guns – Lewis guns were generally more reliable, but their magazine was so small (the largest was less than a hundred rounds) that they required constant reloads – and at least half a dozen were forced to break off their engagements and return to base. Among them was the unfortunate Captain John Palethorpe, both of whose Vickers guns jammed as he attacked a Gotha from below. His aircraft was then raked with gunfire and he was hit in the hip, forcing an emergency landing at Rochford. He noted in his report that 'I doubt if attacking underneath is the best position as they can shoot vertically downwards, as is proved by holes in our planes'.

Meanwhile, the anti-aircraft batteries, silenced no more, were pumping up a barrage of shells at the Gothas. 'Like the wind passing though a field of corn, swaying it hither and thither, so now the machines swerve to left and right, as though in time to the explosions of the bursting shells. Individual machines follow a zigzag course in order to present a more difficult target to the gunners, but always endeavour to close in again upon the leader's machine.'

Despite the barrage, none of them was hit. As the barrage began, Kleine 'made a sudden dive and double-left-hand turn underneath his own flight, emerging a little in front of the centre of his right flank. This he led through a sharp right- and left-hand turn.' The effect was to split the formation in two. As they passed out of range of the barrage, the Gotha formation came back together, 'until it again came under very heavy gunfire . . . It then opened again slightly into two flights, closing again as the fire became less intense . . . throughout the raid they seemingly escaped damage from gunfire by this well-judged division into two main groups. Some observers speak of this being done so quickly that shells which it was thought would have burst among the machines, exploded between them.' In order to confuse the range-finding of the anti-aircraft gunners, the Gothas 'appear to have flown with a sort of individual switchback movement, the difference between the crest and the trough being probably about 100 to 200 feet'.

Once over the sighting mark of Epping Forest, they began their attack runs on London, re-forming their customary diamond formation, the rows of aircraft stepped upwards from front to rear with a height difference of about a thousand feet between the first and last aircraft. The morning was bright and sunny, but in the east, high stratus cloud and a light haze gave the sky a leaden tinge. 'It was out of this haze that the raiders, about half-past ten, came into sight. From a distance they looked like a score of swallows.' Many people fled for shelter at the sound of their approach, but many more at first took them for British aircraft. 'The height at which they were flying was so low, their approach was so leisurely and so well kept was their fan-like formation, that to suppose they were enemies was preposterous.'

Even when it was clear that they were German bombers, astonishing numbers of people remained in the open to watch the 'air show' overhead. One described it as 'perfectly wonderful' before adding the rider that 'I'm glad I've seen a raid, but I can dispense with a repetition . . . It was the most deadly calm, calculating, sinister sort of sight I ever saw . . . we counted twenty-five of them . . . packed together like a flight of rooks.' Among the other spectators were members of the Air Board, watching from the balconies of the Hotel Cecil, who were probably less excited than humiliated by this latest demonstration of German daring and British aerial impotence.

*The Times* published a breathless report on the raid the next day. 'As a spectacle, the raid was the most thrilling that London has seen since the air attacks began. Every phase could be followed from points many miles away without the aid of glasses, and hundreds of thousands of people watched the approach of the squadron, the dropping of the bombs, the shelling of the German aeroplanes and the eventual retreat . . . In the advance, each machine kept its proper station, and as the formation was so accurate and the altitude of the flight so low, people who had received no warning of the raid at first believed that the planes were British carrying out a manoeuvre. This illusion was soon dispelled.'

The Gothas flew a great arc across the capital, first bombing targets in Tottenham, Leytonstone, Stoke Newington, Dalston, Islington, Clerkenwell and Hoxton on the north-eastern approaches. The folly of treating the raid as a spectacle was demonstrated when 'a young officer and his lady friend who had run out of an end house "to see the fun" were blown to pieces . . . nothing was ever found of them, save the officer's military cap with some of his hair in it'. The plate-glass windows of a shop were 'punctured with small holes through which a marble would pass, but by a curious freak, the windows of the restaurant facing the spot on which the bomb alighted were unbroken'.

A woman who had just got back to her home in Hoxton after a night-shift at a munitions plant heard 'the too-familiar drone of engines. I went into the backyard where my father was and said to him, "They must be ours, Dad, look how low they are." He said, "They're not ours, girl, get inside and take cover." We had just managed to get into the passage when Crash! came the house. I remember nothing more until I woke up in the Metropolitan Hospital ... I still carry scars of the burns I received. The man next door, who was standing on his doorstep, had his two legs blown off.'

As the bombs fell, 'the sound was deafening and it seemed as if every-thing was collapsing around us ... every succeeding bomb was nearer than the last ... Death seemed imminent. Suddenly the voice of a woman near me rang out loud and clear. She shrieked to God – nay she commanded him to listen – and there, heedless of us all, she implored forgiveness for sins and faults that one would blush to name in public, and pleaded for "just one more chance".'

A bomb struck Boleyn Road, Dalston, killing five men, one woman and two children, and injuring ten other women and children. Mary Sadler's terrified little son begged her to 'send the Germans away'. She 'put him in the cellar and covered his face and ears with a blanket so that he could not see or hear anything. After the raid he went to bed, but he died within six days of shock through the raid. He was six.'

A soldier on his way home to Leytonstone on leave overheard people talking about an air-raid there. When he got home, he discovered that his father had literally 'been blown to pieces. Neighbours and police searched the ruins but could not find him. He was found early the next morning, lying in a neighbour's garden four houses away, but his hand was found in another street and a limb in a bedroom of another wrecked house. His trousers were hanging in an elm tree.'

Elsewhere, a public house and the next-door fish shop were struck by a bomb. A rescue party of soldiers and policemen dug out alive a man, a woman and three children trapped in the wreckage of the buildings, but they also found four crushed and mutilated bodies. 'In the sidestreet lay the carcass of a horse attached to a fishmonger's cart.' Seven people were killed in 'a dingy street of working-class houses' on the other side of the river. 'A powerful bomb fell in the middle of a granite roadway and hurled the stone setts in all directions. The fronts of half-a-dozen tenements were damaged by the blast, ceilings collapsed and men, women and children were hurled to the floor, some never to rise. Masonry dislodged by another bomb was flung against a church wall and the stained glass windows were broken.' A resolution from the congregation somehow managed to ignore the human misery caused by the raid and instead condemned the Germans only for the 'wanton destruction ... of the east window of the Parish Church, one of the most beautiful examples in London'.

The Gothas rained down bombs right across the City and destroyed buildings and warehouses around the Barbican, Lower Thames Street and Aldgate. A bomb fell just outside Moorgate station, but failed to detonate, and the Mansion House was saved from a self-inflicted wound when a shell from an anti-aircraft gun fell on the pavement in front of it, but fortunately did not explode. Children from the St Giles, Cripplegate Sunday School were on board a tram at the Aldersgate terminus, about to set off on an outing, when the bombs started falling. 'There was no time to transfer, so the driver pluckily started the car ... we rushed through Goswell Street with most of the children crouching on the floor of the tram. At The Angel we hurried the children into a cinema and stayed until the raid was over. On returning to the City, we found buildings at the tram terminus in ruins and great fires burning off Aldersgate Street.'

A car-woman's horse and van were blown from Bartholomew Close into Fleet Street, and a high-explosive bomb devastated the Post Office's Central Telegraph Office in St Martin's-le-Grand. William Baily had just been to the bank for the wages and, 'returning to my place of business, saw police rushing people into the Post Office Tube. Looking towards King Edward Street, I saw about two dozen aeroplanes, rather low. With two others of the staff, I stood behind cloth stacks in our showroom. As the bombs were falling, two officers on leave from the Front joined us, shaking like leaves ... After a few seconds' quiet, the air was filled with falling stone, brick, timber and iron.' A portion of the parapet of the roof fell down on an old soldier who was doing 'sentry-go' (sentry duty) in the street and killed him. A bomb also narrowly missed the Bank of England, demolishing a commercial bank nearby; another struck Billingsgate Fish Market and yet others hit Fenchurch Street and Tower Hill.

A boy working at an office in Tower Hill went out 'to take a last peep' before the raid began. 'I remember the sinister hush of the sunlit street . . . Three horses stood there, all unsuspecting, their carts abandoned. The eighty-odd men and women in our building waited on the ground floor, because the basement, full of papers, would have been a firetrap.' A bomb fell a few hundred yards away and then there was 'a blinding flash, a chaos of breaking glass, and the air thick-yellow with dust and fumes. Five men had been struck by bomb fragments and a boy of my own age, also hit, died in the afternoon. Outside was a terrible sight, the horses twisted and mangled (the carts had disappeared except for a few burning bits of debris), the front of the office next door, which had caught the full force, blown clean away. They brought into our building people from the ruins there and I helped to carry them – it was a relief to do something. All the unfortunates had ghastly wounds. I had never seen a dead man before and I was too dazed to realise until afterwards that they must have been stone dead. A fireman, with his axe, put the last horse out of its anguish. The curious thing is that I did not hear the bomb at all and yet I was quite deaf for three days.'

A clerk in a neighbouring office noticed that 'three of our car-men and a little boy belonging to one of them were outside the premises' as the Gothas approached. 'Several other people rushed in, some of whom I conducted to the cellar, but the car-men and two or three other men remained just inside the door. The head of the firm, a fellow-clerk and I were all talking together when suddenly there was a deafening crash . . . my right arm was hanging limply down and there was a lot of blood. I looked out of the space which had been a window and saw three horses lying badly wounded and bleeding, and the cart, which had contained a hogshead of whisky, was blazing furiously . . . When the ambulance arrived we had to be carried over a heap of dead bodies. The car-men, the little boy, and the other men who were seeking shelter had been killed outright . . . I shall never forget it as long as I live.'

There were many near misses and remarkable escapes. 'A crippled pavement artist displaying a row of his productions, among which was a crayon drawing of a Zeppelin in difficulties surrounded by searchlight shafts', was somehow unhurt, and four hundred schoolchildren starting off for an outing were 'shepherded by a policeman into an underground station not a minute too soon'. 'Three little children lying in bed were buried under bricks from the chimney-piece and roof of their house, but were uninjured, though almost suffocated by dust and soot', and 'four racing pigeons also emerged alive from their loft after it was buried under bricks, rafters and debris for four days'. Two hundred women workers escaped from a bombed and blazing blouse factory and 'not a girl received so much as a scratch', and a crowd of sixty people in a butcher's shop on the corner of Banner Street and Whitecross Street also had a near miss when 'a large bomb' fell into 'a salt-meat tub, which had prevented it from exploding and saved those sixty lives'.

PC G. Asquith found another unexploded bomb that had smashed down through five floors of Barnes's jam and pickle factory in Battle Bridge Lane. He 'obtained a sack, wrapped it round the bomb, then got the same on to my shoulder and conveyed it to Tower Bridge police station. I laid it on the table in the charge-room and, had there been a thousand men attached to this station, they would all have had to handle it – the same as persons will handle a loaded revolver if left on a table. In fact so many intelligent policemen would insist on touching the bomb that it was removed to the cells.' It evidently did not occur to him to question the intelligence of the policeman who had carried an unexploded bomb into a police station in the first place.

The Gothas flew on 'like a flock of huge birds . . . clearly visible as they moved across the sky, contemptuous of the hailstorm of shells that exploded around them. They flew in close formation and very low. Only the aircraft at the heart of the formation dropped bombs, the ones surrounding them concentrated on defending them against attack. Displaying extraordinary boldness, they remained over the City for some twelve or fifteen minutes.' Shells bursting in the air around them left 'puffs of black smoke which expanded and drifted into one another . . . Machines were often hidden in the smoke', which might have explained the bizarre claim by one 'eye witness' that 'when the raiders broke up their formation, several of them seemed to disappear in small clouds of smoke in which it is assumed they enveloped themselves as soon as they were fired at'.

Despite the smoke, 'it seemed impossible that the raiders could escape being hit . . . but they always came safely through. Before the bombing ceased, the formation of the squadron had been broken up. For a few exciting seconds, which seemed as minutes to those who watched, there were signs of confusion. The aeroplanes moved like birds alarmed by the firing of a shotgun. One group held together and still flew towards the west. Other machines began to bank and turn. One or two climbed higher into the sky as though to escape our shells.

'Hopes went soaring up at this stage, but the confusion was more apparent than real. Soon the whole of the enemy had turned and, in an irregular bunch but taking a direct course, they were seen to start their return journey. Within a couple of minutes the haze had swallowed them up. For a little while the ground guns continued to fire, and as the last incident of the attack the crowds saw a solitary aeroplane, probably one of our own, speeding at a great height in the wake of the invaders.' As it flew eastwards 'following in the track of the vanished invaders, derisive laughter burst out, fists were shaken at him and there were mocking cries: "Give the Bosches hell – when you overtake them"', but the Gothas had already 'disappeared into the cloudbanks and only the rolling sound of machine-guns could be heard'.

The raiders shed their last bombs on the Isle of Dogs as they headed eastwards for Foulness and the relative safety of the open sea, holding to their course despite the barrage of anti-aircraft fire and the fighters now buzzing like gnats around them. A total of ninety-five fighters got air-borne, but they were 'an emergency force of very varied elements and of greatly varying efficiency . . . coming from all points of the compass, without much cohesion or experience in working together'. While 'most gallant attacks were made on the enemy formation by individual aircraft', despite the bravery of many pilots, they were most effective in demonstrating the futility of solo, uncoordinated attacks against a formation of well-armed Gothas.

The Gothas' reduced bombload was reflected in reports by British pilots that the enemy aircraft had been 'travelling faster and higher than on previous raids . . . owing to their speed, many of our aviators found it difficult to reach or keep up with them'. Captain James McCudden managed to target a trailing Gotha and poured fire into it at close range. He had improvised an additional armament on his Sopwith Pup, fitting a Lewis gun on the top plane instead of a Vickers gun firing through the propeller 'because the Lewis could shoot forward and upwards as well, for I could pull the near end of it down and shoot vertically above me. This of course would enable me to engage a Hun who had the superior advantage of height. I made myself a rough sight of wire and rings and beads, and very soon the machine was ready to wage war.'

McCudden emptied his first drum of ammunition at the raider, but 'in diving, I came rather too near the top plane of the Gotha and had to level out so violently to avoid running into him that the downward pressure of my weight as I pulled my joystick back was so great that my seat-bearers broke and I was glad it wasn't my wings . . . I put on a new drum, and dived from the Hun's right rear to within 300 feet, when I suddenly swerved and, changing over to his left rear, closed to fifty yards and finished my drum before the enemy gunner could swing his gun from the side at which I first dived.'

Even when he ran out of ammunition, he continued to harry the German formation. 'I flew abreast of the last Gotha at about 200 yards range, in such a position that the rear-gunner could not fire at me, owing to his wings and struts being in the way. My idea in flying alongside was to try to monopolise the Hun gunner's attention so that some of our other machines, of which there were a lot in attendance, could fly up behind the Hun unperceived and shoot at him whilst he was looking at me. However, my comrades had their own attractions and so I escorted this rear Gotha for 25 minutes at 200 yards range and had not a shot to fire at him. My feelings can be much better imagined than described and, owing to my carelessness, the Hun finally put a good burst of bullets through my windscreen, much to my consternation.' McCudden was unhurt, but he now became 'rather fed up with acting as ground-bait', and abandoned the pursuit.

He landed safely, but another pilot, Lieutenant W. G. Salmon of 63 Squadron, was less fortunate. He was hit in the eye by enemy fire and, though he made a valiant effort to reach his home airfield at Joyce Green, he lost control as he came in to land and was killed in the crash. A number of people were arrested at the site as they looted the crashed aircraft and the dead pilot's body for 'souvenirs'.

Second Lieutenant John Young also lost his life when he was shot down as he pursued the Gothas out to sea. His commanding officer told Young's father that he had been caught in a hail of fire 'too awful for words . . . there were twenty-two machines; each machine had four guns; each gun was firing about 400 rounds per minute'; but the CO's claim to have personally witnessed the death was demonstrably false, for he was not even airborne at the time Young was hit, and there is a strong possibility that he was actually shot down by anti-aircraft fire from British guns. Although a Royal Navy ship, HMS *Wolfe*, was at the scene within minutes, Young was trapped in his cockpit and drowned when the aircraft sank. His badly injured crewman, Air Mechanic C. C. Taylor, was rescued but died soon afterwards of a compound skull fracture.

British pilots pursued the Gothas almost all the way across the North Sea and four 'kills' were claimed, though the records of the England Squadron suggest that only one of them was correct. Second Lieutenants Frederick Grace and George Murray of 50 Squadron, a sugar planter and an architect in civilian life, pounced on an already damaged Gotha labouring at low altitude above the waves, and after pouring fire into it they saw 'black smoke coming from the centre section' and it ditched in the sea. The starboard wing 'crumpled' and two of the three crew crawled out on to the port wing. Murray fired off all his Very lights to try and attract the attention of a nearby vessel. The Gotha's tail, rising well clear of the water, would have been clearly visible, but no ships immediately came to the rescue and, low on fuel, Grace and Murray turned for home. No trace of the Gotha crew or their aircraft was ever found.

Despite an official statement the next day that after the raiders were 'engaged forty miles out to sea off the East Coast, two enemy machines were observed to crash into the sea', and 'a third enemy machine was seen to fall in flames off the mouth of the Scheldt', the claims of the pilots – Squadron Commander Butler, Sub-Lieutenant Daly and Flight Lieutenant Scott, all flying Sopwith Pups out of Manston – to have shot down a Gotha each were contradicted by German records. Sub-Lieutenant Loft, also from Manston, caught up with his target just short of the Belgian coast and poured two hundred rounds into its fuselage. He saw it lose height rapidly, as if it was about to crash-land, but then his guns jammed and, short of fuel, he turned for home. He ran out of fuel while still forty miles from his home base, but managed to glide safely to a crash-landing at Manningtree.

The Gotha he had attacked was probably the one commanded by Leutnant Schulte that made a forced landing on the beach at Ostend. His mechanics later counted scores of bullet-holes in its fuselage. He owed his survival to the excellent gliding properties of the Gotha, which could remain airborne for remarkable distances on one or even no engines. The remainder of the England Squadron reached their home airfields at around one o'clock that afternoon but, whether from damage sustained in combat or the aircraft's notorious instability when unladen with bombs and fuel, four of them then crashed as they tried to land.

German newspapers were quick to hail the raid as another triumphant blow against the heartland of the enemy. 'The fortified city, London, came under attack by German airplanes again on 7 July. The raid on the main source of the English war powers was again carried out in daylight. A squadron of our Grossflugzeuge [Gothas] under its commander, Captain Kleine, advanced on London in the late morning. The attack was mainly aimed at the warehouses and armament industries based at the eastern edge of the City and the London and St Katharine's Docks. With clear visibility, the squadron dropped bombs on the stores, warehouses, railways and docks on the north bank of the River Thames, between Charing Cross station and the docks east of Tower Bridge. In a raid lasting one hour and fifteen minutes, the bombs were well aimed and their impact could be seen from the thick clouds of smoke and powerful explosions. Charing Cross station was hit several times and London Bridge also suffered a direct hit. Bombs were also dropped on the fortified port of Margate.

'The defensive fire of the English artillery started when our aircraft approached the coastline, followed the squadron for the whole duration of the flight over English soil and increased to the utmost ferocity over

London. Enemy aircraft rose in great numbers and threw themselves against our planes. However, just like the artillery fire, they were unable to prevent the squadron from carrying out its mission. An enemy plane was shot down during the aerial warfare and with the exception of one [Gotha] that had to go down over the sea because of an engine failure, all our aircraft returned home safely.'

In Britain, newspapers were quick to seize on, or invent, the German connections of people or buildings hit by bombs, as if divine vengeance was being wreaked on the kith and kin of the perpetrators. The deaths of a naturalized German, Philip Frantzmann, and a registered alien, Henry Hoppe, who was with him when a bomb destroyed Frantzmann's shop, were prominently reported, and *The Times* claimed of one bomb that, 'strangely enough, the building on which it fell [the 'German Gymnasium' in Pancras Road] was formerly a popular resort of Germans in London. Its victims were two old men and a boy of seven.' Elsewhere the owner of a shop destroyed by a bomb was 'said to be a naturalised German'. He was killed, and his daughter, son and housekeeper were injured.

'The population of the capital and of the whole of the southern part of the country was deeply roused' by the raid, but 'at bottom was humiliation at the affront which the Germans had put upon us and resentment at the unpreparedness of the Government to repel or avenge it'. A respected commentator, F. W. Lanchester, noted, 'That London should have been subjected to a second raid in force by an enemy squadron cannot have given rise to the least surprise or astonishment . . . What has astonished London and caused widespread indignation is the fact that the attacking squadron apparently found its way over with as little interference as though it had been executing a spectacular manoeuvre at a parade or review in its country of origin.' Other commentators used far less measured terms, their outrage at the attack mingling with disgust at the 'humiliating and incredible . . . dishonour of being outfought in the air'. A reporter had watched 'deeply humiliated, that such a thing should be achieved unhindered in daylight over London', and yet another declared that 'there had not been a more discreditable event in our history' since a raiding Dutch fleet had sailed up the Medway in 1667, burning Chatham and destroying or capturing a dozen British men-of-war.

*The Times* was at pains to downplay such hysteria, claiming that the raid had 'caused no panic' and that Londoners had greeted it with remarkable sangfroid. 'An extraordinary indication of the futility of the raid as a demonstration of "frightfulness" was the rapidity with which people everywhere settled down to their business again when the raiders had disappeared ... Curious scenes were observed in the suburban shopping districts while the raid was in progress. Grocers, fruit and vegetable dealers, and other tradesmen continued to serve customers who, between the ordering of one article and another, would go out into the street to observe progress. It was possible to hear such sentences as "The shrapnel is bursting all around them now. And I shall want two pounds of butter, please."

'Women who were in the streets when they became aware of the raid watched the sky for a time and then walked into shops to do business as much as to take shelter ... For some time the telephone exchanges were overwhelmed with calls. Women waited their turn in queues at the public call offices, anxious to get tidings of the fate of friends and relatives, and the operators who had remained pluckily at their posts throughout the raid dealt with the rush with splendid coolness.'

Despite such claims, there was no shortage of evidence of terror, hysteria, disintegrating morale and the beginnings of mass panic from those areas that had been bombed. When the raid began, fearing a repetition of the horrors of Upper North Street, parents had besieged many schools, demanding their children. Even the rumour of an air-raid was enough to provoke panic, despite a reminder from London County Council's Education Department that 'during danger from an air-raid, all children will remain inside the school building; all gates will be shut and no one will be admitted. Crowding around the school premises only increases the danger. No place is absolutely safe but experience shows that children are safer in school buildings than if sent out into the streets.' Nonetheless, panic-stricken parents were often allowed to take their children home with them.

As nerves settled after the attack, there came the now familiar mixture of hatred for the enemy that had inflicted such suffering, and rage against those who had once more failed to protect London's citizens from attack, or even struck an effective retaliatory blow. Such fury was widespread: soldiers were reportedly beaten up by a mob in Hull after a Zeppelin raid on the city, and an RFC corporal in Beverley was stoned. The anger was only increased by the knowledge that 'a regrettably large number of casualties', including several deaths, had been caused by British shells, not German bombs.

Xenophobia was also widespread as furious Londoners sought any scapegoat for their fear and misery. In the early stages of the war, Londoners moved by stories of their plight had thrown open their doors to an unprecedented number of refugees from Belgium; 265,000 had arrived by June 1915, including fifteen thousand Russian Jews, men previously employed in the Antwerp diamond-cutting industry, and their families. Some of this huge influx had been accommodated in public buildings – a hundred were housed in Dulwich Baths, and hundreds more at Alexandra Palace – but thousands were also taken in by private citizens. There were inevitable tensions in poorer districts where the immigrants were perceived to be competing for jobs or taking scarce accommodation and food 'out of the mouths' of Britons, but on the whole, public sympathy for their plight outweighed any resentment.

Such fellow-feeling did not extend to those of real or apparent German origin, no matter how long they had been British citizens. There were anti-German riots in London Fields where 'a large body of men and women, the latter forming the majority, paraded the Broadway and attacked the premises of several butchers and pork butchers bearing German or German-sounding names'. Houses and shops in Hackney, Highgate and Tottenham were also ransacked, and in one East End street the house of two 'Germans' was wrecked by a mob of women who, failing to find the occupants, smashed their furniture and threw it into the street. Police, including many recently recruited 'Specials', often stood aside and let the mob give full vent to its fury, but even those who tried to intervene struggled to disperse the 'ugly and menacing crowds', among them a man who demanded the right to 'pay those German devils for killing our children. If this Government won't do it, we will.'

Sylvia Pankhurst witnessed the mob rule at close quarters. 'Down the street police whistles sounded vociferously: a babel of shouting, tremendous outcry. A crowd was advancing at a run, a couple of lads on bicycles leading, a swarm of children on the fringes, screaming like gulls. Missiles were flying. In the centre of the turmoil men dragged a big, stout man, stumbling and resisting in their grasp, his clothes whitened by flour, his mouth dripping blood. They rushed him on, new throngs closed around him . . .

'From another direction arose more shouting. A woman's scream . . . in the midst of a struggling mob; her blouse half torn off, her fair hair fallen, her face contorted with pain and terror, blood running down her bare white arm. A big drunken man flung her to the ground. She was lost to sight . . . "Oh, my God! Oh! They are kicking her!" a woman screamed.

' "Do help her!" I pleaded with a soldier who stood watching.

'He shrugged his shoulders. "I can't do anything."

' "You are a soldier, they will respect you."

' "Why should I?" he asked with a curl of the lip. "Look, there's another soldier; can't you get on to *him*?" '

The anti-German riots were also a pretext for looting. Four men were tried for stealing an iron safe from Alfred Wenninger's pork butcher's shop, and many other shops and houses were stripped of their furniture and fittings. In the xenophobia of the mob, victims of almost any foreign extraction would do. Several shops 'belonging to Russian Jews' were attacked in Lambeth, and a Bethnal Green man was arrested after 'shouting that some Germans were in the house next to his and inciting the crowd to fetch them out. The people to whom he referred were of Dutch origin.'

The air was 'filled by the babble of voices and the noise of knocking and splintering wood. Men were lowering a piano through the window . . . A woman and her children raced off with an easy-chair, rushing it along on its castors before them. "I shall sit, and sit, and sit on this chair all day," the mother yelled. "I never had an armchair to sit in before." "Bread! Bread! Bread!" the shrieks rang out. Women and children rushed by, their arms and aprons laden with loaves.

'Looting continued with impunity for days . . . men unknown in the district, with hatchets on their shoulders, marched through Bethnal Green, Green Street and Roman Road to the very end. Wherever a shop had a

German name over it, they stopped and hacked down the shutters and broke the glass. Then crowds of children rushed in and looted. When darkness fell and the police made no sign, men and women joined in the sack.'

Only when adjoining English shops began to be looted did the police stir themselves to intervene. A boot shop in Roman Road 'got its window broken through proximity to a German's and a swarm of children made off with the stock'. A boy employed by the Pankhursts boasted that he had taken some of the boots. On learning of it, Sylvia Pankhurst 'sent for him and told him that if I heard such a thing of him again, I would send him away. Before leaving me, he appeared to agree that it was cowardly to rob defenceless people who were persecuted for no fault of their own. An hour or two later, his mother came to me, a fiery-faced termagant, denouncing me as a German and threatening to scratch my face.'

Thousands of people of German descent were also interned for the duration of the war. One doubly unfortunate pork butcher in Hull, Charles Hohrenhein, had his shop vandalized and was interned because of his German origins, while his son, who lived in his homeland, was interned by the German authorities as an enemy alien. The tide of anti-German feeling in Britain was so strong that the King, whose family name, reflecting his German ancestry, was Saxe-Coburg-Gotha, felt impelled to adopt the invented but less inflammatory and much more British-sounding name 'Windsor'. Prince Louis of Battenburg was forced to resign as First Lord of the Admiralty because of his Germanic name, and felt it prudent to change it to 'Mountbatten'.

There was also widespread paranoia about spies, crystallized in the belief in ' "The Unseen Hand" – a network of spies, traitors and fifth columnists, 50,000 strong'. 'Rumour raced hot-foot: "There were little lights signalling, telling them where to drop the bombs!" . . . "Germans" . . . "Beasts" . . . "They should all have been cleared out at the beginning of the war" . . . The crowds as they passed . . . growled imprecations; wild stories grew there.' German grocers were poisoning the food they sold; German barbers were cutting the throats of their customers; German nurses were murdering their patients. All 'foreigners', whatever their nationality, were equally suspect. A Swiss waiter in one London restaurant was accused of drawing a plan of military installations and dragged off to Scotland Yard; in fact he had been sketching a table plan.

The Government and the authorities charged with London's defence did not escape the popular rage, and once more 'expressions of disappointment and indeed of anger were heard on every hand, because the enemy squadron had got away unscathed'. There was particular fury that lives were lost because either insufficient warning or no warning at all had been given. 'In the course of the last two months we have had numerous warnings of the approach of hostile aircraft but each time nothing has developed. Then on Saturday, when enemy aviators did get over land in this district, the first warning was the booming of the guns ... When squadrons of machines of that size are passing overhead, the noise of their engines cannot fail to give notice of their proximity. The first warning we on this coast had was when the machines were greeted by anti-aircraft guns. One is inclined to suspect that the warnings we have hitherto received by siren followed the actual arrival of enemy machines over some other part of the coast.'

One police inspector estimated that 'four-fifths of the killed and injured' in his district had been in the streets when the bombs fell. 'In many places on Saturday morning a warning was given half an hour before the bombs began to fall and in practically every case people took refuge in basement rooms. Later it was realised how many lives had been saved by this precaution. On the other hand, there were heavy casualties in neighbourhoods where people, surprised in the streets, had been unable to obtain efficient shelter. It is argued that warnings would bring the people into the open, to their greater danger, but the experience of Saturday shows that while men and women in the outer suburbs who could see that the raiders were at a distance remained in the streets to watch the scene, nine-tenths of the people in the area over which the attack actually took place sought shelter.'

In the light of this experience, revised instructions on precautions to be taken in the event of air-raids were issued to the public: 'On hearing the sound signals or at night, the firing of anti-aircraft guns or explosion of bombs, persons in the open should at once take the most effective cover near at hand.' Yet not everyone agreed with using improvised air-raid shelters such as Underground stations and the cellars of public buildings, offices and factories, arguing that these might even increase the danger to the public. 'Unless a reasonably high proportion of the people can get down into the shelter before the bombardment begins, the existence of some refuges may only lead to congestion in the street at the time when there will be masses of shrapnel and pieces of anti-aircraft shells falling . . . The weakest points about the "Tubes" as refuges are their narrow entrances, designed for checking tickets rather than for rapid transit . . . and only a small part of the population threatened is in reach of the deeper Tubes. The east of London is served by lines which are either shallow or are actually exposed and hence likely to attract bombs rather than offer protection.'

Despite the observation of one expert that 'the great mass of English working-class people live in congested areas of poorly constructed buildings, which are completely vulnerable to high-explosive bombs and to which no minor precautionary measures make the slightest difference', many householders spurned the public shelters. Some congregated in the cellars of their local pubs, where there was the added attraction of beer on tap; one Peckham man remembered his family 'would drag me along by the scruff of the neck to take shelter under the Bun House [the local pub]'. Others created their own 'living-room shelters'. The 'old 'uns' often preferred to 'take their chance under the kitchen table with a mattress on top as added protection', surrounded by the buckets of water and the 'supply of fine dry sand or soil or some other incombustible powder . . . kept in pails or scuttles' that the Government urged people to keep at hand to extinguish any fires or incendiary bombs. They were also cautioned that 'on no account should money be expended on powder extinguishers (tubes), glass hand-grenades or similar types of minor fire appliances at present being hawked about, and if provided, they should not be relied upon'.

One family 'congregated in the dining room, where my brother had made a little dugout of his own between the high end of the old-fashioned sofa and a neighbouring chair. There he was snugly ensconced with our pet hedgehog in his charge. The rest of us huddled underneath the big dining room table, which was padded round with mattresses and had on top the *pièce de résistance* of the whole scheme, some baths of water! The idea was that any bomb which hit the house would fall clean through the roof and top storey into the baths of water and so be put out.'

The value of such Heath-Robinson arrangements was more psychological than real; as one air force officer remarked, 'it is dishonest to make people believe that the precautions have much to do with their chance of escaping injury or death'. If a German bomb struck a house, it would normally require a lot more than wood frames, horsehair cushions and tubs of water to protect the inhabitants, though in at least one case they did prove enough. 'There was an almighty bang and a bomb, which must have come through the roof and through three floors, ended up in the kitchen and on the table. Two of the leaves had broken, but it was a very heavy and sturdy table and it saved our lives'; though of even greater life-saving significance was the fact that the bomb failed to detonate. Many people retreated to the cellar of their house, but 'these were often sheer death-traps; the effect of a "delayed-action" bomb is to bring the whole building, except the outside walls, down on the cellar, thus threatening a peculiarly horrible death.'

Lloyd George had made a tour of inspection of some of the bombed areas on the afternoon after the 7 July raid and the local inhabitants left him in no doubt about the popular mood. He returned to Whitehall to chair a meeting of the War Cabinet dominated by discussions about the means by which air defences might be improved. Members of the Cabinet commented 'severely and adversely' on the fact that Lord French's letter to Robertson a week earlier, pleading for 56 Squadron to be kept in England, had not been brought to their attention at the time. In the resulting row, 'much excitement was shown. One would have thought the world was coming to an end,' an unrepentant Robertson confided to Haig.

Although Lloyd George told a parliamentary deputation 'If anyone in this country says "Ourselves first and our soldiers afterwards", well then, they had better find another Government', his War Cabinet resolved to strengthen the home defences by retaining at least one squadron of aircraft in England rather than sending it to the Western Front, and another two squadrons already based in France were to be brought home. A reprisal raid on the German city of Mannheim was also to go ahead, though this was hedged around with the qualification that this should only happen if it did not impinge on Haig's planned Flanders offensive, now due to be launched on 31 July. Haig made a show of acquiescence, but his postscript warning that 'withdrawal of these two squadrons will certainly . . . render our victory more difficult and more costly in aeroplanes and pilots. If a raid on Mannheim is undertaken in addition, our plans will have to be reconsidered entirely and the operations [the Flanders offensive] may have to be abandoned' scared the Cabinet members enough for them to drop the demand for a reprisal attack on Mannheim and reduce the number of squadrons to be returned for Home Defence to just one.

46 Squadron, equipped with fast, modern Sopwith Pups – the aircraft's top speed of over a hundred miles an hour and a rate of climb twice as fast as the ageing Home Defence fighters gave it a menace that belied the inoffensive name – was duly returned to England and based at Sutton's Farm in Essex. The squadron gave a taste of the speed and efficiency it might bring to the air defence of London when all its aircraft were in position with engines running inside two and a half minutes of a 'Readiness' alert being issued, and on the firing of a white flare to signal 'Patrol' all eighteen aircraft then took off within forty-five seconds.

However, too many of the other Home Defence aircraft were still old and semi-obsolescent. Increases in aircraft production were barely keeping pace with the prodigious rate of attrition on the Western Front, where Trenchard's insistence that 'an aircraft was an offensive and not a defensive weapon' and his 'one policy, one method of fighting – to go and find the Hun and make him fight' was reaping a fearsome daily harvest of his own men and machines.

Over the following days the War Cabinet finally approved plans to give all the massive, widely dispersed population of London an advance five-minute warning of an impending air-raid, but until a better one could be devised the warning system would be the near-farcical one of policemen on foot and on bicycle wearing placards 'with the printed inscription, in bold letters and red ink' 'POLICE NOTICE – TAKE COVER'. When the danger had passed, they would tour their districts again with placards reading 'ALL CLEAR'. As *Flight* magazine noted, 'This fore and aft placard business . . . smacks of the ridiculous.'

On 11 July the War Cabinet also approved the creation of a committee on Air Organization and Home Defence Against Air-Raids under the chairmanship of Lieutenant General Jan Christiaan Smuts. A brilliant guerrilla leader against British forces during the Boer War, Smuts had been Defence Minister in Louis Botha's nationalist government but rejoined the South African Army at the outbreak of the Great War and played a leading part in the victorious campaign in German East Africa. Drafted into the War Cabinet by Lloyd George earlier in 1917, 'a fresh and able mind, free from departmental prejudices', Smuts set about his task with characteristic directness, energy and speed. Just eight days later, on 19 July, he presented his findings to the Prime Minister. He warned that 'the air-raids on London were likely to increase to such an extent in the next twelve months that London might, through aerial warfare, become part of the battle front'. Noting that because of its unique importance as not only the administrative hub but also the principal port and prime manufacturing centre 'London occupies a peculiar position in the Empire of which it is the nerve centre', Smuts recommended 'exceptional measures' for its defence.

They included four key requirements: the uncoordinated activities of the RFC and RNAS squadrons should in future be placed under a single, unified command structure; an improved anti-aircraft barrier should be created around London; the deployment of three new squadrons of day-fighters with pilots 'trained to fight *in formation*' should be accelerated; and a reserve force should be established to deal with diversionary attacks on coastal towns and cities, leaving the main defence force to concentrate exclusively on the protection of London.

A new air-raid warning system was also established, with County Hall acting as the command centre for a network of eighty fire stations within a ten-mile radius of Charing Cross. When they received an air-raid warning from County Hall, each fire station would then sound a warning to alert the population of its district. Various more or less plausible alternatives were considered and discarded – gunfire, coloured smoke, lighting the street lights, ringing tramcar bells, blowing factory whistles or sounding the foghorns of ships moored in the Thames – but eventually it was decided to detonate at fifteen-second intervals three 'maroons', also known as 'Socket distress signal rockets', fired from a small brass mortar and normally used by ships in distress at sea.

In order for the alarm to be effective, and to allow a generous four and a half minutes for it to be relayed and transmitted, the warning would have to be given when the raiders crossed a line twenty-two miles from Charing Cross. Unfortunately there was no line of observer posts at that distance, and rather than setting up a new chain, the existing ones – at an average distance of only sixteen miles – were used. That alone made the new system far from ideal, but it was at least likely to be more immediate and effective than cohorts of bicycling policemen. However, the War Cabinet then decided that to avoid undue disturbance to the slumbers of Londoners and to minimize disruption to war production the maroons would only be sounded by day, with placarded policemen on bicycles, ringing their bells, still the purveyors of bad news after dark.

Even before these latest improvements to London's defences, Kleine and the other officers of the England Squadron had already noted that, notwithstanding the success of the 7 July raid, the anti-aircraft system had been reorganized and significantly strengthened since the previous flight. The intelligence that a squadron of Sopwith Pups was now lying in wait for them was passed to Kleine within days of 46 Squadron's move to Sutton's Farm, and that again may have persuaded him to give London a wide berth for a while.

Instead, on 22 July, a flight of twenty-one Gothas – two had turned back with the customary engine trouble – left Gontrode and St Denijs-Westrem at 5.30 in the morning and bombed Harwich and Felixstowe as the inhabitants were settling down to their breakfasts. Just as in the raid on 4 July, most of the bombs aimed at Harwich fell in the harbour, but the RNAS station at Felixstowe and a nearby army base were again bombed and eleven of the thirteen fatalities from the raid were caused by a direct hit on a barracks block. Over 120 British aircraft got airborne, but only one fired as much as a shot at the raiders, who had dropped their bombs and were heading back out to sea within ten minutes of crossing the coast. 48 Squadron, based at Dunkirk, proved more effective, intercepting them off Ostend on their homeward journey, and two of the squadron's Bristol Fighters made a simultaneous attack on one of a group of five Gothas, sending it spiralling into the sea. The wreck of the aircraft was still visible four hours later.

The coastal anti-aircraft batteries around Harwich and Felixstowe had been marginally more successful than the Home Defence squadrons, sending up a barrage that at least forced the Gothas to bomb from high altitude where their accuracy was inevitably lessened, but the only aircraft seriously damaged by anti-aircraft fire were British. Erroneous reports that the Gothas were making for Southend led fighters to scramble to protect the town. The gun-batteries lining the Thames estuary then began blasting away at about 8.45 that morning, half an hour after the Gothas had begun the flight home across the North Sea. Their targets turned out to be the patrolling British fighters.

Lieutenant Barrett made an emergency landing at Rochford after shrapnel punched holes in his wings, and three other aircraft were also hit, including that of the leader of 37 Squadron, Captain Claude Ridley, who also had to make an emergency landing after his engine cowling was shot away at 14,000 feet. His fury can only be imagined, for the previous day he had overflown the same gun-batteries to demonstrate the Sopwith Pup's profile and engine-note to the trigger-happy gunners in the hope of avoiding such incidents. Eight other fighters were also shelled. With a remarkable flair for stating the obvious, a GHQ Home Forces report later noted, 'Gunners do not seem to have realised that the aircraft might not be German'. The gun-batteries continued firing until 9.45, by which time the Germans were already landing back at St Denijs-Westrem and Gontrode.

The new air-raid warning system had also failed to function to maximum effect. The warning of an impending raid was successfully transmitted, but it was not rescinded when it became clear that the raiders were not targeting London and indeed had already begun the flight back to Belgium. As a result, at 8.30 that morning, fifteen minutes after the Gothas left the British coast, County Hall notified its network of fire stations that a raid was in progress and seventy-nine of the eighty at once fired off their maroons, while policemen on bicycles, ringing their bells and wearing their 'Take Cover' placards, rode through the streets. For the most part their message was now heeded. 'In the early days when attack from the air was a vague, unfamiliar terror, the tendency was for people to leave their houses during raids and go star- or sun-gazing. But in the districts where raids have often occurred, people have learnt that cover does minimise the risk.'

The all-clear was not sounded until ten that morning, and meanwhile the transport system ground to a halt as trains stopped, omnibuses and cabs were abandoned in the streets, and tens of thousands of panic-stricken Londoners rushed to find shelter in Underground stations, the tunnels under the Thames at Woolwich, Greenwich, Blackwall and Rotherhithe, and the cellars of public buildings and factories, many of which put out 'Air Raid Shelter' signs when a warning was given. Many more people fled to the parks. But inevitably all of these refuges were more readily accessible to the inhabitants of the affluent West End, where there were far more parks and open spaces and many more Underground stations. In the poorer districts of the East End such means of refuge and escape were far thinner on the ground. Not only were the Tube and rail stations either above ground or too close to the surface to be safe havens but, while there were eight thousand acres of parks (about thirteen square miles) in London as a whole, 'east of Blackfriars Bridge and Whitehall there is practically nothing available, except a few not-too-accessible places like the Greenwich marshes. The great dockland area is appallingly badly provided with parks.'

The inhabitants of these areas, overwhelmingly poor manual workers and their families, had to fend for themselves with little help from the Government beyond well-meaning and often useless advice. Given the disproportionate weight of bombing raids they had to bear and the lack of safe refuges and public shelters in their home districts, it was scarcely surprising that many of them tended to panic in the face of air-raids.

# CHAPTER 7
# HOME DEFENCE

BAD WEATHER PROTECTED LONDON throughout the rest of the month – Kleine tried to launch the squadron against London on 29 July but the Gothas were driven back by the conditions before even reaching England – during which time more of the Smuts committee's reforms took root. On 31 July, the day on which Haig launched his long-awaited Flanders offensive – the Third Battle of Ypres, soon to become notorious as 'Passchendaele' – the London Air Defence Area (LADA) was established. Its commander was the monocle-wearing, moustachioed, Old Etonian Brigadier General (later Major General) Edward 'Splash' Ashmore. Re-called to take up his new command from the Western Front, where he had been commanding artillery in the lines north of Ypres, Ashmore cast a quizzical and perhaps slightly cantankerous look over his new brief, then remarked with characteristic insouciance that he was swapping 'the comparative safety of the Front for the probability of being hanged in the streets of London'.

Ignoring the more eccentric suggestions, such as the *Daily Telegraph*'s proposal that the Thames 'which served to guide the raiders' should be shrouded by artificial fog, Ashmore set to work to provide more effective air defences for London and the south-east, coordinating the work of the observation and listening posts, the anti-aircraft batteries, and the Home Defence squadrons, and reducing, if not eliminating, embarrassing 'friendly fire' incidents. However, his attempts to carry out his duties were hampered by conflicting priorities. The Admiralty insisted on retaining control of the RNAS aircraft that, with the naval and coastal gun batteries, continued to be the first line of defence at the coast, and Ashmore's desire to protect the eastern approaches to London with an unbroken ring of anti-aircraft guns was also compromised. The members of the War Cabinet approved the idea of the ring of gun-batteries, set up at a distance of twenty-five miles from Hyde Park and stretching from Ware in Hertfordshire, north of the capital, to Oxted in Surrey, in the south, but they would not allow more than a third of the necessary guns to be moved from the ports and ships on which they were currently sited.

Nonetheless, it was a modest improvement, and Ashmore then added a refinement to reduce friendly fire incidents by creating defined zones separated by the 'Green Line', in which guns or aircraft would have priority. The system seemed admirably clear in theory: when raiders were approaching, defensive aircraft outside the Green Line would 'fly to a flank' to give 'unrestricted action' to the guns; inside the line, fighters would always have priority and guns would only fire 'up to that time when it becomes plain that our pilots have seen the enemy and are in a position to attack him'. In practice, in the fog of war, with gunners often unable to distinguish the distant, fleeting shapes of aircraft, British fighters continued to be targeted and shelled by their own anti-aircraft batteries.

Ashmore also established an Operations Room in Horse Guards Parade, equipped with a giant map table lit from below by 'an ingenious arrangement of coloured lamps', and divided into five hundred numbered squares, each of which was subdivided into four lettered squares – 'Ack, Emma, Jay and York' – and then split up into four further squares, numbered 'One, Two, Three and Four'. 'Air Bandit, 421, Emma, 3' for example, would instantly pinpoint the position of an enemy raider. Ten 'plotters' stood around the map table receiving information through telephone headsets from twenty-six sub-control centres, instantly moving symbols – discs for single enemy aircraft, rectangles for formations, and aircraft-shaped counters for British fighters – with wooden rakes in response. Although a substantial improvement on what had gone before, the system remained imperfect; according to Ashmore, the 'Air Bandit' system of observer cordons was able to report to the Horse Guards in 'three minutes at best', and 'more often the message took three or four times as long'.

Once a warning was received by the Operations Room, fighters could now be scrambled at high speed. Each squadron had a telephone operator permanently on duty. When an air-raid warning was circulated, the operator sounded 'three large Klaxon horns set up on the roof of the men's quarters and Officers' Mess. The men swarmed into their kit and warmed up their engines. If the air-raid warning was followed by the action signal, machines were off the ground within a minute.' Ground-to-air communications were also slightly improved courtesy of four radio-equipped aircraft patrolling the banks of the Thames, in radio contact with ground stations at Wormwood Scrubs and the Hotel Cecil, but the remainder of the fighters had no radios and were still reliant on the Ingram signals or

'Set us free!' German propaganda postcard of 1914 urging the lifting of restrictions imposed by the Kaiser on the use of German air power against Britain.

Macht uns frei!

*Above:* Gothas of the England Squadron drawn up on the airfield at Gontrode for an inspection by Leutnant-General von Höppner (*at front, saluting*). The massive hangar was originally used to house zeppelins.

*Below, left to right:* General Feldmarschal Paul von Hindenburg, Kaiser Wilhelm II and General Erich Ludendorff; Hauptmann Ernst Brandenburg; Major Wilhelm Siegert; Korvettenkapitan Peter Strasser; Hauptmann Rudolf Kleine.

*Above:* A Gotha of the England Squadron in flight. The white paint was later replaced by grey and black, as mounting losses of aircraft forced the Squadron to switch to night attacks.

*Below left:* Ground-staff help their air-crew into flying gear designed to counter the intense cold at altitude in open cockpits.

*Below right:* Liquid oxygen being poured into containers before being loaded into the cockpit; air-crew inhaled the oxygen through a rubber tu[...]

*Opposite top:* Ground-crew loading 50 and 25kg bombs before a night-raid on England.

*Opposite bottom:* The streamlined shape of a bom[...] photographed a split-second after being dropped [...] a German aircraft.

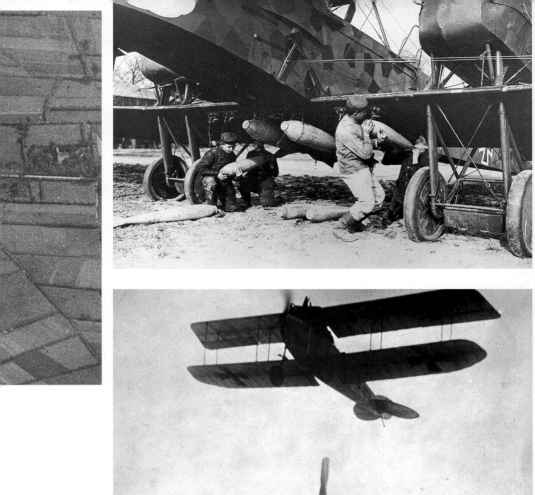
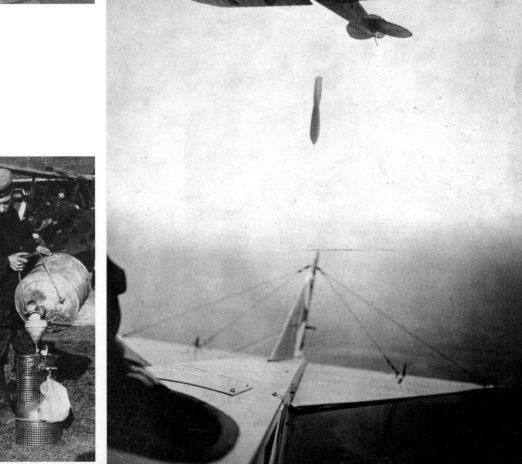

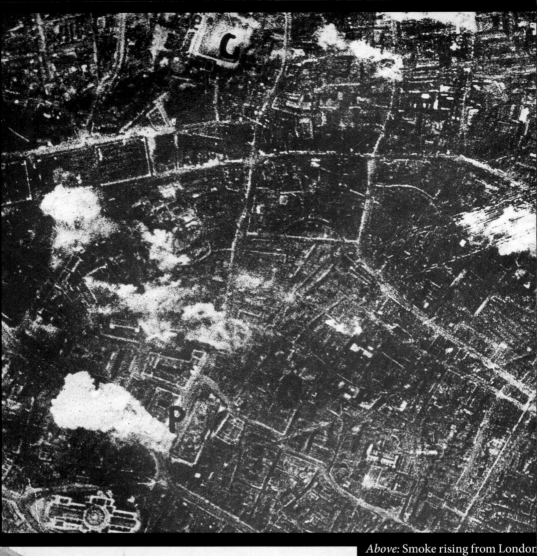

*Above:* Smoke rising from London during the raid by the England Squadron on 7 July 1917. The blaze at the Central Telegraph Office is immediately north of St Paul's, at the bottom left.

*Left:* Lord French and the King and Queen (*centre, beyond the piano*) inspect the destruction wrought by a 1,000kg bomb dropped from a 'Giant' aircraft in Warrington Crescent on 7 March 1918. The piano, dragged from the wreckage of a house, had fallen from the top storey and crushed the owner to death in the basement.

*above right:* The remains of the Eaglet public house in Seven Sisters Road, after a bomb smashed through a delivery hatch in the street and detonated in the cellar beneath the pub.

*below right:* The devastation at Odhams Printing Works in Long Acre on 28 January 1918. Most of the casualties occurred in the basement, which was used as a designated air-raid shelter.

*Right:* A workman clears debris from the basement classroom in which eighteen pupils of Upper North Street School, Poplar, were killed by a German bomb on 13 June 1917.

*Below:* A procession of horse-drawn hearses take the bodies of fifteen of the dead children to a mass funeral.

large white arrows, supplied to all the anti-aircraft units and laid out on the ground to point in the direction of the incoming bombers. The signs could give no indication of distance or altitude, and in less than perfect weather they were invisible to the fighter crews. The only means of recalling them once the raid was over and the bombers had left British shores was a 'general searchlight flashing signal to come down'.

Alongside the other improvements, fighter pilots had also begun to modify their tactics in the light of the realization expressed by Lord French that 'isolated attacks by aeroplanes on these unbroken formations are, it is clear, a useless sacrifice'. The anti-aircraft batteries were now charged with 'the definite role of breaking up the enemy formation', making the raiders more vulnerable to concerted attack by groups of fighters.

The first test of the new air defence system came on 12 August. Kleine's impetuosity and thirst for action meant that, as Walter Georgii complained, 'it was often not easy to persuade the Kommandeur that a certain day might be unfavourable for a raid', and his forecast of poor weather was ignored by Kleine, who made a snap decision to launch a further attack on England that afternoon. So sudden was it that several aircrews were not even at their bases and a number of Gothas could not be readied in time. Only thirteen lined up for the start flag at 2.30 that afternoon and two of those immediately landed again, their pilots once more citing engine trouble. Kleine himself did not take part in the raid, delegating command to Oberleutnant Richard Walter, one of the flight leaders at St Denijs-Westrem.

As they crossed the English coast, one of the Gothas peeled away from the main formation to make the customary diversionary attack on Margate, but RNAS aircraft were already in pursuit and the LADA Operations Room, notified of the raiders' presence at five o'clock, had RFC patrols airborne in numbers soon afterwards.

Strong winds blowing from west-south-west had slowed the formation to only fifty miles an hour and pushed it twenty miles north of its planned landfall. Concerned at the amount of fuel they had already burned in battling the headwinds and perhaps alarmed at the numbers of fighters facing his depleted formation, Walter now signalled the remaining ten Gothas to abandon the attempt to reach London and attack the secondary target, Southend, instead. Over 2,000kg of bombs fell on the town. Fortunately for its inhabitants, half failed to explode, but those that did claimed thirty-two lives and injured another forty-six people. A 50kg bomb fell in Victoria Avenue, leaving 'a heap of torn and mangled humanity'. Seven died there, five of them holidaymakers on their way to the station. Another bomb fell in Lovelace Gardens, 'killing a mother and daughter and injuring the husband who is a cripple', and a man 'watching the aeroplanes' was also blown to pieces.

The death toll might have been lower had a general warning been issued but, although the Southend police and the fire stations, hospitals and railway officials had been alerted to the impending attack, the town's citizens and the throngs of holidaymakers remained in ignorance until the bombs began to fall, because there was 'no system of warning in Southend'. A steam whistle at the local electricity station began to sound only after the raid was over. Irate townspeople, protesting 'the imbecility of the local authorities', marched on the mayor's house and extracted the promise that in future raids a siren would be sounded for one minute, but that was no consolation to the relatives of those already lying dead.

However, the raiders also paid a heavy price. The clouds of pursuing fighters and the barrage of anti-aircraft fire forced the Gothas to abort the attack and flee for home before dropping the last of their bombs. One was shot down over the sea after a dogged pursuit by Flight Sub-Lieutenant Harold Kerby, for which he was awarded the DSC. Kerby saw one survivor clinging to the tail of the Gotha as the sea washed over it and threw him his life jacket. As he returned to base at Walmer, he fired red flares in an attempt to divert four British destroyers to the downed Gotha, but they did not understand the signal and continued on their course. All the German crewmen died.

The bomber that made the diversionary attack on Margate was targeted by five British fighters and hit in one engine. The pilot managed to nurse it back across the sea but had to crash-land on the beach at Zeebrugge, wrecking his aircraft. With night falling and fuel almost exhausted, the remaining aircraft reached their bases only for four more to be wrecked in crashes as they tried to land. Kurt Delang was counting the litres of fuel left 'on my buttons' when he finally reached Gontrode and came in to land. Just then, another Gotha, propellers motionless, slid by below Delang's aircraft, forcing him to go round again. As he did so, his own engines spluttered and died. He just cleared a power line before crash-landing in the soft earth of a potato field. The Gotha flipped over, 'bursting all its joints'. Delang and his crew survived with only bruises and broken bones – Vizefeldwebel Paul Ruhl 'suffered a broken leg when he jumped out of the Gotha just before it touched down, fearing that it would burn up' – but the raid had been a disaster. Six of the eleven aircraft that had crossed the Belgian coast six hours earlier had either been shot down or damaged beyond repair.

On 18 August, undeterred by this reverse and again placing more faith in the sun shining from the cloudless sky than in Georgii's forecast of adverse weather, including the threat of gales, Kleine ordered a further raid. At the briefing before the flight Georgii delivered an update on his weather report and defied his commander by warning the assembled air-crew that it would not be wise to risk a flight to England that morning. Infuriated, Kleine silenced him and ordered an immediate start. 'Although a strong wind was blowing from the south-west, we hoped to find more favourable winds at higher altitudes out over the sea.' Although a high-pressure zone was centred over Germany and the barometer was rising in Belgium, an Atlantic depression over north-west Scotland had brought falling pressure, strong winds, cloud and rain to Britain.

At 8.20 that morning twenty-eight Gothas – at that time the largest force ever to be launched against England – took off from St Denijs-Westrem and Gontrode. The winds were so strong that they were driven close enough to the border to come under anti-aircraft fire from Dutch gunners. 'For a long time it had felt as if we were hardly moving forward at all, but were being driven back by the winds. Our worries were increased by the sight of a menacing bank of black clouds approaching from the north-west.' Kleine still held course for England but, forty miles off course to the north and running low on fuel, 'suddenly there was strong turbulence. There were clouds about 1,000 metres [3,000 feet] below us and the hated country which we had been able to see from a distance disappeared beneath this protective blanket, which looked like a huge mountain of white wool.' Kleine was forced to abort the attack and signal his aircraft to return to base. Only as they turned for home did they fully appreciate what a powerful gale was blowing. 'Now the flying started to become very unpleasant, very turbulent, and going into the clouds there was the danger of hitting the sea which, unfortunately, happened to one of the planes; it dived at full speed perpendicularly into the sea and disappeared.'

'Within a few minutes the squadron formation had been torn apart by the winds.' Gusting to ninety miles an hour with fierce rain squalls, the gale was now almost at their backs, but it was driving them inexorably 'eastwards toward the Dutch islands'. Now and then Walter Aschoff saw another aircraft from the squadron 'appearing and disappearing into the clouds, but most of the time, we flew alone. Hoping that we would find better wind conditions at lower altitudes, we dropped below the clouds and continued on as near to a southward course as we could manage. Battling the winds forcing us towards Dutch territory, we struggled along the western border and received bursts of warning fire from Dutch artillery. Finally, between Zeebrugge and Blissingen, we reached the sanctuary of Belgian territory. Lowering, dense clouds had now covered the sky, so low that we were forced to fly at just 100 metres [300 feet] altitude as we made for our home airfield.'

Although Aschoff's aircraft had managed to avoid the worst dangers, others were not so fortunate. Before they had even reached the coast, three Gothas ran out of fuel. One pilot managed to crash-land on a beach, but the crews of the other two were forced to ditch in the sea, where 'the waves swiftly closed in over them'. Two more Gothas, unable to avoid straying into Dutch territory, were hit by anti-aircraft fire and forced down. The aircraft were impounded and the crews incarcerated. Another Gotha, also hit by Dutch ground-fire, crashed on the Belgian side of the border and was wrecked. Five more ran out of fuel before reaching their bases and had to crash-land, and four more were badly damaged as they tried to land in the teeth of the gales.

Only a few managed to land undamaged, Aschoff and his crew among them. 'Gale-force gusts and rain squalls battered the aircraft and threw it around in such a wild dance that I had to grip the machine-gun stand to avoid being catapulted out. I shot a glance at my pilot and saw sweat streaming down his forehead and cheeks – something I had never seen before. He had fought with the wind for our lives for over five hours, when at 1.30 p.m. we at last touched down on our home airfield – one of very few to do so.' 'We were back home, half-deaf because of the constant thunder of the engines. I pitied my poor homing pigeons which certainly felt very cold at this altitude.'

'During my years with the air force I had been on many flights. Shells had exploded next to me, bullets from fighters whistled past my ears and the aircraft had sometimes been holed by gunfire like a sieve, but even though there had been no attack by enemy guns or aircraft on this flight, it was the worst I ever undertook and one I would never forget. The losses – all due to emergency landings in open country – on this "Holland flight" were the heaviest the squadron ever suffered.' Thirteen of the twenty-eight aircraft that had set out that day were lost or damaged beyond repair.

In addition to the losses of aircraft and their crews, the violation of Dutch airspace and the damage caused when one of the Gothas jettisoned its bombload near a village on the island of Schouwen also provoked a furious reaction from the Dutch. The German High Command was forced to express public regret for the incident and make reparations for the damage caused. Kleine, who was fortunate not to be dismissed or even court-martialled, had to endure a severe censure from von Höppner and give unbreakable guarantees that no future raids would take place in defiance of the advice of the England Squadron's weather officer.

Smarting from the rebukes and desperate to restore his reputation, Kleine seized the next available opportunity, on 22 August, to send the England Squadron on another daylight raid on England; 'it would be the last that we would ever undertake'. Georgii's forecast of light winds allowed Kleine to order the raid with confidence, but the previous losses meant that only fifteen aircraft were now available and 'our flock became smaller and smaller, as unknown reasons forced some Gothas to sheer off and turn back. By the time we were approaching the English coastline, I counted only eleven aircraft in the formation.' The four aircraft that had dropped out included that of the commander himself. Kleine, still desperate for glory, must have had genuine engine problems, but how many of the others were real and how many influenced by the dangers and disasters of the three previous raids is impossible to say.

The eleven surviving Gothas, once more under the command of Richard Walter, were spotted by the Kentish Knock lightship and the alarm was raised. They were making such slow progress that it took another thirty minutes to reach the coast, and by then British fighters were waiting for them. 'The picket ships sent up the first shells and then enemy fighters filled the air around us.' A destroyer, HMS *Kestrel*, and an armed trawler, *Plym*, had fired the first shots at the raiders – both over-optimistically claimed to have scored hits – and a barrage went up from coastal gun-batteries as several RNAS aircraft attacked the formation. Colonel Thompson, commanding the Thanet Gun Defences, had 'recently devised and practised a system of height observation and control, which he now applied with excellent results'. Almost at once, one of the Gothas was hit and plunged into the sea.

Seeing enemy aircraft at altitude ahead, Walter now abandoned any hope of reaching London and signalled the remaining aircraft to turn south to attack the secondary target of Dover, but his signal – three white star-shells in quick succession (Dover was the third target on their list of priorities) – caused some confusion among the other crews who 'failed to understand the signals and the bombs were dropped along the whole coastal area from Margate to Dover'.

The local newspaper reported the next day that the 'morning visit of Hun machines' began between quarter-past and half-past ten, as the sirens warned of the approach of enemy airplanes. 'While many persons then in the streets took shelter, others, out of curiosity, were attracted out of doors to witness what was taking place. About a dozen enemy planes, flying at a very high altitude, were seen approaching from the east . . . one of the German machines was seen to drop suddenly and from those watching there was a general exclamation, "It's hit."' Walter Aschoff saw the stricken aircraft go down. 'The rear-gunner motioned me to look back and I saw one of our aircraft, belching smoke and flames as it plummeted from the sky.' The spectators on the ground burst into 'loud cheering when the first machine began to descend.' It broke up as it fell into a wheat field outside the town and the crewmen were dead before it hit the ground, 'all their clothes having been burned off them and they were practically unrecognisable'.

Almost at once, a second Gotha was hit. Both Flight Commander G. E. Hervey and Harold Kerby claimed the kill, but Hervey was credited with it and was later awarded the DSC. He fired '100 rounds from straight behind his tail at 100 yards' range', and as the Gotha began a slow spin he followed it down and 'fired about twenty-five more into him, to make sure'. 'In the glorious sunlight, one could see the aeroplane turning over and over – alternate patches of grey and flashes of white as the aeroplane caught the sun's rays.' It spiralled down and crashed into the sea in front of the promenade to further cheers from the onlookers. The pilot and observer drowned, but the rear-gunner, Unteroffizier Bruno Schneider, a nineteen-year-old farmer's son, was rescued by HMS *Kestrel*.

The dwindling formation flew on. Ramsgate was 'plastered with bombs' and Dover was also attacked, but the England Squadron suffered a third loss when Flight Lieutenant Arthur Brandon, flying a Sopwith Camel from Manston, isolated a Gotha on the left of the formation and poured fire into it at point-blank range. As Brandon ran out of ammunition, another member of his squadron, Flight Sub-Lieutenant Drake, fired at a Gotha – probably the same one – which then burst into flames and spiralled down out of control.

Brandon's own aircraft was hit several times. When he landed, his mechanics found 'a bullet embedded in an engine cylinder and an aileron cable was holding by a single strand', but he was on the ground only long enough to change aircraft, then took off again and pursued the Gothas all the way to the Belgian coast. Hervey also reloaded and took off again, chasing the Gothas out over the sea and engaging one at 14,000 feet. 'Both gunners must have been hit as I was able to get within sixty feet of him without being fired at.' Other fighters also kept up the attacks on the raiders and few escaped without damage. They were forced to fly 'in close formation, fending off the enemy fighters with the concentrated firepower we could bring to bear'.

Second Lieutenant H. R. Power, observer/gunner in a Bristol Fighter piloted by the CO of 48 Squadron, Captain J. H. T. Letts, was shot through the heart and killed instantly as he exchanged fire with a Gotha. Released from his lifeless hands, his gun struck Letts on the head, momentarily dazing him. As he recovered, Letts fired a green Very flare to signal that he was returning to base, but the other pilots interpreted it as a general recall and broke off the attack. The German raiders suffered no further losses. 'The more we flew towards the east and the open sea, the further the fighters lagged behind us, until at last we lost sight of them altogether.' Although most were riddled with bullet-holes, the surviving Gothas all landed safely at their bases.

Most of the dozen British dead from the raid were from Ramsgate, among them women and children. The deputy mayor said that though God might forgive the Germans, 'our people never could', and the towns-folk retained such bitter memories that there were riots when a German cargo ship tried to dock at the harbour in 1920, two years after the end of the war. Despite the public hatred, traces of the code of honour between flyers that had existed in the early air combats remained. 'The course of aerial combat dissolves into individual battles, like medieval duels, while friend and foe watch the furious spectacle from down below. Maybe it is because of the similarity of these forms of battle that a certain chivalry has been sustained among the warriors.'

It is easy to exaggerate the extent and importance of this aerial chivalry. Among the legendary air aces on both sides, von Richthofen boosted his tally of kills by targeting helpless victims: slow, two-seater reconnaissance aircraft rather than fighters; Albert Ball was 'a social misfit with a talent for taking his enemies by surprise from below'; William Bishop was a 'glory-hunter . . . who may well have invented the episode which earned him a Victoria Cross'; and Mick Mannock, motivated by 'a hatred for all things German . . . enjoyed watching his victims burn in mid-air'. However, as proof that a code of honour of sorts did exist among air-crew, the RNAS sent a burial detail to the farm near Margate where the crew of one of the German raiders had perished in flames. The charred bodies of Oberleutnant Echart Fulda, Unteroffizier Heinrich Schildt and Vizefeldwebel Ernst Eickelkamp were retrieved and carried to their graves on a gun carriage. After a brief service, three volleys were fired over the graves and the Last Post was sounded. The surviving fragments of the Gotha were cut into 1,500 pieces and sold as 'souvenir matchboxes' at 'a minimum price of half a crown, on behalf of local deserving institutions and other charities'.

After these latest heavy losses, an abashed Kleine, his hopes of a Pour le Mérite evaporating fast, was once more summoned for discussions with his Commanding General, von Höppner, that can scarcely have been amicable. In three abortive raids during August, the England Squadron had failed to reach London at all and had lost twenty-one aircraft and twice as many flight crew, though the worsening quality of materials and construction of the replacement aircraft being supplied also meant that the Gothas were no longer capable of reaching the higher altitudes, increasing the danger of being shot down by ground-fire.

'Those last daylight flights to England had clearly shown that the impact of our bombs did not justify the losses of men and aircraft that we were sustaining.' The haemorrhage of men and machines had to stop, and another way of attacking London had to be found. Even so, the ambitious Kleine would not have found it easy to report to his Commanding General that the steadily improving air defences they were encountering meant that the raids on England could only continue if aircraft capable of reaching altitudes of 6,000 metres (19,500 feet) – beyond the 'ceiling' of the current English fighters – were made available, or else 'to carry out the raids solely at night'. As Major Wilhelm Siegert confessed, 'the design of our bombing machines had not kept pace with the opposing anti-aircraft guns and fighting machines, and finally, poor climbing power and lack of necessary speed made it impossible for a bombing squadron to work by day'.

Although Siegert had been an enthusiastic advocate of night attacks, their value had not been 'fully appreciated' by the higher German command and 'insufficient attention was paid to it. Various senior officers announced as their opinion: "There is no inducement to undertake night flying, and no necessity." Perhaps this view was inspired to a considerable extent,' he drily observed, 'by the fear that our opponents might resort to the same practice, and by so doing rob the Staff of their already scanty periods for rest and sleep.' Another officer, Major von Bulow, expressed his frustration that 'apart from the technical difficulties, the failure to grasp the practical suggestions of the squadron on the part of the authorities at the headquarters of the General commanding the Air Forces [a sideswipe at von Höppner with which Siegert would have heartily concurred] made things still more difficult.'

If there had been no inducement to experiment with night-flying before, the British anti-aircraft defences had now supplied one, and a new plan was discussed, to use the improved Gotha G V aircraft fitted with Maybach engines – once enough of them had been produced – as high-altitude daylight bombers, and the existing Gotha G IVs together with the new Riesenflugzeugen 'Giant' R-planes, the first of which were expected within the month, in night attacks.

Work on developing the Giants had begun almost as soon as the war broke out, in September 1914. Ferdinand von Zeppelin understood the limitations of the airships that carried his name as well as anyone; he was one of the driving forces behind the creation of the R-planes and flew in one of the early prototypes on 1 August 1915. Siegert was another enthusiastic proponent. The Siemens-Schuckert and Gothaer Waggon-fabrik companies carried out much of the initial development work and the maiden flight of an R-plane took place as early as May 1915, but, like the Gothas, the early models were beset with problems, and a series of catastrophic accidents forced lengthy delays and redesigns. 'After tedious and expensive experiments' the first production models finally appeared in the late summer of 1916.

Two squadrons, Riesenflugzeugabteilungen (shortened to Rfa) 500 and 501, were formed and the R-planes were first used in bombing raids on the Eastern Front in late 1916 and early 1917, where 'excellent results were obtained ... against the Riga-Petrograd railway and the island of Oesel'. The first Giant to be attached to the England Squadron, a Staaken R IV manufactured in the vast Zeppelin works in the Berlin suburb of Staaken, was not supplied until late July 1917.

These bombers were not the canvas and wire 'string-bags' of the open-ing phase of the war, flown by pilots dropping small bombs by hand over the side. Designed to be 'employed against remote objectives of strategic importance', the Giants had four, five or six engines mounted in pairs with one 'puller' engine and one 'pusher' (with the propeller mounted at the rear of the engine block) generating over 1,000 horsepower. A five-engined

Giant was also the world's first aircraft to be fitted with a supercharger, propelling it to a height of 5,800 metres (19,000 feet). Pusher-type engines had one serious flaw, though: 'in flight, no small object, not even a pencil, was allowed to fly backwards from the cockpit ... such flying objects would invariably cause the propeller to split apart'.

Like virtually all Great War aircraft, the Giants were biplanes. Monoplanes had performed well in pre-war tests and comprised seven out of the top ten machines at the Military Aeroplane Competition of 1912, but a series of accidents involving monoplanes led to a bias against them from all sides in the conflict. The 138-foot (42-metre) span of the Giant's twin wings was almost twice that of the Gothas, and it was also greater than any British or German aircraft of the Second World War, and only three feet less than that of the American B-29 Superfortress. The Giant's tailplane alone was the same size as the Sopwith Pup aircraft that was often sent up to challenge it.

Constructed of wood, aluminium and steel, and painted dark grey or black, the Giant's enormous weight was borne by an eighteen-wheeled undercarriage, with two wheels on the nose landing-gear and sixteen more, all over one metre in diameter, attached to two huge axles extending under the wings. The drag from this cumbersome structure spoiled the Giant's otherwise clean lines and, coupled with the aircraft's enormous weight, helped to further reduce the pedestrian top speed of eighty miles per hour 'flying level and in still air'. The Giants also had enclosed cabins and fuselages, gun turrets, nacelles housing the engines, radio communications, oxygen masks, parachutes and electric light. The full crew of nine even had heated flying suits, connected to a Bosch generator.

The commander doubled as bomb-aimer and navigator. He used a gyro-compass to navigate but could also obtain a fix of the Giant's position by sending a radio signal (the radio operator shared the cockpit with him) to two ground stations on the Belgian coast. However, radio silence was observed on England flights and the system was only used after the glare of searchlights, anti-aircraft gunfire or the presence of enemy fighters made it clear that the Giant had been detected by the air defences. Two pilots sat at the front of the aircraft, immediately in front of the observer, facing a display of sophisticated instrumentation including altimeter, airspeed indicator, temperature gauge, tachometer, a variometer (measuring the rate of climb) and an artificial horizon indicator – the first aircraft to be fitted with this device. Between the pilots were the throttles controlling the massive engines, and there were also a series of switches with which they could send pre-coded signals to the two in-flight mechanics – who could shut down one of the engines in mid-air to carry out repairs – housed in the engine nacelles to either side; the noise of wind and engines made voice communication impossible.

The Giants also carried a fuel attendant who spent each flight constantly transferring fuel between the ten tanks so that the trim of the aircraft was not affected as the weight of the 660-gallon fuel load was reduced. There were two specialist machine-gunners, and the pilots and mechanics also fired guns when required, the mechanics having to brave a climb up an open ladder to reach the upper wing where their guns were mounted.

These enormous bombers had some drawbacks, not least their price. The cost of constructing a Gotha was huge, and it doubled between October 1916 and May 1917, but that of a Giant was so astronomical – well over half a million marks – that only eighteen were ever built. They were also difficult to fly – pilots underwent specialized training at Doberitz and Cologne – and complex to maintain and service, requiring ground support on an unprecedented scale. Each R-plane was assigned a fifty-man ground-crew, including a large number of specially trained mechanics, electricians and radio technicians. Many of the mechanics had transferred from airship ground-crews and their familiarity with the Maybach engines that were used in the Zeppelins as well as the Giants proved valuable.

The Giant's lack of speed and manoeuvrability and its slow rate of climb made it vulnerable to fighter attack in daylight, and though they could pack a formidable counter-punch against fighters, with up to six machine-guns, mounted in the nose and rear, above the fuselage and even on a platform that could be lowered beneath the aircraft to guard against attack from below, the full complement of guns and the personnel to operate them could only be carried by reducing the weight of bombs or fuel. Since their 'large radius of action and the quantity of bombs carried were the very factors which ensured the existence of Giant aeroplanes . . .

they were at once designated as an instrument of night warfare alone.'

The Giant's net 'lift' was as much as four and a half tons, and they could carry almost two tons of bombs, though one ton was the normal limit on England flights. Given the size and engine power of the aircraft, a greater bombload might have been expected. The bombs were 'hung in long, rectangular bomb bays underneath the fuselage floor, between the wings, and enclosed with folding doors', and were released electrically. They ranged from 50kg to 1,000kg in weight. The larger 300kg or 1,000kg projectiles were capable of wrecking blocks of houses 'even if the bombs burst in the street or courtyard'.

Providing sufficiently reliable incendiaries could be developed, the Giants' carrying capacity also made them potentially devastating weapons when loaded with fire-bombs. A single Giant would have the potential to devastate a large area; a squadron of them might be able to lay waste a whole city.

# CHAPTER 8
# NIGHT-TIME EXCURSIONS

THE NEW GERMAN BOMBERS promised to allow the resurrection of the Fire Plan, with squadrons of Gothas and Giants unleashed on perpetual 'rolling day and night raids' using incendiary bombs to create a sea of fire that would engulf the whole of London. However, this could only be achieved with a four- or five-fold increase in the number of aircraft available to the England Squadron.

'Air Attacks on London', a study written by one of Kleine's future flight leaders, Oberleutnant Weese, in February 1917, was a model of clear thinking on the most effective deployment of aircraft to achieve the aims of the Fire Plan. Weese envisaged

1) Simultaneous raids on London by about 120 aeroplanes, divided into two day-bombing squadrons of forty-five aeroplanes each, and one night-bombing squadron of thirty aeroplanes. For this, heavy bomber squadron No. 1, more or less unoccupied on the Macedonian Front, and other bombing squadrons should be employed. If the equipment of two day-bombing squadrons is impossible, the formation of two night-bombing squadrons and one day-bombing squadron is advocated. The mass raids should not begin until the whole formation is complete.

2) Abandonment of the air-raids on Paris; concentration of the raids on the most important objective, viz. London.

3) Continuous daylight and night raids. Provision should be made, on all days when the weather allows, for raids at fairly big intervals by one squadron in the morning, one in the afternoon, and one at night. In this way a lasting and affecting feeling of anxiety will be caused, and it will be possible to instil profound depression and break the determination to carry on the war.

Weese also added a prophetic footnote: 'The possibility of carrying out raids on London by day would be limited to at most three months, as by that time the effect of the A/A defence would be felt, and it would be necessary to carry out the raids at night instead.'

Adopting Weese's ideas of continual mass raids, Kleine and von Höppner made repeated appeals for more night-bombers and an effective force of day-bombers, but, beset by desperate shortages of funds and of every war material, the High Command was in no position to oblige them. Even if limitless funds had been made available, German aircraft manufacturers were suffering acutely from the ever-growing problems in obtaining raw materials and were unable to supply either the quantity or the quality of aircraft required. Labour shortages exacerbated manufacturers' problems as the traditional rivalries between German regions saw workers compulsorily retained in their home areas, even when there was no skilled work for them to do there and manufacturers elsewhere were desperate to employ them. Trained electrical mechanics in Württemberg, for example, were being employed as watchmen and janitors. Strikes in aircraft factories made the supply position even worse.

In the summer of 1917, aware that whatever its limited military potential at that time America's economic might would soon tilt the balance of 'the war of materiel' even further in the Allies' favour, the German High Command had launched the Amerikaprogramm, aiming to increase production of aircraft to two thousand a month and aircraft engines to two and a half thousand a month by January 1918. It was a wildly ambitious, unfulfillable aim; the mere existence of the Amerikaprogramm further distorted the supply of raw materials and disrupted war production, as manufacturers tried to stockpile materials and parts to meet their quotas. Although Ludendorff supported an expansion of the heavy bomber fleet, von Höppner felt that an increase in fighter strength was more important and gave it a higher priority, significantly reducing the number of new bombers available to strengthen the England Squadron and the other *Bombengeschwader* (bombing squadrons). Frontline commanders, including the leaders of the England Squadron, were meanwhile forced to cannibalize some of their aircraft for spare parts and spare engines to keep the rest flying.

The problems they were facing were evident to the Allies too. 'Inspection of our planes shot down on the other side had indicated to them that we had no more copper nor rubber [which was in such short supply that the Army had even requisitioned the cushions from German billiard tables], that the welding work on our steel spars was faulty, that our fuel – a benzol-alcohol mixture – often contained so much water that the engines began to cough.' Fuel oil was so scarce that by November

1917 the air service's annual allocation, scheduled to be 12,000 tons, had fallen to 1,000 tons. Kleine issued repeated memoranda proposing to stage 'continuous day and night raids . . . utilising three or four squadrons and intentionally abandoning any other bombing missions', but, 'for paltry reasons, the scheme came to naught'.

While their commanders argued over the way forward, the men of the England Squadron had the chance of a few days' rest and recreation. Ghent was in the reserve areas, and as the squadron was the only frontline unit based there, 'our reputation as "England Squadron" gave us a bit of a romantic sheen'. Many young Belgian women were seduced by the aura of glamour that surrounded these dashing aviators. Walter Aschoff and his friends often fished for the big pike lurking in the ornamental lakes of the chateaux at Borluut and Drory, though, lacking a rod, he undertook 'not-so-expert fishing with a Luger pistol. My booty is remarkable, the kitchen menu much improved. The biggest pike weighed in at a stout five kilos.' The air-crews also relaxed on the terrace of the chateau, the air full of the scent of the roses and honeysuckle entwined around the stone balustrade; strolled through parkland 'beautiful with lilac and the huge rhododendron bushes'; went swimming or boating on the River Lys and the canals; indulged their taste for 'French red wine and good food . . . explored the art treasures that Ghent has to offer; or acquired a shotgun to hunt the abundant pheasants and hares'.

Their lives 'revolved around our airfields, the nearby city of Ghent and the broad blue skies that for us had no limit . . . We thought only of the next day or the next flight to England. It was pointless anyway to think any further or even to make plans, for tomorrow we might be lying, bones broken, in a field hospital or be a prisoner of war in England, waiting for freedom like a caged animal behind barbed wire. We were all lonely, yet never alone. Even in the face of death, observer, pilot and marksman were connected by invisible nerve cords, like one single creature. I could compare this unity only with the submarine crews; that is probably why the U-boat men became our friends and were always welcome guests.'

Kleine had only envisaged the switch to night attacks as a temporary expedient while the England Squadron was 'speedily and completely equipped with new machines' for daylight attacks, which allowed more precise targeting. However, the performance of the Gotha G V was 'in no way an improvement on that of the Gotha G IV', and in any event neither the G Vs nor the later Gotha models, including the G VIII designed to fly at 6,000–7,000 metres (19,500–23,000 feet), were ever delivered in sufficient numbers to make this a realistic aim. Faced with the shortages of replacements and the depredations on the existing bomber fleet by London's improving air defences, the England Squadron's daylight flights in closed formation were now completely abandoned and replaced by flights of well-separated aircraft flying under the cover of night. Their imprecise targeting instructions were merely to 'raid targets of military importance'.

The Gothas were altered and enhanced for night-flying. They were painted grey and black instead of the white used for day raids, which would have shown up starkly in the glare of the searchlights. Small electrical lamps for the compass and other instruments and a number of other items were fitted in the cockpits, and all flight crew attended classes run by the meteorologist Walter Georgii who taught them to establish their bearings and route by the position of the moon, stars and constellations. 'Soon we knew the northern skies and their stars, the exact times of their position above our targets, and often waved at them grate-fully when they showed us the way to London.' All the flight crews also regularly practised 'shooting with the machine-gun' and attended 'technical training, seminars about navigation and stellar constellations, exchange of experiences during enemy flights, studies of target types and tactics'.

Their first night-flights were a series of short familiarization flights. 'We preferred cloudless skies, though we didn't mind broken cloud, but complete cloud-cover forced us to abort our missions. With only our navigation equipment, we couldn't fly blind within or above the clouds, and were ordered never to remain longer than five to ten minutes above an unbroken cloud-bank.'

The senior pilots' prior experience of night raids in the squadron's early days, beginning with the attack on Dunkirk on 28 January 1915, was helpful, but the training for night attacks on England still proved 'a troublesome business and unfortunately cost us many lives. For the first time the nature and importance of night blindness was recognised. Pilots who flew brilliantly in daylight proved themselves to be quite unsuitable for night-flying, for their eyes would not adjust themselves to the darkness. They also lost their sense of equilibrium in the air, and when landing were unable to judge their distance from the ground with accuracy.' However, 'by systematic training and a gradual increase in the difficulty of the tests put to night-flying pilots, a brilliant pitch of efficiency was attained. Eventually weather, with the exception of mists and fogs, was hardly taken into consideration. Flights were carried out without mishap on pitch-dark nights, without the help of moon or stars, and often through rain or snow.'

However, losses in combat and in training ensured 'a heavy turnover of flight crews. The pilots and observers joining us from the schools and training centres at home were inevitably inexperienced and particular attention had to be given to their further training . . .' 'Although two or three night-flights were enough to give them confidence in their night-flying ability, we did not regard them as fully valid crew members until the general danger areas had been identified and mastered.'

Night take-offs and landings were practised on a daily basis at both the home bases and the emergency airfields. Aircraft taking off lined up facing a red light 'placed at the end of the runway to make possible a straight take-off run'. Special markers and lights were laid out for easier night-time recognition of the airfields when returning from a raid, and the lighting of the flight-path across Belgium was also improved. 'Rocket batteries . . . at given intervals, discharged signal lights that, under good conditions, were visible for fifty or sixty miles', 'that at X being four shots at intervals of three minutes; that of Y being a shot every two minutes, three seconds pause, then a second shot'.

Once the crews had successfully navigated their way to within range of the target, they were able to take advantage of lights that even the most meticulous blackout could not obscure. 'Anti-aircraft batteries could be located by their clearly visible gun-flashes; the signal lamps that were indispensable to railway traffic and the sparks thrown up by engines and steamers afforded an easy means of observing movements of trains and ships. The sea-coast, fires, rivers, canals, lakes, bridges, large woods, railway lines and dry roads provided an easy method of finding one's way by night.

The enemy's searchlights, although used with a diametrically opposite purpose, assisted more than anything else in locating the objective that was to be attacked.'

On the return journey, the signals from Ostend provided a welcoming beacon for aircraft far out over the North Sea. Returning air-crews 'always flew over our airfield at about 200 metres [650 feet] altitude and fired a green flare as a recognition signal to our ground personnel. If there were no enemy aircraft in the vicinity – a fact we in the aircraft could not determine – then the ground position would respond with a green flare.' In case of an unexpected change of weather or a danger of fog, all alternative airfields had to be lit and ground-crews had to fire green flares as soon as German aircraft appeared in the sky.

On the night of 3 September 1917, a still, moonlit night perfect for the attempt, five Gothas took off to mount a trial raid on England. As usual, one immediately reported engine problems, but the other four flew on to attack the dockyards at Chatham in Kent. A practice air-raid alert had been held earlier that evening and warnings of the genuine raid that should have led to the town's lights being extinguished were assumed to be part of the practice and were disregarded. As a result, Chatham was brightly lit and undefended as the raiders swept in.

Observers monitoring the skies grossly overestimated the number of raiders, often confusing defending fighters for German bombers. Although much of the bomb-aiming was equally wayward, two bombs fell on a large drill-hall being used as a temporary dormitory by hundreds of young recruits sleeping in hammocks. Two clocks were blown into the parade ground and showed the exact time the bombs had struck: both stopped at 11.12 p.m. The blast collapsed the roof of the drill-hall, killing 130 recruits and injuring eighty-eight others; 'flying glass . . . thick and heavy, did the damage'. The rescue parties spent the remainder of the night 'picking out bodies and parts of bodies from among glass and debris and placing them in bags, fetching out bodies in hammocks and laying them on a tarpaulin on the parade ground'. 'Everywhere we found bodies in a terribly mutilated condition . . . the gathering up of the dismembered limbs turned one sick . . . The old sailors, who had been in several battles, said they would rather be in ten Jutlands or Heligolands than go through another raid such as this.' In the morning everyone on the base was summoned to try to identify 'any of the lost; it was impossible in most cases'.

Although Sheerness and Margate were also hit again, no fighters managed to engage the raiders and the anti-aircraft fire was sparse and poorly targeted, increasing German confidence that the switch to night-bombing would stem their losses. The LADA commander, 'Splash' Ashmore, had only discovered a few days before that 'an old order was still in existence – I had not been told of it when I took over – to the effect that the guns were not to fire at all at night against aeroplanes. I only got this prohibition removed just in time for the first night raid.' Ashmore also managed to abolish another curious custom, the 'Searchlight Patrol', in which all the searchlights between the enemy raiders and London were turned on simultaneously to 'wave their beams about the sky in the hope of frightening off the attacking aircraft'. In fact it had the opposite effect, serving only to 'give away the position of London and attract any bomber who was still at a distance; in future searchlight beams were only to show when the detachment could actually hear a machine, or to take over a machine already illuminated by another light'.

Although they did not even sight the raiders that night, the achievement of the twenty-two-year-old Captain Gilbert Murlis Green, who had been acting commander of 44 Squadron for less than a week, and two of the other squadron pilots, the South African Captain C. J. Q. 'Flossie' Brand and Second Lieutenant Charles 'Sandy' Banks, in taking off, night-flying and then safely landing their Sopwith Camels was very significant. Until then, the unstable, temperamental Camels were regarded as 'tricky enough to land in the daytime; nobody thought of flying them at night'. They were not fitted with instrument lights, and at night pilots had to fly 'by feel, ignorant of speed, engine revs and the vital question of oil pressure. If this gave out – a thing which happened quite frequently – a rotary engine would seize up in a few minutes and the pilot might be forced down anywhere.' The three pilots took off from an improvised flarepath and patrolled over the Thames estuary for forty minutes before returning safely to base. Their reports of their experiences 'created the most intense excitement and eagerness among the other pilots' to try night-flying for themselves, and Ashmore gave vent to some understandable hyperbole when he called it 'perhaps the most important event in the history of air defence'.

The very next morning, ground-crews 'rushed off to Aircraft Depots' and returned with instrument lighting equipment which they installed in the cockpits of the Camels. Pilots wearing goggles with blackened lenses, simulating the darkness of night, began practising night-flying and landing immediately, and one claimed that within twenty-four hours 'the Home Defence squadrons ceased to be looked upon as anything but night-fighters'.

To aid landings at night, ground-crews set up rows of Heath-Robinson runway lights on the airfield: two-gallon petrol cans filled with paraffin-soaked cotton waste. Later, gas-operated beacons were used. The petrol cans were arranged in an 'L', 'the long arm pointing into the wind and the short arm marking the limit past which the machine should not run after landing. The long arm had four flares and the pilot endeavoured to judge his landing so that his wheels touched at the first flare, thus bringing him to rest about the third.'

Fighter tactics also had to be heavily modified. 'Instead of being able to launch every machine against the raiders, the difficulty was to find them at all. It was futile to loose a hundred machines into the air at night, haphazard, so a system of patrols was worked out.' Fighters patrolled at 10,000, 11,000 and 12,000 feet, and 'each pilot had his allotted beat and had strict orders (and good reason) not to leave it for fear of colliding with another machine'. Each aircraft would patrol for exactly two hours and then return to base, by which time another aircraft was already (or at least should have been) climbing to replace it. However, since there were nowhere near enough men and machines to mount constant night patrols in every area on the off-chance of a German raid, the Home Defence squadrons were still reliant on early warning from observers to get them airborne fast enough to intercept the raiders.

Tactics were further revised after trials using British aircraft to simulate Gotha bombers showed that they could much more readily be spotted at night when viewed from below against the sky than from above.

Even on a moonless night, it was calculated that a Gotha could be seen from 600 to 1,400 feet when viewed from below, and this increased to 4,000 feet when the moon was shining. Ballistics experts had also discovered that a bullet fired from a gun angled at precisely forty-five degrees travelled straight for 600 to 800 yards because the effects of air resistance and the force of gravity on the trajectory of the bullet exactly cancelled each other out. The most effective way to target a Gotha at night was therefore to approach from below and open fire when at a forty-five-degree angle to the raider.

Like most pilots, Cecil Lewis was full of doubt and foreboding as he 'ran up the engine' and taxied along the line of flares for his first night-flight. 'The night was clear but the low-lying country threatened ground mist. The rising moon did not shed enough light to give much confidence . . . It all looked very black indeed and I had the impression that to take off into this would be the same as flying into a cloud, a topless black cloud out of which I would never climb into clear skies above, and out of which I should only stumble back to earth by luck. I paused for a moment before opening up, tested my controls and, with that feeling of fatalism which so many pilots must know, pushed open the throttle . . .

'The machine gathered way and lifted serenely from the ground. A second later I was reassured. This was no black cloud, no impalpable void of blackness, but a lovely dim landscape lit only by the rising moon, with a shining ribbon of water, the Thames estuary, on the southern horizon. I was surprised at the amount of detail visible by night. Every roof made a soft mirror for the moon, railway lines glistened and even roads were lighter lines among the dark network of hedges dividing the fields. Expecting to be keyed up to the highest degree of nervous tension, I relaxed at once. I had entered a new, enchanted world . . . the earth seemed soft, luxuriant, like a cloak of moleskin.

'Soon I could see the flares of other aerodromes marking the ring of squadrons which guarded the city. London itself was a dark, crouching monster within. Here and there a tiny pinpoint of light marked the existence of human beings upon an earth which seemed otherwise reserved to trees and waters and the moon. A passing train, like a golden snake with a long white ostrich feather plume, wound sinuously into the smoke-shrouded obscurity of London. The black silhouette of a steamer passed out to sea. I looked back to the lights of the aerodrome, five golden pinpoints shining from the earth . . . and glided quietly down through the magic of the moonlit sky.

'I watched the slowly falling altimeter, manoeuvred myself into the right position for landing, working my way down in gradual "S" turns towards the flares below, where I could see the mechanics, standing in the glare, listening to my engine and watching for my return. At five hundred feet I fired a Very light. The red ball curled away like a rocket in the darkness. A second later an answering red light curled up from the ground. All Clear! Now I was on alert . . . at fifty feet I was coming straight toward the line of flares. Suddenly they blurred. The first flare, a moment ago plainly visible, disappeared to a glimmer in a bank of white mist . . . the first flare loomed up and flashed past in white drifting vapour. I must be ten feet off the ground. I held the stick back, letting the machine sink a little and then, as the second flare loomed up, buzzed my engine twice. An instant later the wheels and tail touched altogether, and the steady rumble told its tale of a perfect landing.'

'Splash' Ashmore was given an unexpectedly close-up view of his pilots' efficiency at night-flying and a chance to live up to his nickname soon afterwards, when he made a night inspection of 44 Squadron's Hainault base. The red-haired, mercurial 'Sandy' Banks was the only pilot still airborne after a squadron night-flight fuelled by 'a keg of old ale' that the Mess President had broached earlier that evening. As Ashmore, his ADC and Squadron Commander Gilbert Murlis Green were strolling across the muddy airfield, Banks decided to 'buzz' them. 'Down he came like a hawk. The GOC Home Defence was at first amused, screwing his monocle tighter into his eye, but he soon became alarmed, and finally sat, panic-stricken, in the mud while the undercarriage of the Camel shrieked by about a foot above his head and the slipstream from the prop blew his beautiful brass hat off.'

Banks climbed high above the airfield and then returned for a second pass. 'The result was precisely the same except that the General managed to hold his hat on. By this time the seat of his trousers was sopping wet, his dignity had been outraged and he was altogether a very angry General.'

Not content with his handiwork, Banks made a final pass and 'this time he shaved them even closer than before, so that the General thought his hour had come and lay flat on his back, cursing. Meanwhile the rest of us were standing in groups on the tarmac, first on one leg, then the other, divided between wild hilarity at the ridiculous figure cut by the General and a fear of what would happen to the perfect idiot, Sandy, when he came down. Once the machine was safely on the ground with the engine off, the General retraced his steps, recovering indignation and composure at every stride.' Banks's only comment on returning to the Mess was, 'Well, I bloody put the wind up him anyway.' As he later noted in his log book: 'Zoomed at General Ashmore by mistake. Trouble!'

# CHAPTER 9
# *BRANDBOMBEN*

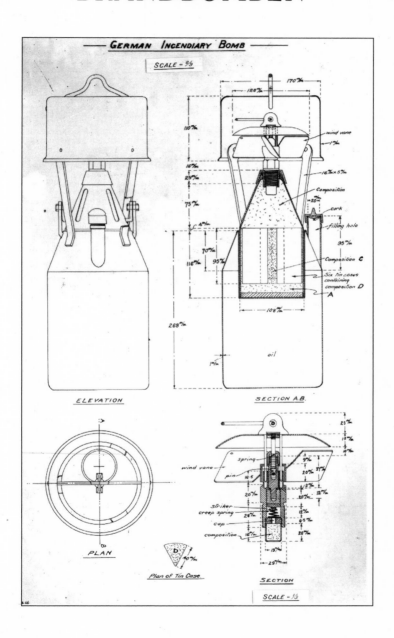

DELIGHTED BY THE SUCCESS OF THE TRIAL night-bombing run, Kleine called the men of the England Squadron together on 4 September 1917 and told them that the first night-raid on London would take place that very evening. The dangers of night-flying, with only a compass and their knowledge of the stars to aid them, were sufficient for him to ask for volunteers rather than ordering his men into the air, but none was willing to suffer the stigma of being seen to be reluctant to volunteer. Kleine then chose his own crew and the four most experienced crews from among the rest.

The close formation that had given the Gothas cross-protection on daylight raids was too dangerous to fly in darkness 'owing to the difficulty of seeing one machine from another and the consequent considerable danger of collision'. As Wilhelm Siegert remarked, 'collisions were subject only to the laws of probability [the 'it's a big sky theory' as it was known to later British pilots]; preventative measures were unknown at the time', and there was greater safety in the bombers flying solo, widely dispersed from their fellows. 'On these long-distance flights, bomber aircraft are released at a few-minute intervals in order to avoid collisions in the air. That way, each pilot flies alone and has to find the route and target all by himself . . . our planes reach the target at very different times, depending on the route they choose; the air-raids therefore last for a good part of the night and spread commotion and insecurity among the population for hours on end', thereby 'producing the maximum moral effect on the British public'.

Additional bombs were loaded on to each aircraft: flying under cover of darkness, the Gothas needed less speed to evade air defences and 500kg bombloads were routinely carried, instead of the 300kg used on daylight raids. Half an hour before the scheduled start time, the mechanics, ground- and air-crews for each Gotha stood by their machine ready to make their final checks. The ground trembled as the twin 260-horsepower engines were run up for the second time, thundering towards full revs as the mechanics and pilots listened intently for any dissonance or faltering of the thudding rhythm that might presage engine failure during the long flight over the North Sea. The ground-crew made a final check that the bombs were fused and secured. Then, climbing into their cockpits, the rear-gunner and observer tested their machine-guns and the pilot and observer set their instrument lights.

As the minutes ticked down, the Startoffizier made his final inspection and then signalled with his lamp to the lead pilot. At five-minute intervals from ten o'clock that evening, eleven Gothas rolled out on to the runway and took off. As usual, two claimed engine problems and landed again soon afterwards, but the others rumbled away into the night, the only visible sign of the other aircraft the distant twin plumes of flame from their exhaust pipes.

It was a fine night with a light south-easterly wind and only slight broken cloud. The moon was just two days past the full and by its light the crews could trace the lines of canals across the landscape. Even roads showed as faint grey lines scored across the fields and through the black, huddled masses of woods. In the dim glow of his instrument lights, the observer in the nose of the aircraft scanned his compass and map, and signalled changes of course to the pilot with his raised hand. The surf breaking on the Flanders coast west of Zeebrugge was visible as a phosphorescent trace in the darkness, but beyond it was an endless black expanse as the Gothas began the long, lonely flight over the North Sea. Despite all the training and practice flights they had undergone, this first night-time London flight was a new and unsettling experience for most of the air-crews.

The skies remained clear, and as they crossed the English coast they checked their bearings to ensure that they were still on course; not all were. Flying solo at night was a rigorous test of individual commanders' navigation skills and some were found wanting as the Gothas made landfalls all the way from Orford Ness to Dover, where the white cliffs, gleaming in the moonlight, were an unmistakable landmark. However, the navigational errors worked in their favour, causing confusion and near-panic in the air defence system and triggering a succession of air-raid warnings. The ground observers – not necessarily men of the highest calibre, since they were largely drawn from the ranks of those unfit for overseas military service – wildly overestimated the number of raiders, claiming that at least twenty-six bombers in seven different formations had crossed the coast.

'The English down below became lively' and the beams of a handful of searchlights sliced through the darkness. The waning moon still cast enough light to illuminate the Thames like a silver highway leading to

London, and the Gothas flew on, following the south bank of the river despite barrages of shells from the anti-aircraft batteries at Chatham and then at Gravesend, firing blind into the darkness, with only the sound of the Gothas' engines to guide them. 'They didn't shoot badly, but still didn't hit their targets.'

To the west, the Gotha crews could now see a bright glow in the sky. London was only partially blacked out – as one pilot noted, 'It was curious that the lights . . . were well screened in some parts and badly in others' – and thousands of lights made the city shine like a jewel in the surrounding darkness. As they began to overfly the eastern approaches of the city, their observers could see every street clearly delineated beneath them. Each man identified his target and squeezed the bomb-release levers. Black, spiralling shapes plummeted away and the bombers bucked and jumped, released from their crushing burden. As the bombs found their targets, vivid flashes – yellow, orange, red – flared up and then were shrouded in swirling clouds of black smoke.

Londoners had not seen a bomber in two months and never at night, and though there had been air-raid warnings on the previous two nights, they had been false alarms. If they had been lulled into a false sense of security, it was rudely shattered by that first night raid. As police ringing their bicycle bells toured the streets with a belated warning, Mrs L. Mercer was roused from sleep by her son calling, ' "Look out. They're dropping bombs." . . . Everything was smashed; windows broke, doors came off and walls fell in. Two doors away there had been a birthday party. The old people had gone to bed, but one woman, who had two children, was just undressing. She took her eighteen-month-old baby and went down to warn the others. Just as she was on the second flight of stairs, a bomb dropped, killing her and her little child; poor thing, she was expecting another baby any day. Her husband, coming down behind her, was carrying the three-year-old girl. A beam hit him across the neck, killing him also, but the little girl was saved . . . We had sixteen fowls and when we went to them they hadn't a feather on them.'

Bombs fell on Barking, West Ham and Stratford, where a 50kg bomb demolished an empty jute factory that had until recently been serving as an internment camp for German immigrants. Many houses were wrecked.

As the Leary family were 'groping our way across the bricks that had been our kitchen, we heard someone groaning . . . the lodger from next door had been blown from his bedroom into our kitchen. My friend Annie Kington and all her little brothers and sisters were killed, and my mother died a little while afterwards through shock. I was then only seventeen.'

'Lockart's Performing Elephants' were on show at the Chelsea Palace that evening. 'When the alarm was given, the manager feared that if the great creatures took fright at the noise they might stampede, and it was decided that the empty streets of the Embankment would be the safest place for them. There they paraded, docile and seeming a trifle bored.' Although that part of the Embankment escaped bomb damage, Cleopatra's Needle and one of the bronze sphinxes at its base were struck by shrapnel from a bomb that hit the road in front of the monument, rupturing a gas main. The driver of a passing tram was killed instantly in the blast, along with two of his passengers. More bombs fell nearby in the Strand, one detonating close to the Air Board's offices in the Hotel Cecil, a forceful reminder of the dangers the public were facing.

A man in a sidestreet off the Strand, outside Charing Cross Hospital, heard the anti-aircraft guns and saw searchlights 'stabbing the heavens all around. In a doorway over against the eastern side of the hospital, two men were sheltering. As I made to join them, a woman came up with terror written on her face. There was only room for one more in the doorway and we three men looked at each other. I signed to the woman to take the place. She did so with profuse thanks. When I crossed the road to the hospital there was a loud report, which sent me to the ground. The bomb had fallen in front of the doorway and one of the victims was the woman.' The two men sheltering with her, both Canadian soldiers, were also killed. The blast blew in the hospital doors and smashed hundreds of windows, sending glass fragments knifing through the air.

Windows were blown in all along the Strand and the next morning, 'with the permission of the manager of a tailor's', a man stood in one of his shattered windows and offered the pieces of broken glass for sale as souvenirs. The money collected went to Charing Cross Hospital, where many people injured in the raid were treated, and 'as the young men came forward to buy, I told them that better souvenirs were to be got in France, also asking them if they would offer themselves. In two hours I collected £35, also a number of recruits.'

The Gothas had arrived over the capital widely separated in distance and time. Kleine was not the first to overfly the capital that night and he also noted that the blackout was only partial. 'Either the Londoners thought that the raid was over after the first attack, or else some of the streets had to be lit temporarily because of fire or some sort of panic.' Yet, though London was a clearly visible target, only five of the nine raiders successfully bombed the capital. The others attacked Margate and Dover, and one, woefully off course, bombed Aldeburgh in Suffolk.

Nineteen people were killed in the raids and seventy-one injured. British pilots and anti-aircraft gun-crews struggled to find the bombers, near invisible in the night, but one was lit and held by a searchlight near Rochester in Kent and, hit by anti-aircraft fire, it went down in the estuary of the Medway. The river was later dragged 'from Rochester Bridge to Halling' for wreckage that would have yielded valuable intelligence about the Gotha, but nothing was found. Unaware of the fate of their fellows, the other German crews flew back over the black expanses of the sea until the beacon of the Ostend light pierced the darkness ahead of them, guiding them home. Thirty minutes later, the aircraft glided down between the landing lights at Gontrode.

Still inexperienced in night attacks, the men of the England Squadron needed the reassurance of moonlight to aid their navigation and bomb-aiming, and for three weeks, as the moon waned and then began to wax again, Londoners slept in peace. Then on 24 September, in fine, settled weather with an anticyclone covering southern England and north-western Europe, and a week of strong moonlight around the time of the full moon ahead, they prepared themselves for what was to become known as 'The Blitz of the Harvest Moon'.

Even more than the daylight raids, the moonlit raids by the England Squadron were specifically planned 'with a view to the moral effect due to prolonged disturbance of rest at night, than to the destruction of any special objective'. For the first time, the England Squadron would now be attempting to initiate the Fire Plan, and as well as the heavy high-explosive bombs fixed underneath the fuselage and the smaller projectiles carried in the racks along the sides of the cockpit, released by a lever marked *magazin,* each aircraft carried 5kg *Brandbomben* – incendiaries – comprising almost half the bombs that would drop on England that night.

Incendiaries had been used in warfare since pre-Christian times. Assyrian bas-reliefs show warriors employing liquid fire, probably derived from oil seeping from what are now the oilfields of Iraq. The Trojans, Greeks and Romans all made use of blazing projectiles. 'Greek fire', a mixture of pitch, sulphur, quicklime and naphtha reputed to have been invented by the Syrian Kallinicus in AD 660, was squirted from siphons like modern flame-throwers. Since the quicklime reacted with water, generating additional heat, Greek Fire would continue to burn even on water, adding to the terror it inspired. It was said to have saved Constantinople from capture on many occasions. In medieval times balls of burning pitch were hurled from catapults, and archers fired flaming arrows.

Even when the introduction of gunpowder to the West opened the way to a range of more devastating weapons, fire remained a potent part of the military armoury on land and sea. Fireships played a vital role in the defeat of the Spanish Armada in 1588, forcing the dispersion of the Spanish fleet at the battle of Gravelines; together with fire-rockets and cannon firing blazing missiles, fireships were used in sea-battles until the introduction of steel-hulled vessels in the nineteenth century. The development of artillery and high-explosive shells seemed to have rendered fire weapons obsolete, but the invention of airships and aircraft, and the start of 'total war' targeting a combatant nation's war industries, transport, food stores and civilian population, brought incendiaries back into military use.

They were of two broad types: '1) the intensive type, where the heat and flames are concentrated in a limited space in order to set fire to heavy construction and targets generally difficult to ignite; 2) the scatter type, where the incendiary materials are scattered in a number of small burning masses over a relatively large area, in order to initiate fires at a number of points simultaneously in large targets of inflammable or easily ignited materials'.

It was perhaps natural that military scientists would first turn to modern refinements of ancient fire-raising materials such as Greek Fire, and the first air-dropped incendiaries relied on oil derivatives as the principal combustant. The *Brandbomben* used by Zeppelins until well into 1917 were crude devices: ungainly, snub-nosed, steel-encased bombs weighing between 9kg and 12kg, hand-dropped with the aid of a carrying handle. On impact, a chain reaction was begun by a fuse igniting a yellow phosphorus plug. It fired a thermite charge that in turn ignited the tarred cotton waste packed around it. Further combustible material – a tarred rope coil – was wound around the outside of the casing. Despite this ingenious combination of incendiary materials, the bombs often failed to detonate, and those that did were very rarely successful in igniting sub-stantial fires. One such bomb, dropped near Braintree in February 1915, was said to have been picked up by its handle by a soldier and thrown into the Blackwater river.

The early aircraft incendiaries were also hand-dropped. Half the diameter and weight of the Zeppelin bombs, they were of simpler con-struction, with a core of black powder surrounded by an incendiary mixture, usually 'solid oil' – a wax-like mixture of soap with oil, or an oil derivative such as kerosene. They too were temperamental and unreliable devices, often failing to ignite at all, and of those that did, few generated blazes widespread or intense enough to trouble the fire crews sent to extinguish them.

The greatest problems were caused by the use of oil-based fuels, which have a relatively high flash-point and also require huge amounts of oxygen to combust satisfactorily: a pound of kerosene requires the equivalent of all the air in a two-hundred-cubic-foot room. In areas where oxygen was restricted – and that meant almost any building on which they fell – the oil-based incendiaries often generated only slow, smouldering fires that gave fire crews ample time to reach and extinguish them.

The use of phosphorus was also ineffective. It would ignite readily inflammable materials but was of little general value as an incendiary because of its low temperature of combustion and the fire-deadening qualities of the oxides formed as it burned. However, it was very effective as an anti-personnel agent, since particles of phosphorus readily burned through clothing and left painful and very slow-healing burns. For this reason it was greatly feared by troops and produced a 'demoralising effect, far beyond the actual casualties produced'.

A larger and slightly more sophisticated incendiary with a streamlined shape, five inches wide and thirty-two inches long, was introduced in 1915. The fuse detonated a core of priming mixture (thermite), but once again the core was surrounded by 'solid oil' and tarred rope, and these newer incendiaries were only a little more reliable than their predecessors. A succession of variants – the Karbonit-Brandbombe, the Traiser-Brandstreubombe (a scatter bomb, dispersing the incendiary material over a wider area) and the Wollersdorf-Brandbombe – were all tried in turn, but all weighed around 10kg, restricting the number that could be carried, and none overcame the twin problems of inadequate ignition rates and ease of extinction.

Writing before the war, the Italian General Giulio Douhet had pointed out that 'the construction of aerial bombs does not call for high-grade steel, other special metals, nor for precision work. What it does demand is that the active ingredient of the bombs – the explosives, incendiaries, and poison gases – have the maximum efficacy and that research be directed to this end.' Throughout the first three years of the war, Germany's scientists, engineers and manufacturers had completely failed to fulfil that simple dictum, but now another new incendiary would be tested on London. 'Made of streamlined shape' with a vaned tail, it was fitted with a small explosive charge to 'burst open the upper portion of the casing and thus to scatter the incendiary material . . . semi-solid paraffin wax, partially dissolved in benzol, which contains either potassium chlorate or barium nitrate to provide an additional supply of oxygen. This component prevents the hydrocarbons burning with the excessively smoky flame which usually characterises their combustion.'

The efficiency of these new incendiary weapons and the resolve of Londoners to resist them were now to be put to the test in a new and even more devastating series of raids.

# CHAPTER 10
# THE BLITZ OF THE
# HARVEST MOON

O N THE WARM, still night of 24 September 1917, the England Squadron completed their final preparations for take-off, but Walter Aschoff and his crew had to sit out the raid as their Gotha was under repair. He waited as 'the evening twilight set in; soon it would be pitch black. The weather conditions were flawless and the orders to prepare for the night's raid had already been issued. We heard the rumble of the engines on trial runs, and saw the searchlights flare up in turn as they were tested, then all were extinguished, leaving an even deeper darkness behind.'

At last, on the signal from the Startoffizier, the twin searchlights were switched on, their beams intersecting in a 'V' of light, and the first bomber took off and disappeared into the blackness of the night sky. The runway lights were immediately extinguished until the next aircraft was ready, lest their beams identify the airfield to marauding English bombers. At five-minute intervals, the remainder of the squadron followed the leader into the sky, the double-note of their engines still heard for some time after they had been lost to sight, fading eventually to a faint rumble like distant summer thunder on the wind. Sixteen Gothas had taken off, but three landed again soon afterwards, blaming the eternal scapegoat 'engine trouble'.

Fighting was still raging on the other side of the Channel as the already infamous Passchendaele mud swallowed ever-growing numbers of troops, but in London, on that drowsy late-September evening, the war seemed a long way away. The capital had expanded during the war years; 'it seemed to thrive upon slaughter. The city's economy was fuelled by full employment, with so many of its young males detained elsewhere, and as a result the standard of living improved.'

For the rich, life went on much as it always had, albeit practised with a little more discretion than before the war. Most felt that conspicuous consumption was both unpatriotic and provocative to 'the lower orders' and very few people, rich or poor, bought new clothes; for some it was a matter of necessity, for others 'it was considered bad form'. For those in work the war brought rising wages and limitless overtime, but a dwindling range of goods on which to spend their money, and there were shortages of even the most basic foods. Sandbagged statues and monuments were constant visual reminders of the threat from the air, lack of petrol cut the traffic on the streets, and among the pedestrians there were ever-growing numbers of wounded and convalescent soldiers clad in uniforms of hospital blue. In the early years of the war there were also hordes of black-clad mourners, for at first virtually all bereaved people had continued the old pre-war mourning rituals, including the wearing of black suits or 'widow's weeds', but the sheer numbers of bereaved parents, wives, brothers and sisters eventually led to the old customs being abandoned. Most may have felt it was somehow unpatriotic to draw public attention to yet another death; 'one should not show the face of grief to the boys home on leave from the trenches'.

The war had impacted on every area of daily life. The striking and chiming of public clocks, including Big Ben, was banned between sunset and sunrise, as was whistling for cabs between 10 p.m. and 7 a.m., partly to ensure that air-raid warnings were clearly heard and unmistakable, but also, perhaps, to avoid unnecessary disturbance to the slumbers of munitions workers. There were other 'local hazards and difficulties. Building work was suspended . . . parks and squares were used as kitchen-gardens, while hotels became government offices or hostels. But there were more foreign restaurants and patisseries than ever as a result of the presence of émigrés, while the dance halls and music halls were full.'

There were also many less reputable pleasures on offer. There were an estimated sixty thousand prostitutes working the streets, many of them émigrés from occupied Belgium, servicing the thousands of soldiers of the Empire on leave or in training for the Front. Sexually transmitted diseases were so rife that a law was eventually introduced making it illegal for any woman infected with venereal disease to have intercourse with a soldier. Prostitutes suspected of being infected could be held in custody for a week while compulsory medical inspections were carried out.

Abuse of drugs, primarily opium and cocaine, and alcohol was also widespread. Munitions workers could earn all the overtime pay they wanted, and with cash in their pockets drunkenness and absenteeism affected safety and production. The teetotal Lloyd George, then Minister of Munitions, seized upon the 'shell scandal' of 1915 – which highlighted shortages of munitions at the Front and the defective quality of many of the supplies that were getting through – to push through a package of measures to counter drunkenness. Between April and October of that year, Britain's first ever licensing laws were introduced, limiting the hours that public houses could open to an average of five hours a day, restricting supplies of grain for brewing and distilling, banning 'heavy beers' such as stout and porter, and sharply reducing the alcoholic content of other beers and of spirits. 'Treating' – the practice of buying rounds – was also banned. The misery of manual workers was heightened by three- to five-fold increases in the prices of drinks that were still available. Even more stringent regulations were introduced to control drinking in areas such as Enfield Lock, Carlisle and Gretna, where some of the country's largest munitions plants were sited, giving the Government power to close pubs and breweries altogether and restrict opening hours as required.

The attempt at prohibition was sometimes counterproductive as workers displayed considerable ingenuity in getting round the new regulations. Men coming off the evening shift at Gretna would pass the hat round to bribe the driver of the last train into Carlisle to get there ahead of schedule; the faster he went, the more he was paid. The owners of every pub within range of the station lined their bars with pints and whiskies, and the workers would tumble off the train as soon as it had screeched to a halt, fill themselves with as many drinks as they could down in the few minutes available to them before closing time, then spill into the streets in a brawling, spewing mass, leaving the citizens of Carlisle to wonder how this could possibly be helping the war effort.

In London that September evening, the roads were 'strangely quiet and deserted . . . petrol restrictions had reduced motor traffic almost to zero', but the pavements and parks were full of people, strolling in the last of the sun. As nightfall approached, however, the streets and public places emptied rapidly. Clear skies and the strong light of a harvest moon had once been welcome autumn sights; now they were full of menace. As dusk fell, 'street lights were no more than glowing pinpoints along the shadowy chasms between the houses. Darkened London seemed like a dim underwater world . . . Pedestrians hurried by quickly in the shadow of walls, glancing apprehensively at the sky – would they come tonight? London seemed breathless, in the tense expectancy of disaster.'

When the alarm was raised, the LADA Controller relayed the warning at once to Hainault and a score of other fighter airfields. One of them, on a narrow plateau above the wooded slopes of the North Downs, was in use for the first time. Previously a wireless testing park where air-to-air and air-to-ground telephony systems were developed, the grass airfield on its windswept hilltop was still surrounded by a ramshackle collection of sheds and buildings festooned with aerials. Now it was the new home of 141 Squadron, flying Bristol Fighters emblazoned with a red cockerel. When the alarm was raised, the pilots scrambled from their makeshift quarters and sprinted for their aircraft. Within seconds the air was full of the noise of engines, as they taxied out and took off into the ever-darkening sky. These were the first fighter sorties ever to be flown from the airfield, then unknown but destined to become famous the world over: Biggin Hill.

As the air-raid warning was given, policemen rode through the London streets on bicycles, ringing their bells and wearing their 'Take Cover' placards. A few civilian volunteers also toured the streets in placarded cars, sounding their horns to reinforce the warning, and in Chelsea 'special constables ran a motor-car with the words "Police Warning. Take Cover" printed on canvas stretched on an iron framework across the front and illuminated from behind by electric lights'. However, no maroons or sirens were sounded; while it had been agreed that visible and audible alerts could be used in daytime, the fear of confusion and panic, and even of disturbing the slumbers of London's workers, meant that no general air-raid warnings were sounded after dark 'as they would unnecessarily disturb persons already under cover'.

Nonetheless, word of the raid was rapidly spread by police bicycle and word of mouth, and people at once began hurrying down to their cellars and improvised shelters, or rushing through the streets to the Tube stations, the tunnels under the river, and the parks and open spaces. Not all were in fear. As one paper sardonically observed, 'We Britishers are not going to sit mum at home whenever there is a sight to be seen, out of mere consideration of safety', and, although the vast majority fled for shelter, a number of people gathered in Hyde Park ready to watch 'the Hun air show' over the City.

So many people packed the Underground that on many platforms it was impossible for passengers to get on or off the trains. The City of

London Police Commissioner, Sir William Nott-Bower, visiting Old Street station, found it 'difficult to alight from the train and move along the platform because of the crowd. The rear ranks were sitting with their backs to the wall and the front ranks standing. All the corridors were blocked, with barely room for one to move along in single file. The staircases were solid with people. I estimate there were 3,000 people on the platform and not less than 10,000 inside the station.' The scene was repeated at every station and, understandably, irrespective of the notional closing time of the station, they would not leave until they were sure that the danger was past.

Soon the drone of aircraft engines became audible and the fierce beams of searchlights probed the night sky over London, sweeping to and fro in search of the silvery glimmer of an enemy plane. The thousands of anti-aircraft guns surrounding the capital began pumping up a barrage, firing blind with no real idea of where their targets might be, but blasting so many shells that it seemed to onlookers as if the sky itself was on fire. Not a single shell hit its target.

Lit by a quarter-moon, the first Gothas could now be glimpsed between the patches of broken cloud drifting across the sky on the westerly breeze. As Dr R. D. MacGregor made his way home across Bloomsbury, the sound of explosions began to echo through London's deserted streets. Unlike three weeks before, a full blackout was now in force. 'The streets were in total darkness and everything was as still as death. I walked (I had to), keeping in touch with the houses as I made my way gingerly along. I could hear the movement above of the aeroplanes but kept on. At one of the blocks of flats in Southampton Row, a policeman sheltering inside the doorway shouted to me to come in. I did so and waited for about ten minutes, but then, being hungry, I said to him, "I'm going to risk a bolt across to the hotel [the Bedford Hotel in Southampton Row]."

'He advised me not to as the noise above was getting very loud. However, pulling my hat well down, I said, "Well, here goes, goodnight," and made a dash. I was within twenty yards of the door when a terrific screeching from above nearly paralysed me. I knew it was a falling bomb. With one spring from the pavement, I cleared the steps through the doorway of the hotel. The door at that moment was being cautiously opened by some of the porters, waiters and guests of the hotel. I shouted "Get in!" and barged in, coming in contact with one of the men, knocking him down and falling on top of him just as the torpedo [bomb] exploded. That fall saved his life and mine. Everyone else at the door and in the lounge was killed . . . I was the only witness at the inquest on the dead.' The blast hurled 'persons inside across rooms and down stairs like the leaves of a tree in a storm' and sent splinters and shards of shattered glass knifing through the lobby. It was packed with people, hotel guests and passers-by seeking cover from the raid. Thirteen were killed and many others seriously injured.

The hotel was 'chiefly patronised by provincial visitors, to the majority of whom an air-raid was an unusual and spectacular event'; men from Bristol and Woolloomaloo in Australia were among the victims. Four of the dead, according to one of the next day's papers, had 'invited disaster – they ignored the peril of loitering in doorways which has been emphasised again and again in the *Daily Mail* and paid for their folly with their lives . . . Two of the hotel porters and the stoker, just off duty, were on their way home. The warning of the raid had reached the hotel and many of the guests had gathered in the hall downstairs. Half a dozen of them were actually in the doorway outside. A passing constable urged them to get inside. Reluctantly they obeyed him and the last had only just turned his back on the street when the bomb fell. The three hotel servants, still outside, were killed outright. The door and most of the front windows of the place were destroyed, some of the guests were cut by the flying glass, a waitress was very seriously injured and the chef was rendered unconscious by shock, though no injuries could be found upon him. There were some marvellous escapes. Guests lingering over their coffee in the dining-room were smothered in broken glass, but no one of them was badly hurt. A neat round hole was cut in the glass over the girl cashier's head, missing her by inches and shattering the clock above her desk. The clock stopped at 8.55.'

Guests at The Ritz narrowly missed a similar fate when a bomb blasted a large crater in Green Park near the hotel's south-west corner. On the other side of Piccadilly, Burlington House was hit by a bomb which burst through Gallery Nine and penetrated the basement, causing 'damage to the building and some statuary'. Another bomb fell in the Thames opposite St Thomas's Hospital, sending a towering column of water skywards, and Westminster Abbey also escaped when a bomb landed in Dean's Yard and failed to detonate, but another struck the Embankment with deadly consequences.

A tram was 'just swinging round off Westminster Bridge when the driver of a single-decker shouted, "Hi, mate, I'm two minutes late, will you let me pull off in front of you?" We waited while the single-decker shunted on to our lines. Then we followed along closely behind it. A bomb dropped into the Thames as we were nearing Charing Cross Bridge. The next hit the single-decker, for little remained of it. Our tram seemed to rise in the air and wobble. The driver of the other tram appeared to kneel down suddenly, still pulling at his controls. I saw him fall and that his legs had been blown off; so, while dying, his last thoughts were to stop his tram.'

A thirteen-year-old Camden boy, James Sharpe, also showed his own doomed heroism that night. After carrying his little brothers and sisters to a cellar across King's Cross Road from his own house as the air-raid began, he returned to check on his bedridden grandfather. As he was about to enter the house, a bomb struck it, blowing him off his feet and burying him under rubble and debris. The grandfather was rescued and 'taken to the infirmary, suffering only from severe shock', but the boy died.

The moon set at 10.21 that night and by that time the last of the Gothas was already well out over the North Sea on the way back to Ghent. Twenty-one people were killed and seventy injured in the raids and not a single one of the attacking Gothas was shot down. However, the effect of the incendiaries that they had carried was far less severe than the Germans had hoped and the British might have feared. The bulky devices proved completely unreliable: at least 50 per cent failed to ignite at all and many of the others burned out ineffectually. The number of incendiaries dropped on the capital was also far smaller than planned, because only three of the thirteen aircraft that had crossed the English coast reached London. Six others made 'a specially heavy attack on Dover' – where many residents had taken to spending the night in the huge caves, previously used as store places, carved out of the chalk cliffs – and the remainder, whether by accident or design, attacked Chatham, Tilbury, Southend and the Isle of Sheppey.

The Gotha crews flew back to Gontrode and St Denijs-Westrem, where 'the approach to the runway was marked by two intersecting cones of light. A line of green lights was used to show the start of the runway and a line of red lights marked the last possible point at which it was possible to touch down and come to a halt before the end of the runway. A returning aircraft wanting to land identified itself from a predetermined point on its inbound course, using flares or morse code signals from the lamp that the observer carried for this purpose. If the runway was clear and there were no enemy bombers overhead, the launch officer signalled permission to land. The landing lights were then illuminated as the aircraft circled the field and came in to land between the cones of light.'

It was an eerie experience for Walter Aschoff to stand on the airfield as the returning night bombers, drawn like moths to the columns of light stabbing up into the sky, hovered with their engines throttled back, almost silent and barely visible in the enveloping darkness, before rumbling in to land. 'The last minutes and seconds before they touched down seemed an eternity to those who waited on the ground, fearful that even now, there might be a fatal ending to the long and perilous flight.'

As Aschoff watched, 'suddenly, an aircraft swept out of the black, moonless night, flying at very low altitude. The landing lights were illuminated, marking the runway in the middle of the field, but the aircraft was not heading for the intersecting cones of light but straight towards us as we stood well to the left of the runway. The aircraft's drift to the left grew ever more pronounced and, bracing ourselves for disaster, we threw ourselves flat as it thundered over us. The Gotha's wing clipped the lighting stanchion; it was a glancing blow but enough to send the aircraft rearing up like an eagle hit in flight, and then it plummeted out of the sky, drilling its nose deep into the ground.

'Responding even before an order had been given, the emergency vehicle roared across the airfield to the crash site, while soldiers and ground-crew ran there as fast as their feet would carry them, but fire was already licking over the fuselage. The rescuers tried everything they knew to pull out the trapped crew but the flames kept soaring higher and higher, the roar and crackle of the flames punctuated by the rattle of the remaining rounds of the Gotha's machine-guns, detonating in the heat. The fires blackened and destroyed everything in minutes . . . and the hand that only a moment ago tried to help rescue a friend flinched back powerlessly. A sea of flames now engulfed the aircraft, turning night into day and making any further rescue attempt impossible. Under our very eyes, helpless, we could only watch a brave flight crew meet their end.'

In England there was once more a curious mixture of wonder and fury about the raid. Some found it a thrilling experience. 'About 7.30 our ears are disturbed by the sound of bombs or guns and someone comes in saying excitedly, "Raid on." We give a careful look round to see that our blinds are all right and no glimmers of light shining out, and then go upstairs to try and locate the danger, but tonight it seems to be all around: gunfire, shellfire, little spurts of flame, searchlights, bombs dropping, shells screeching.'

Newspaper reporters again mirrored that excitement, writing as if theatre critics at an opening night. 'As a moving, thrilling, tremendous demonstration, Monday night's raid was by far the most sensational "show" we have experienced in London. The searchlights were whirling in great, broad sword-blades of light; amid the flickers, our own questing aeroplanes darted like gnats, trailing lights hither and thither, and finally disappearing in the distant blue. Far away to the south-eastward, guns were rumbling and growling, the sound of them grew nearer and nearer . . . and then with a mighty roar the nearer batteries leapt to the attack. I heard four or five bombs drop into London, the smash of their impact quite unmistakable, and it occurred in the interval between the ending of one deafening barrage, or curtain fire, and the start of another. All the rest was one magnificent but frightening display of pyrotechnics. The sky streamed shells, and for twenty minutes the whine and wail of them cut the air like whiplashes. Out of that red hot sky our grisly visitors were glad enough to turn tail and run for home, leaving only a small toll of dead and injured behind. The bombs were dropped at random – anyhow in the bewildering chaos. In the racket of the night people imagined – and naturally enough – that half of London had been destroyed. But most of the devilry of shattering noise was the strident, determined work of our concentrated defence. It drove the Hun home and upset his plans completely.'

However, even the most jingoistic correspondent was forced to concede that, 'magnificent as was the work which the air defences of London did against the raiders on Monday night, it had a manifest draw-back in the return to earth of thousands of fragments of exploded shell-case. In several cases considerable damage has been traced to these missiles of defence, although no loss of life is attributable to them. The lesson is obvious. The danger of the unexploded shell or the fragment of shell makes it more important than ever that cover should be promptly taken and that persons should not expose themselves at open doors or windows. Yesterday the children of London reaped a great harvest of these fragments. Every other child seemed to have a proud souvenir of the raid, which was often enough wrongly described as "a piece of bomb".'

Ordinary Londoners were in more sombre mood as they assessed the damage, discussed the likelihood of another raid that night and vented their anger at the lack of adequate air-raid warnings. 'London is weary of the system which gives warnings by day and not by night, and yet provides night warning for a few while refusing it to thousands. Repeated demands for night raid warnings have all been met by refusals . . . The Lord Mayor who had forwarded many petitions and resolutions to the Home Office in favour of night warnings, has now been informed that the matter is "under consideration". This is probably the Home Office way of saying that it is going to do what the public wants . . . A meeting at Tower Hill yesterday, convened by the People's Fairplay League, passed a resolution demanding effective warning of night raids by means of coloured rays or otherwise, and the vigorous and sustained bombing of German towns and cities.'

Some took their defence into their own hands and formed their own neighbourhood night-watches. One was 'composed of aged fathers who had worked hard all day and undertook these tiring all-night vigils'. A soldier home on leave, Frank Equart, 'took the opportunity of relieving one of the watch at the first chance. The job was to watch a mirror that was fixed to catch the SOS flare from the local Town Hall roof. The old 'uns were pleased to have a real live corporal who had seen and been through the real stuff, to talk to. I refrained from relating the real things that happened out there.'

In Poplar, scene of the slaughter at the Upper North Street School, residents of some streets set up the 'Poplar Patrol'. Each household paid threepence a week into a communal fund that paid for rent, fire and refreshments in Mrs G. Stilwell's 'small front room, where three men, each in his turn, used to sit up every night. In the event of a raid, as soon as they got the first warning, they used to run and knock on every door where there was a P.P. On the brick wall at the side of our street door can still be seen faintly two large letters: "P.P", for Poplar Patrol.'

After the previous night's raid, City offices and West End shops closed early so that their staff and customers could get home before night fell. Restaurants, music halls and theatres ran advertisements proclaiming 'Moonlit Nights – Open As Usual – Ample Bomb-Proof Shelter', but few were willing to take the risk, and it is doubtful if Londoners found much to laugh at in *Punch* magazine's Home Front equivalent of the multiple-choice postcards sent home by soldiers to let their families know that they were still alive and well:

At the Front – Somewhere in England.
I am quite well/ill.
My windows are smashed/intact.
I have a/no crater in my front/back garden.
I slept/did not sleep a wink the whole night.
Grandmother behaved like/unlike a brick.

They were even less likely to have been amused after the German bombers returned again that night. 'We generally left at dusk, while the sky was still red in the west . . . Our planes must have looked like some great prehistoric birds, struggling to get airborne against the red twilight of the primeval world. Bearing such a heavy load, our bombers rose very, very slowly. You couldn't force them to climb, you had to rely on a favourable wind and the steady rhythm of the engines.'

Fifteen heavy-laden Gothas had taken off, only one of which returned to base with engine trouble – a tribute either to the good work of the mechanics, or to the fact that the lack of fighter attacks on the previous evening had emboldened some of the fainter hearts in the England Squadron. They should have had no difficulty in finding London, for one of the defending fighters reported that he could 'see the moon-glint [on the Thames] from over twenty miles away to the North', yet although the capital was 'always clearly visible despite patches of low cloud and mist which temporarily obscured some districts', only three raiders actually reached London, the others bombing the Kent coast south from Margate as far as Folkestone. Only one British fighter crew even sighted a Gotha that night and then lost sight of it again within fifteen minutes without inflicting any serious damage upon it.

Sylvia Pankhurst was 'writing at home' when 'on the silence arose an ominous grinding . . . growing in volume . . . throbbing, pulsating . . . filling the air with its sound . . . Then huge reports smote the ear, shattering, deafening, and the roar of falling masonry . . . the angry grinding still pulsated above us. Again that terrific burst of noise; those awful bangs, the roar of the falling buildings, the rattle of shrapnel on the roof close above our heads . . . Next morning there were pieces of shell on our flat roof. Swarms of children were out in the road, picking up shrapnel, prising up with impromptu tools the bits of metal which had embedded themselves in the road.' The bombs destroyed several houses in Bermondsey and Camberwell, but two bombs exploded harmlessly in the Thames near London Bridge and the raid was much less sustained and damaging than the previous night.

On the night of the first raid of the Blitz of the Harvest Moon, 'a concourse of people estimated at 100,000' had rushed to take shelter in the Underground. By the following night the number had increased to 120,000, and on the two succeeding nights, even though no raids took place, 'people began to flock into the Tubes in the early evening without waiting for any warning'. Others simply boarded a Tube train and remained on it 'on its journey from one terminus to the other until the "All Clear" is sounded. But they sometimes find themselves in trouble at the end; for the train might stop for the night at the wrong terminus for them . . . getting home often involved a long walk through deserted streets.'

Many middle-class parents sent their children out of London to stay with friends or relatives, or to board with country families willing to take them in for payment. The London working class had no such option; their children had to stay with them and face the consequences. Tens of thousands of them, 'urged by fear, were not content to await the usual warning before setting out. They had often to face long journeys across London and knew also that there would be competition for the best places, so they watched the skies to see whether the atmospheric conditions and the state of the moon appeared favourable for raiding . . . and set their faces to the west.'

The nightly migration was 'spontaneous, infectious and unorganised. It defied policemen, the Underground railway staffs and park keepers. Officials were scandalised. It simply would not do.' Faced with an ultimatum by irate park-keepers to leave or be locked in for the night, the virtually unanimous choice was to spend the night there. Tens of thousands more people boarded trains and buses to spend the night in the open country around the capital or in whatever accommodation they could find.

The numbers seeking shelter in the Underground continued to grow on each subsequent night until they had reached an estimated total of three hundred thousand. 'The majority of people behaved bravely while raids were in progress, but the dread of their coming, the hasty flight to Tubes and other recognised places of shelter, wore down the nerves of many, especially in districts where houses were overcrowded and families had but poor rooms to shelter in. Everywhere working women looked exhausted from sleeplessness, anxiety and fear. Each night at this time, queues formed outside the Tube station, waiting to go down if an alarm was given.'

'People took up their places as soon as darkness fell, or even before, prepared to camp out until all possibility of danger had passed. They blocked the stairs and the platforms, and the majority of them, it was said, did not prove amenable to efforts of the railway officials to distribute them to best advantage.' 'The sights in the Tubes were the most extraordinary imaginable . . . women were dressing on the platforms and taking their hair out of curling pins; some were pulling on their stockings . . . The staircases and platforms of the Tube station were like a huge bedroom and "night nursery".'

Some stations were so full that the gates were locked and no more people were admitted. One man escorting two young women to Clapham

Common station found 'the iron lattice door of the station was closed and through its chequered bars I could see that the booking hall was packed with men, women and children. Its congestion afforded no proper shelter from the raid – the people would have been better off in their homes – and its state could only mean that the safer places, the platforms below and the stairs leading to them, were so crowded as to be inaccessible. Two policemen were inside the gates . . . one of them, when the girls and I asked for admission, lifted up a large piece of cardboard, on which was printed, in bold lettering, "Full up; no more room".'

Wind, rain and poor visibility kept the England Squadron grounded on the nights of 26 and 27 September, but on Friday, 28 September they returned once more, and for the first time the Gothas were aided by two of the massive new R-planes – the Giants. It was the largest raid yet mounted, with twenty-five Gothas taking off alongside the two Giants. The weather at first seemed perfect. Oberleutnant Fritz Lorenz, Flight Leader of Staffel 14, was observer in a Gotha painted with the motto *Eisern und Irre* (Iron and Madness). In keeping with that motto, Lorenz and his pilot, Kurt Kuppers, normally dispensed with the services of a rear-gunner and his machine-gun in order to carry a heavier bombload, but on this occasion they had a passenger, Hauptmann Muehlich-Hoffmann, a staff officer at headquarters, who 'wanted to get a picture of what we were doing'.

They flew on towards England 'over a milk-white sea of clouds' flooding in from the west. 'A full moon was shining above with a brightness that was almost unreal. In addition to our compass, a beautifully clear, star-filled sky showed us the way.' The crews had learned that at that time of night 'Arcturus, a fixed star of the first magnitude, was an exact finger-post to the target of London'. The star had been punningly nicknamed 'Sturius' by a member of the squadron, Leutnant von der Nahmer – *stur* meant 'stubbornly or straight ahead' – and he had even constructed a 'Sturometer', 'a big fork, located at the front machine-gun ring, so that the pilot could navigate to London by keeping the "Sturius" in that fork'.

Despite the beauty of the scene, the weather was turning against them, the dense cloud layer below counter-pointed by strengthening winds. In addition to the customary engine problems, a stream of Gotha crews, perhaps remembering the disasters of the previous month, gave up the struggle with the wind and weather and turned for home, and only three Gothas and the two Giants actually reached the English coast. The cloud cover protected the handful of raiders from the probing beams of search-lights and the anti-aircraft fire that was lighting up the sky 'from Dover to the river Thames . . . Where a devil's cauldron of bursting shrapnel had never let a machine pass without inflicting at least some hits, there pre-vailed this time in the silvery solitude, a peace that was like something out of a fairy-tale. The ghostly moonlight cast the faint shadow of our machine onto the white blanket beneath.'

With even the course of the Thames invisible beneath the clouds, Lorenz had to navigate by 'stars, compass and clock' but believed he had found London by the play of the numerous searchlights around it. 'Their faint glow shimmered within the clouds all around . . . sometimes for a fraction of a second, there were streets of lights below us, the streets of a big city . . . a few twists of the levers, a slight shudder of the machine and the long, torpedo-shaped missiles silently found their way down through the clouds.'

In fact, though Lorenz and all the other crews had dropped their bombs over what they thought was London, they fell harmlessly in Kent, Essex and Suffolk. There was not a single casualty and damage was estimated at a laughable £129, though there was a near-miss when four bombs fell close to the Uplees Powder Works in Faversham, but buried themselves in the estuary mud before detonating. Even worse for the squadron, just as on 18 August, many of the Gothas – six – crashed on landing and a further three were shot down.

Lorenz and Kuppers were fortunate not to join the missing list after descending through the clouds over the North Sea to pick up a bearing to steer them home. As they went down through the overcast they found themselves in 'an impenetrable darkness, an indescribably oppressive sensation, suffocating and stifling. Even from a distance of only a few centimetres, the eye could barely read the instruments through the fog and damp.'

Kuppers, at the controls, became disoriented and the Gotha went into a spin. A strut snapped under the strain and still they plummeted downwards. Kuppers, not even sure whether they were over land or sea, was convinced they would either crash and burn, or drown. Lorenz felt the pressure of the dive like 'a ring of iron pressing my chest', and was 'searching desperately for some point below on which to fix the eye'. He stood upright in the nose and held out his arms horizontally to try to give Kuppers an artificial horizon on which he could fix. 'The needle showed only fifty metres' when the Gotha at last burst through the bottom of the cloud layer. 'Very near below us there was the boiling sea', the waves 'so close, we thought we could touch them', yet somehow Kuppers managed to drag the Gotha out of its death-dive and regain control.

With the compass spinning crazily, and the skies above them completely obscured by cloud, they still had little idea in which direction to fly. Lorenz's compass 'finally offered two directions'. He chose the one he hoped was north and set a course that would 'reach the coast of Flanders soon – if not, a wet grave would be awaiting us'. As they frantically scanned the horizon, they saw a light flashing over the waves – 'long-short; short-long-short; short' – and recognized it as the signal light at Ostend. They landed at Gontrode five hours after taking off, by which time the other flight and ground-crews had already given them up for lost.

Undaunted by the squadron's heavy losses, Kleine again launched the raiders at England the following night, and this time London 'suffered heavily'. A small force of seven Gothas and three Giants took off, but once again three of the Gothas abandoned the flight and landed almost at once. The remaining bombers flew on as thick fog spread across the landscape below them. It was too late for any others to abort the raid now; 'landing with full fuel tanks and bombs on board would have been suicide'.

The raiders crossed the coastline between Foulness and Deal and the thunderous noise of the multiple-engined Giants sowed confusion among the ground-based defences. British Intelligence had discovered little about the Giants at the time and disseminated even less. Information obtained on 19 September that as many as six new large bombing aircraft had been deployed in Belgium and a reconnaissance photograph taken on 25 September of an aircraft twice the size of a Gotha on the airfield at St Denijs-Westrem were never circulated.

To observers in listening stations, straining their ears for the first sound from the skies that would signal another German air-raid, the rumble of the four or five huge engines of a single Giant was so loud – 'on a still night their effect on the tympanum [eardrum] when twenty miles away equalled that of a Gotha near at hand' – that they thought they were hearing not one aircraft but an entire squadron of Gothas or a group of Zeppelins. The human eye was as fallible as the ear, for the 'five aeroplanes' reported as caught in the beam of a searchlight by a London unit that night were without doubt a single Giant. The official communiqué issued after the raid reflected those erroneous beliefs, claiming that there had been 'a determined and simultaneous attack by three groups of raiders', and a German report stated that the sound of a Giant pilot testing his engines prior to take-off was 'picked up by the enemy listening posts . . . Bruges [German] naval station, which possessed the British code and key, shortly afterwards heard the Giant aeroplanes being reported by wireless to the London Air Defence as Zeppelins'.

At least two of the raiders bombed targets in Sheerness but the others flew on to London where, despite the thickening fog, they saw enough of the target for two bombs to hit Waterloo station, tearing up tracks and wrecking carriages. Houses were also destroyed in Kensington, Notting Hill and Kingsland, and a bomb smashed through a wooden trapdoor outside the Eaglet public house in Seven Sisters Road, Holloway, and exploded in the cellar. 'The floor of the saloon was blown upwards and many of the refugees were hurled into the street.' Four people were killed and thirty-seven injured, 'many seriously'.

The licensee, Mr Crouch, had taken his wife, their children and their nanny down into the back part of the cellar to shelter from the raid and was 'counting cash in the bar' when the bomb went off. He was concussed but otherwise unhurt and his children suffered only minor injuries, but his wife, who had left her refuge 'to turn off a running tap', was killed instantly.

A soldier home on leave had been playing snooker in the pub with a friend. 'We had scored one game each when an air-raid warning was given. We decided to play the third after the all-clear. In the meantime I popped along, a few doors down the road, to see that my wife was all right at home. I had just got my key in the front door when there was a terrific crash and

I was thrown off my feet.' He arrived back at the Eaglet to find 'nothing but ruins and what had been the billiard room a huge crater . . . I never saw my friend again and the only souvenir I have is a tiny piece of slate from the table we had played on.'

Another German aircraft, well off course, dropped its bombload on Putney Common. The All Clear had already been given and a young couple, George Lyall and his wife, had left their children at home and gone for a walk on the common. They sat down on a seat by a lamp-post. Two other passers-by noticed them. 'There was a bright moon shining over the lonely stretch of damp grass and bushes and by its light we saw a young couple sitting clasped in each other's arms under one of the trees . . . The sound of a gun made us quicken our steps . . . It was the dreaded air-raid warning.' 'At that moment a German aeroplane, wishing to get away quickly, unloaded its remaining bombs above the Common; it had evidently lost its way. The couple were blown to pieces and all that remained to tell of the tragedy were a shrapnel-scarred seat and lamp-post, and the large hole across the road.' They were among fourteen people to die that night, with another eighty-seven injured, but 'nearly as much damage was done by anti-aircraft fire as by bombs'.

One Gotha was shot down by a gun-battery after it was pinned by searchlights near Dover. The crew of the searchlight claimed that they had seen the German aircraft spin out of control and crash into the sea about two miles offshore. A second raider was lost after encountering a patrol of specially converted British Handley-Page bombers north of Ostend. Carrying no bombload, they had been fitted with five Lewis guns each to deliver a formidable barrage of fire. One of them poured three drums of ammunition into a Gotha, which just managed to reach the Dutch coast before crash-landing.

A third raider, piloted by Kurt Delang, crash-landed after losing its elevator controls to anti-aircraft fire over Sheerness. As they crossed the Belgian coast on the return flight, the aircraft went into a dive. Delang 'turned off the ignition for both engines so that they would cool off during the final dive', lessening the risk of the Gotha becoming engulfed in fire on landing. As he brought it in for a crash-landing, it 'hit a row of poplar trees that took the impact of the crash'. His observer, 'almost without injury, ended up safely in the top of a tree', the rear-gunner suffered a broken arm, and Delang himself was 'found under the wreckage. I had a slight brain concussion.'

In England, newspaper reports of Gotha losses did nothing to stem the fear that now gripped London. Thousands spent their nights in ' "Dugouts" in railway arches and factories', 'sleeping under the table', or 'fully-dressed waiting for the alarm'. One puzzled child 'sat and watched the enemy aeroplanes fly over and vaguely wondered why my aunt cried'. Vast numbers of London families were no longer willing to wait for warnings of air-raids, but left home before sunset each night. An army of the dispossessed, carrying bedding and baskets of food, and taking their pets with them, they disappeared into the Underground. 'It was pitiful to see the people trying to get into the already crowded station. There were brave mothers with their little children clinging to their skirts; sometimes a kiddy would be seen carrying a bird in a cage.'

One woman 'made a dash for the Leicester Square Tube station. The lifts were not working, one was being used as a sort of hospital. In all the corners and even on the stairs people were sitting who had come there for refuge. As the incoming trains carried away ten or a dozen people – all that could be squeezed in – a few more were allowed out of the packed staircase and on to the platform to await their turn. It was horrible that platform. The poor folk from the surrounding districts who had taken refuge there at the first signal early in the evening were lying all over it. Some had brought their bedding or rugs and bundles, and were leaning against these or against the walls, fast asleep, and wherever there was an inch of platform uncovered by human beings, there was broken food, banana skins, orange peel – much worse than that too. One poor white-faced mother with a tiny baby looked up at me and said, "It's an awful life, isn't it?" '

Every station was choked with humanity and the lack of sanitation left the Tubes reeking of urine and excrement. 'So vile does the air become that many people say they would rather be bombed than take such shelter', 'so noisome that only the very strongest could endure it without being affected. Every now and then a man or woman who had fainted had to be brought up to the fresher air of the booking-office.'

Whenever there was a lull in the gunfire 'people would insist on going outside' to escape the crush and the stench. Then when the firing began again 'there was a mad rush for re-entrance'. Even with 'the danger of violent death hanging over their heads, the crowd did not lose their happy-go-lucky sense of humour; but some of the laughter sounded hysterical'. Many people found themselves pushed and trampled as they fought for a space to rest, and scuffles and fights broke out. The crush was so great in one station that a man was pushed on to the line 'just in front of an in-coming train and was cut to pieces'.

Some soldiers 'home on leave or convalescent . . . fainted when they got down to the Tube station, and told me they were less afraid to face the enemy in the trenches than to face the unseen, unknown dangers of a London air-raid . . . When the "all clear" sounded, we had difficulty in getting the people to leave the shelter of the Tubes and go home. They feared the enemy would return. I have stood over a poor woman who was sitting in a doorway at three o'clock in the morning with her baby wrapped in an eiderdown, huddled in her arms, using all my persuasive powers to convince her that the danger was over and get her home to bed.'

By now, a million Londoners were spending the night in the Tube or public buildings, and many thousands more slept in the royal parks or the open fields around London. To ease the overcrowding in the Underground, Government buildings and police stations were thrown open and those who preferred to take their chances at home were offered sandbags 'in large or small quantities' to shield their doors and windows and place in their lofts, though people were warned that overloading joists 'could cause a roof to collapse, and so anticipate the intentions of the Huns'. At first sandbags were hawked round from house to house by any local entrepreneur with a wheelbarrow or a horse and cart, who sold them 'off the barrow' at 2d each in the poorer areas, but at prices rising to as much as a shilling in more affluent districts. They were eventually distributed free by the Government, but only when the worst of the raids were already over.

# CHAPTER 11
# THE SERPENT MACHINE

S UNDAY, 30 SEPTEMBER was a perfect autumn day, but the sun shining from a cloudless sky on the yellowing leaves of the plane trees merely terrified most Londoners: clear skies and the full moon due that night were guarantees of yet another German raid. 'Glorious moonlit nights will ever be associated in my mind with these terrible experiences.'

At St Denijs-Westrem and Gontrode the England Squadron's ground- and flight crews were making the familiar round of final checks. For Walter Aschoff, 'midnight had just passed as our car stopped at the airfield. Everywhere there was movement, shouting and action. The sound of engines starting up tore apart the peace of the night. Above us, the big bomber aircraft of the neighbouring Staffel 18 were already taking off one by one and were swallowed up by the darkness.

'Our Serpent Machine's engine shivered impatiently, propellers slowly turning in the glare of the floodlights. One last time the engineer and I used our torches to inspect the undercarriage and the other key parts of the aircraft, then I turned to my pilot, gave him a nod and sat down on my folding chair in the turret. The engines increased to full power, groaning and growling like prehistoric beasts. We rumbled forward, the ground blurring beneath us. The air pressure increased on my chest and breathing became harder as we rose into the uncertain darkness of the night.

'I still clasped the flare-gun ready to fire it to throw light – however meagre – on the airfield, if we had to make an emergency landing, but after a few seconds we had risen a few hundred metres, and the greatest danger had passed. We completed the obligatory safety lap of the airfield while the rear-gunner and I once again illuminated the engines and wheels to make sure that everything had survived the take-off.

'Gontrode and the blacked-out city of Ghent were now far below. I switched on the light over the compass, raised my arm to signal the course to my pilot and let it fall again when he had adopted the right heading. The night was foggy, but the higher we climbed, the clearer the air became and the further our eyes could wander. Orientation lights were lit at the take-off of the first aircraft, and the emergency landing fields were sending up their recognition signals. Strings of white, green and red lights marked the direction to take and the rapid-fire guns near the Dutch border at Zeebrugge and further to the west at Ostend sent up the agreed number of star-shells that shone like pearls against the night sky. We made for the westernmost leading lights – the shortest route to the target.

'Flanders was immersed in deepest darkness; only very rarely could a weak glimmer of light be seen from the towns and cities below us. In the military area around Bruges, some searchlights were scouring the sky and the muzzle flashes of the guns flared up here and there. The bursting shells formed an immense firewall to destroy or disperse enemy bombers, but we were on course for an even hotter hell than this. The Front at Wytschaete-arch was silent. Now and then a stray flare rising from the trenches got lost in the night sky and then dropped between the lines of friend and foe, burning out slowly . . . As so many other times, we flew over the emplacements while countless flares and rockets rose like wraiths into the black sky, shells and shrapnel dropped their steel rain and the shell-bursts showed us the ferocious battle below us.'

'Before we crossed the coastline, we made a last round of checks – the enemy might already be lurking in ambush. Then we were out over the sea – enemy territory. We relied on our vigilance and the two good Mercedes engines to keep us safe. I peered into the darkness, fully alert, the gun in front of me at the ready. The tension in all of us was palpable. Suddenly, the silhouette of a big aircraft loomed out of the darkness 200 metres [650 feet] above us. I hardly had time to swivel the machine-gun and warn the rear-gunner before it had passed like a ghost in the night. It was probably an enemy bomber on its way to its target, just like us.

'On the French coast, a number of searchlights, woken by the sound of our engines, sought us out, their beams groping ever higher and wider into the night. Even the sea below us looked restless. My eyes were everywhere: on the millions of stars in the sky, peering into the distance ahead, watching the detonating bombs and shells over Dunkirk, and scanning the ocean surface, observing the movement of picket ships and patrol boats.

'The "light blockade" between Dover and Calais was clearly visible. Destroyers, fishing trawlers and motor boats, with powerful lights and magnesium flares, were on guard here every night to prevent German submarines from passing through the Channel. The nets of steel cable hung underwater had made the passage too dangerous, even for U-boats, and raids by our squadron on this blockade had been considered several times.

'We had already done many hours of night-flying, but this particular night was strangely heavy with stars, sparkling like diamonds on the dome of the sky, hinting at unreachable worlds. The Milky Way glowed like a band of silver across the heavens; the Great Bear that had served us well as a guide shone brightly through the cold of the night. My thoughts drifted in the endless space of the universe; despite the dangers, this flight felt almost like a dream. It was an indescribably beautiful and uplifting experience, flying and gliding through the night, detached from the gravity of the imperfect earth below, and ever more aware of our insignificance under the heavens. None of us thought of our lives today or the death tomorrow that might already be casting a dark glance towards us. We flew on, wrapped in this enchantment, as if we could float forever in the sky until the end of the world.

'Time passed slowly, with no land in sight. We had been flying above the sea for over an hour and the rocky coast at Deal had yet to appear. I assumed that the wind had driven us northwards. Finally, after an hour and a half, we reached the coast between Harwich and Southend. We reoriented ourselves and turned south-west to follow the north bank of the Thames towards London.'

The air defences awaiting them were in some disarray. The fighter squadrons were at readiness but lack of experience of night-flying, poor aircraft and tactics, and the sheer difficulties of finding the enemy raiders in the vast blackness of the night sky – 'of every eighteen of our pilots that went up in defence, seventeen saw nothing of the enemy' – made their combat patrols an often dispiriting business. Anti-aircraft gun-batteries were in an even more parlous state. Many had not yet been able to replenish their stocks of shells after the sustained fire on the previous nights' raids, the gun-crews were close to exhaustion, and their weariness increased the likelihood of dangerous or fatal mistakes. A loader rendered temporarily deaf and stupid by the continual firing of the guns 'supplied two rounds of wrong ammunition at a critical moment' and another gunner 'placed his hand in the breech of the gun instead of the shell'. As the breech was snapped shut, the man's hand was mangled.

A London air defence commander noted some of the other difficulties. '*First*, the establishments of personnel in the defences had been cut down to the very smallest number of men which would suffice to work the guns; *Secondly*, these men were necessarily of indifferent physique, such as did not permit of their employment at the Front; *Thirdly*, they were hurriedly and recently trained, and were, for the most part, quite un-familiar with military discipline; *Fourthly*, there were no reserves, and it was therefore necessary to keep every man, however exhausted, *at his post at all costs*; *Fifthly*, the greater part of the previous night had already been spent "in action" and, as nothing could be more urgent than the necessity for preparation for further attack, there had been no rest for any member of the defence force for at least twenty-four hours; *Lastly*, and most im-portant, the system of defence which the men were called upon to carry out was of a most elaborate nature, and its successful operation therefore depended absolutely upon the efficient co-operation of many widely scattered individual posts, the failure of any one of which would seriously impair the efficiency of the whole system. If these facts are borne in mind . . . it may perhaps be realised that it was with deep anxiety and a certain diffidence as to our powers that I, on this occasion, received the "warning" that the enemy were again on their way to attack us.'

Although the days were still warm, the approach of winter was casting a chill over the night air. Mist seeped over the dew-sodden ground, filling dips and hollows and tracing the course of streams and rivers. As the Gothas flew on towards London 'searchlights had now come alive every-where on the island, their long white arms reaching menacingly upwards on the horizon. Tendrils of mist lay over the land below us, with only the occasional glimpse of a light breaking the darkness, but looking back towards Sheerness or further south, and everywhere on our flight-path, I saw the same picture: searchlights – gunfire – flares! How many people and machines were on alert and in motion in order to prevent the England Squadron reaching the capital? How many thousands of eyes were looking at us? How many hearts were beating in fear and worry?

'As we overflew brightly-lit airfields I could see fighters taking off in pursuit, but we flew on over open land, towns and cities, determined to reach our target. From the west I saw a thin bank of approaching cloud. Was London covered by this, too? Within minutes the clouds had completely obscured the land below us. We had only the stars above our heads and white, shining mountains and valleys of clouds under our feet.

'Ahead, two, four and ever more of the hungry night eyes of search-lights pierced the darkness, painting white circles on the canopy of the clouds. We were close to the metropolis now. A slight impatience crept over me. I glanced at the bomb levers, leaned over the aircraft's side and peered into the depths. Finally the layers of cloud ended and the first ranks of houses came into view. The defensive fire increased; clouds of shell-bursts hissed past us. Mechanically my hands clutched the machine-gun tighter as my eyes drilled the darkness . . .

'Were those sounds shells exploding or our engines missing a beat? Clouds of smoke and shell-bursts surrounded us as we circled right over the centre of the immense city, surrounded by a curtain of shell-fire. The bends of the Thames and the rows of streets with badly blacked-out lamps were clearly visible. Thirty or forty searchlights swept the sky, groping for us with their long, thin fingers.

'We turned southwards towards the arsenals at Woolwich and the ammunition depots. I pressed down one lever after another, releasing the bombs, then leaned over the side of the aircraft to see the impacts. A fire broke out, small at first, but growing hungrily, lighting up the whole area around it. The deadly searchlights were now closing in on us, missing us at first, but returning again and again until all at once our aircraft was drenched in blinding light. We jinked, dived and swerved, trying to escape the danger, but the cursed lights were holding onto us tightly, and new ones were seeking us too. A few seconds later we were held in the merciless grip of ten or twelve tentacles.

'All evasion had now become pointless. I ducked lower below the edge of the cockpit to avoid being dazzled by the light, searching on all sides for enemy aircraft, for which we would be easy prey. We were flying as fast as this aircraft could go, south of the Thames, heading for the sea. The flak gunners had taken up the battle, spitting fire at us, and each time we escaped one area of searchlights, the next ones picked us up. Our only hope was our lucky star that had shone on us during so many previous flights. We kept flying a straight course, driven on by the need to escape this hell and reach the safety of the open sea.

'London now lay far behind . . . In the distance we saw many airfields and the defensive fire glowing over Chatham. At last we breached the last blockade north of Dover and were out over the sea. The pale crescent of the moon rose higher in the eastern sky. I checked the time – 3.20 a.m.; we had been in the air for more than three hours. Another half an hour and I could see the flares sent up by the guns at Ostend.

'Several enemy searchlights flashed up close to La Panne. I waved my pilot towards them as we wanted to pay them a small visit. We dived towards the emplacements and let our machine-gun fire rain on them. In a split-second the lights were extinguished. We climbed again and took up our old course. The glow of street lights from Blissingen reflected from the distant clouds and our orientation lights shone through the darkness, guiding us home. We had reached Flanders, our safe haven; it was still fast asleep.

'In a while, the outlines of towns and cities became visible, as the line of the dawn inched across the land. I could now make out the long Zeppelin hangar and the buildings at our home airfield. As we spiralled gently towards the earth, I became aware of a bank of fog rolling in from the east – we had to hurry. We were barely 300 metres [1,000 feet] above the ground and preparing to land when suddenly the whole area was blanketed by thick fog.

'The ground-crew at the airfield at once switched on two vertical searchlights to help us estimate the position of the buildings and hangars. As we descended through the fog, we suddenly saw the ghostly shapes of branches and treetops reaching for us. Our pilot immediately climbed again and we circled around the airfield once more.

'The fog showed no sign of thinning, but staying airborne for much longer was impossible; our fuel reserves were almost exhausted. Our pilot tried again to land, making an approach from a direction that in any other circumstances would have been forbidden. We sank into the fog, with no feeling for our position in the air, dropping into the unknown. Our hearts beating close to bursting, we hardly dared breathe or move, three pairs of eyes searching desperately for the first glimpse of the ground through the opaque layers of fog. Death lurked below us, ready to pounce. Seconds lasted for eternities, then: There! The ground! We were safe!

'Friends, engineers and ground-crew came running. We could see the strain in their faces. None of them had thought the crew of the Serpent Machine would make it back alive this time. The hands on my watch had crept to 5.22; our flight had lasted over five hours. Our reports were quickly given to the Night Officer of the squadron, then the car drove us to our nearby quarters. The dog "Bor" that I inherited from my predecessor was the first to greet us in front of the door and then went for an interrogative wander around the rooms to see whether everyone had made it back.

'In the house next to us a window opened quietly; I called to the dog loudly enough for them to recognise my voice; the window was closed again. We were hungry and thirsty and drank tea and ate bread, then emptied a few bottles of good wine to celebrate the life that we had won back.'

Not all were so fortunate. 'Even when all the surviving aircraft had returned and the runway and equipment had been readied for the next launch, still the officers and ground-crew would wait for the missing ones ... We had to endure the agony of uncertainty, not knowing if the missing crews already lay dead, shot down over England or the North Sea, or had managed an emergency landing elsewhere but had not yet been able to send a message. Each engine-note heard in the far distance raised our hopes as we stood silent under the starry night skies; each time the sound faded and died, it buried our hopes with it. The squadron leader remained at the airfield until every one of his men had either reported back or until the elapsed time showed that there was no longer even the faintest possibility that the aircraft could return to our base. As the minutes ticked away, more than once I saw tears trickling down the cheeks of ground-crewmen mourning the death of their young lieutenants.'

The official German report issued later that morning crowed, 'Last night our planes attacked England. Bombs were dropped on military buildings and stores in the heart of London, on Dover, Southend, Chatham and Sheerness, fires gave evidence of the impact.' Although no Giants took part in the raid, ten Gothas had crossed the English coast, four hitting targets in Kent while the other six bombed London.

In addition, one pilot, Immanuel Braun, whose Gotha had been damaged during the previous raid, took off in 'a small aircraft used only for *Spazierfluge* [local flights] which had been sent back from the front lines as it was no longer usable there'. Nursing his fuel, he crossed the Channel, saw 'the hell of shells and shrapnel' over London and dropped his four 12.5kg bombs on Dover. 'It was a great feeling to see such a large part of England below you and everybody frightened to death.' He flew home 'followed by two big naval vessels which fired constantly but either did not see me or did not hit me'. He landed at an airfield near the front lines to refuel and then returned in triumph to his home base.

The barrage from the anti-aircraft guns had sent fourteen thousand shells skywards, once more without recording a single hit, but killing two people and injuring fourteen others in London alone. Many guns 'fired over 500 rounds apiece . . . in many instances the guns were red-hot and fire had to be temporarily ceased to allow them to cool, in spite of the constant streams of water which were poured over them. Everything breakable in the gun-stations quickly succumbed to the constant concussion; the men, in many instances, were temporarily blinded by the flashes of the guns, and deafened by the incessant concussions, until they became entirely bewildered and practically useless.'

Several times guns were silenced by rounds jamming in the overheated weapons; the response was 'instantly given, and was always the same, albeit one which is in no way authorised by the regulations – namely "Jam another round behind it and *fire it out*." Needless to say, on such occasions the gun's crew were instructed to take precautions . . . as the danger of that "heroic" method of clearing the bore of a gun is considerable.'

When some of the gun-batteries ran out of conventional shells, their local commander ordered them to use incendiary shells intended for use against Zeppelins, which emitted 'a cloud of burning gas during a definite portion of their flight'. Although these were ineffective against aircraft, the sight of 'magnificent clouds of burning gas . . . hurtling through the sky' not only misled watching reporters who claimed to have seen enemy aircraft 'falling in flames', but may well have deterred some Gotha crews from continuing with the raid; 'the fact that the attack at once ceased and the retreat began is not thought to be entirely due to the use of that form of ammunition having been adopted', the commander claimed with understandable smugness.

Even using the conventional shells, the cost of each barrage blasted into the sky was enormous. 'A three-inch shell costs at least £2 and the life of a three-inch gun was only some 1,500 rounds. Yet there were occasions when 20,000 rounds were fired in one barrage alone, at a cost of £40,000 and a wastage of thirteen or fourteen guns.' Admiral of the Fleet Hedworth Meux, MP for Plymouth, dismissed the barrage as 'an infernal nuisance' and, to the amusement of his fellow MPs, compared it to his experience of a lunar eclipse in China, when 'tom-toms were beaten and crackers were let off'. When the eclipse ended 'there was general rejoicing, it being assumed that the tom-toms and crackers had driven away the devil from the moon'. Even worse, in Winston Churchill's view, the thousands of artillery pieces ringing the capital were near-useless 'instruments of self-bombardment' – a remark echoed by one irate citizen, who called 'this infernal Barrage . . . a remedy worse than the disease. We have lived under showers of this odious shrapnel (purely home-made) and it is costly in life and property. A woman close to me was killed in bed thereby.'

Another victim of friendly fire was on his way home from work when he heard an air-raid warning and stopped to help the woman owner of a coffee-stall put up her shutters so that she could take cover. As they did so, 'one of our own shells fell on the pavement outside the Wheatsheaf public house in Goldhawk Road, Shepherd's Bush, making the public-house look like a pepper-pot full of holes', and killing him outright. 'A bit of the shell nearly took his leg right off. The woman was more fortunate, she only had two toes taken off. He died thinking of others, although he knew the danger he was in. His name was Thomas Weight.' Seven others met the same fate in that week alone, and sixty-seven were seriously injured. In a single raid shrapnel and shell fragments from anti-aircraft fire damaged three hundred houses, 'about half of them seriously'. Most dangerous of all were the French nineteen-millimetre guns firing only shrapnel for, unlike explosive shells, the shrapnel shell-cases came down intact. 'Many lives were lost and much damage done by the fall of the empty and unbroken shell-cases, which were of more danger to the inhabitants of London than the shrapnel bullets which they had contained ever were to the enemy.' It was yet another source of terror for those huddled in their houses and improvised shelters. The nineteen-millimetre guns were eventually moved to

Birmingham, 'which was not, at the time, considered liable to aeroplane attack'.

Not everyone saw the guns in the same threatening light. Some found the boom of the gun-batteries reassuring, audible evidence that at least someone was fighting back, and Londoners gave 'nicknames to their big guns just as the men do on sections of the Front. The big gun whose voice cracks ceilings, stops clocks and shivers electric lights (if the gun-braggers can be believed) is known as "Fat Hannah". A brazen-voiced virago has been given the singularly gentle name of "Clara". "Bronchial Bill" is the name of another. It is even harder to find the Londoner who doesn't live close to the biggest gun around London than it is not to find the Londoner whose house "they flew right over". When the thunder of the guns at last ceased, it was 'followed by a profound stillness. Not a sound could be heard from the streets of the beating of London's mighty heart. It gave an uncanny feeling of loneliness. We seemed to be in a vast solitude.'

At 7.45 the following night, Monday, 1 October, the silence was torn apart once more as the German bombers returned yet again, in the last and, in financial terms, the most damaging of all 'the raids of the Harvest Moon', continuing until after ten o'clock. The alarm was raised by the men manning a huge new concave 'sound-mirror' carved into the face of the chalk cliffs of Fan Bay, between Dover and St Margaret's. They claimed to have picked up the first faint drone of aircraft at a distance of fifteen to twenty miles, though sceptics claimed that what they were hearing was actually the boom of heavy guns firing around Boulogne. A second twenty-foot double-disc sound mirror on a movable mounting was subsequently installed at Joss Gap near Broadstairs.

A few minutes later the sound of the raiders' engines was heard at other listening stations by observers wearing stethoscopes connected by tubes to two sound locators – 'gramophone trumpets'. The idea was imported from Venice, where the defence against air attack had been aided by 'two microphonic ears on either side of a spade-shaped board, horizontally balanced on a pedestal about five feet high, each of these microphones being telephonically attached to the right and left ears respectively of a skilled listener'. By swivelling the equipment until 'the cadence of sound in each ear is identical, he will then know that he is pointing directly at the aeroplane'.

By the end of 1917, a more sophisticated version was in use in London, using two pairs of twenty-four-inch trumpets, one pair mounted vertically, the other horizontally. By moving them until the sound was of equal intensity in both the listener's ears, it was possible to pinpoint the compass bearing of the noise and its angle to the horizon with surprising accuracy. Many observers were blind men, whose hearing was particularly acute; 'they would now hear for others who so long had seen for them'. Their information was not only used to raise the alarm, but transmitted by radio to the gun-batteries and searchlight stations, allowing them to target the right area of sky, corrected for the 'sound-lag' – the time the aircraft was estimated to have travelled while the noise of its engines was reaching the listener some distance away.

As policemen and volunteer corps roamed the streets with their 'Take Cover' signs, and telephone exchanges spread the air-raid warning to their subscribers, the flight of people from London was even greater than on previous nights. Only eleven of eighteen Gothas actually reached the British coast – an engine failure forced the Serpent Machine of Walter Aschoff to turn back '20 kilometres before Dover' – and five of those failed to find London because of mist and cloud. The remaining six targeted Victoria station, but the bombs missed their mark and landed among the fine houses of Belgravia. One fell in South Eaton Place, damaging over fifty houses and covering the streets with broken glass; another hit Pimlico, damaging a similar number of houses and wrecking St George's Row School, and yet another fell on numbers 2 and 4 Glamorgan Street, 'tenements of twelve rooms each, accommodating a considerable number of persons'. Four men who were standing in the doorway of one of the houses heard the whistle of the falling bomb and dashed inside, but all were killed. Seven people were injured and another eighty-five houses damaged.

A 50kg bomb also fell in the Serpentine and the concussion of the detonating bomb reportedly killed all the fish. Highbury and Edmonton were also bombed. In one house a girl, her father, brothers and sisters had just gone to bed 'when a terrible flash went across my bedroom window. I jumped out of bed and went into my father's bedroom to tell him what had happened. He said, "All right; the first gun we hear, we will get up." I stood at the foot of his bed for a few seconds, when I heard something rushing through the air. It sounded like an express train . . . I had just managed to say "What is it?" when our house collapsed, and several others. I don't remember anything else until I came to in hospital, where I remained six weeks . . . My father, two sisters and brother were all killed.' Another little girl buried in the debris was 'rescued alive after seven hours and taken to hospital with both legs broken'. Eighteen years later, she was 'still an inmate of the lunatic asylum'.

No bombs fell on or near Liverpool Street station but there was a double tragedy as people panicked by the air-raid alarms rushed to take shelter in the Underground. Crowds were still pushing their way in, though the station was in darkness, and special constables were urging them to go back. People were 'climbing over the banisters on the top of people's heads . . . At the bottom of the stairs was a heap of women and children.' Among them were the bodies of a sixty-eight-year-old woman and a little girl, who had been trampled to death.

Once more the anti-aircraft barrage had fired to no effect and fighter pilots had searched vainly for their targets. Once airborne, they were effectively on their own. Radio communication between the ground and the aircraft had again been vetoed by the Admiralty on the grounds that it might interfere with naval signals traffic, and the only guidance that could be given by day were the ground signals, indicating the approximate direction of the enemy aircraft; by night there was nothing. The sound of the German bombers was masked by the noise of the British pilots' own engines, and many took off, flew for two hours and then landed again without glimpsing the enemy at all.

Later that evening a mist spilling from the Thames obscured the city, sparing it further damage as two bombers missed the capital altogether and dropped their bombs around Luton, while the other three abandoned the attempt and bombed Ramsgate, Margate, Sheerness and Harwich instead, but another twelve people had died and damage totalling over £45,000 had been caused.

# CHAPTER 12
# LONDONERS UNNERVED

LONDONERS DID NOT KNOW IT YET, but the Blitz of the Harvest Moon was over. In the space of eight days, six raids had taken place and 5,000kg of bombs had been dropped on London. Sixty-nine people lay dead, four times as many were seriously injured, and damage ran into hundreds of thousands of pounds. The anti-aircraft batteries were on the point of collapse; it had already been necessary to reduce the volume of fire directed at the raiders because of shortages of ammunition and the wear and tear on the guns. Some were already beyond repair, and Lord French warned that if the raids continued with the same frequency and intensity it would not be long before 'the gun defences of the London area ceased to exist'.

Quite apart from the physical effects, the waves of night attacks had also had a psychological impact far in excess of the actual deaths and damage inflicted, causing 'a tendency of a section of the public . . . to give way to panic' that paralysed London for days on end. As a German officer noted with grim satisfaction, the raids had 'yielded excellent results, creating constant panic among the population of London'. Churchill later offered confirmation of the accuracy of that view when he predicted that three or four million people would flee the capital under a renewed onslaught from the England Squadron. Coupled with the U-boat campaign that was decimating Britain's merchant fleet and severely disrupting supplies of food, raw and war materials, this dual offensive 'awoke in Britain a realisation of the possibility of defeat, not of the armed forces in France but of the British will to war . . . The Gotha offensive bypassed not only the strength of the BEF as a whole but also the bulk of the RFC, just as the submarine offensive bypassed the strength of the Grand Fleet.'

Although jingoistic newspapers continued to claim that Londoners were displaying the traditional British stiff upper lip in the face of the bombing, their claims rang increasingly hollow. An American engineer, probably as dispassionate a witness as could be found, noted that 'the September air-raids with their constant recurrence have aroused extraordinary fear among all classes of the population . . . Domestic servants have left their employers, the omnibus and tram employees refused to go on night duty and abandoned their vehicles as soon as the alarm was sounded. The working classes, whose night's rest is perpetually broken, failed to go to work, schoolchildren had to be given permission to sleep during school hours. As soon as there was a moon, it became impossible to use the underground railways for huge crowds of women and children besieged the entrances and staircases and remained below, usually for the night, until finally forcibly expelled by the police. This led to big disturbances which in some cases ended in serious riots.'

There was a widespread and sometimes justified feeling that the whole truth about the raids was not being told: 'on Saturday and Sunday more raids, and on Monday [1 October] a very bad one of which the papers suppress details'. Rumours also grew wilder in the telling: the asylums were said to be 'full of nervous cases', and the reported statement by 'a doctor in London' that 'after an aerial attack there were 28,000 cases of nervous breakdowns and nerve-shock, which would require from three to ten months to cure' can scarcely have allayed the feelings of panic. Rather more credibly, the *Morning Post* reported that on a single day there were eight cases of suicide, which 'at the Coroner's Inquest were ascribed to "nerve collapse, following on the air-raids"'.

Although not recorded in the official casualty figures, many other deaths were attributable to the effects of the raids. After a bomb exploded near her, a woman of forty-two, though unwounded, was taken home 'in a collapsed condition' and died soon afterwards. 'Death was due to cerebral haemorrhage which brought on a fit and apoplexy, and the doctor was of the opinion that this was probably caused by the excitement of the raid and consequent fear.' The deaths of Rosa Silverman and 'Eliza Revell, a widow' were also said to have been 'hastened by the excitement' of an air-raid, and John Ward, 'a linen buyer on the staff of Messrs Hitchcock, Williams & Co, who had been with the firm for some sixty years, died from shock' due to a false alarm of another air-raid, two days after an actual attack on London. Gertrude Binstead, 'very much terrified by the raid', died of a heart attack, and Louise Alice Budd, the thirty-four-year-old wife of a Quartermaster Sergeant in the Machine-gun Corps, committed suicide at her house in Streatham Hill after she was 'terribly frightened last Saturday by the air-raid over London. She was of a very nervous temperament indeed.'

Lord Curzon's alleged sneering comment that the people of London had been 'cowering in cellars' during the air-raids was widely reviled, but the effect of the bombing had both 'filled the Tubes and raised the rents in Maidenhead and Brighton' as many affluent Londoners fled the capital. One woman had been as far as Lyme Regis, but 'after thorough and patient search we had found it quite impossible to get apartments. You see, it was safely out of the raided area and people were flocking in this direction . . . At Weymouth people were sleeping in bathing-vans, stations and even the gaol – unless I had actually proved it, I should not have found it possible to believe.'

The reaction of Londoners to the stress of repeated raids seemed to bear out Trenchard's opinion (expressed after the war) that 'the moral effect of bombing, especially night bombing, does not decrease with experience. I have often heard people say that, although the moral effect of bombing may be very great for the first two or three times, people soon get used to it. Personally, I believe the reverse is the case.'

There was no doubt that Londoners had been 'put to the test' by the raids, one young woman wrote, 'and I confess we might have shown our-selves to better advantage'. 'Our nerves have been somewhat shaken. For a week German airmen . . . succeeded in seriously disorganising the lives of the whole population. As soon as the signal "Take Cover" is heard, one by one the taxis stop and refuse to take up passengers, the buses turn out their lights and line up in some wide thoroughfare, the Underground trains cease running and the stations are darkened. And one is stranded.'

Children in Kent had to get up 'in terror in the night, the dreadful anti-aircraft barrage from Faversham, Conyer, Sheerness and Chatham, night after night. And we had double doses, for after they had gone up towards town, we had to wait for them to come back (with the same accompaniment) before our "all clear" was sounded. In the mornings, in school, we fell asleep, and were encouraged to do so by the teachers. We slept on our desks, knowing that we should get very little sleep in the night. It was so regular that we children came to look on it as part of our lives to sleep in school.' Schoolchildren also practised air-raid drills 'crouching under our desks in case the enemy should attack in school hours'.

Their elders were often just as terrified. One air-raid started during a concert at an infants school, at which the audience was 'mainly wounded soldiers in hospital blue. When the guns started booming, many of the soldiers collapsed and were taken into the corridor ... The sight of those soldiers fainting has stayed with me always – it made us little ones begin to realise.' Some children were born during air-raids. The 'poor mother' of one, not able to get up, 'lay trembling in bed; we children huddled underneath, thinking our last hour had come'.

Those living on the outskirts of the capital witnessed a nightly diaspora of terrified Londoners fleeing the city. 'On the Saturday night of one harrowing week in September 1917, a week of perfect weather, the nights being brilliant with the glories of a full moon, London was raided. On Sunday they came again and on Monday evening the late trains brought to our south-western suburb a crowd of distracted creatures from those parts of London which had suffered most. They stayed in our neighbourhood that night and went back on the Tuesday morning. That night another raid came, and on Wednesday evening. Again dozens of terrified families poured out of our station. I remember them going through the street to camp in the fields.

'By the end of the week, hundreds of nerve-shattered and hollow-eyed mothers and families were spending the night in the fields, because the houses were crowded. As each night closed in, more and more of the strangers arrived. I heard some pray for deliverance and saw mothers hold up their hands and curse the brilliant moon. The natives of that part felt the strain, and soon we children were terrified of going to bed. On the Sunday a storm of wind and rain arose. The people gazed up at the ragged clouds and blessed the wind, and began to trickle back to their homes in London. I never see the full moon without remembering that ghastly week.'

Even in rural areas 'careful preparations' against air-raids were being made, in 'remote villages, preparations far more effective than in parts which ought to be considered natural targets. This probably does little harm but ... the first and real duty of villages is to consider how many refugees they can take.'

It was easy for those in the remoter suburbs and districts outside London to appeal for more of the British 'bulldog spirit' in the face of the bombs. The vast majority of those in the shadow of the nightly raids, however, lived in constant dread and fear that could rapidly escalate into blind panic. 'The noise of the guns and shells bursting and the bombs exploding was terrific . . . Women simply went off their heads and were difficult to control. I locked my lot, wife and all, in the kitchen, but in less than half a minute they were out through the window.' The postmaster of King's Cross Road Post Office, close to the site of a bomb-blast, spoke of 'his little son, who had said he wasn't frightened, but nevertheless was now unable to button his clothes owing to loss of power in his hands caused by the nervous strain of the frequent air attacks'.

There was precious little evidence of any 'blitz spirit' under this air assault. 'The prevailing feeling in political circles was that if the German raids continued unabated, the British will to continue the war would crumble.' Sir Malcolm Campbell, an RFC pilot during the war, also admitted how close events came 'to cracking the morale of London . . . The "stop the war" cry was heard far more frequently than was flattering to our belief in the sticking-to-it qualities of our people. Who that lived or spent any time in London . . . will ever forget the scenes of panic terror to be seen immediately the warning maroons were exploded?' Sickeningly, there were people who saw opportunity and profit in the terror of the city's population. 'Whilst the scared people are away from their homes, the roughs go in and pillage food, clothing or anything portable. Surely the war calamities are enough without such grievous wickedness.'

The widespread credence given to ever wilder and more alarming rumours about German secret weapons – poison gases or poisons disguised as cakes or sweets – also gave a fair indication of the state of the public mood, and the paranoia was further fuelled when a series of alleged incidents was splashed across the front pages of the popular press. Special Constable A. Aldridge produced 'two chocolate sweetmeats' found after an air-raid which he thought 'might contain poison, and probably dropped from hostile aircraft'. A sceptical Home Office official carried out a series of tests which, while their academic rigour might have been challenged, seemed to point to the correct conclusion. 'There appears to have been no direct evidence of these things having been dropped from aircraft and I think the condition in which they were found is pretty conclusive evidence . . . Two of the chocolates, which I return herewith, have been dropped down the Home Office stairs and in spite of their somewhat solid construction they show palpable signs of this treatment, while the others are quite undamaged. We do not propose, therefore, to spend money in having these things analysed.'

Other officials were less sceptical. A 'liquorice lozenge' was 'seen to fall in Greenwich when the aircraft was over. The man who reported it (a chemist in the employ of the South Metropolitan Gas Co.) had been struck in the face by it. In the early afternoon the lozenge (looking like an ordinary "Pontefract Cake") was received from New Scotland Yard in a bottle.' Along with another twenty or thirty sweets of various kinds 'found at Limehouse', the liquorice lozenge was sent for analysis.

'Some gelatine sweets in two lots, each having some paper adherent to it' were found near Waltham Cross in Hertfordshire, and once more they were 'presumed dropped from an enemy aeroplane . . . From the position of the bag and the manner in which the sweets were scattered, I concluded that they had fallen from a height.' They too were passed to the Government analyst. All were examined for 'pathological bacteria or poison . . . typhoid, cholera, glanders or Malta fever . . . anthrax, tetanus . . . smallpox, but no trace was found'. Two calves and two rabbits were also injected with 'the solutions and sediments of the sweets in saline' without ill effects.

The scientific debunking of these stories did not prevent their dissemination. Next there were accounts from Calais of hundreds of poisoned cakes 'resembling "Madeleines" . . . covered with a substance resembling chocolate icing, which the chemists are analysing', and the *Daily Mail* carried a report about 'poisoned soup powder' having been dropped in Paris by German aeroplanes. 'Analysis has shown that the packets contain an extremely violent poison and *Le Temps* states that all the families who took the soup have died.' The *Mail* then went on to claim that children in eastern France had been 'killed by poisoned sweets and explosive pencil-cases dropped from aeroplanes'. A Home Office official noted the report: 'I am trying to find out the truth about this . . . The German authorities . . . do not seem to regard the use of such things among the civil population as a contingency to be excluded.' Just as in the other cases, the scare story enjoyed far greater currency than the subsequent admission that scientific analysis had showed 'that no poison of any sort was present'.

Not to be outdone by its rival, the *Daily Express* reported that, after 'a curious patter was heard' on the roofs of houses in Southend, sweets 'about the size of sparrow eggs' had been found. The local Medical Officer of Health had detected 'traces of arsenic' in them. The *Daily Graphic* took up the story the next day with even greater relish, quoting an unnamed official at the War Office as saying that there was 'reliable evidence' that the sweets had come from a German aircraft, and the *Daily Mirror* referred to the same 'arsenic-loaded sweets' the following day. It was left to the *Globe* to defuse the story, reporting that the sweets 'could not have been dropped from an enemy aircraft' and that the 'small trace of arsenic discovered on analysis . . . was probably due to the presence of the poison in the glucose which was used in their manufacture, an impurity frequently met with, but without significance'. None of the other papers chose to publish the correction, which allowed fear and rumour to grow.

Already concerned about the collapse in public morale, incensed Home Office officials launched an investigation. 'These reports of poisoned sweets have been rife and this "official" confirmation was particularly unfortunate. The reports have been contradicted by the Secretary of State in the House of Commons but it is very difficult to catch up such stories when once they have got hold.' An official who interviewed the *Graphic* reporter thought 'from his statements and manner he concocted the whole story' of War Office confirmation; after representations to the editor, the 'delinquent reporter . . . a shifty young man' was sacked.

Poisoned sweets were not the only subject of wild rumour. Even the august *Times* was persuaded that 'the latest production of [Germany's] highly skilled scientists is the *Nebelbomben* (the fog bomb) to be used "when the big attack on London takes place". Workers in the factories who are usually so secretive are as enthusiastic as schoolboys over the successful experiments made with the new contrivance, which explodes in the air and sheds over a large area a fog-like cloud sufficiently dense to obscure the airship from the rays of the most powerful searchlights.'

There was no shred of evidence to back up this story, but claims that the Germans were using poison-gas bombs seemed to be justified when an inquest was held at Wateringbury police station on a ten-week-old baby, Lilian Alice Trower, 'who died in a hop-pickers' hut at Green Farm, Nettlestead'. She had been sheltering with her parents in a Shoreditch flour mill when 'several bombs were dropped . . . and gas and sulphur fumes penetrated into the building'. The baby died the following night. The coroner's jury returned a verdict that 'death was caused by irritant gases caused by bombs dropped from enemy aircraft at Shoreditch', but the Metropolitan Police dismissed the suggestion. 'Had there been any testimony whatsoever in support of the gassing theory, we should have told you so . . . Many houses were hit and gas mains damaged and it is not impossible that the child may have been thus affected. There is no gas in the flour mills and enquiry fails to disclose that any of the persons taking refuge there were affected by gas from the bombs.'

The only authentically toxic substance that could with confidence be linked to the German bombs was the greenish-yellow powder associated with TNT. Workers in British munitions factories were often derisively referred to as 'canaries' because of their yellow skin colouring caused by exposure to TNT dust. The flippant nickname concealed a deadly threat. Even though women workers wore 'rubber gloves, mob-caps, respirators and leggings' and coated their faces with flour and starch to protect them, their skin still turned yellow and there were fifty-two deaths from 'toxic jaundice' in 1916 alone.

The detonation of high-explosive bombs smothered every surface in TNT powder. Although not fatal in small doses, it was a potent irritant and the Government even offered guidance, reported in *The Times*, on how to avoid injury from 'Air Bomb Powder'. 'The removal of the powder from surfaces on which it has fallen is best effected by a weak alkaline solution; one teaspoonful of soda (bicarbonate or ordinary washing soda) to a quart of water. The powder should not be mixed with ordinary dust as it might be sent to a destructor and possibly cause damage. The explosive should be mixed with earth and buried . . . It is better not to wear gloves to handle the powder, as the glove soon becomes penetrated with the powder and the skin is more easily irritated. Moist rags are best employed. If the skin of the hands is stained, an endeavour should be made to remove the stain at once with pumice stone and the soda solution. At the first sign of inflammation of the skin, i.e., small swellings containing fluid and irritation, a doctor should be consulted.'

Even without fears about poisoned sweets, toxic powders and noxious gases, many Londoners were simply too frightened by the prospect of further air-raids to leave their homes. Beckton School's log for the week of the Harvest Moon raids noted 'Attendance very poor due to air-raid of last evening', and later in the week 'only thirty per cent of children came in answer to the bell'.

Adults were no less frightened. Munitions workers could not be 'compared with the steel-hardened mass into which fighting troops are forged', and 'nothing even remotely approaching the casualties required to destroy the moral[e] of an army' was required to demoralize 'the un-disciplined civilian workers of all ages and sexes, in a war-factory'. When Winston Churchill, who had become Minister of Munitions in July 1917, asked for a report on the effects of the raids on output from Woolwich Arsenal, it disclosed that between 53 and 73 per cent of the night-shifts in the various sections of the arsenal had failed to turn up for work on the night of 24 September, the first of the Harvest Moon raids. Production was even worse affected, suggesting that those who did turn up had their minds more on self-preservation than filling munitions. In the sections manufacturing rifle-grenade cartridges, 7.62mm ammunition and .303 rounds, for example, output was respectively only one-quarter, one-fifth and one-sixth of the normal rate. Even though the raids took place at night, the output of the next day-shifts was also significantly lower.

Throughout the rest of the week absenteeism remained high and out-put well below normal, and Churchill concluded that it was 'typical of what was taking place over a wide area'. Seventy-five per cent of munitions workers stopped work altogether throughout the lengthy period between an air-raid warning being given and the sounding of the All Clear, and, though the claim that air-raids over London 'had reduced our output of munitions from the metropolitan area by almost fifty per cent' was prob-ably an overstatement, a more credible estimate suggested that as much as one-sixth of the total war production of Britain's munitions factories might have been lost as a result of air-raid disruption. 'On receipt of air-raid warnings – and there were many false alarms – work was suspended, sometimes over vast industrial areas, traffic was disorganised and an adverse moral effect was produced both on the workers and on the population.'

Other industries were equally affected. A single raid caused the Great Western Railway's services 'in the London and Birmingham districts' aggregate delays of 195 hours to passenger traffic and 650 hours to goods traffic, yet 'the only damage done to the company's property was a small fire ... readily extinguished'. In Birmingham, bombed by Zeppelins but never by aircraft, an attempt to give nineteen key industries advance warning by telephone of air-raids was vetoed by the management of the factories involved, who argued that 'it would be practically impossible to prevent this knowledge becoming known throughout the works without panic and disorganisation. The workmen would discontinue their work for that day at least. This warning would have to be given ... on a very large number of occasions on which enemy aircraft would not visit this neighbourhood and on each occasion the output of practically the whole of the city would come to a standstill. The loss to the general output of the country and the injury to the morale of the workpeople would be immense.'

The largest clothing manufacturer in England, whose factories were sited in the East End, complained that the result of a single raid, 'or even of a warning, was that the factories ceased to work for twenty-four hours, as the workers could not be induced to return that day. If the raid took place at night, the work for the ensuing forty-eight hours was seriously affected.' During the Harvest Moon raids 'work ceased almost entirely, output dropping from 40,000 suits to 5,000'. Iron and steel works suffered even worse disruption. Not only was production lost as a result of the raids and the attendant absenteeism, but the interruptions could also cause severe damage to furnaces and equipment, and even the destruction of the entire plant. After three raids in rapid succession, one company warned that 'the position at our blast furnaces on each of the nights was one of extreme gravity, the whole of the plant being in positive danger of destruction by explosion at times'.

False alarms and rumours of raids heightened the problem of absenteeism. A report of a phantom Zeppelin off Scarborough on 10 February 1916 led to factories as far away as Gloucester stopping work and railway lights being extinguished in Nottingham, Bath and Worcester. The problem of false alarms became so serious that a law was passed under the Defence of the Realm Act making it a criminal offence 'punishable by fine or imprisonment, to spread false reports of an air-raid warning'. However, much of the blame for the mass panic that saw people fleeing their homes and places of work at the first rumour of a raid was laid at the door of the press: 'panic paid the newspapers'.

Two papers even suggested that Prime Minister David Lloyd George had abandoned his official duties and fled to his country home. He at once sued and received damages and 'unreserved apologies'. He also summoned newspaper editors to a meeting at which he pointed out that, over the previous eighteen months, six times as many Britons had been killed in traffic accidents as in air-raids, and then ordered them to moderate their lurid accounts of the bombing and in particular to cease publishing photographs of bomb damage, which he regarded as particularly in-flammatory. Laws were hastily pushed through Parliament requiring owners of bombed-out buildings to erect hoardings to screen them from passers-by and ghoulish sightseers, and a Defence of the Realm regulation allowed Government and local authorities to requisition suitable buildings for use as bomb shelters.

It was unfair to blame the press for mass panic; Londoners did not need to read the papers to feel the impact of German bombs, hear the screams of wounded and dying and see the darkness torn apart by explosions and fires. The terror that gripped London's citizens during the relentless Harvest Moon raids was entirely understandable, for they had neither expected nor experienced such an airborne 'blitz' before. It had been carried out by an astonishingly small number of aircraft. Only ninety-seven bombers had taken off for London that week, and of those only fifty-five reached the English coast, the rest falling victim to the mechanical failures inevitable when pushing such new technology up to and even beyond its limits. The bombers were also operating at the limit of their range. Thirteen were lost – the majority to mechanical failure or crashes on landing rather than the air defences – and only twenty actually reached London. Yet this tiny number of bombers was enough to paralyse the capital.

The incessant raids fed the public thirst for revenge and reprisals against Germany. Even the normally restrained *Financial News* was now warning that 'the longer the question of reprisals is shelved, the greater will be the dissatisfaction of the general public over the delay. And this may finish in a revolt which will either shake some of our dilatory rulers into energy or else sweep them from office.'

The only reprisal raids being staged were the day and night raids flown by British bombers operating on the Western Front against the bases in occupied Belgium from which the Gothas and Giants flew every night. As Walter Aschoff remarked, 'we appear to lie damn heavy on their stomachs'. On 29 September, the old Zeppelin hangar at Gontrode was set ablaze, and the following night a hangar at St Denijs-Westrem was ignited by a bomb, causing a fire that could be seen from thirty miles away. Whenever an unfamiliar engine-note was heard, signalling the arrival of British aircraft over the England Squadron's bases, there was 'a wild rush for the dugout; those who do not reach it throw themselves flat on the ground'. As soon as the raiders had dropped their bombs and the sound of their engines had faded, the ground-crews hurried out of the dugout to search for craters that might be ten or twelve feet deep. If there was time, they would roll out farm-carts loaded with rocks and gravel to repair the runway for the returning Gothas and Giants. If that was not possible, the position of the landing lights was altered 'so that there should be no bomb-holes in the path of any machine landing'.

Kleine responded to the raids by dispersing his flights to other air-fields near Ghent – Staffeln 13 and 14 transferred to Mariakerke, and 17 and 18 to Oostakker – but the attacks appeared to have no significant impact on the ability of the England Squadron to launch raids on London, and in any event, the British public would not be pacified by the mere bombing of German airfields. They wanted retaliation in kind, targeting German cities and German civilians. One newspaper summed up the popular feeling. 'There unfortunately are days when the enemy and not the British government acts on Cromwell's doctrine "A word and a blow, but the blow first" . . . The effective method of protecting our large towns and in particular our poor districts, is to attack the Germans in their own homes. Instead of doing that we have all through permitted them to attack

us, and East London and Thanet have suffered to please the sentimentalists. To those who honestly and sincerely oppose operations against
German towns, we would give this word of counsel: their duty, it seems to
us, if they hold these views, is to go and live in the area constantly attacked
and threatened . . . The *Berliner Tageblatt* has pointed out "the measures of
air defence taken in England demand considerable personnel and much
material. Numberless defence stations have been created which require the
attention of many thousands of officers and men, including the crews
needed for handling the guns and manipulating the searchlights." All these
are detained in Britain by Germany's plan of attack, but in Germany not a
man is kept at home. The policy of our sentimentalists has not only killed
and wounded many hundreds of British women and children, it has also
deprived our generals at the front of a whole army corps.'

The preferred targets for reprisal raids were spelled out by one newspaper correspondent with chilling logic. 'The only possible rejoinder, if
enemy aircraft killed our women and children, was for us to kill theirs,
preferably in greater quantity. But it must be the right sort of women and
children whom we kill. Small-town folk are no good at all, because they are
not of much account in any case and the vocal efforts of the insignificant
can be disregarded, while those of more important sections of the
community can be loud and resonant.' A second correspondent made a
similarly brutal calculation: 'Another very strong reason for concentrating
on working-class areas is that these are usually very badly built. The high-
explosive and the incendiary bomb are infinitely more effective against
"boxes of bricks" than against steel-framed modern buildings.'

Early that summer of 1917, C. G. Grey, the editor of *The Aeroplane*
magazine, had called for the wider use of air power, but in attacks targeted
on German war production. 'Behind Germany's army lie the sources from
which it is fed. The iron mines, the steel works, the armament factories . . .
lie within reach . . . Instead of bowing to popular clamour for reprisals –
mere retaliatory raids in revenge after every enemy attack – let us take the
invasion of Germany from the air as a serious problem of the war.' In
the inflammatory atmosphere that followed the raids, such reasoned arguments were never likely to hold sway. Grey might remark that 'the very
word "reprisal" is enough to make one sick', but that was precisely what the

public wanted. A mass meeting sponsored by the *Daily Express* protested 'the brutality and horror of high-explosive bombs being dropped upon small children who were blown about like bloody rags', and the Lord Mayor of London, chairing the meeting, proposed a resolution demanding that Lloyd George's Government 'initiate immediately a policy of ceaseless air attacks on German towns and cities'. It won overwhelming support.

During the Harvest Moon raids riots had broken out in the streets of London, and following a rowdy gathering on Tower Hill a telegram 'paid for by the pennies of the people' was sent to the King, asking him 'to instruct your Ministers at once to make vigorous and continual air attacks on German towns and cities'. If the Government would not do so, the King was urged to 'dissolve Parliament and appoint Ministers who will do their duty'. If all else failed, the telegram advocated revival of the system of 'Letters of Mark' granted to state-sponsored pirates such as Sir Francis Drake in Elizabethan times, so that 'privateers of the air' could 'carry havoc and destruction as reprisals into Germany'. The 'League of Londoners' was formed at the same time. Lord Tenterden, addressing its first rally, complained that Britain had been 'fighting too much under Queensberry rules and the time has come when we should attack the Germans with "knuckledusters"'.

Cecil Lewis of 56 Squadron, who won the Military Cross for his valour in air combat, did not share the popular revulsion at the German 'baby-killers' who had 'laid their explosive eggs' on London. 'Actually that raid was a very stout effort, and nobody in their right mind would deny that the Germans were perfectly right to bomb the capital of the British Empire. Their objectives were Woolwich, Whitehall, the Houses of Parliament – the very nerve-centres of the whole organism. The Allies would have bombed Berlin without hesitation if they had happened to have machines good enough to get there. [The Gothas] did not actually do very extensive damage but their appearance was quite enough to scare the civilian population very thoroughly and raise an outcry. Barbarians! Dastards! Bombing open towns! Waging war against defenceless women and children! The daily hymn of hate rose to a frightening scream.'

Another airman, a future Air Commodore, remarked that 'indirectly we were baby-killers too, of a much higher order, by inducing food shortage in the enemy country' (through the blockade of Germany's coast). General Sir Ian Hamilton also argued both then and after the war that the 'fierce anger against the Germans . . . is unjust. The soldier who pulled the trigger was not letting death fall at random from the sky . . . we were at war.' He went on to advance the theory, adopted decades later by some advocates of nuclear weapons, that the development of ever more sophisticated and horrific weapons would end in the elimination of war altogether. 'Go on improving arms, go on preparing to kill babies and you will put an end to wars of the future. Your little martyrs of Poplar have taken the first step.'

The citizens of Poplar were unlikely to appreciate the subtleties of such arguments; their mayor's warning that Britain was 'a nation of lions governed by asses . . . unless the Government are extremely careful they will find themselves heading for a revolution' was probably a more accurate reflection of his fellow citizens' opinions. Already alarmed by the gathering revolution in Russia and the unrest in France that had seen four cavalry divisions deployed to 'break strikes and suppress agitation', Lloyd George, ever attentive to the popular mood, chose the occasion of a visit to bomb-damaged areas to promise the mob that surrounded him, 'We will give it all back to them, and we will give it to them soon. We shall bomb Germany with compound interest.' In a note to General Haig, Sir William Robertson was scathing about the Prime Minister's 'most harrowing description of . . . the sight of blood on the walls. They really lost all sense of proportion.'

In the face of the crisis, the commander of the Royal Flying Corps, Major General Hugh Trenchard, was recalled from France by an imperious summons sent to Haig on 1 October 1917: 'Continuous aircraft raids on England are causing interruption in munitions work and having some effect on general public. Cabinet desire immediate action against those German objectives which can be reached from neighbourhood of Nancy. Send Trenchard over at once to me to discuss scale on which you can undertake these operations and necessary arrangements for them.'

When Trenchard arrived in England early the next morning, he had an immediate sight of the terror and collapsing morale the German air-raids were causing. A flight of three RE8 aircraft brought him and some of his staff officers across the Channel. They 'took off in visibility that worsened as they approached the English coast', and the sound of their engines was enough to set off air-raid warnings throughout the south-east, sending Londoners fleeing in terror. Trenchard's aircraft made an emergency landing at Lympne near Folkestone and he was driven to London from there, but another pilot flew on over the Thames and was met with 'a violent barrage from all the aircraft guns along its course'. Panic-stricken Londoners had meanwhile packed the Underground stations and public buildings or fled into the parks. The streets were still largely deserted when Trenchard reached London later that morning. He was 'amazed at the half-empty pavements and thoroughfares. As a portent of nervous confusion in high places, the spectacle was not reassuring.' He was still less amused to see the way in which a few misidentified aeroplanes could bring the nation's capital to a virtual halt. The All Clear was not sounded until two that afternoon.

Lloyd George lectured Trenchard on the vital importance of re-taliatory air-raids on Germany to lift 'the morale of the people at home', and he showed no outward dissent while facing the Prime Minister, assuring him that the first bomber airfield at Ochey, near Nancy, was ready and that RFC bombers would be able to begin operations six days after arriving there. However, the man whose 'loud grunting noises . . . when anyone addressed him and he had nothing to say' had caused him to be nicknamed 'The Camel' was still dismissive of the military value of strategic bombing and shared with Haig a detestation of moving any military resources away from the battlefields where the Third Battle of Ypres (Passchendaele) was still in full flow. Despite his agreement to retaliatory raids, Trenchard confided to a journalist that 'the long-range bombing squadrons are not ready yet, and will not be till winter', and after his return to France he insisted that he would not 'alter his offensive battlefield tactics until the present operations are suspended'. Although the British attack was already drowning in Flanders mud, Haig showed no sign of doing that.

The original commander of the military wing of the RFC, Major Frederick Sykes, had an altogether more acute appreciation of the strategic value of aircraft. Sykes 'never thought that bombing alone' could win the war, but 'it could have crippled industrial and aeronautical production and destroyed communications. It could have increased war-weariness and, used correctly, it would have shortened the war.' However, he and Trenchard were bitter rivals and any course of action favoured by Sykes would have been opposed by Trenchard on instinct alone.

Sykes's opinions and advice went unheeded and both Haig and Trenchard remained in 'complete harmony' in their view that aircraft had only a tactical role, not a strategic one. When the Admiralty – which, through the Royal Naval Air Service, had been carrying out limited bombing operations in Germany – had proposed basing 'at least 200 bombers in France', Trenchard had condemned it as 'a luxury of war' and Haig had sent 'a real snorter' of a letter to the Cabinet, demanding that priority be given instead to the production of aircraft for air defence and ground-attack over the front lines. A further proposal to bomb German cities by Sir William Weir, Secretary of State at the Ministry of Munitions, received the withering dismissal from Trenchard, 'You prove that your factories can deliver the machines, then leave the bombing to me.'

Even if Haig and Trenchard had not been so obstructive, barely any British aircraft suitable for strategic bombing had been produced. In December 1914 Winston Churchill, then First Lord of the Admiralty, who 'had the foresight to see that large planes were necessary to carry war into other countries', commissioned Sir Frederick Handley-Page to design and build a heavy bomber. Problems in developing the aircraft delayed its production until November 1916, and though it proved an impressive aircraft – faster, longer-ranged and capable of carrying a heavier bombload than the German Gothas – by September 1917 only eighteen were in service, all with the RNAS, assigned to the naval squadrons in Dunkirk. The RFC did not order a single one until compelled by Cabinet demands for reprisal raids. As C. G. Grey complained, 'The Germans have developed a special branch of warfare which we have neglected in a manner which can only be described as idiotic . . . It was never worth the while of any designer to design a machine specially for bombing because the authorities did not want it . . . and yet we are surprised when the German goes to the trouble of building as good a bombing machine as he knows how, and proceeds to use it for the purpose for which it was built.'

That purpose – the complete devastation of London – had yet to be achieved, but the raids of the Harvest Moon had still brought the city to the brink of collapse.

# CHAPTER 13
# AIR DEFENCE REVISITED

THE NIGHTS OF BRIGHT MOONLIGHT had now ended for another month, and as deteriorating weather prevented further raids by the England Squadron, both sides had an opportunity to assess the results of the Blitz of the Harvest Moon. German pride in the success of the raids was reflected on 4 October 1917 when Kleine at last achieved his ambition: 'the squadron's performances and the glorious example of its Commander were honoured by the Supreme Commander with the award to Kleine of the highest war decoration, the Pour le Mérite'. Walter Aschoff noted that the award had produced 'great joy in the whole squadron. We celebrated this event appropriately that night in Drory.'

However, privately German commanders were less euphoric than their public pronouncements might have suggested. Although Gotha losses in combat had been relatively modest and not a single Giant had crashed or been shot down, the disaster of 28 September, when nine Gothas were lost, weighed heavily against the perceived benefits of the London raids. Such levels of losses could not be sustained. The morale of the British people had clearly been badly affected by the bombing and there had been substantial disruption to war production, but the decisive blow had yet to be struck.

The Fire Plan had failed so far and could scarcely be implemented when the incendiaries supplied by German manufacturers were of such dubious quality and reliability. In the absence of a new Great Fire of London, there were insufficient signs of the wholesale mass panic and civil disturbances that would force Britain to the negotiating table. Had the German authorities produced aircraft and ordnance in the quantity and quality that the commanders of the England Squadron had requested and expected, a different outcome might already have been obtained, but 'neither the strength of the squadron, nor the properties of the bomber aeroplanes and amount of bombs available, were adequate to have a really devastating effect'. The steady attrition of aircraft and air-crew was also too heavy a burden upon a squadron already stripped of many of its most experienced pilots. Kleine had pursued his task with dogged and sometimes foolish persistence, but he was now coming to realize that, with the resources currently available to him, the frequency and weight of the raids on England could not be increased sufficiently to achieve the aim of the complete demoralization of London's population.

On the British side, although the gun-batteries had poured thousands of shells into the sky, usually in vain, and the patrolling fighters had found German raiders as elusive as moths in the darkness, a coherent defensive system was forming. If the bombers were not being shot down in large numbers, their targeting was being disrupted by the altitudes at which they were being forced to fly. Many were also being deterred from even approaching London by the gun-barrages and the prowling fighters.

The Harvest Moon raids had also led to one further modification to London's air defences: the installation of balloon barrages. Balloons were already in use in Germany and in Venice, where they were attached to rafts floating on the canals to protect the city from attack by Austrian aircraft. Edward Ashmore's innovation was to link a number of balloons together to form a barrage, each one comprising 'three Caquot captive balloons, 500 yards apart, connected by a horizontal wire from which were suspended at twenty-five-yard intervals, steel wires 1,000 feet in length', 'in the pious hope', as Cecil Lewis remarked, 'that some unfortunate Hun might fly into their cables. (We all regarded this as ludicrous.)'

Initial trials of the system were not encouraging. A test in Richmond Park saw gusts of winds tear the balloons from their moorings, carrying two riggers aloft. One, Air Mechanic W. J. Pegge, working a thousand feet above the earth, fell to his death almost immediately; the other man, H. E. James, clung on for some time but then also plunged to his death 'from an immense height' as the runaway balloons, still rising, were swept over Croydon.

Despite this inauspicious beginning, the lumbering whale-shapes of barrage balloons trailing their curtains of steel cables far below them, and straining against their tethering ropes as the wind caught them, were soon a familiar sight in the sky. Despite Cecil Lewis's scathing comment, the aim was not so much to entangle aircraft in the cables – though that would have been a welcome bonus – as to 'deny to an enemy the lower air', forcing the raiders to an altitude where their bomb-aiming would be less accurate; moreover, 'induced to fly in the narrow range of heights between the aprons and the ceiling of their machines', 'both guns and fighters could engage them with a reasonable expectation of success'. Lewis guns were also added to the armoury of the anti-aircraft batteries to stop raiders from 'descending below heights at which anti-aircraft gunfire ceased to be effective'. By early October ten balloon screens had been set up. Another ten had been planned, but they were never installed.

Improvements were also made to the range-finding and targeting of gunfire from the anti-aircraft gun-batteries. In the early stages of the air campaign, Army- and Navy-trained gunners used the standard-issue range-finders and the traditional methods of their services, which assumed that the target, located in two dimensions, would not move appreciably in the one minute or so it took to calculate (from the shots already fired) how the gun should be trained. This system was useless when firing at a target such as an aircraft that was both relatively fast-moving and operating in three-dimensional space.

The key was to establish a means of determining the height of the target aircraft, and eventually a method was developed that used simultaneous measurements from two conventional range-finders, modified to determine the angle of sight, and located at sighting stations around a mile apart. They were in radio communication with each other, and with a 'plotting station' where the information was computed and relayed to every gun-battery in the area. While the target was still tracked by eye, the elevation of the gun-barrels and timing of the fuses was adjusted in the light of the information from the plotting room.

Other proposals to improve London's defences, of varying credibility, were considered and discarded. One suggestion to illuminate with flood-lights the night-time skies over the whole of south-east England was rejected on the wholly logical grounds that 'it would have been cheaper to move London'. Another idea was 'to blow carborundum powder into the air to stop the engines of the raiders . . . an engine was set revolving on a bench and carborundum was blown at it. The more the engine got, the better it liked it.' Yet another, even more demented proposal was to sprinkle the German bombers with sulphuric acid as they overflew London. Quite how this was to be accomplished, let alone without dousing the capital in acid as well, was not specified.

Rather more logically, a communications net was set up linking the dozen fighter bases ringing the capital with each other and with HQ. Each group of fighters had a designated zone to defend, ensuring complete coverage of the sky. At night, the search for the enemy was aided by powerful searchlights, while anti-aircraft gun-crews readied themselves to pump a barrage into areas that were designated 'no-fly zones' for British aircraft. The skies over London were also divided into a notional grid of numbered squares and, tracking the bombers by sight or sound, the gun-crews blasted 'curtains' of fire along the edges of succeeding squares, seeking to deter or divert the raiders attempting to reach the heart of the capital. Barrages produced a screen of shell-bursts extending about 2,500 feet from top to bottom, and gunnery commanders could order fire at five different heights : 'Very Low', 'Low', 'Normal', 'High' and 'Very High', ranging upwards from 5,000 feet to 17,500 feet. Different forms of barrages could also be ordered, known by 'fancy names' such as 'The Ace of Spades', 'Mary Jane', 'No Trumps' and 'Cold Feet'.

One innovation of rather less long-term value was the system of sounding the All Clear. When the experiments with police whistles and car horns proved unsatisfactory, the authorities turned to bugle calls. After all future raids, in addition to the customary placard-wearing, bicycling policemen, the All Clear was given by hundreds of Boy Scouts and members of the Boys' Brigade 'who blew bugles as they were driven round the streets in motor-cars'. Enfield Council arranged to transport its bugle blowers 'to selected points to sound the alarm and to return with them when the danger was past to sound the "All Clear", for which service they were to be paid 2/6d', and a businessman promptly offered to pay £50 to the bereaved parents of any 'little patriot killed by bombs or shrapnel' while blowing his bugle.

This panoply of new measures was not brought into play until the day before the next full moon. The 'Hunter's Moon' had reached its first quarter on 23 October 1917 but strong winds, cloud and rain prevented any raids for several days. A large-scale raid was planned for the night of 29 October, but it was then aborted because of forecast poor weather and instead just three Gothas were sent to bomb the Kent coast. Although British observers claimed to have seen or heard three or four detachments of enemy aircraft come over, only one of the Gothas succeeded in reaching England and its crew bombed Burnham and Southend instead of the target, Sheerness. No damage was recorded.

Two nights later, on 31 October, with a full moon and light south-easterly winds, a much larger force, twenty-two Gothas, made a fresh attempt to reactivate the Fire Plan. They were loaded with over six tons of bombs, two-thirds of them 4.5kg incendiaries of an improved design; the claim was that the failure rate of previous models had been eradicated, or at least much reduced. Precise targeting with these weapons was neither necessary nor desirable; the aim was a 'scatter raid' in which the Gothas would strew incendiaries across London like farmers scattering seed in a field.

For only the second time in the England Squadron's history, none of the Gothas turned back with engine trouble. The raiders were widely spaced: the first was recorded crossing the British coast just after 10.30 that night and the last one did not arrive until almost three hours later, at a quarter past one the following morning, but fewer than half of the aircraft – ten – actually reached London. The others, pushed to the north by strengthening winds and struggling with poor visibility, sought targets of opportunity wherever they happened to find them, the majority in Ramsgate and Dover.

Of the 274 bombs dropped by the Gothas, 181 were incendiaries, but although one crew reported 'a fierce and distinctively visible fire on the eastern rim of London', and a gasometer in Ramsgate was struck and burned out, once again the vast majority of the incendiaries failed to detonate or fell uselessly on open ground, parkland or in the Thames. Of the five that fell on Greenwich, for example, only one achieved any result at all, and even that one failed to ignite, just damaging the roof it fell on. Five more were dropped on Charlton, where one hit a small but highly combustible target, a storehouse at the Silicate Paint Works, and burned it out. Another damaged a barge on the river, the rest caused no harm at all. One bomb landed on a perfect site for an incendiary, a timber stack at Pier Wharf in Deptford, but yet again it failed to ignite, and one that did detonate after falling on a school in Silvertown was extinguished 'owing to the prompt action of some local residents, who threw a bucket of water on the flaming bomb'. The most damaging fire of the night was probably the one that consumed a Gotha as it crash-landed on its return to base, killing the crew.

Considering the scale of the raid, British casualties of ten dead and twenty-two injured were surprisingly light, though one bomb, which fell on a house in Romberg Road, Tooting Bec, killed three of the occupants and seriously injured the rest, including a young boy. 'Up till this time, an air-raid had seemed to me rather a novelty than a grim and terrible form of warfare. I can remember my father shaking my brother and me into wakefulness that night and saying, "Quickly boys! The raiders are coming nearer." Half-dressed and more asleep than awake, we were hustled downstairs and took shelter in the drawing-room under an improvised dugout constructed by father, consisting of a settee inverted upon two chairs. A similar shelter had been made in the dining room for Mother, my sister and a woman friend. The droning of the enemy aeroplanes became louder and louder, while the shrapnel from our anti-aircraft guns could be heard thudding on the roof. A dull whine, a crash, and then oblivion. Our home at Tooting Bec was razed to the ground. My father and brother and the woman friend were killed. My sister was temporarily blinded. Mother became a nervous wreck after being buried under debris from 1.40 a.m. until 4.45 a.m.' Three tenants of the next-door house were also killed.

The closest the British defences came to a 'kill' that night was achieved by a mobile anti-aircraft battery. The crew at first thought that they had shot down a Gotha, but daylight revealed that the 'wreckage' amounted to no more than a copper fuel pipe and other parts of the Gotha's fuel system. The bomber's pilot had been able to switch to his emergency fuel supply and returned to base, though his aircraft may have been one of the five Gothas that crashed on landing. The aircraft's notorious instability when not fully loaded and the fragility of its undercarriage remained design flaws that had never been eradicated.

Dark nights and 'storms and rain' then kept the England Squadron grounded for five weeks, during which time Kleine took the opportunity to transfer his headquarters from the Villa Drory – 'not well suited for the winter season' – to the townhouse of the Countess Hemptin in Ghent.

In Britain, fears about a resumption of the German raids were compounded by growing unrest. Friction in key industries had been growing throughout the war. There were many general grievances – shortage of food, scarcity of accommodation, rising prices, resentment that workers had to apply for permission to change their jobs – but worker and union anger became focused on one factor in particular. The loss of hundreds of thousands of male workers to the forces had necessitated the employment of women on a huge scale. Full employment and labour shortages had caused wages to rise, but unions feared – correctly in many cases – the process of 'dilution' by which, under cover of the wartime replacement of male workers by newly recruited and predominantly female workers, many categories of traditional jobs were being permanently 'de-skilled'. Many workers even believed that skilled men were being deliberately conscripted to allow dilution to take place. The result was a wave of unrest and strike action in manufacturing and munition plants.

The Government was so concerned about the industrial and social unrest, fearing it might even be pre-revolutionary, that a highly secret contingency plan, 'Emergency Scheme L', was put in place. The scheme led to the retention of eight divisions of troops in Britain, aligned military and police districts, and replaced civil authority with military control. Although the purpose of the scheme was never explicitly stated, it was clearly devised to maintain Government control and suppress revolution if it arose. The lack of confidence that could be placed in the police was demonstrated when the Metropolitan Police themselves took strike action, on 31 August 1918, which brought armed Guardsmen on to the streets to maintain order. 'Specials', 'mainly civil servants from the government departments' in Whitehall, took over some police duties; 'the strikers hustled them with much booing and cries of "blackleg"', and some blows were struck.

The public remained largely indifferent to the police action, even when Lloyd George bought off the strikers with an increase of 'thirteen shillings a week to their pay', but a strike by aircraft workers in Coventry provoked particular fury. A chaplain was sent to the city from the Western Front to 'preach patriotism', military aircraft overflew the factories dropping leaflets calling for a return to work and increases in production, and the strikers were roundly abused in the press, with Coventry described as the focus of the 'contempt of the British Empire'. One editor pointed out that the next generation of German aircraft might well bring Coventry within range of the bombs that had fallen so often on London and the south-east, and that the city would then 'get precious little sympathy' as 'the Hun raiders' bombs will pay Coventry as a whole for the results of last week's disgraceful work'.

Faced with a far more immediate prospect of German bombs, Londoners watched and waited as the moon waxed and then waned again. Whenever the weather appeared promising, Kleine despatched Rumpler reconnaissance aircraft equipped with two-way radios to report on weather conditions off the English coast, but there were only two nights in the entire month when 'clear moonlight coincided with anticyclonic conditions. On both occasions a raid was attempted.' On 5 December, with the moon entering its final quarter, the Rumpler pilots finally reported good visibility and, accompanied by Georgii's forecast of fine weather, Kleine felt confident in authorizing a raid.

British Intelligence about the existence of the R-planes and their capabilities remained patchy at best. An American Intelligence report of 9 November 1917 noted that 'last week during a gale, when the wind was blowing fully sixty miles an hour, a telephone message was received in Dunkirk that a German aircraft was approaching. The British simply laughed at the idea that anyone could fly under such conditions and paid no attention to the telephone message. A short time later, Dunkirk was bombed by this large German airplane.'

Strengthened by the addition of two of these 'large German airplanes', nineteen Gothas took off in the very early hours of the following morning, 6 December, to make another attempt to 'burn down London and terrorise the surviving population'. They were armed with yet another improved model of incendiary.

It was a bitterly cold and frosty night, with hardly a breath of wind and a 'half-moon, ringed with haze'. The windows of London's houses were frost-glazed and the roofs 'covered with rime'. Three Gothas turned back soon after take-off but the remainder, spaced at five- to ten-minute intervals, kept crossing the English coast from two in the morning until 4.30.

Although London was the prime target, once more only a few of the raiders – six of the eighteen – actually attacked the capital. Navigation by night was never easy, but even with a waning moon, the silvered waters of the Thames should have been an unmistakable landmark, and it must be supposed that at least some of the raiders made little, if any, effort to reach London. Either they lost their way or they preferred to drop their bombs on the first coastal targets that presented themselves – Sheerness, Dover, Margate, Ramsgate and Whitstable – and then turn tail and flee back to Belgium.

The raiders had gained some element of surprise over the air defenders, who, after a five-week hiatus since the previous attack, were at less than full alert, particularly at an hour of the morning when raids had never previously been launched. Cecil Lewis's squadron at Rochford was already in holiday mood and earlier that night he had laid on some Christmas lights for his fellows. Their fighters were fitted with magnesium flares at the wing-tips that could be ignited electrically in case of a forced landing.

' "If," ' Lewis said to his fellows, ' "you went up to three thousand [feet] and then lit your flares and came down in a spin, wouldn't it look awfully pretty?" "Probably," they said, thinking me the idiot I was . . . I had my bus wheeled out and rose into the air. At three thousand, I touched off the flares, threw a loop and a couple of rolls and then went into a spin. I dropped a thousand feet before the flares finally burnt out and came down to land. Meanwhile the wind had changed. I landed across it, bounced, wiped off the undercarriage and turned over. It was a very ignominious ending to the exhibition. I was greeted with loud guffaws. "Not so good," said the Major. "Drinks all round." '

Lewis and his fellows settled down to the rest of their night duty. While on standby, pilots were fully dressed in their flying kit, waiting for the hooter that would signal an air-raid. 'There was nothing to do but play poker, put on the gramophone and drink – but not too much, in case of a raid.' As the night wore on there was 'the feeling of the whole world going slowly to sleep, lapped in waves of silence. Then suddenly the raucous Klaxons right overhead. Their nerve-shattering blast jolted our hearts into our throats. Instantly everything was confusion. "Where's my helmet?" "Give me a hand into this." "You've got my gloves." Pilots dashed about, frantic, picking up odd bits of kit, and tumbled through the door of the Mess, pell-mell.' They sprinted across the frost-covered grass to the sheds where their aircraft were waiting and 'within a minute' came the roar of their engines as they began taking off into the night.

Having wrecked his own aircraft, Lewis went up in a new one that he had ferried in from the factory only that afternoon. It had not yet been checked over by the ground-crew, its oil pressure was 'twenty instead of the requisite forty-five', and it had not been fitted with instrument lights, but 'if the Huns were over, our place was in the air, and I didn't feel like giving the excuse that I'd wiped off the undercarriage of my bus doing a stupid stunt'. Lewis merely shouted to a ground-crewman, 'Get me a torch!', and went into the familiar routine of starting his engine: ' "Switch off. Petrol on. Suck in." Slowly the prop was pulled round, jerking against the compression. "Contact!" Click went the double-switch. "Contact!" A sharp pull and away she went.'

Snatching the torch from his ground-crewman and waving away his concerns, Lewis took off, 'rose over the river and climbed up to patrol height' using his torch to read his instruments. Despite the earlier optimism of the Rumpler reconnaissance crews, 'the night was overcast, starless, moonless, the very darkest kind of night'. The tips of the exhaust pipes glowed in the darkness 'like coals. Blue flames flickered about them.'

Despite steadily falling oil pressure, Lewis patrolled up and down for half an hour without even glimpsing a Gotha, then caught his hand in the long flex connecting his torch to its battery and tore it out. Unable to read his instruments and disoriented in the pitch-darkness, Lewis went into his second spin of the night, this time accidentally. He 'cut off the engine, straightened the controls, pushed the stick forward and came out into a dive', but deciding that he'd had enough excitement for one night, he then landed, too fast, at Rochford, touching down 'tail up, well short of the flares and ran down them, beyond the end of the "L", and came to rest in darkness. Thank God Rochford was a large aerodrome.'

Another wave of German bombers passed over an hour or so later, by which time Lewis was off-duty and fast asleep in his bed. A ground-crewman burst in and woke him to tell him that a Gotha had crash-landed on the edge of the airfield; its crew were now prisoners in the guardroom. The Gotha had been hit by anti-aircraft fire over Canvey Island and had lost a propeller. Aircraft returning to Rochford fired red, green and white flares – the sequence of this 'visual password' changed daily – to signal that they were friendly aircraft, not German raiders. Unable to maintain height, the pilot had seen the dimly lit airfield and had by sheer chance used that day's correct sequence. The landing lights had been switched on to guide him in but, battling his unstable, faltering aircraft, he had missed the runway, hit a tree and finally come to rest on the edge of the golf course just beyond the perimeter of the airfield.

Lewis decided that both aircraft and its crew would still be there in the morning and went back to sleep, thereby missing a chance to examine a Gotha at close range, because before daylight it had been reduced to a charred wreck. It had still been carrying its full bombload and a few British officers and men had turned out to inspect their prize and remove its ordnance. By this time it was surrounded by pools of spilled fuel from its ruptured tanks. The squadron's equipment officer helped himself to a souvenir, slipping the Gotha's Very Light and cartridges into the pocket of his mackintosh. As he walked away from the aircraft, he pulled out the Very pistol to show to one of his comrades, but the trigger caught on the flap of his pocket and it went off, sending a white-hot magnesium flare blasting along the ground. It ignited the petrol surrounding the Gotha, which was completely destroyed in the blaze.

When Lewis got up the next morning, all that was left were 'the charred ironwork of the fuselage, the engines and the wires', much to the pilots' chagrin, because no Gotha had ever come intact into British hands before. The ones shot down had either fallen in the sea or been so burned and mangled that no information could be gleaned from them, and they had hoped to seize this unique opportunity to settle the argument about whether the Gothas had a firing tunnel down through the fuselage to protect the blind-spot under the tail, necessitating a change in tactics against them.

The Gotha's crewmen, unhurt but 'very quiet and rather sorry for themselves', feared that they would be subjected to mob violence; as Lewis conceded, with considerable understatement, 'raiders were not popular with the general public. However, whatever the public thought of them, we knew they were brave men and had a fellow-feeling for them, so we gave them a good breakfast, and took them round the sheds.'

Lewis was part of the escort that took them to London later that morning. They travelled by train in a closed first class compartment, with the blinds drawn, but 'somehow the news had got out and at every station there was an angry crowd. The officer in charge had to keep them off at the point of a revolver, otherwise we would all have been lynched.' One of the terrified Germans cut off the flying badges on his tunic and gave them to Lewis as souvenirs; 'I suppose he thought they made him a little too conspicuous. At Liverpool Street there was a heavy armed escort and the wretched men were marched away, through a hostile mob, to the safety of an internment camp.'

Their aircraft was not the only one lost to the England Squadron during the night. Although the Giants returned unscathed to their base, another Gotha had also been hit by ground-fire. Its port engine overheated and caught fire and, after jettisoning his secret, specialist equipment over a gravel pit, the commander, Leutnant Schulte – who, like his pilot Vizefeldwebel Senf, was making his thirteenth raid on England – made a crash-landing at Hackington Marsh near Canterbury. Once again the crew escaped unharmed and managed to set fire to their aircraft before surrendering to a special constable – the vicar of the local church. Two more Gothas were lost, one after crash-landing in Belgium, the other, listed as missing in action, probably forced to ditch in the North Sea.

The six aircraft that had reached London had been laden with incendiaries, and 395 were dropped altogether, by far the largest number yet used in any raid on England. Of the 276 bombs that landed within the Metropolitan Police District – encompassing the whole of Central London in a rough circle, fifteen miles in radius, centred on Charing Cross – 267 were incendiaries. They all fell within forty minutes of one another, and this 'most formidable effort to implement the Fire Plan in the history of the War' ignited scores of fires in the capital, 'four of them serious', including blazes at a furniture warehouse in Curtain Road, Shoreditch, a cigar box factory in Hanbury Street and a wholesale clothiers in Whitechapel Road.

However, although one of London's air defence commanders thought the number of fires 'afforded convincing proof that these "infernal machines" had now been rendered much more effective', once again more than half the incendiaries failed to ignite and the 'futility of a *scattered* fire over a city so copiously provided with open spaces and "dead spots" was conclusively demonstrated'. Furthermore, forewarned by the previous raid, the London Fire Brigade had also called in every available man and machine from outlying districts to guard the most vulnerable quarters of the city. The firefighters had to deal with fifty-two emergency calls between 4.30 and six that morning, but managed to contain the large fires and prevent them from spreading, though there were many narrow escapes. 'One incendiary crashed through a house roof but extinguished itself in the water tank, another fell into a dustbin and burned itself out harmlessly . . . many of the bombs fell in open spaces and did no damage.' Many of the small fires that were observed may simply have been caused by 'the ignition of the combustible in the bomb itself . . . in any case, in no locality were a larger number of fires observed than during previous raids when H.E. bombs were used [and] the incendiary bombs lacked the great moral effect of the H.E. bombs.'

Had all the incendiaries ignited, or had more than one-third of the raiders reached London, the death toll of eight people and the bill for damage of over £100,000 would have been far worse, and London's fire services would have struggled to control the blazes. As it was, although they had been severely stretched, they had not been overwhelmed, and the German aim of creating an ocean of fire to engulf the entire city remained nothing more than a dream. As one German officer later complained, 'a great deal of time and effort had gone into the design of these incendiary bombs, on whose effect on the densely settled London area such high hopes were based. The bomb was a complete failure . . . the sound idea of creating panic and disorder by numerous fires came to nought because of the inadequacy of the materials employed.' Confirmation was offered by a report from the Chief Officer of the London Fire Brigade, who noted that 'although fires were started in practically every one' of the air-raids on London, 'in only six were serious fires caused'.

Kleine had always been a much less enthusiastic advocate of the Fire Plan than his predecessor or his superiors. He was dismissive of the effectiveness of the incendiaries and claimed that British reports of the fires generated by the raid were made 'to trick us into continuing the use of incendiaries instead of heavy calibre demolition bombs'. He also drew General von Höppner's attention to the rapidly improving night defences his men were encountering over England. The lines of search-lights were laid out in semicircular arcs 'so organised between the coast and the capital that any route followed by the bomber aeroplanes cut one of these semicircles', and the lights then 'caught and held our aeroplanes in spite of all efforts to escape ... picked up by one group of lights after another'. The curtain of fire put up by the anti-aircraft guns extended 'far to the north and south of the Thames', and Kleine's men had seen 'many enemy fighters' and at least a dozen illuminated airfields, though they felt that 'the ground anti-aircraft defence was far superior to the fighters ... and was practically alone effective'.

Perhaps as a result of Kleine's generally pessimistic report, the England Squadron's raids on London were temporarily suspended after this latest pyrrhic victory and instead they were re-tasked to fly tactical bombing missions over the Western Front, 'a dispersal which was quite contrary to the whole object of the squadron ... an operational error which, though excused by the serious position of the Army, did away with any idea of any decisively successful air-raids on Great Britain in the future'.

On one of these tactical missions, against an ammunition dump near Ypres on 12 December 1917, an overcast, bitterly cold winter's day, Kleine's aircraft was attacked between Le Touquet and Croix-le-Bois by Canadian pilot Captain Wendell Rogers. He riddled the Gotha's fuel-tanks with a mixture of tracer and explosive shells, and saw fire streak along the fuselage from the burning tanks. As he watched, two figures – pilot Leutnant von der Nahmer and rear-gunner Leutnant Bülovius – leapt from the burning aircraft. They had no parachutes but had opted for a swift death rather than the lingering agony of being burned alive. Kleine stayed with his aircraft, and from an altitude of 2,800 metres (9,200 feet) he was almost certainly dead before it hit the ground. Neither of his crew-men's bodies was ever found. Kleine's aircraft and his burned and battered corpse were discovered behind German lines by a soldier who recognized the cross of the Pour le Mérite around Kleine's charred neck. The body was retrieved and sent back to the England Squadron for burial. 'The loss of this, our best and most successful crew and our outstanding Commander

... is felt deep in the heart by each member of the squadron and particularly the flying crews.' Kleine's commander, General von Höppner, added his own eulogy the next day. 'The brave and exemplary commander of the squadron, Captain Kleine, has died in the field with the best of crews. Oberleutnant Kleine has led the squadron to great successes. In him, the Air Force lose one of their knights of the order Pour le Mérite, one of its best and most merited, of whom I still expected much. His name and the raids on England carried out under his name will stand forever, engraved on the Roll of Honour of the Air Force. The confidence and attacking spirit of the squadron will be sustained by following the example and the successes of these fallen comrades.'

Oberleutnant Richard Walter took temporary command of the England Squadron, and on 18 December he led it on what was, in terms of the financial cost of bomb damage, the most successful raid by the squadron in the entire campaign. Fifteen Gothas and one Giant, R12, took part in the raid, crossing the English coast between six o'clock and 7.15 that evening. British observers on the banks of the Thames showed even more than their usual confusion, describing as many as 'five separate divisions, each consisting of numerous groups of aeroplanes, advancing in succession on a broad front on both sides of the river'.

'It had not been thought probable that there would be sufficient light to enable the enemy to attack' as the thin sliver of the new moon was only 'four days, twelve hours old, setting at 9.07 p.m.' but, although the moon cast only a pale light on the landscape, snow had been falling and the dark course of the rivers, particularly the broad sweeps of the Thames, stood out clearly against the whitened land. Nonetheless, once again only six aircraft reached London, the remainder attacking targets in Kent and Essex.

The House of Commons was still sitting when the raid began and the Speaker suspended the session so that the members could shelter in the basement, to the disgust of one MP who likened it to cowardice in the face of the enemy. One of their constituents, in Clerkenwell, was 'hurrying to find shelter after the "Take Cover". The streets were fast emptying when a cripple girl called to us to follow her to shelter. We were led to what was then Groom's Crippleage, the basement of which was used as a refuge. Men were hurriedly bringing down the poor cripples and already the room was half-filled with women and children. A gas jet flickered feebly and an old harmonium stood in the middle. One side was skirted with a glass fanlight. As soon as the bombs started we were called upon to sing hymn after hymn in a vain endeavour to drown the terrible noise. Never shall I forget the St John Ambulance man with his formidable axe in his belt, the nurse flitting to and fro and the wheezy harmonium playing "Jesus wants me for a sunbeam" . . . During the whole time we seemed to be the centre of the inferno and the last bomb lifted us entirely off the form [bench] we were sitting on and also blew out the windows.' 'Very few escaped injury. In the roll-call by torchlight we found that what we thought to be water was blood.' In all fourteen people lost their lives, including two killed by falling shrapnel from the anti-aircraft barrage.

The Giant R12 was one of the aircraft to bomb the capital. It dropped streams of incendiary and high-explosive bombs, including a 300kg projectile – the heaviest bomb dropped during the England Squadron's campaign so far – that exploded in Lyall Street, near Eaton Square. The Gothas also dropped incendiaries, one of which fell in the gardens of Buckingham Palace, though many fewer than on the previous raid. Almost a quarter of a million pounds' worth of damage was caused by the high-explosive bombs and the thirteen fires started by the incendiaries, one of which was said by a Gotha crew still to be visible from fifty miles away as they returned to base – possibly the blaze at a 'pianoforte manufactory' in Farringdon Road, which was burned out during this raid.

Although the alarm had been raised in time in some districts of London, in others the police were alerted only eight minutes before the raiders appeared overhead, and did not have time to tour the streets with warnings. Since the firing of maroons was still only allowed by day – the War Cabinet had decided that firing the charges after dark would only increase public panic – many people had no warning of the raids at all and were left unprotected, on the upper floors of their houses or in the streets, as the bombs began falling. As a result of the raid the system was modified once more and maroons would henceforth be sounded by day and by night, except that 'in deference to invalids, the aged and the feeble' they would only be fired after the nation's notional bedtime of 11 p.m. if the police did not have sufficient time to issue warnings by the conventional means. A resolution passed by Bermondsey Borough Council urged the Government to ban the ringing of church bells on Sundays in case the sound masked the noise of an air-raid warning. One councillor added this footnote: 'if you stop the ringing of bells, you should stop the barking of dogs, as they make more noise and confusion than the bells'. The resolution and the footnote were ignored.

If the raid had been costly for London, the England Squadron also paid a heavy price. Captain Gilbert Murlis Green, the commanding officer of 44 Squadron based at Hainault, was later awarded a Bar to his Military Cross for showing remarkable persistence and no little courage after a Gotha was caught by the searchlights 10,000 feet above Goodmayes. Flying a Sopwith Camel, he made the classic attack from below and behind his target, closing to within thirty yards before discovering that his starboard Lewis gun had frozen in the cold. He had to take evasive action to avoid being hit by the Gotha's bombs as they began to drop on Bermondsey but, though often blinded by the searchlights and his own gun-flashes, he kept the Gotha in sight and made four separate attacks on it, pulling away until his gun-blindness faded and his night vision was restored, and then returning to the attack.

As the Gotha pilot, Leutnant Friedrich Ketelsen, dived to try to shake off his assailant, Murlis Green's aircraft was buffeted by the slipstream and thrown off its tail, but his gunfire had already done its work – the Gotha's starboard engine was ablaze. Losing altitude all the time, Ketelsen crossed the coast but had gone only a few miles before he realized that his crippled aircraft would not survive the crossing of the North Sea. He tried to return to England to crash-land but was forced to ditch in the sea off Dover, and though his two crewmen, Oberleutnant von Stachelsky and Gefreiter Weissmann, were rescued by the armed trawler *Highlander*, the unfortunate Ketelsen lost his hold on the upper wing moments before the rescue and drowned. The trawler crew tried to tow the wreckage of the Gotha ashore so that its construction and equipment could be examined, but as they did so the aircraft was blown apart when one or more of its bombs exploded – either a delayed fuse set by the crew or, perhaps more plausibly, the result of striking a submerged rock. The trawler suffered only slight damage but the Gotha was completely destroyed.

It was fitting that the first Gotha to be shot down by a British fighter since the German switch to night attacks had been claimed by Murlis Green, the man who had first demonstrated that Sopwith Camels could be flown at night; however, as General Ashmore observed, a large number of British pilots were still 'risking their necks for pitifully small results'. Anti-aircraft batteries also claimed two unconfirmed 'kills' that night and the damage caused by British aircraft and ground-fire may have contributed to the number of Gothas that crashed back in Belgium. Two burned out after crash-landing and catching fire, two others suffered major damage after forced landings in open fields, and another two crashed while trying to land on their home airfields.

After the Wanstead gun-battery reported that they had fired at a far larger aircraft than a Gotha, and observers had commented on the thunderous noise of a six-engined Giant flying alone, away from the Gothas, the first official confirmation that Giants were joining Gothas in attacks on London finally appeared in a note circulated to anti-aircraft gun-batteries and searchlight units by their commander, Colonel Simon, the next morning – almost three months after the Giants had first appeared in London's skies. An official report compounded the error, claiming that the raid of 18 December marked 'the first advent of the "giant" aeroplanes over London'.

On 22 December a final, token raid of the year by a Gotha and two Giants, R12 and R39, was foiled by poor weather. All the raiders' bombs fell in the sea off the Kent coast, and though the Giants returned to base safely, the Gotha made an emergency landing near Margate. Its crew managed to burn the aircraft before surrendering to four local policemen, who had commandeered a taxi to transport them to the scene of the crime.

Two days later, the much-delayed reprisal raid on Mannheim finally took place when ten RFC bombers made a daylight attack on the city. A river bridge was destroyed and the crews reported a number of fires. The Kaiser, travelling in his special train, had left Mannheim station only half an hour before the raid began.

# CHAPTER 14
# A FAILURE OF STRATEGY

THE NEW YEAR BEGAN disastrously for the England Squadron. On 17 January 1918 two complete air-crews were killed without even leaving Belgian airspace. Both aircraft were on test flights, carrying heavy bombloads, when the accidents happened, one near Oostakker, the other at Landeghm. Among the dead were three noblemen including the Reichsunmittelbare Graf Adelmann von und zu Adelmannsfelden, whose hereditary title had been granted under the Holy Roman Empire. The King of Württemberg sent a telegram ordering the body to be shipped home, but the aircraft had been carrying 450kg of bombs that had detonated in the crash and 'all they found of the entire crew were one piece of shoulder and one arm. The airplane itself had disappeared.'

The first raid on England of the year did not take place until 28 January, at the time of the full moon. An attempt three days earlier had been aborted because of fog, and this time, although thirteen Gothas and one Giant took off in clear starlit conditions, heavy mist again began to spread, and six Gothas returned to base without even sighting Britain. The rest crossed the coast around eight that evening. One of London's air defence commanders thought that the Gothas had evolved new tactics of stopping their engines and gliding in silence, and he also conjectured that they had been fitted with 'silencers and cut-outs' to reduce the noise of their engines, but there is no evidence that this was the case, and it is more likely that it was simply the wind and weather conditions that made the sound of the raiders' engines appear to fade from time to time.

As the alarms were sounded, including maroons and two steam sirens that were alleged to be audible five to ten miles away, the familiar exodus to the Underground began; but those who had predicted that the sounding of maroons at night would only increase the likelihood of panic were given grim confirmation of their fears.

The Bishopsgate Goods Depot in Shoreditch was an officially designated air-raid shelter but so many people had been pouring into the station and staying there all night, whether there was an air-raid warning or not, and 'so much damage was done to the goods, and the habits of the visitors were so insanitary', that the railway company had decided on 'a new precaution tried out that night for the first time'. The station gates were now to be kept locked until an air-raid warning had actually been sounded. 'On this night there was a beautiful moon and, as was usual in those times, when there was a moon, most of the women and children from round about were getting near the station, in case. Also it was opposite the Olympia Music Hall where people were queuing for the second house.' Crowds had already been milling about in front of the station for over an hour, 'begging to be let in', when explosions were heard.

The sound was the maroons being detonated to give a three-minute warning, but mistaking the noise for exploding bombs, the crowd surged towards the station. The two main iron gates were still locked and people were 'forced against them by the pressure behind'. A railway policeman managed to open the narrower gate of the workmen's entrance and there was a 'mad rush' as 'the mass of people surged through the narrow opening'. 'Someone must have stumbled and fallen' (another observer suggested that 'someone seems to have dropped a camp-stool and in stooping to pick it up was overwhelmed by the pressure behind'). 'Women and children were piled on top of each other. To make matters worse, the people who were lined up outside the music hall ran over and added to the pressure.'

Many people were trampled underfoot. Some were suffocated, others crushed against pillars. 'A woman had a baby swept from her arms. She next saw it in the mortuary.' Mr H. Jones 'struggled hard to pull the people off one another, thinking my wife and the two children were underneath. I did manage to pull one man and his wife and two children from underneath, and was nearly dragged under by the clutching hands of people who were trying to save themselves. I got two little girls out too, but found they were dead. After that, willing porters came and eased the crowd, pulling them off the pile, and we carried the dead and laid them out on the bank.' A similar incident at Mile End station left a total of fourteen dead.

In both cases the authorities chose to blame the incident on foreigners – 'mostly aliens of the lowest type . . . great hulking men, pushing aside women and children in their anxiety to save their own miserable skins' – further inflaming the xenophobia that was already ruling the East End. A police inspector told an inquest that the cause of the panic was 'the behaviour of young men . . . practically all Russian . . . they ought to be in the Army [the Military Service Act of July 1917 gave every able-bodied 'friendly alien' the Hobson's choice of conscription or deportation] but it is hard to get hold of them'. The coroner described the alleged conduct of the 'foreigners' as 'entirely unworthy of men and nearly approaching the conduct of the lower animals'.

There was further carnage elsewhere in London. One man hurried down into the Aldwych Tube station when the alarms sounded. The small platform was soon crowded with women and children, and 'the wounded soldiers from the huts that then stood on the Strand Island site were brought down . . . When the bombs began to fall, the sound came down the stairs with a roar and the whole Tube seemed to tremble. The soldiers who were suffering from shell shock were a sad sight – still Britons, but their limbs could not keep still.'

Out in the streets, George Bentley was hurrying to his house when 'a man a few yards in front of me dived to the ground and shouted to me to lie down. I did, though I was only twenty yards or so from home. There were three deafening thuds and flashes . . . One house was demolished. Suddenly we heard a groan. I pulled and wriggled my way into a cellar which was full of gas and water, and in the darkness came across a young woman, only just alive. Most of her clothes were blown off her. With help, I managed to get her to the surface, but by that time she was dead. Next morning the bodies of the wife and five children of a friend of mine, Sergeant-Major Kerby of the Middlesex Regiment, were found.'

One bomb wrecked a public house and ninety-four houses in Kilburn, another fell within a few yards of the Savoy Hotel, where a thousand people were sheltering. Fighter pilots 'stood by for night raids in relays, so they were able to take it in turns to go to town', and Cecil Lewis was off-duty and in the Savoy when the bomb fell on the pavement and blew in the front wall of a four-storey building at the corner of Savoy Hill, 'thirty feet from the hotel . . . It was about 11.30. The Savoy was crowded after the theatre . . . the waiters hurried, the people chattered, the smoke rose like mist over the tables . . . Crrrrump! The whole building shook.

'If everyone had been suddenly struck dead, the silence could not have been more absolute. The band broke off in the middle of a bar . . . Bombs! Bombs! Then a terrific shattering roar just outside the restaurant. The whole crowd stood up and rushed, panic-stricken, up the steps to the foyer. A woman fainted. Another leaned against the wall, sobbing. Pause. Everyone waited, breathless, for the next bomb. Silence, nothing happened. The machines had passed over. People began to whisper. A man laughed and then, like a flood, a wave of forced hilarity swept over everyone.'

The building damaged by the bomb presented a weird sight. The outer wall had been completely stripped away, but the exposed interiors were almost untouched. 'Pictures, notice-boards and drawings remained undisturbed . . . from the ceiling of the fourth floor electric lamps with their shades and bulbs unbroken, still hung by the cords.'

Bombs also exploded near three of the Thames bridges – Vauxhall, Waterloo and London Bridge. 'A mighty disturbance of the waters followed, something like a tidal bore, the waves of which, sweeping up the river under the arches of Westminster Bridge, rose so high that they poured onto the Terrace [of the House of Commons].' The worst casualties and damage were in Long Acre, near Covent Garden, where a 300kg bomb dropped by the Giant R39 struck the Odhams Press building housing the presses that, among other things, printed the jingoistic British newspaper *John Bull*. The basement was a designated air-raid shelter and 'when the "take cover" sounded, as usual, down we trooped to our shelter'.

The basement was reached by a short stone staircase that led first into the room where the rotary presses were housed; from there, a connecting cast-iron door led to a paper warehouse that also served as the public air-raid shelter. There were two exits from it, one leading into Wilson Street behind the building, and one into Arne Street at the side. About six hundred people were in the basement when the bomb, narrowly missing the actual building, burst through a toughened-glass 'pavement light' immediately outside and detonated in the basement.

The blast pulverized the main walls and blew out the supporting piers of the building, causing the collapse of the upper storeys with concrete floors nine inches thick, and 'grossly overloaded with rolls of paper'. 'The outbreak of fire which followed added to the agony of those imprisoned in the debris.' The Arne Street exit was blocked by the blast and, trying to escape the flames, 'the terrified refugees appear to have lost their bearings'. Instead of using the Wilson Street exit, they 'made frantic efforts to escape through the iron door to the machine room'.

One woman who had run to the basement to take cover, cradling her baby in her arms, 'had just got settled down inside when there was a flash, followed by an explosion. I was wearing a comb in my hair which caught fire, setting my clothes alight before I could do anything. The force of the explosion blew my baby out of my arms and she was never found again. I had all the fingers blown off one hand, a leg taken off, the top of my head injured (I have to wear a plate) and my body burnt all over. I am just a piece of the woman I was before the air-raids came. All I have to do is sit in a chair day after day, with people waiting on me, because I am useless for anything ... I was in hospital for two years ... When I could remember, they told me about my little baby.'

Three boys had been 'playing on a big roll of paper' when the bomb went off. One, knocked unconscious, regained his senses to see that 'everything seemed to be alight and falling on me. I was pinned to the ground with a piece of machine across my legs. My two playmates were missing and no trace was ever found of them. I can vividly remember women and children bleeding and burning, lying near me, and one woman with her dress blazing actually ran over me. How I was injured and covered with printers' ink, fought my way out to the firemen who were waiting to help us, I have no idea. The last I remember of that terrible night was that a fireman (I know it was a fireman because he promised me his helmet if I was a brave boy) carried me up a blazing wooden staircase to what seemed safety.'

Fire crews and police were quickly on the scene and rescued 'a considerable number of people' through the Wilson Street doors, but five minutes later part of the wall at that end of the building collapsed, blocking that escape route. The only way in or out of the basement was now by way of the stone stairs and the main entrance of the building in Long Acre. Firemen were playing hoses on three sides of the burning building, 'deluging the whole place with water which, soaking through the floors, gradually filled the basement to a depth of several feet'. Those trapped there, who had managed to escape being burned alive, now faced death by drowning instead. Risking their own lives, coughing and choking, volunteer ambulancemen and local doctors ventured into the smoke-, fume- and steam-filled basement, sometimes wading through water chest-

or neck-deep, to rescue the few people who might still be alive. 'In order to gain access to those still living, the dead bodies were carried into the adjoining room and laid out on the covers of the printing machines . . . In one case, where a victim was firmly held under some fallen timber, an amputation was contemplated to save him from drowning. A massive reel of paper . . . was sawn through to save another.'

On the streets, 'it seemed as if the whole of Holborn was one big fire. The John Bull office . . . was a great mass of flames. We watched all the dead and injured being carried out during the night.' 'Right around the building were line upon line of plain grey ambulances, and hundreds of voluntary workers were helping the ambulance attendants. These workers wore long rubber gloves and every now and then paused to run their hands down them from arms to fingertips to free them from accumulations. Policemen were besieged by scores of people giving descriptions of their missing relatives and I saw here a sight to make angels weep – two little boys, one about five years old, the other about three, the one with his head bandaged, the other with his little arm in splints, crying for their mummy. Their mother's body was never found.'

Thirty-eight people were killed in the building and almost a hundred injured or badly burned. 'Everyone who was working in that basement death-trap was so dumbfounded that hardly a word was spoken all night.' A young man of about twenty who escaped from the building found his way to Bow Street police station, where he 'sat shivering'. A policeman asked if he could help. The man said, ' "Look what they're dropping now," and he held out greasy black hands. "That, my boy," I said, "is printers' ink. Have a drink of water." '

Even after the raiders had long departed, the streets of London 'lay in a dead hush under the moon . . . absolute silence and loneliness . . . There were always pedestrians about; always, at first, carriages and hansoms; and, at a later period, always taxis and motor-cars. A policeman on point duty . . . "nightbirds" male and female were to be encountered. Tonight . . . I met no policeman or special constable, no prowler or drab. Those benefactors of the London streets on winter nights, the hot-potato man and the roasted chestnut man, were gone with the glowing braziers of their trade. That other friend of night-wayfarers, the coffee-stall, with its red lights, its tea and coffee urns, its cups and mugs, its loaves and cakes, and its packets of cigarettes, had also disappeared.'

Margate, Ramsgate and Sheerness were also bombed that night, and in total sixty-seven people were killed and 166 injured, while £187,000 of damage was caused. Eleven of the injuries were caused by shrapnel from anti-aircraft fire, which also damaged 311 houses. One Gotha was shot down by Second Lieutenant 'Sandy' Banks and Captain George Hackwill, who mounted a coordinated attack, showing that British pilots had at last learned the lessons from the failures of previous solo attacks on the well-armed Gothas.

Both men were flying Sopwith Camels fitted with a new gunsight, named after its inventor, Lieutenant H. B. Neame of the Technical Directorate, and manufactured by the Mayfair gunsmiths Purdey at a cost of £1 15s (£1.75) each. A ring-sight illuminated for night-flying, it was calibrated so that the seventy-seven-foot wingspan of a Gotha bomber was at the ideal range of a hundred yards when its silhouette exactly filled the gunsight. While this proved effective against a Gotha, a Giant was twice as big and, unaware of its true size, British pilots using the Neame sight emptied their machine-guns at it when it filled their sights without registering a single hit, because the enormous aircraft was still well out of range. Perhaps for this reason, R12 survived an exchange of fire with a fighter that forced the British aircraft to make a crash-landing, but the Gotha that Banks and Hackwill had targeted went down in flames, still carrying its bombload, causing a massive explosion as it crashed on farmland in Essex. All three crew – Leutnant Friedrich von Thomsen, and Unteroffiziers Walter Heiden and Karl Ziegler – were killed.

On top of the already heavy losses at the end of the previous year, the shooting down of the Gotha and the serious damage sustained by another four after they crashed while landing forced von Höppner to impose a temporary suspension of attacks on England until the squadron had been reorganized, retrained and resupplied. Richard Walter's reign was now over, and though barely recovered from the severe injuries that had left him with an artificial leg and using crutches, Brandenburg was restored to the command. He had just returned from honeymoon after marrying the nurse who had looked after him while he was hospitalized, but his good humour did not survive his first meeting with the men of the England Squadron. He was so shocked at the depleted and demoralized state of the squadron that he maintained the suspension of raids on England for several weeks.

In the meantime, under his energetic direction, replacement air-crews were drafted in and trained, new Gothas arrived from the factories – though in both quantity and quality they left much to be desired – and morale was improved. By March all was ready for a resumption of the attacks, but events on the Western Front frustrated this plan as the squadron was again redeployed to fly tactical bombing missions against 'railway hubs, troop camps and ammunition dumps', this time in support of the huge last-ditch German offensive Operation Michael. For over three months no Gotha flew over England and the bombing campaign was maintained only by sporadic raids by the R-planes.

On 29 January, four Giants took off from Gontrode and St Denijs-Westrem. One, the R12, suffered engine problems over the Channel and turned back, dropping its bombs on British positions around Gravelines, east of Calais. The other three – R25, R26 and R39 – crossed the English coast just north of the Thames estuary. Once more confused by the thunder of the Giants' multiple engines, British observers sent a warning that at least fifteen German bombers were attacking and eighty fighters were scrambled to repel the raiders. The R26 developed problems in two of its engines soon afterwards and, after dropping bombs on Rayleigh in Essex, it turned for home. The other two pressed on towards London.

As the R39 overflew them, confused observers once more described the single Giant as 'a "V" of five aircraft' or 'a group of seven'. The R39's commander, Hauptmann von Bentivegni, and pilots Leutnants von Lenz and Buth struggled to find their target in the fog and darkness, and then mistook Hammersmith Bridge for Tower Bridge. As a result their bombs fell on Acton and Richmond rather than in the heart of London. A series of 50kg high-explosive bombs killed ten people, and the R39 also dropped showers of incendiaries, but in leafy suburbia and parkland they did little damage. Nineteen fell in gardens at Isleworth and in Richmond Old Deer Park alone.

The R39 was repeatedly targeted by fighters almost from the moment it crossed the coastline. Captain Arthur Dennis of 37 Squadron at Goldhanger fired a whole drum of ammunition from his Lewis gun into it over the Blackwater river, but was then thrown around by the wash from its engines, and when he regained control of his aircraft he had lost sight of the Giant in the darkness. Another Sopwith Camel pilot, Second Lieutenant Robert Hall, spotted the R39 over west London but suffered one of the perennial gun jams as he tried to engage it. Captain F. L. Uxmoore of 78 Squadron was next to try his luck. He made two diving passes, firing off fifty rounds on each one, but his synchronizer gear was faulty – it was less reliable when an aircraft was diving than in level flight – and one of the bullets, instead of passing between the propeller blades, struck and broke one. A piece flew off and hit him in the head, and by the time the dazed pilot had regained his composure the Giant was nowhere to be seen. Captain George Hackwill of 44 Squadron then fired six hundred rounds at the R39 before he ran low on fuel and had to break off the fight, and Second Lieutenant F. B. Bryant also attacked it near Faversham in Kent, as it made for the coast, but his BE12b fighter lacked the speed to close to killing range.

The R25 was even more hard-pressed. It was first spotted by Second Lieutenant R. F. Kitton of 37 Squadron, who emptied a drum of ammunition into it but lost sight of it while reloading. Second Lieutenant Hall then encountered his second Giant of the night, but managed only five rounds before his guns again jammed. He cleared the jam and overhauled the R25, by now also being attacked by Second Lieutenant H. A. Edwardes of 44 Squadron, who also had the misfortune to shoot off part of his own propeller. Unable to maintain the attack himself, he had the presence of mind to switch on his landing lights, attracting other British aircraft to the fight. Hall and Edwardes were now joined in the attack by Second Lieutenant T. M. O'Neill and Major Gilbert Murlis Green. Walter Aschoff had observed how often it was the same few pilots who demonstrated the courage to attack London while the other bomber crews turned aside, and the same seems to have been true of British fighter pilots, for the same names – Murlis Green, McCudden, Banks, Hackwill, Palethorpe – keep recurring in accounts of aerial combats with those bombers. The unfortunate Murlis Green made his attack run seconds after O'Neill had made a diving pass at the Giant and Murlis Green received the full force of the R25's counter-fire. He still unleashed a drum and a half of ammunition before his guns jammed.

By now, fire from one of the fighters had hit one of the Giant's radiators, causing one of the port engines to overheat. Forced off course by the balloon screen near Southgate, the R25's commander dropped his bombs on Wanstead and then made for home. The Giant was steadily losing height and speed – it was reduced to flying at fifty-eight miles per hour – but, although Murlis Green landed, rearmed and got airborne again within eleven minutes, neither he nor the other fighter pilots could prevent the raider from reaching the relative safety of the open sea. It was another tribute to the astonishing durability of the Giants that R25 eventually reached its landing ground safely; after touching down it was found to have eighty-eight bullet-holes in it.

A British official report later claimed, on the basis of an interrogation of a captured German air-crewman, that the crew of this Giant had been 'paralysed by fright' when under attack and were 'within an ace of landing from pure fright, and had they been further pressed, even though our men had no ammunition left, would have done so'. The report went on to cite this as 'proof' that Giant crews were 'not usually among the first rank of German airmen. They can be thoroughly frightened and might be forced down by concerted attack.'

The Giants had dropped seventy-four bombs in total, and of the fifty-four that fell on Central London, nineteen were incendiaries. Once more they often failed to detonate, and those that did ignited no substantial fires. Pending the delivery of yet another new model incendiary that was already in an advanced stage of development, the Fire Plan was put on hold and the next raids by the Giants used only high-explosive bombs.

Quite apart from the inadequacy of the projectiles being used, the fire-raids on London were also hampered by other constraints. Even the limited improvements in the design and manufacture of incendiaries up to this point in the war had not been matched by any parallel refinement of the techniques for deploying the weapons on the chosen battlefield – the streets of London. The use of high-explosive demolition bombs alongside incendiaries, as was the case in every single fire-raid on

London, was arguably a mistake. As far back as AD 64, the great fire of Rome had been extinguished on the sixth day 'by demolishing a number of buildings and thereby leaving a void space where, for want of materials, the flames expired'. The Great Fire of London in 1666 had eventually been brought under control using similar means, yet German commanders in the First World War were sending planes loaded with equal quantities of incendiaries and demolition bombs. Any value that HE bombs might have had in 'opening' buildings and exposing their combustible interiors was likely to be neutralized by their negative effects. HE bombs did have a valid function as an adjunct to fire-raids, if used in the immediate aftermath of the main assault, targeting road junctions and traffic choke-points to hamper the movement of fire crews; but this was never done.

The way that the incendiaries themselves were used was also deeply flawed. The staff officers at the German High Command responsible for directing the use of the bombing squadrons were not well enough informed 'to counteract the mistaken views of the High Command at the Front' – another sideswipe at Kleine and von Höppner. Their error 'lay in not concentrating the available squadrons in mass raids on the most dangerous enemy or the politically most important objective'.

The critical point for an incendiary attack and 'the point to be aimed at as an act of war, is that at which the extinguishing appliances of the community are beaten or overcome. Up to this point the damage done may be taken as roughly proportional to the means and cost of its accomplishment; beyond that point the damage is disproportionately great: the city may be destroyed *in toto*.' 'Had the German commanders been better trained for their work and possessed a more intimate knowledge of the topography of London, a blaze might have been started which would have been exceedingly difficult to control', but they had formulated virtually no strategy or tactics beyond the overall aim of destroying London by fire.

Hauptmann Erich Linnarz had shown the way as far back as 31 May 1915, when he overflew London in the first Zeppelin raid on the capital and dropped a concentrated pattern of bombs. 'His chief concern was to release incendiaries at the shortest possible intervals. In doing this he was following the logical dictates of the Plan, because fires started in close proximity tend to burn their way towards each other and thus merge into a greater conflagration.' Most of Linnarz's bombs fell on districts of 'a poor residential character', and the resulting blazes tested London's firefighters to the limits.

No subsequent raid by Zeppelin or aircraft had followed that pattern; the average density of bombs in the 'Cock-crow' raid of 6 December, which had seen more incendiaries fall on London than in any other raid yet flown, was no more than seven to the square mile. Yet setting isolated fires was not enough. Only if a large number of individual fires came together to form a conflagration could the Fire Plan hope to succeed, and if the aim was to generate an inferno, the bombing of a series of widely dispersed targets was a crass error. There was no technical reason why densities of three or even four times that number should not have been achieved, and the potential for generating a massive fire raging out of control would have been hugely increased.

A concentrated attack on a tightly defined and carefully chosen area of densely packed combustible buildings was much more likely to generate a firestorm. Older properties were particularly vulnerable; 'the old-fashioned roof of fragile slates, lathing, boarding, dry rafters and a loft with an accumulation of dust, practically invited an outbreak of fire from the smallest incendiary'. Yet there is no record of a methodical plotting of districts of London that were vulnerable either because of their poor con-struction – densely packed slums and tenements, for example – or their concentration of vulnerable industries or warehouses. Nor were there any attempts to study patterns of wind or precipitation. The only evidence of research to back up the Fire Plan appears to have been the information supplied by German Intelligence, probably after a trawl through old news-paper files, that the 'great fire' of 1897 in the close-packed garment manufacturing districts north of St Paul's had killed twenty-two people and caused half a million pounds' worth of damage.

As the disruption of British war production was a major secondary aim of the Fire Plan, the failure to subject to regular and sustained attack the cluster of arsenals and munition factories at Woolwich, packed with inflammable and explosive materials and offering 'a heartening target of two square miles to the bomber', was equally incomprehensible. It was well defended, but despite the gun-batteries and airfields surrounding it

*picture*: The two in-flight mechanics on German 'Giant' aircraft doubled ...achine-gunners, but had to brave a climb up an open ladder, with the ...tream tearing at them, to reach the upper wing where their ...s were mounted.

...: The massive four-engined aircraft could carry two tons of bombs. ...wingspan of 42 metres (138 feet) was bigger than any German ...ritish aircraft in the Second World War.

*Left:* The Operations Room from which London's air defences were co-ordinated. Save for the addition of radar, the air-defence system was virtually unaltered in the Battle of Britain during the Second World War.

*Middle left:* Sir John French, whose extraordinary order that anti-aircraft guns should not fire on aircraft 'even if recognized as hostile', was not rescinded until June 1917.

*Bottom left:* An anti-aircraft gun crew examine the results of their handiwork after shooting down a Gotha on 29 January 1918. Such successes were rare and casualties among British civilians from falling shrapnel far exceeded those of German airmen.

*Opposite top:* An RFC Air Technical Diagram demonstrating 'good and bad looping'.

*Below:* Queen Mary, Major General Hugh Trenchard and other senior officers watching a British airman 'looping the loop' in July 1917. Earlier in the war such aerobatics, though vital in air combat, were dismissed as 'cheap selfishness' and forbidden.

ENGINE OFF

DIVING

**GOOD LOOP**

ENGINE ALL OUT

**BAD LOOP**

MACHINE ENTERING LOOP

BUMP CAUSED BY BACK WASH

NO EXCESSIVE STRAIN

ENGINE OPENED OUT

MAXIMUM SPEED - EASY CURVE

**BAD LOOP**

MAXIMUM SPEED - SHARP CURVE - EXCESSIVE STRAIN

MAXIMUM SPEED - SHARP CURVE - EXCESSIVE STRAIN

SUDDEN CHANGES IN DIRECTION AT VERY HIGH SPEEDS GIVE RISE TO EXCESSIVE AND POSSIBLY DANGEROUS STRAINS.

IN FLATTENING OUT FROM A DIVE OR GOING INTO A LOOP AT HIGH SPEED THE STICK MUST NOT BE JERKED BACK BUT PULLED SLOWLY AT FIRST IN ORDER THAT THE CURVE MAY BE GRADUAL WHERE THE SPEED IS HIGH

Note.—The extra stress due to the curved path is proportional to the square of the speed and inversely proportional to the radius of the curve

This diagram is the property of and is intended for Offic

*Above:* Parisians sheltering from an air-raid in a wine-cellar pass the time by playing cards.

*Left:* 'L'heure des Gothas': a saucy French postcard combines titillation with a reminder of the need for a black-out.

*Below:* Citizens of Dover took refuge from the bombing in old caves carved out of the soft chalk of the White Cliffs.

e: 'British means Pluck': London
olchildren are taught about the danger of air-
 in February 1916. Within a few months the
bers of the England Squadron would pose an
 graver threat than the zeppelins.

t: As in this London lawyer's office,
eholders and businesses were urged to
 buckets of sand handy as a defence against
diaries.

w: Queuing to enter an air-raid shelter at Hither
n. The orderly queue, from smallest to biggest,
 children first, women, then men, suggests that
was a rehearsal rather than a real alert, when
c often ruled.

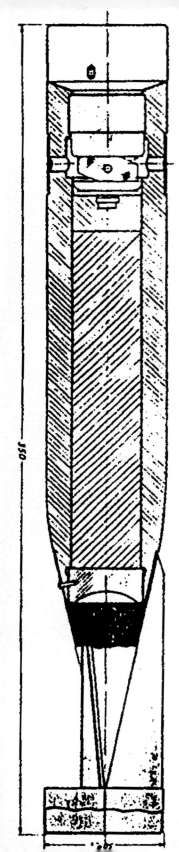

## Der Feuerplan –The Fire Plan

*Left:* A diagram of an Elektron incendiary, showing the thermi[?] core surrounded by the Elektron alloy casing. Weighing only 1[?] every part of the bomb was inflammable and once alight it was almost impossible to extinguish.

*Below:* The blistered door of a burned-out building shows the intense heat generated by a successful incendiary bomb.

*Opposite top left:* A German incendiary dropped on an East End Street in 1917. After the failure of the crude and unreliable incendiaries, the England Squadron discontinued their use un[?] the development of the new and deadly Elektron bomb.

*Opposite top right:* A chief constable examines one of the many early-model German incendiaries that failed to detonate.

*Opposite bottom:* After a raid by the England Squadron, Londo[?] firefighters extinguish fires before beginning the search for victims.

From Alpha *(inset)*: the modest impact of the first bomb to drop on the City of London . . .

. . . to Omega *(main picture)*: Dresden 1944 – how London might have looked the Fire Plan raids of September 1918 not been called off at the last moment The incendiaries that engulfed Dresd were virtually indistinguishable from German Elektron bombs of 1918.

Woolwich could not have been much better sited for German bombers, well to the east of London and with the Thames acting as an unmistakable marker. Yet Britain's greatest arsenal had so far never been targeted for a concentrated attack by German bombers. 'In over three and a half years, the enemy airman only once succeeded in reaching it', and even then damage was slight.

Two other obvious targets, the Small Arms Factory at Enfield Lock and the Royal Gunpowder Factory at Waltham Abbey, led equally charmed lives throughout the conflict. Nor was there a single focused raid on London's docklands. Like the streets and wharves where the Great Fire of London had broken out in 1666, the docks and the surrounding wharves and warehouses were 'a lodge of all combustibles' packed with oil, timber, grain, spirits, textiles, sugar, tobacco and a thousand other inflammable materials. Even worse, from the point of view of London's fire services, the docks were serviced by a relatively small number of major roads. High-explosive bombs dropped on the junctions of no more than three roads in the vicinity would have paralysed traffic-flows and greatly hampered crews racing to deal with fires. Yet, like the other vulnerable areas of London, the docks were never subjected to sustained, concentrated attack. Instead multiple individual targets were chosen, few of which were ever hit, and bombs were scattered in small numbers over huge areas, rendering the job of London's sorely stretched firemen much easier.

The sheer scale of incendiary attack needed to guarantee success was another crucial factor. In even the most densely populated city, no more than 15 to 20 per cent of its ground area is occupied by buildings; the remainder is taken up by public or private open spaces – streets, pavements, squares, parking lots, gardens and parks. In any fire-raid, therefore, at least 80 per cent of incendiaries will fall uselessly on open ground. Since perhaps 50 per cent of the remainder that actually strike buildings will be deflected off the roofs or penetrate but fail to ignite, an absolute maximum of 10 per cent of the incendiaries dropped will have the potential to start fires. Many of these will also fail, either falling into water tanks or other 'safe' areas, or being spotted and extinguished, or will cause only local damage.

In order to achieve the objective of combining a number of individual fires into a major conflagration or firestorm, a fire-raid on a massive scale was essential, requiring huge stockpiles of incendiaries and large numbers of aircraft and air-crew to deliver them. Given all these negative factors, until enough aircraft and sufficient quantities of incendiaries of a sufficiently reliable design could be put in place, the Fire Plan had to be put into abeyance.

# CHAPTER 15
# GIANTS IN THE NIGHT SKY

WHILE THE R-PLANE RAIDS on London had been taking place in late January, two squadrons of Gothas had bombed Paris, killing and injuring over 250 people, and a third squadron, temporarily transferred away from Flanders, overflew the Alps to attack Venice. News of the near-simultaneous assaults on three great European cities sent shockwaves across the Atlantic, where the spectre of German raids on the eastern seaboard of the US was raised. The *New York Times* gave prominent coverage to a call for a one-billion-dollar budget to create air defences to protect New York and Washington DC. The potential threat was real enough. If the USA remained out of reach of German aircraft, the newest-model Zeppelins, now nearing completion, had the range to cross the Atlantic, bomb New York, Boston or Washington DC, and then return to Germany. The shock to public opinion of such a brutal violation of American territory and domestic peace and security would have been as traumatic in 1918 as Pearl Harbor or 9/11 was for later generations.

Two more Giant raids on London followed in mid-February, once more sending millions of people scurrying for shelter. The first, on the bitterly cold night of 16 February, saw five Giants over England, one of which, the R39 commanded by von Bentivegni, dropped a devastating new weapon – a four-metre-long 1,000kg bomb. His target was the City but instead he hit the Royal Hospital, Chelsea, designed by Christopher Wren. The bomb had a massive impact, flattening the north-eastern portion of the three-storey building and severely damaging many surrounding ones. Among the victims were a member of the hospital staff, his wife, her sister, two sons and a niece who was staying with them at the time, and it was perhaps fortunate for London that night that the remaining four Giant crews had opted to continue using the existing smaller bombs that they believed – erroneously, on the evidence of the impact of that first 1,000kg bomb – to be more effective.

Two of the other Giants had narrow escapes. R33 lost power to both its port engines, and when one of its starboard engines also began to labour, causing the aircraft to lose height at an ever-increasing rate, the panic-stricken crew threw overboard every movable item of equipment, including their machine-guns. They had fallen from over 7,000 feet to just 650 feet when one of the mechanics discovered that the problem was the

281

lubricating oil which had become so cold that it would not flow. The quick-thinking mechanic then punctured one of the oil tanks with his knife, warmed some oil in his cupped hands and poured it into the rear port engine, which was then induced to start again. The R33 made it back to base.

The R12 had an even more incredible escape after flying into one of the steel cables trailing from a balloon screen. The impact was 'so severe that the starboard mechanic fell against the glowing exhaust stacks, which severely burned his hands', and the aircraft was 'first pulled to starboard, then port, and finally sideslipped out of control to the port side'. It plummeted a thousand feet in seconds, but it was a tribute both to the solidity of the Giant's construction and to the cool head of its pilot, Leutnant Gotte, that the lives of the crew were saved. Gotte instantly shut off all his engines, and then fired the port pair to stabilize the spinning aircraft before it plummeted to the ground, though the violent manoeuvre shook loose two 300kg bombs, which fell on Woolwich. The mechanic crawled along the R12's wing in mid-air to assess the damage and, reassured that it was not terminal, Gotte even flew on to unload the rest of his bombs on Beckenham, before turning for home. Once more the Giant reached base safely.

Because of damage from gunfire, steel cables and engine troubles, only one Giant, the R25, piloted by Leutnant Max Borchers, was able to return to raid London the following night, Sunday, 17 February. Once again it was enough to send the panic-stricken population fleeing for shelter. Steering a north-westerly course, the R25 dropped the first of its stick of eighteen bombs near Eltham in Surrey. Another fell on the Cambridge University Press building in Fetter Lane, penetrating through five floors to the basement, where it failed to detonate and was picked up 'alive'.

The last five bombs fell on and around St Pancras station and the great 'gothic revival' Midland Grand Hotel that formed the station's southern façade – 'a fine piece of shooting by the man responsible' according to an Air Board official. The first struck the steps of the station in Euston Road and the second burst in the entrance to the archway leading to the departure platforms, where many people were sheltering. The next, even though it failed to explode, sent two of the stone pinnacles crashing from the tower of the building and 'knocked out the side-wall almost entirely'. Tons of falling stone, brick and other debris smashed through the glass-roofed main carriageway leading to the station platforms. The fourth in the sequence fell by the entrance to the booking hall where more crowds were sheltering. 'All the surrounding glass is shattered and the brickwork for a height of about nine feet is much damaged.' The fifth fell near Weller's Court in Pancras Road, killing a woodcutter and his dog.

George Jellicoe had been working late in his office and had booked a room at the Midland Grand Hotel that night. He left work about eleven that night and caught the Tube at Piccadilly Circus. A train for King's Cross was standing at the platform, but as he ran to catch it 'the conductorette (as they then were) slammed the gates in my face . . . that girl saved my life. I left by the next train after waiting a minute or so and arrived at King's Cross to find the doors shut and no one allowed to leave. As I was in uniform, they let me through into the street, which was in pandemonium – fire engines, people, police racing about in all directions. Bombs had been dropped less than two minutes before in the street and on the hotel itself, killing a number of people in the street between the hotel and Tube station . . . At the hotel, which was rapidly being turned into a first-aid station, I could not get to my room on the top floor. When at last, at 3 a.m., I was allowed up, it was to find the roof off, while the adjoining rooms were blown out. I heard that a man who had been asleep there had been killed.'

Edith Gooday had also sought shelter at the hotel with her family. 'My mother was strangely restless and kept saying she was not going to stay in the hotel itself, for she could feel that something awful was going to happen. Friends told her not to be silly, but she took our hands and led us through a long passage and down a flight of stairs until we found ourselves in what must have been a disused coal-bay. A young man-friend of ours, too young to go to war, said he was going to see if it was all clear, but as he stepped outside into the street he was hit by flying shrapnel. He staggered back saying, "It's awful outside."

'Then there came a terrific crash and darkness descended. Showers of splintering glass fell round us and coal dust fell, it seemed, by the ton.

Those of us who were not lying on the ground bleeding and groaning were practically choking. From all sides came cries for water but no water was to be had. How long we stayed like that I do not know. Suddenly a ray of light descended and framed in the doorway was a man in uniform. He told us it was daylight and the raid had been over for some time. So we tried to leave; all this time we had been in a corner behind a pillar. When we moved, we seemed to be ankle-deep in broken glass, and as we left the ruins, matches flickered and in their light a ghastly sight met our eyes: dead and injured lay everywhere. Picking our way out carefully, we at last came out into the air to see in the distance flames leaping up to the sky.'

'Crowds and crowds of poor people from the slums all round King's Cross' were also sheltering in the arches beneath St Pancras. They 'brought their beds and furniture and babies, and had encamped there under this concrete archway ... they come every night and stay all night.' On this night, two members of the Kane family were among them. They lived near King's Cross and since the raids began they had 'never properly undressed, the members of our family taking it in turns to wait at the police station for the first warning every night. My mother was a midwife, and [that night], as my brother came running home with a warning, she was sent for to attend a case. We had never left our home before, because my mother had a dread of crowded places and preferred to keep us close either in the passage or front room of the house. We were usually alone, us three; my father was a soldier. This night, hardly knowing what to do, my mother begged a neighbour to take my brother and me (he was twelve and I was eight) to the railway granaries at King's Cross, which were usually crowded by families taking shelter. The place was packed tight; it was dreadful, and as the raiders came nearer, the lights were lowered.

'Suddenly there was a sound that, even now, in memory, turns me sick. It was a whizzing, cutting sound, almost as if a huge knife was being sent through the air. A woman screamed, "My God! They've got us!" There was a terrified rush to the doors. It was pitch dark and my brother grabbed hold of me and dragged me under a table. I struggled to get away, to run anywhere. The air was full of screams and children crying; as long as I live I can never forget it. My brother sat on me, pinching me and daring me to move. I thank heaven now that he did. We never knew how many people were trampled to death there. We heard later that twins a month old were suffocated in the rush. My mother had heard the people running through the streets and almost frantic with worry had to carry on with her patient . . . I had air-raid shock and we were forced to take refuge in Glasgow.'

Rescue work in the Midland Grand Hotel and the station was 'carried out with considerable difficulty, the electric lights having failed . . . The lanterns of the ambulancemen, seeking in the dark for the dead and injured, made a weird, unforgettable picture.' Given that air-raids invariably paralysed train traffic and often led to thousands of people being stranded at stations waiting for services to resume, it was a miracle that the death toll was not even worse, but the solitary Giant's bombs still killed almost twice as many people – twenty-one – as the previous night's raids, severely injured twenty-two more, and caused twice as much damage.

In his report, the R25's commander suggested that even raids by a single aircraft would be enough to cause 'the whole of the anti-aircraft defences in England' to go on alert and 'an enormous amount of ammunition would be wasted' by anti-aircraft batteries putting up 'curtain barrages'. He noted that on 17 February, 'apparently from nervousness', anti-aircraft guns were fired 'not only in the vicinity of the aeroplane but also wildly into the air at a distance of thirty kilometres away'. Once again the guns also fired at a number of British fighters. Cecil Lewis's aircraft was holed by fire from the Benfleet guns, and several Bristol Fighters of 39 Squadron were targeted, one pilot temporarily losing control of his aircraft after a near-miss. In their defence the gunners claimed that 'two Bristols sounded like one Gotha'.

The jittery condition of the men manning the gun-batteries and the state of mind of London's defenders and its population could also be gauged from an incident the following night. Not a single German raider left Belgium's coast that night, but the faint sound of German bombers attacking Calais on the far side of the Channel was enough to set air-raid warnings sounding over London at ten to eight that evening, and fifty-five aircraft were scrambled. Anti-aircraft batteries pumped more than 2,500 rounds into the air, directed in part at ghosts and shadows, and in part at their own fighters. Some were damaged but, by a miracle, none was shot down. 'These alarms and excursions', the official chronicler of the air war admitted, choosing his words with care, revealed 'how sensitive the nerves of the public and of some of those responsible for the protection of the public had become'.

Further proof was offered by the tragic tale recounted by the registrar of deaths for St Pancras. A family from Leyton – father, mother and two teenage daughters – had narrowly escaped from their house in an earlier bombing incident. Their younger daughter, 'who was having a warm bath' at the time, rushed out 'inadequately clad, and in the chill night air contracted a cold which developed into pneumonia, from which she died a few days later'. Her death and the memory of the bombing raid preyed on her sister's mind and she became 'a physical wreck'. Hoping that a change of scene would help her to recover, her parents moved to a house near St Pancras. They moved in just hours before the raid of 17 February. Once again, a bomb exploded near their house. The windows of their daughter's bedroom were blown in and 'splinters of glass covered the bed on which she was lying'. Although physically uninjured, 'the shock proved too much for her weakened constitution and she followed her sister to the grave a few days later'.

The nerves of the surviving members of her family, and of the rest of London's population, were soon tested again. On 7 March the Giant squadron, RFA 501, previously based with the England Squadron at St Denijs-Westrem and Gontrode, was transferred to a new, purpose-built base at Scheldewindeke. Sited in low-lying farmland six miles to the south-east of Ghent, the ground was so wet and marshy that miles of ditches had to be dug to drain the airfield. It was probably the first airfield in the world to have concrete runways; there were two of them, 400 and 500 metres long, intersecting at right angles in a T-shape.

That night six aircraft were 'rolled out on the T-shaped concrete apron and parked in preparation for the take-off. We have been ordered to ready the machines for a night attack . . . Under the commander's supervision, every crew member bends to his assigned task.' The wireless operator tested his equipment, the fuel attendant checked the levels in the ten 245-litre tanks, the mechanics tuned the engines and the gunners armed the four machine-guns that each aircraft was carrying. The raid would be the first to be carried out on a completely moonless night but, unlike the Gothas, the Giants were equipped with radio equipment to fix their position and were not dependent on moonlight for navigation.

Hauptmann Arthur Schoeller, piloting R27, just had time for 'a frugal supper and dissemination of orders. A last comprehensive study of charts and orientation material with my observer, Oberleutnant Gunther Kamps, and the second pilot, Unteroffizier Buhler, then out to the armed R27, whose idling engines sing a song of subdued power. At exactly 20.00 hours, Hauptmann von Bentivegni fires the starting flare and the first of the R-planes strains forward with an ear-deafening roar. We are next to taxi to the take-off strip and ten minutes after the first aircraft, with full throttle, R27 heads into the the clear, dark night.'

The heavily loaded R27 rumbled over the concrete and climbed ponderously into the sky, belching black smoke from its multiple exhausts as the thunder of the straining engines drowned out every other noise. It flew a wide curve around the airfield and then headed north, following the 'pin-marked course on our maps. Inside the fuselage, the pale glow of dimmed lights outlines the chart-table, the wireless equipment and the instrument panel, on which the compass and other navigation instruments are mounted, to help us through the darkness.'

Schoeller 'saw the beacon at Ostend sending up flares into the night skies on which we could orientate ourselves. As we approached the coast, it was so dark that we could hardly discern the line of the surf; then we were out over the sea, setting course for Margate. Beneath us was a black abyss, with no visible lights that would hint at any type of vessel and not even a white wave crest to be seen. In the far north, there was a weak glow of light – the Northern Lights – but ahead of us was only a black void.

'We had set out under clear skies, but now thin shreds of clouds drifted past us, becoming thicker and thicker as we flew on. We rose above the cloud cover; beneath us we could see nothing, though judging by the flight time, we should now have been above English soil. Had we missed the English coast? Then, at last, searchlights flashed up, making circles of light on the clouds without fastening on us. Every other light appeared to have been blacked out, as if we were flying over a wasteland.

'We were obviously over England, but where? As the enemy had now heard our engines and activated the searchlights, we could break radio silence and request our bearings. The radio operator sent the signal to the two coastal stations in Belgium, they fixed our position and transmitted it to us: we were to the south-east of London. Tracked by the beams of searchlights that seemed to pass us on down the line from one light to the next, we set course for the Thameside dockyards that were our target, wondering if we could find them despite the poor visibility and the blackout.

'The landing lights of English airfields flashed into life; they were now scrambling to the attack. Our rear-gunner strafed the searchlights and Leutnant Kamps dropped four bombs on one particularly brightly-lit airfield, in retaliation for the raids on our own bases. The impact of the bombs was clearly visible. Ahead we could make out parts of the screen of barrage balloons that surrounded the southern and eastern outskirts of the city and, through a gap in the cloud cover, we briefly made out a grey ribbon in the surrounding blackness – a stretch of the Thames. We steered towards it and, as the next break in the clouds occurred, Oberleutnant Kamps, standing in the bow, pressed the levers that set our bombs falling to the earth below.'

Six R-planes had taken off, but one suffered engine trouble and returned to base. Only three of the Giants – R13, Schoeller's R27 and von Bentivegni's R39 – reached London, the other two bombing the Essex coast near Southend and, presumably through poor navigation, Ware in Hertfordshire. Twenty-three people were killed in the raids, the majority when von Bentivegni released his sole projectile – another 1,000kg bomb. Probably aimed at Paddington station, it instead struck Warrington Crescent in Maida Vale, demolishing a row of four five-storied houses 'of the type largely built fifty or sixty years ago for the merchant class of tenants, with spacious rooms and substantial materials' and devastating another 140 houses in the neighbourhood, 'a very large number so badly shattered . . . that they will have to be pulled down'. 'The whole area from Portsdown Road to Sutherland Avenue and Formosa Street appeared to the startled and bewildered residents as though a tornado had passed over it.'

A nine-year-old girl living across the road from the focus of the blast had been 'very excited and happy' as she went to bed. 'The next day I was going to a new school and on the chair by my bed was the first gym tunic I had had, which I was longing to wear. I never wore it. Long before the morning, I was awakened out of a sound sleep by the most terrible noise imaginable and it felt as if all the house was falling to pieces. We were in the front room of a semi-basement flat, immediately opposite the houses on which the bomb fell. Mother told me to put the light on and I found the switch, but of course [there was] no light. Suddenly we seemed to realise our position. We were in complete darkness, and we clung to one another, Mother with my baby sister in her arms. We felt as if we were standing on the edge of a hole and did not dare to move. Presently sounds of calling came from the people in the house, who were making their way down to us. We answered that we could not move to open the doors – if we could only have seen, there was not a door standing to open. How thankful I was to see them appear at last with torches and candles. I looked out of the window and saw a mass of flames, the houses opposite having caught fire. I can hear now the awful cries for help above the roar and crackle of the flames and the falling of masonry. Two children had come down from upstairs and the older girl and I kept the two younger children from looking at the fire, pretending the bright light was a sunset.'

Another young woman was found 'high up in a shattered house, hanging on to a beam by her hands'. She was rescued by fire crews and taken to hospital. The vicar of the nearby church heard 'the barking of the anti-aircraft guns, the roar of aeroplanes and whistle of falling bombs. Suddenly the darkness of the room was broken by a vivid flash, as bright as a fierce lightning flash, and a terrific roar caused the whole house to tremble. Our top window panes fell to the ground with a shattering noise. A soldier in our company, who was on short leave, pale and trembling, cried out, "My God! This is worse than the trenches!"

'When we ventured forth, the broad roadway off Sutherland Avenue was littered with splintered glass; not a window remained intact. It was much as though one was walking over a shingle beach, so thickly did glass cover the road . . . The next morning we heard that a piano which that very day had been tuned by our church organist had fallen from the top storey of its owner's house and crushed him to death in the basement.'

One young woman, kept alive for five hours as rescuers made frantic attempts to free her from the rubble of her home, died just as the last obstacle was being removed. She was one of twenty-three dead. A neighbour was luckier: trapped in his basement for twelve hours and given up for dead, he emerged with only a few scratches and bruises to show for his ordeal.

The shocked survivors of the bombing came out in daylight to see that the four houses where the bomb had fallen had been 'reduced to hideous piles of wreckage. Across the road, great branches of plane trees were torn from the stem, massive iron railings were thrown down and smashed, paving stones were torn up, and the contents of half a dozen houses were tossed around about in a broken and tangled litter . . . For a couple of hundred yards in every direction, hardly a window, even in basement rooms, was left intact . . . Here and there along the stricken road, phlegmatic householders were loading trunks and bags into taxi-cabs and starting off to find lodgings in places more habitable than their own windowless and shaken homes.'

The bombed-out wreckage of Warrington Crescent that they left behind – including the piano dragged from the ruins of the building that had housed it and deposited in the middle of the street – became a bizarre tourist attraction. 'Great crowds from all parts of England' flocked there to see the piles of rubble almost blocking the street and the collapsed and tottering houses, some with curtains still fluttering at glassless windows and pictures hanging on interior walls exposed by the collapse of the remainder of the building. Among the sightseers were the King and Queen, who were conducted round the ruins by Lord French.

After dropping their bombs, the Giants 'peeled off, homeward bound, along the banks of the Thames while the gun-batteries pumped shells up at us. The cloud cover thinned and broke up as we neared the coast, exposing us to the beams of the searchlights. Shells burst alarmingly close to us – we could almost touch the glowing fragments flying past us.' One shell-splinter sliced through the upper deck of the R27, without causing serious damage. 'Beneath us I saw the exhaust-flame of a fighter following us, but it never came close enough to threaten danger.' The British fighters had failed to trouble the Giants; even worse, two of them – Captain Alex Kynoch of 37 Squadron and Captain Clifford Stroud of 61 Squadron –

were killed when they flew into each other while climbing through cloud over Rayleigh in Essex.

R27 reached the open sea at Margate and set course for Ostend, 'its familiar signals guiding us home once more. We had just switched to the last two fuel containers when, as the coast came into view, the bass note of all four engines, so constant and reassuring until now, began to fade. It became slower and slower and suddenly the whirling discs of all four propellers ground to a halt. The pipes from the fuel containers we had just connected had frozen because of water in the fuel. Melting them was impossible, an emergency landing in the darkness of the night inevitable. Fearing that we would not make it to dry land, we put on our life vests, but even with no engines, the tremendous gliding ability of our R-plane still took us to shore, so close behind our front lines that we could see the artillery firing to our right.

'As the aircraft glided towards the ground, we fired flares to light up the terrain beneath us, but all we could see were hollows and zigzagging trench lines. To hit them or any other obstacle would mean almost certain death for us all. I saw a patch of level ground and rammed the column forward. The aircraft crashed down, rebounded hard a few feet into the air and finally came to a halt just in front of a wide canal. The right undercarriage was cracked and the lower deck on the right broken, but no crew member was badly injured.

'The time was 4.30 a.m. We had landed close to the dugout of an infantry brigade [near Courtrai] and they gave us castaways a warm welcome. We notified our division that we were safe and they were able to salvage our valuable instruments and the engines, before the wreckage fell victim to enemy artillery fire.' Another Giant was seriously damaged that night after crash-landing at Ghistelles – the airfield used in emergencies by aircraft unable to reach their home base, suggesting that it too was suffering from fuel or engine problems.

The same night Bogohls (bomber squadrons) 1, 2, 5 and 7 ('Bogohl' was the abbreviation for Bombengeschwader der Oberste Heeresleitung) had launched a raid on Paris, dropping 'more than 23,000 kilograms on the military establishments of this important fortress city', as von Höppner put it, still careful to maintain the nice distinction between 'fortress cities' and 'open towns'. While the British press renewed its calls for more frequent and heavier reprisals on Germany, Paris 'gave expression in its press of the desire to come to an understanding with Germany on the subject of bombing raids'. Such sentiments can only have encouraged those in the German High Command who believed that a truly devastating assault on the French and British capitals would bring them to the negotiating table. Von Höppner also had hopes that continuing raids might drive a wedge between the Allies: 'The opposing views on the subject which were held by the British and French . . . might take on a more serious aspect if we made further attacks.'

On 11 March German bombers again targeted Paris and, in a hideous echo of the Bishopsgate station disaster in London, seventy people were crushed to death against the locked doors of the Métro station Bolivar when the crowd surrounding the station panicked at the sound of anti-aircraft guns. A planned raid on London the following night, 12 March, never took place. Three Giants took off, but two developed engine trouble. One returned to base, the other, R13, bombed Boulogne before returning to Gontrode. Von Bentivegni, unwilling to venture over England alone, then turned the R39 around and bombed Boulogne as well.

All strategic bombing raids were then suspended as the Giants, like the Gothas of the England Squadron and every other available German aircraft, were redeployed in support of Operation Michael, launched on the Western Front on 21 March 1918. There were huge initial successes for the German forces in which all the Allies' hard-won gains of the previous three years were rolled up in a matter of days. Many British forces broke and ran, and the situation was so bleak that on 15 April Trenchard resigned and Haig delivered what sounded like his final address to his men: 'With our backs to the wall and believing in the justice of our cause, each one of us must fight to the end.'

However, the offensive was costing the already exhausted German forces men, machines and munitions that could no longer be replaced. Allied counterattacks, including the first large-scale deployments of American troops, stopped the German advances and began pushing them back. Operation Michael had failed to achieve a decisive breakthrough and the grinding war of attrition was resumed with the German armies now in a parlous state and increasingly outnumbered in manpower as more and more American troops were committed. Even more crucially, they were hugely outweighed in every kind of materiel: aircraft, tanks, artillery, shells, mortars, machine-guns, rifles and ammunition.

What Germany needed to prevail, or even to achieve parity in negotiations, was a *coup de main*, a lightning-bolt, a massive, coruscating assault on the twin pillars of the Entente, France and Britain. German armies no longer had the capacity to strike such a blow, but Ludendorff and the High Command believed that the weapon that could deliver such a victory from the jaws of defeat now lay almost ready to hand.

# CHAPTER 16
# THE WHIT SUNDAY RAID

IT HAD BEEN ALMOST FOUR MONTHS since a Gotha last crossed the English coast, but Brandenburg had not been idle. His England Squadron, refreshed, re-equipped and revitalized, was now ready to launch a fresh assault on London with by far the greatest concentration of bombers ever sent there. On 9 May, von Bentivegni was to lead four Giants of his 501 Squadron against England. Brandenburg was eager to pitch his force of Gothas into battle alongside them, but Georgii argued forcefully against it, warning him that dense fog was likely to form, obscuring the target and shrouding the airfields to which they would be returning. Brandenburg was persuaded and stood his Gotha crews down, but von Bentivegni, as headstrong and as eager for glory and medals as Kleine had been, ignored the forecast and the Giants took off as planned.

Georgii was vindicated when dense fog forced the Giants to divert to targets on the French coast, and it had indeed spread to their home airfield by the time they returned. It became a night of disaster for them. At one in the morning, R32 appeared overhead at Scheldewindeke. Despite the searchlights casting 'washed-out circles of light' on to the fog banks, R32's pilot could not make out the runway. He made several circuits of the air-field, trying and failing to detect the approach path, and then, as he came in low, hoping for a glimpse of the sheds or some familiar landmark, his undercarriage clipped the tops of the trees beyond the perimeter of the airfield. The aircraft crashed into a meadow half a mile away and an un-released bomb was detonated. One man survived, badly injured, the remainder of the crew was killed.

The pilot of von Bentivegni's R39, Freiherr von Lenz, was next to try his luck, and he was able to read the dim glow of the light beacons well enough to make a near-textbook landing, though even he only managed to bring the shuddering Giant to a halt a few inches from a ditch at the end of the runway. By the time the last two Giants were approaching Scheldewindeke the fog was even thicker; a signal was sent to them telling them to divert to Ghistelles, which was clear for landing. The message was either ignored or not received and the Giants continued to circle over the fogbound airfield. With their fuel running low, a second message was sent: 'Land at Ghistelles; otherwise use parachutes'. This too elicited no response, and in turn, the pilots attempted 'blind' landings. R26 flew into the ground and burst into flames. A mechanic was thrown clear and survived; everyone else was killed. The pilot of R29 tried to glide in, his landing lights casting a glow that was diffused to uselessness by the fog. He saw trees looming ahead of him and gunned his engines to try to climb again, but it was too late. The undercarriage caught in the branches, and the Giant smashed its way through the wood, tearing off its wings and bursting its fuel-tanks. The pilot managed to avoid another inferno by killing his engines before the spilt fuel ignited and he and most of his crew escaped with minor injuries, but their aircraft was another wreck.

Like Kleine before him, von Bentivegni's hubris had led his squadron to disaster; unlike Kleine, he was never to receive the Pour le Mérite he coveted. The loss of the Giants, halving the number Brandenburg could put in the air, was a bitter blow, for they had demonstrated themselves to be the most reliable, durable and formidable of the raiders. However, when Georgii was at last able to give Brandenburg the weather forecast he had been seeking, he was still able to launch the largest force ever sent against England. The England Squadron had been diverted to a series of tactical raids against Allied targets on the Western Front over the previous days, but despite the inevitable losses no fewer than thirty-eight Gothas, three Giants – R12, R13 and R39, making its seventh raid on England and once again carrying a 1,000kg bomb – and two reconnaissance aircraft were ready when the raid was launched on the evening of Whit Sunday, 19 May 1918.

There was only a gentle easterly wind as the first raiders took off from their bases in Belgium around nine in the evening and set course for England. It was a tribute to the improved reliability of the latest-model Gothas, and probably even more to the improved morale of the England Squadron under its first and finest leader, that on this occasion not a single aircraft turned back claiming engine trouble.

If the England Squadron's equipment, training and morale were much improved, however, the same also held true for the air defences that awaited them. London was now defended by 166 'actively efficient' aircraft and hundreds of anti-aircraft guns, searchlights and height-finders, not to mention 'an effective system of listening posts, chiefly manned by the police'. Although there were still fewer aircraft and guns than Ashmore had requested, they were well capable of exacting a heavy toll on the raiders.

The fighters' zones of operations had been completely reorganized. Squadrons based at Biggin Hill, Detling, Throwley, Sutton's Farm, Rochford, Bekesbourne, Hainault, North Weald Bassett, Goldhanger and Stow Maries straddled every possible attack route from the Kent coast to Suffolk. The facilities of these new bases varied enormously. North Weald Bassett was a gently sloping field on the north-facing side of a hill outside Epping. The officers were billeted in local houses but the ground-crews lived in tents around the airfield, vulnerable both to the weather and to shrapnel from German bombs. Rochford, just outside Southend, had a 'magnificent aerodrome almost a mile square', whereas Hainault, in low-lying, flood-prone fields requisitioned from the farm that had given the base its name, was a damp, grey and miserable place from which the aircrews escaped as soon as their turn of duty was over.

The aircraft flown by the Home Defence squadrons were equally varied. Some were still outmoded models that lacked the speed, rate of climb and 'ceiling' to trouble the German raiders, but several squadrons had been re-equipped with new Sopwith Dolphin aircraft, though their improved rate of climb and speed did not wholly compensate for difficulties of handling that required highly experienced pilots to fly them, particularly at night, and difficulties of access that made it necessary to strip down the engines completely to effect even quite minor repairs and maintenance. New ammunition combining explosive and incendiary properties was also in use, and the tactics of both fighter crews and gun-crews had been modified in the light of the experience of earlier raids. They were about to receive a thorough testing.

The waxing moon was well past its first quarter and the night was fine and dry, though a mist was seeping from the Thames and drifting through the streets of London on the faint easterly breeze. At 10.17 that night a 'suspicious aeroplane' was spotted off the North Foreland. It was a Rumpler acting as a pathfinder, dropping flares to indicate to the following bombers that the weather ahead was favourable for the attack. It was also carrying a few small bombs, and after completing his pathfinding duties the pilot made his own bombing run over London before wheeling away, unmolested, to return to base.

The first of the heavy bombers, a Gotha, was spotted approaching the coast twenty minutes after the Rumpler, and the British squadrons were ordered to begin their defensive patrols at seven minutes to eleven that night. The first in action was Major Christopher J. Quinton Brand, commanding 112 Squadron at Throwley. The twenty-four-year-old Brand, who already had six German victims to his credit, saw searchlight beams knifing through the darkness west of Canterbury and, spotting a Gotha near Faversham, he at once attacked from below and behind. Ignoring the fire from the Gotha's rear-gunner, Brand closed to within a hundred feet and fired two short bursts which silenced the bomber's starboard engine. The pilot took evasive action, swinging on to a north-easterly course, but Brand pursued him and three more rapid bursts caused the Gotha to burst into flames 'which also enveloped my own machine for an instant'. By then he was so close on its tail that the flames scorched the noses of both Brand and his Sopwith Camel and singed his moustache. He followed the Gotha down to 3,000 feet, seeing it break up and fall 'over the south-east side of the Isle of Sheppey', before he pulled out of the dive.

A second Gotha was shot down by nineteen-year-old Flight Lieutenant Anthony Arkell and his gunner, Aircraftman Albert Stagg, of 44 Squadron, patrolling at 11,000 feet just north of Hainault in the Bristol Fighter that Arkell had christened 'Devil in the Dusk'. At five past midnight, Arkell saw what he thought were 'the lights of some ordinary-sized machine' about a thousand feet below him. 'I dived down under it, as it was hazy, and saw against the starlight the shape of a Gotha. What I thought were lights were the exhausts of the engines . . . I was much faster and could climb better than it. After a little manoeuvring, I got under its tail, about 150 yards behind.' Arkell and Stagg, who was flying with him for the first time, both fired repeated bursts into the raider and 'saw sparks flying off the engine several times'. Then the starboard engine caught fire and, as the Gotha went into a spin and flames swept the aircraft from end to end, two of the crew were seen to jump to their deaths. The other, already dead or paralysed by fear, perished as the burning Gotha crashed into the ground 'in a sheet of flame' in a field off Roman Road, '200 yards away from the Albert Dock at East Ham, near the north bank of the

Thames'. 'Sirens near and far sounded a shrill note of victory' and, 'electrified by excitement when they saw the enemy visitor burst into flames and crash to earth', the watching crowds on the ground gave 'a long and satisfied roll of cheering'.

Arkell, whose 'first meeting with the Hun' this had been, felt more sympathy for the Gotha crew. 'I couldn't help feeling sorry for the poor fellows. For after all, they were only acting under orders, and it must take very brave men to come all that way at night over the sea and hostile country.' Arkell, who was awarded the Military Cross for shooting down the Gotha – the non-commissioned Stagg, who 'displayed the greatest coolness, taking no notice of much tracer which was going all round us' had to be content with a Military Medal – went to the crash-site the next morning. The body of one of the Gotha's crew had not yet been found and was 'presumed to be buried in the ground under one of its engines'. Arkell picked up a fragment of the Gotha's dark blue camouflage canvas, 'a bit of charred wood, and one German cartridge case as small souvenirs', together with 'a three-ply box that contained the belt of ammunition for the Hun machine-gun, slightly charred'. Hundreds of other people also turned up to stare at the 'compact heap of wreckage not more than a dozen yards square'.

Major Frederick Sowrey, CO of 143 Squadron at Detling, claimed the third kill that night, though it is probable that another crew actually shot it down. Sowrey fired a drum of ammunition from his Lewis gun into one Gotha near Maidstone, and put two drums into another, but lost both before he could apply the *coup de grâce*. The second aircraft was then targeted by Lieutenant Edward Turner and Lieutenant Henry Barwise of 141 Squadron, based at Biggin Hill. Turner manoeuvred on to the Gotha's tail and Barwise then raked it with the combined explosive/incendiary RTS ammunition. The Gotha's port engine was silenced and both starboard wings and the fuselage were riddled before Barwise's guns suffered the customary jam. Turner then lost sight of the damaged Gotha in the darkness.

Losing height fast, it fired distress signals in the apparent hope that it might be able to make an emergency landing at Harrietsham airfield, but, uncertain if it was a genuine airfield or a decoy laid out with false landing lights to fool German bomb-aimers, the pilot eventually crashed nearby. The rear-gunner, Unteroffizier Hermann Tasche, was the only survivor and he later confirmed that Turner and Barwise's aircraft had fired the fatal shots. Both men were subsequently awarded the Distinguished Flying Cross. The Teutonic cross insignia was cut from one of the Gotha's wings and hung in the 141 Squadron Mess at Biggin Hill, the first of many trophies that would one day adorn those walls.

Several other Gothas were attacked by fighters and survived, but three others were shot down by anti-aircraft fire and a seventh was lost after one of its engines failed as the pilot flew at low altitude beneath the cloud layer, trying to get his bearings. The observer, Leutnant Wilhelm Rist, had lived in London before the war and married a woman from Southend; he should have been familiar with the area, but he mistook the Blackwater estuary for the mouth of the Thames. Although he jettisoned his bombs in the river, the aircraft could not gain height fast enough to clear the rising ground and it crashed at St Osyth in Essex. His two crew members survived the crash but Rist, who had received the Knight's Cross of the Royal Order of the House of Hohenzollern just a week earlier, was killed.

Although many raiders were sufficiently deterred by anti-aircraft fire and fighter attacks to drop their bombs on easier targets – over half the bombs fell on Essex and Kent, not London – enough penetrated the capital's defences to cause further carnage. As the air-raid warning was given, passengers jumped off a train at Bethnal Green and 'followed the crowd to find ourselves under some railway arches with hundreds of others. The sight was pitiful: old people and little kiddies all looking deathly-white, some crying and everyone half-frozen with cold and apprehension.'

The Reverend Vernon Jones received a message asking him to go to the Metropolitan Hospital, Hackney, to help a deaf-and-dumb girl who was seriously ill after an operation. 'An air-raid began, but amidst all the tension and noise, there was no sign of panic in the ward. The nurses and patients were singing hymns. The deaf-and-dumb girl did not hear the bombs exploding or the anti-aircraft guns firing, but sometimes she felt the vibration, and once she said, in the sign language, "Why are the trains running so late at night?" I did not tell her what was happening. About

1 a.m. . . . there was a great crash and I found myself on my back, covered with broken glass . . . A number of babies were born deaf as a direct consequence of these air-raids, which terrified expectant mothers.'

A row of a dozen 'fairly good class houses' near the Bricklayer's Arms in the Old Kent Road were 'reduced to hideous piles of wreckage' by one bomb. The wallpaper of upper bedrooms was left 'flapping in the air' and fireplaces 'suspended as if in mid-air'. A 300kg bomb hit the Carlton Tavern in Carlton Vale, flattening the pub and killing 'the landlord and his dog, also injuring his wife', and in Packington Street 'two eight-roomed houses' packed with families and their lodgers were devastated by another bomb. Two women, who 'had apparently retired to bed, were found in their night attire on the pavement outside their house', and another seven people, caught in the open, were killed in the street. A man who visited the ruins of the houses the next morning noted that 'there was a bird in a cage, still merrily singing', but eight people had lost their lives and one of the survivors, a one-year-old girl, was so traumatized that seventeen years later she 'still suffers from fits'.

Another bomb demolished Delahoy's Dairy in Sydenham Road in south London. The owners and their three daughters were killed outright, and four members of the Milgate family also died in the bakery next door. A woman gave birth to a son the next morning 'amid the ruins' of their home in Hither Green. Several children rescued from the wreckage of another house in Camberwell 'made for St Bartholomew's church down the road, and rushed in there during a service, still screaming and crying for help. Women took off their coats to wrap around us, as we were wearing only thin night-dresses and had nothing on our feet. For a week we lived in the church, sleeping with hassocks for pillows, and every day we were fed by the Salvation Army.' Before dawn, on the morning after the raid, Whit Monday, Salvation Army volunteers were also 'round the road with a travelling kitchen, issuing hot soup and tea to the survivors'. Later that day, Miss S. Lansdowne saw 'four small coffins being carried out of a church. They were those of four little children who had attended Sunday School there the day before.'

The raiders had dropped 10,000kg of bombs, killing forty-nine people, injuring another 177 and causing £177,000 of damage, including at least 'one big fire' that had been seen when over London by the rear-gunner of the Gotha shot down near Harrietsham airfield. However, the England Squadron had lost eight Gothas in the raid: six were shot down, one was forced to crash-land in England, and the other was wrecked as it tried to land back at its Belgian base.

London's air defenders had been forced to endure abuse from people, press and politicians alike, but on this occasion their efforts earned them praise, and not all of it grudging. A fulsome note was circulated to fighter bases, expressing London's 'admiration and gratitude for the splendid defensive measures taken by the Air Services against the enemy's attack'. The anti-aircraft gunners also had reason to feel satisfied with their night's work. Thirty thousand shells had been pumped skywards, reaping the customary harvest of killed, injured and damaged houses from falling shrapnel, but, though 'most of the fire was of the barrage-kind, by sound and often wild', three raiders had been downed and several must have been diverted from their targets by the intensity of fire.

Brandenburg had planned a further series of raids on London after the Whit Sunday attack, but his squadron was once more diverted to tactical operations in support of a fresh German offensive on the Western Front, launched on 27 May. When that petered out, Brandenburg once again focused on London, scheduling raids for around the time of the full moon on 1 July and then when the moon was again near the full on 31 July. On both occasions the raids were called off by his superiors a short time before the aircraft were due to take off; but still the Fire Plan remained in place, and the means to implement it – Germany's new secret weapon – was now ready to be used.

# CHAPTER 17
# THE ELEKTRON FIRE BOMB

LORD FRENCH HAD BEEN MADE Viceroy of Ireland immediately after the Whit Sunday raid, and Sir William Robertson – replaced as Chief of the Imperial General Staff by Sir Henry Wilson – was appointed Commander-in-Chief, Home Forces, in French's place. It was a job that appeared something of a sinecure at first, but General Ashmore remained far from complacent, warning that 'the 3rd Hun bombing squadron [the England Squadron]' was at full strength and had taken delivery of 'special aeroplanes' that would enable them to overcome the current air defences arrayed against them. However, his warning faded from the public mind, and from Robertson's, as the bombers did not return during the weeks that followed, though the first of a series of high-speed reconnaissance flights took place just two days after the Whit Sunday raid, on 21 May 1918.

The aircraft, a Rumpler, crossed the coast near Shoeburyness, at an altitude of 18,700 feet. It passed over London at half-past eleven that night and had returned to its base in Tournai by two the following morning without a single shot being fired at it. Few in Britain were even aware of it, but that sortie and the series of daylight reconnaissance flights that followed, always by solitary aircraft criss-crossing London and the south-east, photographing targets and defensive installations from a height few British fighters could reach and none could attain before the Rumpler had flown out of range, had a significance that dwarfed all the combined horrors of the previous raids.

Amid the carnage of the Whit Sunday raid, it is unsurprising that, though the authorities recorded that among the 157 bombs dropped two had been incendiaries, they saw no particular significance in that. Yet those two must have been the prototypes of the England Squadron's newest and most deadly weapon of all. It was 'a war of engineers and chemists quite as much as of soldiers' and, spurred by the previous failures of the bombs required by the Fire Plan to set London ablaze, German scientists and engineers had been constantly working on improved incendiary devices. Much of the work was carried out by the giant Griesheim-Elektron company. With plants at Griesheim, Bitterfeld, Spandau, Rummelsburg, Döberitz and Horrem near Cologne, Griesheim-Elektron had already 'rendered indispensable services above all to the electro-technical and weapons industries ... aiding warfare with products and devices of all kinds', including aluminium and zinc, red phosphorus – 'exceedingly important for warfare' – and other 'chemical products for ammunition'. As the Allied blockade of the German coast choked off supplies of essential raw materials, the company was also in the forefront of the development and production of ersatz (synthetic) substitutes for war materials.

An incendiary had to satisfy four requirements. It should:

1.  Burn for a considerable time with a very large, hot flame.
2.  Actually render very inflammable not only the combustible material upon which it rests, but the material around it for a considerable area.
3.  Contain practically no material which is not extremely inflammable or which would not aid in the combustion.
4.  Present no great problems of manufacture, cost, transportation or use.

Although not specifically stated, a fifth requirement was equally obvious: the device had to successfully ignite in as close to 100 per cent of cases as human ingenuity could ensure.

By April 1918, the scientists and engineers at Griesheim-Elektron had found the solution: the B-1E Elektronbrandbombe (the Elektron fire bomb), an incendiary device named after the Elektron alloy from which its casing was made. Major Wilhelm Siegert could hardly contain his delight at the news. 'Since 1914, I have been a keen advocate of using the incendiary bomb against the enemy capitals. I regard them as more effective than demolition bombs, with the exception of my favourite 1,000kg bomb. From the 4.5kg Karbonidt bomb that spat out some remarkable incendiary material and a small 5-litre barrel of benzol that usually led to duds, via the tar-drenched Thermit- and Seil-Goldschmid bomb, in April 1918 we finally arrived at the effective Elektron incendiary bomb.'

The Elektron alloy was principally magnesium and aluminium – one formula prescribed 86 per cent magnesium, 13 per cent aluminium and 1 per cent copper, while Italian engineer Renato Ravalli described an Elektron incendiary composed of 92.5 per cent magnesium, 4 per cent aluminium, 3 per cent zinc and 0.5 per cent manganese – filled with a powder made of magnesium or aluminium and iron oxide. An alloy was used for the bomb casings because it had a high tensile strength and could be machined much more readily than pure magnesium; Elektron 'melts and is moulded very easily: the only difficulty in the production of the bombs is making the fuse'.

The use of magnesium in incendiaries conferred three huge advantages. First, magnesium and its alloys have densities of less than a quarter of that of steel so, though still strong enough not to shatter on impact, incendiaries constructed from magnesium alloys were a fifth the weight of the previous bombs. Second, there was no dead weight at all: whereas the previous incendiaries had a non-flammable steel casing, the casing of the Elektron bombs was as inflammable as its core. Third, magnesium combines rapidly with oxygen and burns fiercely in air when heated only slightly above its melting point – 650°C – and, whereas a pound of kerosene requires three and a half times its own weight of oxygen to combust, a pound of magnesium needs less than its own weight of oxygen. Its rapid and violent combustion is helped by one other property: as soon as it starts to burn, the heat generated raises the metal's temperature to its boiling point of 1,100°C, giving off magnesium vapour. This vapour, mixed with air, burns with a ferociously hot flame at a temperature of around 1,800°C.

A thermite charge was used to bring the magnesium to its ignition point. Thermite, a mixture of one part metallic aluminium to three parts oxide of iron, is an extraordinary substance. Only certain oxides of iron and particle sizes of aluminium or oxide are suitable and the material is so inert that it can be handled without danger, so stable that it can even be dropped on to molten iron without starting a reaction. However, once any part of the thermite is heated to around 2,000°C, a fierce reaction begins like 'a furnace from which gaseous products are not evolved and in which metals themselves are used as fuels'.

In the Elektron incendiary bomb, a small percussion charge of black or smokeless gunpowder ignited a priming mixture of finely powdered magnesium and an oxidizing agent such as barium peroxide. That in turn started the thermite reaction, and because no gases or vapours formed to conduct the heat away, the temperature of the reaction soared to around 3,000°C. The resultant white-hot fluid flowed like water, igniting any combustible substance with which it came into contact and burning straight through brick and cement. The reaction was so fierce that even dropping the thermite into water had no effect; it continued to burn until the reaction was complete.

The burning thermite's intense heat itself contributed to the incendiary effect, but that heat also melted the magnesium and started it burning. Such is magnesium's tendency to unite with oxygen that it will take oxygen out of many compounds, even though they would not normally be classed as oxidizing agents. For example, water thrown on to molten magnesium will not extinguish it. Instead the oxygen contained in the water will be given up to fuel the burning magnesium and the hydrogen released as gas. The hydrogen gas then also burns with a long, very hot flame as it mixes with air above the magnesium, and if some of the hydrogen fails to combust at once, perhaps because the water has temporarily cooled the flame below its ignition point, it forms an explosive mixture with the air that can then detonate with savage effect. Molten magnesium will also combine with the oxygen in carbon dioxide, so neither water nor carbon dioxide fire extinguishers were of the slightest use against the burning magnesium of Elektron bombs, since they only served to fuel the flames. 'Their enormous combustible temperature sets fire to any flammable object within reach' and, 'once the fuse is lit, it is impossible to extinguish them; the casing burns with the rest'.

The British Fire Prevention Committee's standard advice for dealing with incendiary bombs, still current in 1918 and widely disseminated to the public, was therefore completely useless. It stated that 'fires caused by incendiary bombs may be prevented from spreading, regardless of the high temperatures generated at the actual seat of the outbreak, if water be promptly applied in fair bulk, force and continuity, say from a series of buckets energetically thrown, or hand-pumps vigorously worked.' Any attempt to follow this advice when dealing with the new incendiaries would simply fuel the fires. The only way to extinguish an Elektron bomb was to remove the oxygen supply to the fire using sand, fire-blankets or the Heath-Robinson contraptions British fire brigades eventually devised:

large bowls of fireproof material on the end of eight- or ten-foot poles, which could be clamped over an incendiary to starve it of oxygen.

The cylindrical Elektron bombs, fitted with stabilizing fins, were just 350mm long by 50mm in diameter, and weighed just 1kg; some experts thought that even 'a 200 gram bomb would have sufficed'. They were not designed to penetrate deep inside buildings. If dropped from a height of 5,000 feet, the Elektrons struck with a velocity of around 380 feet per second – powerful enough to penetrate slate or shingle roofs, but not to smash down through all the floors of the house. If the attic floor was of flimsy construction, the Elektron might break through it to the floor below, but it would very rarely travel further than that. As a result, fires would break out in the roof-voids or upper stories of target buildings rather than on the lower floors, and 'residents who had gone down into the cellars' as a precaution during an air-raid 'would often not have noticed until too late that the upper storeys were on fire'. Even if the occupants were not taking shelter in their cellars, the small size and lack of explosive impact of the Elektron incendiaries, and the relative silence of their combustion – neither the ignition of the thermite nor the burning of the magnesium generated anything more than a hissing noise, audible only for a distance of a few yards – made them likely to remain undetected amid the rattle and thunder of large steel fragments from the anti-aircraft shells raining down on rooftops and streets.

Subjected to rigorous testing, the Elektron incendiaries proved to have none of the flaws of their misfiring predecessors. With a weight of only a kilogram they could be dropped in their thousands over the target, and their thermite and magnesium charges, ignited on contact, burned at up to 3,000°C and were almost impossible to extinguish. 'The operational orders for their use had already been written, which in particular envisaged the generation of several small incendiary fires capable of combining into one giant conflagration or firestorm.' Elektron bombs may have been used during a raid on Paris on 15 June 1918 during which the Paris-France department store was completely burned out. If so, this was only a test-drop of a handful of projectiles. As soon as sufficient bombs had been manufactured and stockpiled, the new weapons were to be unleashed in two overwhelming incendiary attacks – the final realization of the Fire Plan that Germany's commanders had nurtured throughout almost four years of war.

Bogohl 3, the England Squadron, would carry out a massive fire-raid on London, aiming to 'engulf the capital in flames, the like of which had not been seen since the Great Fire of London some 250 years earlier'. Simultaneously three other squadrons – Bogohls 1, 2 and 4 – would bomb Paris, 'the nerve centre and seat of the main resistance of the Entente'. German optimism about the impact the fire-raids would have on Paris was reflected in Hindenburg's view that 'at the time, the political atmosphere of Paris seemed to be heavily charged. Our shells and attacks from the air had hitherto not produced the explosion [of popular protest], but we had reason to hope that there would be an explosion.' The disparity in squadron numbers targeting the two Allied capitals was because those attacking Paris would have to cross the Allied lines on the Western Front on their flights to and from the target, and would inevitably suffer heavy losses from the thousands of fighters and anti-aircraft guns stationed on and behind the Front. The statistics of previous raids bore that out: in the course of the war, while ten airships and 116 aircraft had successfully bombed London, only two airships and fifty aircraft had reached Paris, and of those, one airship and sixteen aircraft – a third of the total – were shot down.

At least one man was looking even further afield. The faith of Korvettenkapitän Peter Strasser in the Zeppelin fleet he commanded had never wavered despite a catalogue of failures. On 18 July 1918, Strasser, an intense, brooding man, with a black moustache and goatee beard, pre-sented the Chief of Naval Operations, Admiral Reinhard Scheer, with a plan to unleash the latest-model Zeppelins not only against London but also against New York City. The vast new Zeppelins, like the multi-engined, 694-foot L70, had the range to cross and re-cross the Atlantic. With each one capable of carrying a 4,000kg bombload, just three of them, Strasser argued, could drop enough high-explosive and incendiary bombs to paralyse New York and deal a devastating blow to American morale. Scheer considered the proposal for twenty-four hours, then returned the plans, annotated with a single word: 'Nein'. Two weeks later Strasser was dead, shot down in the L70 as he staged a final futile Zeppelin raid on England, perhaps in an attempt to persuade Scheer to reconsider.

Whatever the merits or demerits of Strasser's proposal, the Fire Plan to use aircraft in waves of incendiary attacks on London and Paris retained the wholehearted support of the German High Command. Every Giant and Gotha aircraft that was fit to fly was to attack its designated target, return to base, reload and take off again at once, raining down incendiaries on London and Paris over and over again, until every single aircraft had been shot down or the surviving air-crews had become too exhausted to fly.

All knew that this was effectively a suicide mission. There would be an element of surprise as the first wave went in – there had been only half a dozen isolated bombing raids on London in the whole of 1918 and defenders and population alike would inevitably have grown a little complacent – but by the time those pilots who survived that first raid returned to the attack the air defences would be ready and waiting for them. As the numbers of surviving Gothas and Giants dwindled, the odds on their returning safely to base would lengthen exponentially. Most, perhaps even all of them, would eventually be shot down, but by then, blitzed by Elektron incendiary bombs, London and Paris would be twin oceans of flames none could extinguish.

Based on experience of fire-raids on the Eastern Front, 'the area of towns hit by the bombs varies from 15% (Graz) to 50% (Danzig, Breslau), from which an average of 35% can be assumed. If half the bombs do not break through the roofs or do not ignite, and only half both break through and ignite, a squadron of a hundred planes, each carrying a tonne of bombs, would nevertheless cause 17,000 fires, a not inconsiderable number.'

'Even supposing that of the hundred planes which set out, only five succeeded in flying over a city like Paris, that equates to 5,000 Elektron bombs falling on the city . . . that means more than 800 fires. Whether there are 17,000 or 800 fires starting simultaneously, the result is roughly the same if the meteorological conditions are favourable for fanning the flames, i.e. if the wind is in the right direction. Faced with such an attack the Parisian fire service, even though it is made up of an elite corps of well trained and well equipped personnel, would have been overwhelmed:

whole districts of Paris would have been ablaze. The catastrophe would have caused enormous loss of human life as well as destruction of supplies and resources.'

A similar catastrophe would hit London. One very conservative estimate suggested that, even allowing for the depredations of the anti-aircraft defences and the number of aircraft turning back without reaching the target, a minimum of 2,250 Elektron incendiary bombs would fall on London in the first raid alone. Since a single Giant could carry almost that number, a more realistic estimate might have been five to ten thousand.

Now, at last, as Paul Behncke, the Deputy Chief of the Naval Staff, had threatened at the outbreak of war, 'England shall be destroyed by fire'. The horror of the repeated attacks and the swelling firestorms left in their wake would cause devastation and mass panic, sweeping London and Paris and spilling out into the country beyond, and forcing the Allies to sue for peace. That, at least, was the belief of the German High Command.

London now faced 'one of the gravest perils which ever menaced the capital', and Parisians, in similar peril, were already being softened up by another German innovation. Since 21 March 1918, 'as a sort of intro-duction to the raids, an extraordinary "wonder ordnance" was firing its shells 130 kilometres to the French capital'. This Paris-Geschütz (Paris Gun) was the largest artillery piece used in the war, firing a 200lb shell. Batteries of standard Army artillery were located in the area a few miles around it, firing simultaneously to create a 'noise-screen' to prevent Allied spotters identifying and targeting the site of the giant gun. The shells reached an altitude of twenty-five miles before plunging back to earth almost three minutes after being fired and led Parisians to think that they were being bombed by a new type of high-altitude Zeppelin, as the explosion of the shells was preceded by neither the sound of an aircraft nor the audible firing of artillery. Although it was a hugely expensive, in-accurate and inefficient weapon in purely military terms – each firing wore away the gun-barrel so much that numbered shells had to be used, each slightly larger than the previous one, and every sixty-five firings the barrel had to be rebored – as a device to generate panic and sap the morale of Parisians it was much more successful. In total between three and four hundred shells were fired, killing 250 people, wounding 620, and casting a pall of fear over the whole city.

That fear might soon turn to terror and mass panic as the Fire Plan was reactivated, with a genuine prospect of success. Bogohls 1, 2 and 4 had already been 'drawn forward to the area of Ham' in preparation for the attacks on Paris, and at St Denijs-Westrem, Gontrode and Scheldewindeke, although the rumble of Allied guns was every day a little closer and louder, the England Squadron and Giant Squadron Rfa 501 were also at readiness. Tens of thousands of Elektron bombs were stored in stockpiles at or near the bombing squadrons' bases, ready for the onslaught to begin.

The order to launch the Fire Plan – or the 'fire circus', as one German pilot described it – was twice issued, in August and again in early September, and twice countermanded at short notice. The weather then intervened as England and the Low Countries endured the wettest September on record; in many parts of Britain it rained on every single day of the month and it was unseasonably cold and windy as well. Time and again the German squadrons assembled, waited and then stood down as Walter Georgii's forecasts of dense cloud, high winds and rain over either the target or the Ghent bases precluded the launch of the aircraft.

Finally, on 23 September, Georgii was able to offer a window of settled weather. The order to attack was received from Germany's High Command, and Bogohl 3 (the England Squadron), the Giants of Rfa 501, and the Gothas of Bogohls 1, 2 and 4 at once began their final preparations. At the airfields near Ghent and Ham, and at the Giant base at Scheldewindeke, mechanics carried out their last checks on the engines and equipment while armourers ferried endless loads of Elektron bombs from the bunkers and bomb-stores. Shining a ghostly silver-grey in the fading light, like shoals of fish in the depths of a lake, the bombs were laid out in rows on the grass by each aircraft, ready for loading into the racks.

The air-crews assembled for their final briefings; some were held in huts and sheds, others took place in tents pitched on the edge of the air-field. The men of the England Squadron talked in murmurs as they waited in their briefing hut, the only sounds the creak of leather and canvas as they shifted in their seats, and the slow pulse of a ceiling fan turning lazily overhead. The familiar smell of cigarette smoke and stale sweat in the room mingled with the taint of aviation fuel and exhaust fumes drifting through the open window from the airfield outside.

When Brandenburg and Georgii entered, the men fell silent, the stress etched in every line of their faces. The meteorologist's report outlined the weather conditions and Brandenburg then briefed his men on routeing to the target and the disposition of air defences. If there was an air of suppressed excitement, there was also an almost palpable sense of foreboding. Every member of the air-crews of the England Squadron, and of the other squadrons at their airfields, sitting attentive and motionless as Brandenburg, von Bentivegni or the other squadron leaders spoke, knew that the bonds formed during the years of training and the combat flights over London or Paris, or the battlefields of the Western Front, were now to be severed. These moments before this final mission for the England and Paris squadrons would be the last time that many, perhaps even all of them, would see one another.

Those who survived the swarms of enemy fighters lying in wait on the outward and return flights and the forests of flak-bursts over the target would return knowing that their fate had only been postponed, not averted. After refuelling and reloading they would immediately be running the gauntlet of those air defences a second, a third, a fourth and a fifth time, returning endlessly to the target until exhaustion or death claimed them. Yet enough patriotism and pride burned in them to know that this was a defining moment that could decide the conflict that had raged so long, bringing victory to their Fatherland and eternal glory to them, and none of them – outwardly at least – showed any weakening of his resolve.

Years after the war, a pilot with one of the Paris squadrons could still vividly recall the scene on his airfield at sunset that evening, 'the half-circle of tents silhouetted against the sky, rapidly disappearing in the dusk. I still hear the noise of the motors making a test run and drowning out every other sound. Then we could see a long stream of sparks from the exhaust until the throttle was eased and the engine, after releasing a long blue flame from the exhaust, was idling again smoothly. When all engines had been tested, the ignition was cut. The sudden silence gave us an unreal feeling of peace and of suspense.

'We were tense when we emerged from the tent of the squadron leader, who had given us the meteorological report and the itinerary for our separate take-offs, the route going out and the return, the latest intelligence reports about the anti-aircraft guns, the searchlight defences and the information about the 150 night-fighter airplanes that were supposed to defend Paris against us ... Only a week before we had launched a heavy attack on Paris with high-explosive bombs totalling twenty-two tons, a terrific amount for that time. We had seen the huge explosions and the fires that we had caused, and a few days later we were able to read reprints from Swiss papers with exciting reports of the terror we had created.' Now Paris was again to be the target, while 'other German bombers were to visit London that night. The aim was to start so many fires with this first incendiary attack that the fire brigades would not be able to put all of them out.'

# CHAPTER 18
# LUDENDORFF'S
# INTERVENTION

BARELY A HINT ABOUT THE FIRE PLAN had reached Allied Intelligence. Among the few elliptical references was an Air Board report that 'information, which should be accepted with reserve, concerning a new incendiary bomb was given by a prisoner. This bomb is believed to be very light and fifty or sixty can be dropped simultaneously'; in fact, a single Giant could drop a minimum of a thousand of them. A report from Frankfurt also noted that, 'according to a friend of Baron von Jenin, an air-raid on Paris on a large scale is being prepared'.

There is no evidence that either piece of intelligence was acted upon, but, although the timing was coincidental, a vast offensive by British, French and American forces on the Western Front had now tipped the balance of the war against Germany. On 8 August, as the stockpiles of Elektron bombs at last reached the required levels, the Allies launched a massive ground attack. It was prefaced by an artillery barrage of brief duration but such horrific intensity that the ground seemed 'to boil', and hundreds of tanks, backed by ground-attack aircraft, then led an assault on the German positions. The depleted enemy, weakened by long attrition and the mountainous casualties suffered during its own spring offensive, was driven back and the retreat turned into a rout. German losses on the day were estimated at thirty thousand – five times the Allied casualties – and collapsing morale saw a further 16,500 German troops surrender. '*Der schwartze Tag des Deutschen Heeres in der Geschichte dieses Krieges*' – 'the black day for the German Army', in Ludendorff's phrase – signalled to both sides that the tide of the war had now taken a potentially decisive turn.

German forces would continue to offer stubborn resistance, and Ludendorff and his commanders still clung to the belief that the Fire Plan could yet snatch a victory, or at least an honourable peace, but the relentless tide of Allied advances over the remainder of the month suggested otherwise. Others felt that, while the timing of the end might yet be uncertain, the result was no longer in doubt, and Germany's deteriorating position on the battlefield now made them fearful of the consequences for the nation if the planned incendiary raids went ahead.

One other factor was beginning to weigh heavily on German minds. However belatedly, the popular clamour in England for retaliatory air-raids had been answered. The Smuts reports in 1917 had argued for a single unified air service and for the bombing of Germany. The proposal was nearly abandoned, but was revived after the intercession of Rear-Admiral Mark Kerr of the Air Board. He wrote 'an alarmist report of German air strength' that became known as 'the Bombshell Memorandum', correctly claiming that the Germans had a massive new bomber 'ready for use', though the five-ton bombload he cited was a considerable overstatement. Using information obtained from Italian sources, he also warned that the Germans were building four thousand heavy bombers and would soon have the ability to devastate large parts of London and the south-east. 'Woolwich, Chatham and all the factories in the London district will be laid flat, part of London wiped out'. To counter this, Kerr argued that an Air Ministry 'with executive power' was required, deploying two thousand heavy bombers 'as a minimum'.

The Air Force Bill was duly pushed through Parliament, but even before it became law, 41 Squadron, using the RFC's handful of new Handley-Pages, took off from the Ochey airfield on 17 October 1917 to make a daylight raid on the Burbach iron factory near Saarbrucken. A week later the Navy's Handley-Pages joined a night attack on the same target, the first British strategic night raid. A civic group in Manchester promptly offered a bounty of £1,000 for 'the British aviator who dropped the first bomb on Berlin'. Confronted with the brusque rejoinder that 'British officers were prohibited from "accepting tips"', the group then offered the sum to charity. The reward was never to be claimed.

The Air Force Bill was passed into law on 29 November 1917, and the Air Ministry duly established in January 1918. In April the two air forces, the RFC and the RNAS, were at last merged into a single arm: the Royal Air Force. To his volubly expressed disgust, former president of the Air Board Lord Cowdray was passed over for the job of Air Minister; after Lord Northcliffe turned it down, Lloyd George awarded it to the press baron's younger brother, Viscount Rothermere. He announced his plans with considerable brio, claiming that 100 to 150 aeroplanes 'carrying bombs enough to lay the place attacked level with the ground' would soon be launched against German cities, and asserting that every future raid on London would be answered by a retaliatory strike that would 'absolutely wipe out one or two large German towns'.

Rothermere wanted Major General Hugh Trenchard to be Chief of the Air Staff and overcame his, and Haig's, initial reluctance. Trenchard returned to England by destroyer on this occasion, avoiding the possibility of triggering further embarrassing air-raid false alarms. However, the two men disagreed over almost every aspect of the role of air power, not least Rothermere's belief in the efficacy of bombing Germany. As Trenchard remarked in a withering aside, it was 'easier to bomb Berlin in headlines' than from the cockpit of a bomber. Rothermere's proposal that the Allied bomber fleet be increased to sixty squadrons also fell foul of Douglas Haig and the Allied Supreme Commander, Ferdinand Foch. Both felt the emphasis on bombing Germany was diverting men and equipment needed for the ground war, and distracting the Allies from what should have been their true priority: victory on the Western Front.

Nonetheless, raids on German cities by British and French bombers were intensified, provoking a furious reaction from Major Wilhelm Siegert. 'Two of our bombing squadrons carried out a punitive raid against Paris with the concurrent announcement that in case of a repeated attack on German cities, Paris will suffer the treatment of re-offending criminals. And what do those brothers do? Immediately they drop bombs on Trier. Well, you'll see! Instead of two there will be four squadrons, including some R-Birds, paying you a return visit so that it may rain on the roof of the Frenchman right and proper.' A few weeks later he was still complaining that 'the "Frogs" just won't learn. They bombard Stuttgart and Mainz. Our loud answer to the Parisians follows promptly during the night.'

Siegert's response to an article in the French newspaper *Journal du Peuple* was even more scathing. It reported that 'The flight from Paris on the rail tracks towards the South is increasing in numbers on a daily basis. Moreover, innumerable wealthy Parisians are living in the distant outskirts and are busy in the city only during the day. But what about the proletarian who lives in a flat in the fifth floor with his children, where they are the first to be at the mercy of the bombs? Renting a single room in the outskirts is also out of the question as there is a genuine price war going on for these commodities. Safety measures have to be put into place.' The newspaper went on to applaud the call from the Federal Committee that, 'In the light of the fact that in these days the voice of humanity has to be made heard as often as possible and that the bombardment of open cities does not shorten the duration of the horrible suffocation, but must bring the feeling of hatred to its peak, all governments are called upon to accept the suggestion of the Swiss Red Cross asking for the suspension of unnecessary crimes.' 'How hoity-toity!' Siegert sneered. 'If your fuel tanks were big enough to take you on raids to Berlin, then the proposal would sound somewhat different.' But he was offering a dangerous hostage to fortune with his comments, for development work on new aircraft that would at last bring Berlin within range of Allied bombs was now well advanced.

Although the feud between Trenchard and Rothermere had reached such proportions that both men resigned, Trenchard was not long out of the public eye. British raids on Germany accelerated after the formation on 5 June 1918 of the 'Independent Force', the British equivalent of Germany's England Squadron. The new Air Minister, Sir William Weir, offered the command to Trenchard, who turned it down. He continued to show no desire to undertake any active role in the war effort until he overheard two officers comparing his resignation as Chief of the Air Staff to desertion in the face of the enemy, and remarking that if they had the power they would 'have him shot'. Shaken, Trenchard at once wrote to Weir to say that he had changed his mind and would accept the post after all.

It was not the least of Great War ironies that Trenchard had previously been one of the most obdurate opponents of strategic bombing, but he now took to his poacher-turned-gamekeeper role with all the enthusiasm of a religious convert, and was soon urging ever larger raids on German cities. In June 1917, a British pilot had said that every British airman 'would ten thousand times rather fight ten Boche birds [aircraft] single-handed on the Western Front than bomb a quiet German town and kill women and children, but,' he added, 'if any squadron is ordered to bomb a German town, it will, of course, be done.' That order had now been issued, and the tempo and weight of raids on German towns and cities was increasing.

Trenchard identified the two aims of his bombing force as 'a) Do military and vital damage by striking at the centres of supply of war material. b) Achieve the maximum effect on the moral [i.e. morale] by striking at the most sensitive part of the whole of the German population – namely, the working class.' However, to the often expressed fury of officers of the Air Staff, Trenchard then directed his bombers to attack railway stations and airfields far more often than chemical plants and steel works. To his critics, whatever his public statements, he was continuing to subordinate the air forces he controlled to the tactical requirements of the Army in the field, rather than pursuing the strategic role he had been given. However, the reason for the attacks on railways at least 'was obvious – rail sidings were the easiest target to hit and the most congested railway centres were in the middle of industrial towns. Hence, the targeting of railways provided the greatest measure of success, regardless of where the bombs landed,' and 'if houses are hit, it produces panic and lowers the production'.

British politicians and generals were privately not unhappy that German civilians were now discovering the terror that German bombers had inflicted on Londoners. An officer at the Directorate of Flying Operations advocated bombing by daylight rather than at night because factory workers would feel more exposed in a daylight raid at work than in their own homes at night, and Weir told Trenchard, 'If I were you, I would not be too exacting as regards accuracy in bombing . . . the German is susceptible to bloodiness and I would not mind a few accidents due to inaccuracy.'

To increase the possibility of 'accidents' there was a British equivalent of the Elektron bomb, the disarmingly named 'Baby' incendiary, and even a British equivalent of the Fire Plan. 'In an incendiary system we are harnessing the element fire and applying it as a war weapon. In deciding on this element, we need no stronger warranty than the universal dread in which fire is held by humanity . . . No ordinary populace' could withstand the effects of a sustained incendiary campaign. Weir wanted an incendiary raid to 'start up a really big fire in one of the German towns', and others in the Air Ministry were also pressing for a fire-raid on the congested and largely wooden old quarter of one of Germany's towns or cities, creating a firestorm that would raze it to the ground and break the spirit of the German population to continue the war.

That the Allies possessed effective incendiaries was demonstrated to the German High Command on 28 August 1918 when 'the enemy dropped many incendiary bombs' on a petrol dump at Saarbrucken. 'We could hear all the noise and our windows were broken by the explosion.' In another raid near Offenburg a farm was destroyed and woodlands ignited by 'some incendiary fuses dropped by enemy aviators . . . This must act as a warning to our people to take such precautions as are necessary.'

Britain also paid a heavy price for these raids. Aircraft losses under Trenchard's policy of 'relentless offensive' – those who followed a more prudent policy were condemned by him for 'a lack of ginger' – were as horrendous for the Independent Force as they had been for the RFC. In one period of 'eleven flying days and twelve flying nights', Trenchard lost 81 per cent of his total establishment, and one authority claimed that 'the expense of the RAF's destroyed aircraft exceeded the cost of the damage it inflicted on Germany'. Yet still the raids continued. Berlin remained just out of range of Allied bombers, for the moment at least, but Germany's industrial cities in the west – Cologne, Frankfurt, Mannheim, Offenburg, Kaiserslautern, Karlsruhe, Saarbrucken, Trier, Hagendingen and Saaralben – were pounded.

In Cologne, the marketplace 'looked as if they had been slaughtering animals'; 'one walked over nothing but debris. The mourning is great.' The station at Offenburg was also 'completely wrecked by an air-raid', and 'the people who were under cover were all buried, but the newspapers don't mention anything about it'. 'The uproar that goes on here is terrible . . . No one has rest any more, day or night'; 'a permanent and mighty thunder fills the air'. 'Who knows what may yet happen to us. There is great uneasiness here.'

A 'reliable source' of British Intelligence applauded 'the excellent moral effect' of the air-raids. 'The panic created at Cologne, in especial, was intense, and if we had only continued these bombing expeditions for a few days consecutively, the result would have surpassed expectations.' Just as in London, the pervasive atmosphere of fear and tension, waiting for the next wave of bombers to appear from the night sky, bred rumour and panic in the German population. 'No one saw the machines and the people seemed convinced that it was caused by Americans flying new machines at altitudes hitherto unknown. The terror of raids grows day by day.' 'At Herstal a bomb fell forty metres from the Pieper works without causing any damage. All the workmen fled in a panic and since then over 300 of them have refused to work, on the pretext that the Allies will come back to bomb the factory again.' There were also constant false alarms. Out of 107 air-raid warnings in one German city, only seven raids actually followed; the alarm was sounded three hundred times in Bous but again it was attacked only seven times; and the Roechling Works at Volklingen had fifty alarms but was never bombed at all. Just as in England, each false alarm was almost as disruptive of production as an actual raid.

The threat and the actuality of bombing raids prompted a delegation of Rhineland town mayors to travel to the headquarters of the German High Command. They petitioned Hindenburg and Ludendorff to cease bombing London, Paris and other British and French cities since that only invited reprisals, and warned of strikes and riots if air-raids on Germany continued. Hindenburg heard them out with barely concealed impatience, then dismissed them with a curt statement that the conduct of the war would remain unaltered.

Meanwhile the morale of the population continued to disintegrate under the combined pressures of the ever-mounting toll of German war-dead, the hardships caused by the Allied blockade and the terror of the day and night bombing raids. German society as a whole was fragmenting and divisions were widening, between Prussian and Bavarian, middle class and working class, even neighbour and neighbour.

Two German POWs, both Warrant Officers, 'expressed the opinion that it would serve a better purpose if the Prussian towns were raided . . . as Prussia is the culprit all the way through'. An intercepted letter from Cologne noted that 'the bombs fell in the centre of the town and the killed and wounded were mostly among the working class. It would have been better in every way if some of the bombs had fallen on the villas [where the middle classes lived].' During another attack 'a terrible panic occurred among the population because the people refused to allow others to take refuge in their houses. This doubtless on account of the numerous cases of stealing . . . an order has been given out by the General Commanding the 18th Army Corps with a severe penalty attached . . . commanding all householders to open their doors when the alarm is sounded and to give shelter to all who ask it, until the danger is passed [sic].'

As a reprisal for air-raids on Karlsruhe, British officer prisoners of war were used as human shields and 'interned in hotels near the factories', but this merely served to emphasize to the local population the lack of any more effective response to the raiders, and, just as in England, that only increased the popular fury. In its edition of 9 August, the newspaper *Trierische Landeszeitung* called for Germany's leaders to be housed in bomb-damaged areas where they would have 'ample opportunity for collecting information in the hospitals, in the schools, in the underfed families, from the woman with child, from the man with a weak heart, from the bedridden invalid, and from other similar cases which are equally susceptible to this modern method of waging war'.

The leaked news that Prince Joachim of Prussia had given orders to the garrison at Strasbourg not to use the anti-aircraft guns 'so as not to frighten the Princess' who was about to go into labour at the Imperial Palace was also seized upon as an example of the way the poor were being made to suffer a disproportionate share of the burden of the raids, and there was fierce criticism of affluent citizens who, just like their well-off cousins in England, moved out of the areas threatened by bombing and rented houses in 'less threatened locales of the Fatherland ... As no sufficient accommodation exists in these towns ... the local people have either to pay the correspondingly high rents offered by these rich intruders or clear out into the streets, as of course the house owners exploit the occasion to the utmost.'

Food shortages bit ever deeper, too, exacerbating the misery of the poor. 'One is deprived of everything, food is rare, clothing is difficult to obtain and even the best-dressed women wear shoes with wooden soles.' 'One is suffering a great deal from lack of food. At Frankfurt the meat ration, which for a time was 150 grammes for each person per week, was later on 150 grammes for a fortnight, and now is only allowed every three weeks. Vegetables are difficult to obtain, there is no oil and little fat.' The shortages worsened and the air-raids continued. 'My eyes won't keep open while I am writing. In the night, twice in the cellar and again this morning in the shelter. One feels as if one were no longer a human being. In my opinion this is no longer war, but murder. Finally in time one becomes horribly cold and one is daily, nay hourly, prepared for the worst.' 'There are times when one doesn't wish to live.'

Popular discontent soon turned to unrest and open rebellion. One British agent quoted a letter from Dusseldorf claiming that 'the authorities are powerless to keep the terrorised population quiet', and a woman agent reported from Mannheim that 'scenes of disorder' after a British air-raid 'lasted most of the day . . . Soldiers took part in the demonstrations . . . an appeal was made to the cavalry, who were powerless until sections of a machine-gun battalion started firing, first of all in the air, and afterwards at the crowd. There were no deaths, but a number of wounded.' A Frankfurt woman in an air-raid shelter began 'to protest violently against the continuation of the war. The police tried to interfere but the crowd took the part of the woman. Those manifestations could only be stopped after a great deal of trouble.' A German prisoner of war also revealed that riots had occurred in Cologne in May after an air-raid and the unrest had increased as the raids intensified. The revolution in Russia was only a year old and there were strong signs in street demonstrations, civil unrest, troop mutinies and the rise of the Spartacus League – revolutionaries who named themselves after the slave who rebelled against Imperial Rome, to symbolize their war on the German ruling class – that Germany too might be ripe for an insurgency. If the Allies were to launch fire-raids on German cities in retaliation for Fire Plan attacks on London and Paris, the whole of Germany might erupt.

Had Germany's disintegrating economy and domestic unrest not given Germany's High Command pause enough for thought, the rapidly deteriorating position and morale of their forces on the Western Front would have done so. Allied advances were continuing at a relentless pace and increasing numbers of German troops were surrendering or deserting. Ludendorff himself acknowledged that there were tens of thousands of German deserters in neutral countries, and many more, 'unmolested by the authorities', simply went home; one of Ludendorff's staff officers, Colonel von Thaer, claimed that there were nearly thirty thousand in Cologne alone. Trains carrying wounded men back from the Front were commandeered by able-bodied troops to carry them away from the front lines, an entire trainload of veterans from the Eastern Front refused en masse to enter the front lines, and an estimated forty thousand German soldiers abandoned their trenches and voluntarily surrendered to advancing American troops. By contrast, Allied morale, so close to collapse in the spring of that year, was now sky-high and every week saw thousands more fresh American troops arriving to augment the exhausted soldiers of Britain and France.

On 23 September, as the men of the England and Paris squadrons made their final preparations and thousands of Elektron incendiaries were loaded on to their aircraft, Ludendorff's nerve failed. The failure of the March offensive, Operation Michael, had hit him doubly hard: the bitter knowledge that the last chance of victory by force of arms on the battlefield had gone was compounded by his grief at the death of a son, the second of his sons to die in the war. Ludendorff was now close to breaking point, railing against incompetent civilians, socialists and defeatists, and erupting into frequent outbursts of wild, irrational fury. His cold fixity of purpose had carried him through almost four years of war, indifferent to reverses, uncaring of the growing disparity in men and materiel, certain always of the final outcome. Now, for the first time, he was shaken into a bitter realization.

The devastation of London and Paris was only a handful of hours away. '36 planes were to attack London with Elektron bombs' and 'Bombing Squadron 3' had '45 heavy bombers at the ready to deliver 20,000 of these promising projectiles to Paris'. The pilots of one of the Paris squadrons were already in their cockpits and making their final checks before starting their engines. The officer of the launch service and his adjutants, responsible for the preparation of the runway before take-off and, hours later, for the landings of the returning aircraft, were already on the manoeuvring area. The *Startdienst*, the ground-crew who prepared the airfield for the departure of the bombers, stood ready on the dew-soaked ground. Next to them was their starting cart, loaded with flares, and the saws, hatchets and wire clippers that might be needed to rescue trapped crewmen from a crashed aircraft. Two mobile searchlights, mounted on the back of lorries, had been driven down the airfield to their positions, the runway lights and red and green landing lights had been laid out, and the signal pistols with ammunition in corresponding colours stood ready for use. The emergency crews were standing by, ready to clear the runway and repair bomb craters from enemy raids, using gravel stored in a row of requisitioned Belgian farm carts parked behind the hangar. A doctor also stood ready to deal with any medical emergencies.

'In the near impenetrable blackness, lit only by the faint glow from their instrument lights, the flight crews settled in their cockpits as their air-craft, in turn, were rolled out by the engineers . . . Handshakes and good wishes were exchanged as the engineers and runners bade farewell to "their" crews.' 'We took our seats and I was about to start my motors . . . Suddenly, through the darkness a car came racing.'

The yellow glow of its headlights, diffused by wisps of ground mist, had announced its presence before the sound of its engine was heard. Everyone – ground-crew, air-crew, officers – froze, their heads slowly turn-ing to look at the speeding car. It was as black as the night, its paintwork shining softly in the starlight, but the fluttering pennants it carried showed it bore an emissary from the High Command. It sped across the airfield, bumping and rattling over the rutted ground, driven flat out. Each Gotha, momentarily caught in the glare of its lights, loomed ghostly grey out of the darkness, then faded to a shadow as the car roared on.

As it reached the head of the line of aircraft, the car braked to a sharp stop, throwing up a cloud of dust that drifted slowly away on the faint breeze. The Startoffizier, still standing open-mouthed, his hand half-raised from his side, waited in a silence broken only by the metallic tick of the cooling engine. Then the driver jumped out, threw open the rear door and 'a staff officer jumped out and rushed towards us. Orders from General Headquarters. We were not to take off . . . That sudden change of orders came as a severe shock to us.'

The decision was also communicated to the England Squadron at Ghent at the last possible moment: 'the supreme commander of the German army forbade the use of these bombs half an hour before the commencement of the attack'. 'Then came something that should have tipped us off. We were requested to drop leaflets over the [French sector of the] enemy lines. Up to that point none of us fliers had doubted for a moment that Germany was going to win the war.' Entitled *Pourquoi?*, the leaflets, written in French, said that Germany was eager to make peace and

France was being prevented from doing so by England and America 'which had decided to continue the war until the utter destruction of Europe was achieved. Well, that hadn't sounded too good but somehow we never thought that the reason for such leaflets was that our war was already lost.' Yet 'that day it had been decided to send a request to President Wilson to start negotiations for an armistice. Incidentally, the request did not leave Imperial Headquarters at Spa till late on October 3 – ten days later.'

Barely suppressing his disgust at the decision to call off the incendiary raids, Major Siegert, the father of the Fire Plan, commented in his diary that 'as Ludendorff is not, inherently, a defeatist, I must conclude that highly political considerations were responsible for the cancellation of this mission. Maybe negotiations with France and Belgium were opened in this way: "We retreat one kilometre every day, destroying all settlements, facilities and infrastructure. Furthermore, we will avail ourselves of a new means of war against Paris and London if the Entente does not come to the table." Well, the banning of bombs for this hope of "peace" is the biggest folly of this war that we have ever allowed ourselves.' He later added that 'Something is going on that led to the non-execution of the incendiary bomb raid on Paris ... It has to be of <u>such</u> significance that this subsequent order was necessary ...

Further production of Elektron bombs is to be ceased, only those already in production shall be finished. Delivery to Bogohl 3 [the England Squadron] is cancelled. Entire stock of those already produced and those still to be manufactured is to be delivered to Air Force Depot North at Maubeuge. Report delivery count. All existing bomb-throwing devices and those still to be finished also to be delivered to Maubeuge. All Elektron bombs without exception and the corresponding bomb-throwing devices of Bogohl 1 and 2 are to be checked by an Officer familiar with these devices and to be forwarded to Maubeuge, where they are to be stored in the Air Force Depot North according to the rules. Bogohl 1, 2 and 3 as well as Maubeuge have been notified. Any action taken is to be reported.

Der Kommandierende General der Luftstreitkräfte [KoGenLuft]

... instead of burning down their house nice and proper so that, in comparison, the fire of Rome would have seemed a minuscule, match-box affair. But we will see.'

The date Siegert cited for this decision, 8 September, differs by fifteen days from that given by one of the pilots involved, whose detailed account stated that the fire-raids were scheduled for 23 September. Since the England Squadron's war diaries were lost or destroyed at the end of the conflict, there is no objective confirmation of either man's version, and it is most likely that both are correct, in the sense that the raids may well have been scheduled for 8 September and then postponed until the 23rd – the weather alone would have precluded any attempt in the intervening two weeks – before being cancelled altogether by Ludendorff's last-minute intervention.

'Because of the gravity of our position,' Ludendorff later wrote, 'the Supreme Command could not hope that air-raids on London and Paris would make the enemy more disposed to sue for peace. Permission was therefore refused for the use of a particularly effective incendiary bomb, expressly designed for attacks on the two capitals, which had been produced in great quantities during the month of August [1918] and which was to have been used in the air-bombardment of the two capitals. The considerable destruction which would have ensued would no longer be enough to influence the course of the war; one could not tolerate carrying out such destruction for its own sake.'

Ludendorff was writing for public consumption in the aftermath of the war and may well have ascribed loftier motives to himself than had really been the case. The Chancellor, Count von Hertling, articulated a more pragmatic reason for abandoning the raids when he ' "begged the Supreme Command not to use these new incendiaries because of the reprisals that the enemy would take against our own cities". The state of the war,' Ludendorff added, 'led me to concur with that decision.'

His reasons for abandoning the fire-raids, so incomprehensible at the time to Siegert, were made clearer just five days later, on 28 September, when he informed first Hindenburg and then the Kaiser and the Chancellor that the military situation was now so bad that it required Germany to sue for peace without delay. When the Kaiser asked 'what the officers and troops were still capable of accomplishing', Ludendorff answered that 'the Supreme Army Command and the German Army were finished; the war could no longer be won; only an inevitable and conclusive defeat awaited Germany. Bulgaria had already been lost. Austria and Turkey, both at the end of their powers, would also soon fall.' Even the German Army had been so 'contaminated with the poison of Spartacus-socialist ideas' that the troops were, he said, no longer reliable. Since the 'black day' of 8 August, the situation had deteriorated so fast that some troops had had to be hastily withdrawn from the front lines. Other soldiers, still willing to fight, had been denounced as 'strike breakers'. 'Any day now,' Ludendorff warned, 'our Western Front could be breached by an enemy boosted by battle-hungry American troops.' A decisive breakthrough would cause the German armies to retreat in disarray across the Rhine, carrying revolution back to Germany. 'This catastrophe must be averted by all means.'

Ludendorff added that he had never been afraid to demand the utmost from his troops but he realized that continuing the war was pointless and an end needed to be found as quickly as possible in order to avoid the useless sacrifice of the brave men who were still loyal and willing to fight. As Supreme Army Commanders, and de facto rulers, Hindenburg and Ludendorff 'demanded of His Majesty the Kaiser and of the Chancellor that a peace proposal be made to President Wilson of America without delay, to bring about an armistice based on his "14 Points"'. The Chancellor then announced that he would resign with immediate effect. 'An old man, after so many honourable years, he could not and would not end his life by tendering a petition for ceasefire.'

Three days later Ludendorff, his face 'pale and lined by deep worry, but his head still held high', broke the news to his senior officers, including a shocked staff officer, Colonel von Thaer, who described the 'terrible and appalling' meeting in his diary. Almost all Ludendorff's audience had 'involuntary tears running down their cheeks' as he outlined Germany's impossible position and the decision to sue for peace. Already seeking to blame socialists and defeatists for Germany's plight, he told them that he had asked the Kaiser to 'bring those circles into the government whom we can mainly thank that we have come to this. We will now see these gentlemen brought into the Ministries. They should make the peace that must now be made. They made their bed, now they must lie in it!' Ludendorff then 'lowered his head slowly, turned and went to his adjoining room'. He was relieved of his command on 24 October, after making a public reversal of his views about Germany's ability to continue the war.

As soon as he was appointed, the new German Chancellor, Prince Max von Baden, contacted President Wilson to sue for peace, but another five weeks were to pass before an Armistice was declared, and meanwhile the fighting, and the German retreat, went on. Although the Fire Plan had been abandoned, 'ordinary raids' on London and Paris were continued 'to keep enemy anti-aircraft material far from the front and to prevent the troops noticing the reduction in our strength'. In fact, London was never bombed again, but a hint of what the raids might have produced had the decision to use the Elektron bombs not been aborted at the last moment was offered by a raid using conventional high-explosive bombs, when 'Paris was bombed with 22,161kg of bombs . . . in a joint attack by Bogohls 1, 2 and 4' – the same bombing squadrons that would have launched the Fire Plan with the Elektron incendiaries. The 'strongest resistance from Allied aircraft and the three-tiered flak and searchlight belts around the great fortress' that sent up a barrage of anti-aircraft fire that gave the city the appearance of a 'volcano in eruption' caused heavy German losses. According to a British artillery officer, 'only three airplanes out of fifty in the raiding squadron got by the anti-aircraft fire of the outer defence of Paris and flew over the city', but the German raiders that did get through mounted devastating 'concentric air-raids on Paris'. Once they had passed through the screen of barrage fire that barred the way to the city, German pilots found that they were able to drop their bombs 'undisturbed in the interior of the circle of fire'.

French newspapers reported that a 'more elevated part of the city was a particular target for the raids. Numerous bombs were dropped within a limited perimeter' and 'fires broke out in several locations. One outer district of the city in particular suffered heavily. All sites where bombs fell were damaged considerably. The suburbs apparently suffered far worse devastation than Paris proper. Numerous shacks were destroyed in a large community in the south-west. At other sites residential blocks were partially destroyed. One bomb fell onto a barge that subsequently sank.'

A 'credible agent' reported to the German High Command that the raid had been 'the most damaging since the beginning of the war. In Pantin, in the outskirts, some bombs hit an artillery troop's camp and more than 800 people were killed and injured. A bomb destroyed three houses in the Avenue de l'Opera. Twelve dead and six wounded were found under the rubble. Three consecutive bombs fell on rue Touron and caused heavy damage to twenty houses. The Senate building in the Jardin du Luxembourg was destroyed almost in its entirety, the access roads had to be closed off by police.' The 'powerful attacks produced results that could have led to complete demoralisation if the High Command hadn't, on humanitarian grounds, banned the use of the incendiary bomb – the most terrible weapon of the attack bomber, the construction of which had already been completed – even though the English were draining the energy out of our people by means of the inhumane starvation blockade.'

Their war-winning mission abandoned, the dispirited, demoralized air-crews of the England Squadron were reduced to flying ground-attack missions against Allied trenches. Inexperienced in this form of aerial warfare and vulnerable to the enemy fighters filling the skies over the Western Front, they suffered their heaviest losses of the war. Among the dead was Walter Aschoff's pilot Erwin Kollberg, though he was killed in a training accident at Gontrode when a wing detached and his aircraft plunged into the ground. Aschoff was not flying with him that day and was plagued for years by 'survivor's guilt': why had he lived when his friend and crewmate had been taken? 'It had never occurred to us that one of the crew would die alone without the others. We always thought that, if we were to die, we would do so together, flying against the enemy.'

Once taken, the decision to abandon the Fire Plan was irrevocable. Siegert's last flicker of hope that it might yet be resurrected was extinguished when the Allied advances through Flanders forced the evacuation of the bases near Ghent. The England Squadron retreated to Evere outside Brussels, and Aschoff saw for the last time the airfields and the city that had been home to the squadron through all the raids on

England. 'We flew low over the chateau where we lived, our eyes took in once more the familiar scene: the old city, the streets and church towers, until finally everything was lost from sight in the mist.

'From that night in September until the day of the Armistice, we changed airfields four times and were bombed more and more often by the Allies. That was the end of the strategic air war as far as we were concerned. We had to assist the infantry on the battlefield. We were sent on reconnaissance. We had to strafe the ground and do some low-level bombing flights in order to support the "planned retreat" of our troops – yes, already then it was called that . . . One night a German anti-aircraft battery near our airfield fired at my plane and with the first salvo shot off half my tail. This was the first time I had been hit by flak during the whole war. It seemed highly symbolic to me. What was the use of precisely calculated and daringly executed forays when everything around us was crumbling?'

When the Armistice was declared, the surviving members of the England Squadron left their last base at Evere by lorry, not aircraft. The remaining Gothas and Giants were left behind. One of the conditions of the Armistice was that military aircraft were to be handed over to the Allies, but this was too much dishonour for many air- and ground-crews. The engines of some aircraft and the rigging on the wings were 'all rendered useless by shots from our weapons'; others were destroyed 'in huge bonfires' or sabotaged in more subtle ways. As Aschoff slyly observed, although they were duly handed over, the mechanics of the England Squadron and the other bombing squadrons had left dangerous surprises for any British pilot foolish enough to try to fly them. 'Outwardly they looked perfect, but our ground-crews would never have allowed us to fly those machines.'

The men of the England Squadron were transported to Frankfurt and demobilized there before the end of November 1918. They packed up their belongings and began the journey home, sharing the bittersweet feelings of so many others as the conflict that had dominated their lives for four years came to an end: the sadness and shame of defeat; guilt that they had survived while so many of their friends and crewmates had not; relief that the war was over and they could return to their homes; and the knowledge that the special bond they had forged in adversity was now at an end, and they might never again experience such times and such intensities of feeling and emotion, despair and elation.

'Even if our time was always overshadowed by dangers, still it seemed a great and beautiful thing to us, because what does life mean without battle and danger? They test a man's inner core and spirit, and only in the face of danger and death is the value of an individual's personality revealed in its clearest and most selfless form. Among the old, experienced flight crews there were a good number of people who would not leave their squadron to the very last. They wanted to stand in the front line, ready to fight at all times and, if that was their fate, then to die, too. In our innermost beings we wanted nothing but to be warriors for Germany.'

The England Squadron was no more, and the fuel for the Fire Plan, the Elektron incendiaries, had already been destroyed. As the retreat from Ghent got under way, the stockpiles of Elektron bombs – tens of thousands of them – were dumped in the River Scheldt. It was done either to prevent a maverick commander launching a last-ditch assault with the incendiaries, thereby condemning Germany to even more terrible reprisals, or in the futile hope of concealing the secret of their invention and construction from Allied commanders. As Germany slid towards defeat in this war, some German commanders at least were already planning for the next. So were some of their British counterparts.

A demand voiced in the months following the war that the surviving pilots of the England Squadron should be brought to London and put on trial for war crimes was vetoed by the Air Ministry which, after hostilities with Germany had ended, soon began further bombing raids on civilian populations in a succession of colonial 'policing actions'. Trials for war crimes, as an Air Ministry official noted in a document never intended for public consumption, would 'be placing a noose round the necks of our airmen in future wars'. British air attacks on German cities had also been designed 'to weaken the morale of civilian inhabitants . . . by persistent bomb attacks which would both destroy life (civilian and otherwise) and if possible originate a conflagration which would reduce to ashes the whole town'. The application of the Hague convention would 'defeat the very purpose of bombardment'.

No firestorms would now rage through London and Paris in the Great

War; that fate would be reserved for Hamburg, Coventry, Dresden and Tokyo in the next. The British incendiaries that rained down on German cities in the Second World War – 650,000 of them on Dresden alone – were almost identical in chemical composition to the Elektron bombs that German scientists and engineers had invented, perfected and then manufactured in huge quantities in the spring and summer of 1918. By a matter of a handful of hours, the French and British capitals had escaped a terrible fate.

Berlin had also survived the Great War unscathed, but, like London and Paris, it had been a very close-run thing. On 26 October, Hugh Trenchard was made Commander-in-Chief of an Allied Air Force combining British, French, American and Italian squadrons. The Armistice came before the new force was tested; had the war continued, air-raids on Germany would have been mounted on a scale dwarfing anything thrown at England even at the height of the England Squadron's raids. New 1,650lb bombs had just been introduced, and Handley-Page, Farman, Vickers and Voisin all had four-engined bombers in production in late 1918. The new Handley-Page V/1500s, nicknamed 'The Bloody Paralysers', were powered by four Rolls-Royce engines and were capable of carrying 7,500lb of bombs and remaining airborne for twelve hours.

When Austria-Hungary surrendered on 3 November there were plans to base the Independent Air Force in Prague and bomb Berlin from there; pending that move, three Handley-Page V/1500s were delivered to a base at Bircham Newton in Norfolk, ready to stage the first British air-raid on Berlin on 12 November. The Armistice, announced twenty-four hours earlier, brought the war to an end just in time to spare Berlin's citizens a taste of what Londoners had been forced to endure at the hands of the England Squadron. The first British bomb would not now fall on Berlin for another twenty-two years.

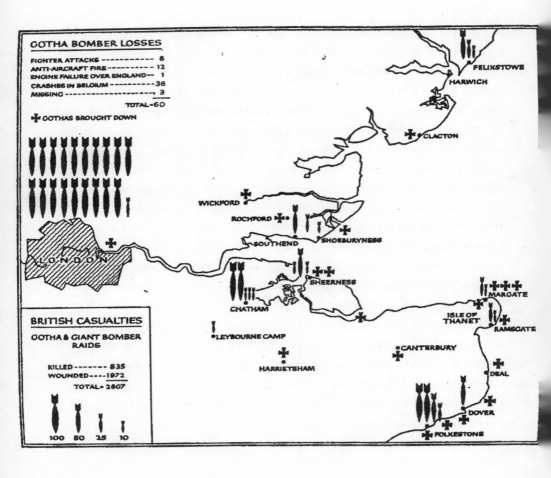

**GOTHA BOMBER LOSSES**

| | |
|---|---|
| FIGHTER ATTACKS | 8 |
| ANTI-AIRCRAFT FIRE | 12 |
| ENGINE FAILURE OVER ENGLAND | 1 |
| CRASHES IN BELGIUM | 36 |
| MISSING | 3 |
| | **TOTAL-60** |

✠ GOTHAS BROUGHT DOWN

**BRITISH CASUALTIES**

**GOTHA & GIANT BOMBER RAIDS**

| | |
|---|---|
| KILLED | 835 |
| WOUNDED | 1972 |
| | **TOTAL= 2807** |

100  50  25  10

FELIXSTOWE
HARWICH
✠ CLACTON
WICKFORD
ROCHFORD
SOUTHEND
SHOEBURYNESS
LONDON
SHEERNESS
CHATHAM
• LEYBOURNE CAMP
HARRIETSHAM
• CANTERBURY
MARGATE
ISLE OF THANET
RAMSGATE
DEAL
DOVER
FOLKESTONE

# EPILOGUE

THE TURKENCREUZ (TURK'S CROSS) 'blitz' on London lasted for almost exactly a year, from the first daylight raid on 25 May 1917 to the last night raid on Whit Sunday, 19 May 1918. In that time the Gothas of the England Squadron and the Giants of Rfa 501 dropped a total of 105,000kg of high-explosive bombs and 6,500kg of incendiaries on England, killing 836 people and injuring 1,965, a death toll comfortably exceeded by a single day's losses on the Western Front. Bomb damage of around £1.5 million had also been caused; in comparison, it has been estimated that rats destroyed crops and other material worth £70 million a year.

The number of German bombers reaching British shores was consistently exaggerated by British observers, through fear, the uncertainties of shapes dimly glimpsed among clouds or against dark night skies, and the thunder of the multiple engines of the Gothas and Giants. One of the conditions of the Armistice was that the Germans would surrender all their surviving heavy bombers to the Allies. Even making full allowance for those already destroyed, British officers were astonished when they saw how few of those Gotha and Giant aircraft there actually were, and initially suspected the Germans of concealing squadrons of bombers from them.

The pilots of the England Squadron had flown a total of 450 sorties, and barely a quarter of them – 114 – reached London. Yet by the time of the last raid on England, these modest numbers were enough to force the British Government to install 469 anti-aircraft guns, 622 searchlights, 258 height-finders and ten sound-locators, and have ready 376 aircraft (though only 166 of them were listed as 'efficient'); 660 officers and 4,000 other ranks flew and serviced those aircraft, another 82 officers and 2,573 men served with the Balloon Wing, operating the balloon barrages, and unquantifiable thousands of other men built and maintained the infrastructure, facilities and equipment that all these men and machines required. The British Government had been forced to commit these vast quantities of men and materiel to Home Defence rather than sending them to the Western Front.

The output of munitions factories and of many other industries was also severely affected, and the disruption of production occurred over a far wider area than that which was actually bombed, and continued long after the bombers had returned to base. Germany had 'aspired to cause alarm and despondency, to delay munition output and to constrain us to withdraw guns and aircraft from the front in France for the needs of local defence. In all these aims, she well succeeded, and, as regards the latter, it is worthwhile to note that in each case it was popular clamour, rather than a strictly military necessity, which induced the Government to elaborate the various schemes of defence until the odd score of Gothas employed in raiding were immobilising, on the home front, more than twenty times their number.'

Yet despite these secondary successes, the England Squadron's primary aim – the Fire Plan, the devastation of London by fire, causing the collapse of British morale and the will to continue the war – remained unfulfilled. Although the raids had often generated mass panic in the capital, they were never sustained over a sufficiently long period to break public morale completely. The one exception was in the period of the raids of the Harvest Moon from 24 September to 1 October 1917, when, even though relatively few German bombers were involved, their activities brought London to the brink of collapse. As one German officer noted, 'It is perhaps no exaggeration to state that the period of these six raids constitutes the climax of all the raids on Great Britain, because they were carried out in the rightful assumption that only continuous raids, even though no very considerable numbers were involved, would provoke a high degree of nervousness and unrest.'

The 'blitz spirit' so often lauded in the Second World War existed in the Great War mainly in the minds of British propagandists and wishful thinkers. Those who witnessed public morale in the bombed areas for themselves, at close quarters, came away with an entirely different impression: a population on the verge of nervous collapse, riven by fear and rumour, xenophobic and violent, and perhaps even in a pre-revolutionary ferment. Had the raids continued at the intensity of the Blitz of the Harvest Moon for a few more weeks, the Government might have been forced to act or to resign, but German commanders could not and would not make enough aircraft available, and as the autumn nights passed without further raids London's panic and terror began to subside once more.

The high cost and relative frailty of the German bomber fleet, and the escalating losses to Britain's steadily improving air defences, were undoubtedly factors in the failure of the Fire Plan, but the England Squadron was also hampered by the lack of a clear vision of its aims and the strategic grasp to maximize its assets and advantages, and the failure to identify the most effective means of delivering the projectiles on to the target. Concentrated bombing of strictly defined target areas would inevitably have caused greater problems for the defenders and the fire services than the multiple targeting that led to the almost random scattering of small quantities of missiles over large areas.

Above all, however, it was the limitations of German science and industry and failures at the highest levels of command that doomed the Fire Plan to failure. General von Höppner's was a triple failure. Unable to grasp the strategy required – even though it was laid out with admirable clarity in Oberleutnant Weese's paper of February 1917, months before the first London raid – he also failed to obtain either the quantity or quality of bombers required, and then failed to concentrate the resources that he could command to maximum effect. Bombing squadrons flew sporadic raids against London, Paris, Allied positions on the Western Front and the Allied ports on both sides of the Channel, when what was called for was a concentrated mass assault on a single target: London. In the whole of the night-bombing campaign, only on two occasions, 31 October 1917 and 19 May 1918, were as many as twenty bombers available. Shortages of supply, losses to the air defences and the far more substantial numbers wrecked in crash-landings were exacerbated by reliability problems. No Giants were ever lost on raids over England, but only on one occasion out of the eleven Giant raids was it possible to launch all six aircraft of 501 Squadron against England, and only on two others did five or even four get airborne.

The Gothas were even more unreliable. On every mission, several were grounded by mechanical problems, and one in every eight that actually took off returned to base without even crossing the English coast. Even worse, despite huge strides in aircraft technology in the course of the war, the Gothas' performance actually declined. 'The acceptance conditions required that the Gotha G IV, fully-loaded, should climb to 5,500 metres [18,000 feet] in one hour. The maximum altitudes reached during the first raid on Great Britain were on an average 4,900 to 5,100 metres [16,000 to 16,700 feet], during the second raid 4,500 to 4,900 metres [14,800 to 16,000 feet], and during the third raid 3,800 to 4,100 metres [12,500 to 13,500 feet].' By the time of the last moonlight raid on 19 May 1918, the maximum altitude reached by some of the German raiders was just 1,200 to 1,700 metres (3,900 to 5,600 feet).

At squadron command level, Kleine's reckless leadership often dissipated precious air assets for little tangible reward, and for all the bravery of some of the air-crews of the England Squadron, the numbers turning back with reported engine failures or bombing the Kent and Essex coast and countryside instead of attacking London cannot all be explained away by diversionary raids, bad weather, fuel shortages or poor engineering.

Failures in the leadership and sometimes the men of the England Squadron were matched by the shortcomings of German science and industry. Beset with shortages of raw materials because of the Allied blockade, German manufacturers failed to produce aircraft with sufficient speed, rate of climb, altitude 'ceiling' and bomb-carrying capacity to match the improvements in Allied aircraft and air defences. They also failed to produce a sufficient quantity of heavy bombers, and those that were produced were often defective. German scientists also failed to deliver an effective incendiary weapon until the closing stages of the war – and by then the reluctance of the German High Command to use the fiercely efficient, truly terrible fire-weapon that was eventually produced doomed the England Squadron's campaign, and with it the Fire Plan, to ultimate failure.

For that, humanity must be grateful. Had London and Paris been engulfed by flames in the late summer of 1918, the outcome of the First World War might have been different. What is certain is that tens of thousands, or even hundreds of thousands of innocent people in those two capitals – and in Berlin and other German cities when the inevitable reprisals followed – would have died in one final holocaust of the most blood-soaked war in human history.

*

If the First Blitz on London during the Great War was ultimately a failure, it was to have profound consequences for the conduct of the Second World War, and in particular the outcome of the Second Blitz in 1940–41. The air defence system that was to serve so effectively in the Battle of Britain over twenty years later was forged in the crucible of the Great War. With the single exception of the incorporation of radar, everything – the ring of fighter bases and the air defence zones, the listening stations, barrage balloon screens, mobile and static anti-aircraft batteries, LADA, the communications net, even the Operations Room with its giant map table manned by staff plotting the movements of attacking and defending aircraft with the aid of counters and wooden rakes – was already in place in 1918. Ashmore's description of the Operations Room in September of that year could, with little alteration, have been applied to Fighter Command's Ops Room in 1940. 'I sat overlooking the map from a raised gallery. In effect I could follow the course of all aircraft flying over the country as the counters crept across the map. The system worked very rapidly. From the time an observer . . . saw a machine over him, to the time when the counter representing it appeared on my map, was not, as a rule, more than half a minute.'

The targeting of civilians, reprisals and the use of incendiaries – new and shocking in the First World War – became routine in the Second, but the differing conclusions the two sides reached from their experience of air war between 1914 and 1918 also led directly to the failure of the 1940 Blitz and to British victory in the Battle of Britain.

The editor of *The Aeroplane*, C. G. Grey, wrote as early as July 1917 that 'Captain Brandenburg deserves some signal mark of recognition from this country for convincing so many thousands of people that an aerial invasion of enemy territory must be an important part of our war policy in this or any future war.' Great War experience also suggested that the psychological impact of bombing an urban population far outweighed its physical effects. Speaking in the immediate aftermath of the war, that enthusiastic convert to the cause of strategic bombing Hugh Trenchard claimed that 'the moral effect of bombing stands to the material effect in a proportion of 20 to 1, and therefore it was necessary to create the greatest moral effect possible [when bombing German towns and cities]'. The

Allied Supreme Commander, Foch, a sceptic about strategic bombing for most of the Great War, was also converted before its close: 'It is clear that aircraft attack on a large scale, owing to its crushing moral effect upon a nation, may impress public opinion to the point of disarming the government and thus become decisive.'

The mass panic that greeted the bombing of London during the Great War and a misunderstanding of the number of aircraft involved, further fuelled by doom-laden prophecies of the wholesale slaughter and destruction future wars would bring, led British politicians and military strategists greatly to exaggerate the potential impact of strategic bombing in a future war – described by Churchill as a way 'to make the enemy burn and bleed in every way'.

The most typical entries under the bomb damage and casualty reports compiled during the Great War were those that read 'Nil', 'Unexploded' or 'glass broken, garden damaged', and 'occasionally a "K" or "W" for one or two people killed or wounded', but 'air power theorists were still making great play with the Chatham drill hall [in which 130 died] twenty years after, and were careful to ignore the broken windows and the damaged garden'. A parliamentary paper produced a few months after the Armistice crowed that the moral and material effect of the raids on Germany 'can hardly be overestimated'. A purportedly more dispassionate report by two officers who toured German cities to assess the impact of the raids for themselves conceded that material damage had been small, but went on to assert that 'the progress in air science' would make it possible for 'a powerful military nation . . . to obliterate cities in a night and produce the stunning moral effect necessary for victory'. That report and the later verdict of the official history of the air war were both strongly influenced by Trenchard's views; 'there is no doubt that the documents pronouncing on the effectiveness of RAF bombing were strongly influenced by the field commander's desire to justify and defend his record'.

Prime Minister Stanley Baldwin showed the power of the myth over the reality when he warned Parliament on 10 November 1932, 'I think it well also for the man in the street to realise there is no power on earth that can protect him from bombing, whatever people may tell him. The bomber will always get through . . . The only defence is in offence, which means you have got to kill more women and children quicker than the enemy if you want to save yourselves.' Fighter pilot Cecil Lewis reached much the same conclusion. 'An army could stop an army, a fleet a fleet, but a thousand aeroplanes could not stop a thousand enemy aeroplanes. Wire netting would not keep flies out. *Both would get through to their objectives.*'

A former RFC instructor in aerial bombing noted that the 258 incendiaries dropped on London by the England Squadron on 6 December 1917 had fallen over an area of thirty-eight square miles, diffusing their impact, and warned that 'under the modern system of zone bombing from high altitudes, there is nothing to prevent three or four times that number falling within a *single* square mile'. Basing their calculations on the raids by the England Squadron in 1917 and early 1918, Air Ministry officials predicted that Britain would suffer six hundred thousand deaths and twice as many casualties in the opening months of a new world war, as the Germans rained down 3,500 tons of bombs in an initial blitz and then 600 tons a day thereafter.

In a speech to the House of Commons in 1934, Winston Churchill also painted a vivid picture of 'the dreadful act of power and terror' that German fire-raids on London with Elektron bombs would have represented, and warned that in a future war, under the pressure of saturation bombing of London with high-explosives and incendiaries, 'at least three or four million people would be driven out into the open country . . . without shelter . . . without food, without sanitation'.

In response to these fears, as war approached, over a quarter of a million hospital beds were made ready to accommodate the casualties of a German air assault, one and a half million women and children were evacuated from the capital, and twelve regional controllers were appointed, who were to take over the government of Britain if 'Whitehall and Westminster were wiped out'.

When, prior to his infamous meeting with Hitler in Munich in 1938, Neville Chamberlain asked the British chiefs of staff what would be the consequences of going to war with Germany in defence of Czechoslovakia, their unanimous response was that the war would be lost. As Field Marshal Lord Ironside wrote in his diary, 'We cannot expose ourselves now to a German attack. We simply commit suicide if we do. At no time could we stand up against German air bombing.' He added that the Cabinet was 'terrified now of a war being finished in a few weeks by the annihilation of Great Britain', and noted that 'the authorities have insisted upon the parcelling out of troops all over London during air-raids' to try to quell the threat of mass panic, riot and revolt.

The effect on the British public of this constant repetition of the terrible power of the bomber was vividly demonstrated on the day war was declared, 3 September 1939. When the sirens began to wail in what turned out to be a false alarm of an air-raid, two million Londoners duly voted with their feet and fled the capital in panic, fearing that Armageddon was about to be unleashed upon them from the skies.

German commanders, drawing diametrically opposite conclusions about the effectiveness of the First World War bombing campaign, turned their backs on strategic air warfare and, concentrating virtually all their aircraft production on battlefield, ground-support aircraft such as the Stuka, went into the Second World War without a single four-engined air-craft. General Max von Wever, the first Chief of the German Air Staff, was virtually the only senior Luftwaffe officer to advocate the use of heavy bombers, and he had commissioned prototypes, but the project was aban-doned when he died in an air crash. Goering dismissed the concept with the remark that 'the Fuhrer will not ask how big the bombers are, but how many there are'. Although *Blitzkrieg* tactics were a huge initial success on the battlefield, the Luftwaffe thus had no heavy bombers for strategic attacks.

Britain was far better supplied. Believing that 'the only defence in the air likely to be effective in the long run is an offensive more powerfully sustained than that conducted by the enemy', much of Britain's planning for war centred on the counter-use of heavy bombers; 'Plan WA8' called for a massive night attack 'to produce an immediate dislocation of German war industry'. Chamberlain had assured the House of Commons that his Government would 'never resort to blackguardly attacks on women and other civilians for purposes of mere terrorism', and Bomber Command was confined to 'legitimate military objectives' at first. However, senior air force officers, backed by Winston Churchill, had few such scruples and a raid was carried out on Munchen-Gladbach on the very night, 10 May

1940, that Churchill replaced Chamberlain as Prime Minister. Pressure of public opinion, especially in America, required that Germany should be perceived to have struck the first blow, but in fact the first attack in the air war was made by British bombers, and Air Chief Marshal Sir Hugh Dowding spoke openly of 'a bombing raid on the Ruhr in order to draw reprisals upon this country'.

The excuse for an all-out assault on German cities was finally provided on 24 August 1940 when a dozen German aircraft, tasked to bomb oil tanks at Thameshaven and Rochester, lost their bearings and dumped their bombloads on Central London. The 'phoney war' was over. Reprisal raids on Berlin lasting a week drew Hitler into pledging that in revenge German bombers would raze British cities to the ground. The Blitz was duly launched on London on 7 September, when three hundred bombers – almost every aircraft Germany could put in the air – attacked the city, causing 1,600 casualties. But Germany did not have the heavy bombers to deliver a decisive blow, and over the succeeding months the Battle of Britain was lost.

The spectre of the Fire Plan was resurrected by the German raid that turned Coventry into an inferno – fulfilment of the Great War warning after the aircraft workers' strike that 'the Hun raiders' bombs will pay Coventry as a whole for the results of last week's disgraceful work' – but it was Britain, not Germany, that carried it to its logical extreme. 'Area bombing', a dry euphemism for mass destruction and extermination, was born in the thousand-bomber attack on Cologne in May 1942, which ignited twelve thousand fires in the city. Supposedly launched 'to capture the imagination of the British people', its true purpose was surely its effect on the German imagination.

Operation Gomorrah – the destruction of Hamburg in July 1943 – followed, and in February 1945 the ancient, largely wooden and previously unbombed city of Dresden was consumed by a firestorm that claimed 135,000 lives – more than twice as many as had been lost in Britain in all the German air-raids of the war. The seeds sown by the German Fire Plan of the Great War had grown into a whirlwind that engulfed its creators.

# NOTES

vii: *Fliege nach England* . . . burned down: Frank Morison, *War on Great Cities*, p. 26.

vii: 'In comparison . . . match-box affair': diary of Major Wilhelm Siegert, vol. VI, p. 15.


## Chapter 1: The First Blows

3: A German seaplane . . . three days earlier: Myron J. Smith, *World War I in the Air*, p. 211.

3: but this was the first aircraft that Tommy had ever seen: Raymond H. Fredette, *The Sky on Fire*, p. 8.

3: When he picked himself up . . . vegetable patch had been: ibid.

3: The windows of the surrounding houses . . . Christmas decorations: Thomas Fegan, *The Baby Killers*, p. 135.

3: 'might almost be compared . . . prehistoric days': Georg Paul Neumann, *The German Air Force in the Great War*, p. 52.

4: The gunners at Beacon Hill . . . their own telephone wires: Christopher Cole & E. F. Cheesman, *The Air Defence of Great Britain*, p. 21.

4: 'We heard a noise . . . some of the guests fainted': W. Wicker, in the *Evening News*, 12 March 1935.

5: 'Parisians, attention! . . . German aircraft': Alexander McKee, *The Friendless Sky*, p. 88.

5: In a second raid . . . killing three civilians: Myron J. Smith, op. cit., pp. 208–9.

5: 'Undisturbed by defensive fire and aircraft . . . the autumn sun': Peter Supf, *Das Buch der Deutschen Fluggeschichte*, vol. 1, Berlin, 1935, p. 285.

5: 'assemble along the River Seine . . . *les cinq heures du Taube*': Arthur M. Soltan & James Davilla, *The Bombardment of Paris*, p. 250.

5: 'Aerial bombardment . . . is prohibited': Article 22, Air Warfare Rules drafted by a Commission of Jurists at The Hague, December 1922–February 1923.

5: 'The complete destruction . . . military and non-military objectives': General Giulio Douhet, *The Command of the Air*, quoted in Eugene Emme, *The Impact of Air Power*, p. 163.

6: 'The conduct of war . . . the object of war will allow': *Kriegsbrauche im Landkriege*, pp. 1–3.

6: 'fortresses . . . occupies them': ibid., pp. 55–6.

6: 'with all his heart' . . . 'even how to do sums': John H. Morrow Jr, *German Air Power in World War I*, p. 21.

6: 'the death of an old woman': McKee, op. cit., p. 88.

6: 'if what we do is frightful . . . Germany's salvation': quoted in Aaron Norman, *The Great Air War*, p. 382.

6–7: 'not in favour of the evil policy . . . concentrated on that city': Admiral Alfred von Tirpitz, *My Memoirs*, vol. II, pp. 271–2.

7: 'England shall be destroyed by fire': Fredette, op. cit., p. 31.

7: 'render it doubtful that the war can continue': Douglas H. Robinson, *The Zeppelin in Combat*, p. 50.

7: 'confer an enormous advantage . . . a small army': Sven Lindqvist, *A History of Bombing*, p. 58.

7: 'we do not consider . . . war purposes': J. A. Chaumier, *The Birth of the Royal Air Force*, p. 2.

7: 'more nerve-shattering . . . adequate air force': *The Times*, 9 March 1916.

7–8: 'We stood to gain nothing . . . our sea power': CAB 38/22/32.

8: 'useless and expensive fad . . . unworthy of attention': Andrew P. Hyde, *The First Blitz*, p. 19.

8: 'What strikes the viewer . . . defenceless buildings below': Michael Paris, *Winged Warfare*, p. 131.

8: 'from sunrise to sunset' . . . cover their retreat: Lindqvist, op. cit., p. 47.

8: 'The floodgates of blood and lust': *The Times*, 31 October 1911.

8: 'was not war. It was butchery': *Daily Chronicle*, 6 November 1911.

8: The first man to drop a bomb . . . on 1 November 1911: Lindqvist, op. cit., p. 4.

8: 'large targets – villages, markets, grazing herds': ibid., p. 74.

9: 'as many living targets as possible': ibid.

9: 'be set on fire by aerial bombardment': quoted in Paris, op. cit., p. 110.

9: As early as 1910 . . . attack and demoralize enemy troops: John H. Morrow Jr, 'Expectation and Reality: The Great War in the Air', p. 29.

9: 'aerial terrorism . . . kill both': H. A. Jones, *The War in the Air*, vol. V, p. 8.

9: German aircrews . . . *Fliegerpfeilen* (flyer's arrows): Oskar Kuppinger, *Bomber Observer*, Part I, p. 119.

9: 'as an instrument of war, *c'est zéro*': Morrow Jr, 'Expectation and Reality', p. 29.

9: two hundred French 'aviation deaths' were recorded in 1913 alone: Soltan & Davilla, op. cit., p. 250.

9: 'more of Jules Verne than of reality': Morrow Jr, 'Expectation and Reality', p. 29.

10: 'the greatest German of the twentieth century': John H. Morrow Jr, *The Defeat of the German and Austro-Hungarian Air Forces in the Great War, 1909–1918*, p. 100.

10: 'far superior . . . quite extraordinary': Morrow Jr, 'Expectation and Reality', p. 29.

10: 'aerial war-games . . . huge searchlights': Paris, op. cit., p.72.

11: 'undefended towns . . . such action would involve': Charles Frederick Snowden Gamble, *The Air Weapon*, vol. I, p. 263.

11: 'I hope none of you gentlemen . . . the use of cavalry': quoted in Hyde, op. cit., p. 16.

11: 'made full use of aerial reconnaissance': Paris, op. cit., p. 186.

11: in 1913 Henderson . . . 100 horsepower: ibid., p. 155.

11: One 'air expert' . . . were developed: James M. Spaight, *Aircraft in War*, pp. 9–10.

11: 'equipped with machines . . . enemy machines or ground fire': Paris, op. cit., p. 156.

12: In August 1914 . . . on his biplane: Louis Strange, *Recollections of an Airman*, p. 42.

12: 'merely cheap selfishness' bringing 'discredit': Sykes papers, RAF MFC 77/13/12.

12: 'When asked . . . could not get the money': Winston Churchill, *The World Crisis 1914–1918*, p. 265.

12: Nor did they have any engines . . . dependent on France for supplies: Morrow, op. cit., p. 12.

12: 'had about eleven . . . we are what you might call behind': Andrew Boyle, *Trenchard*, p. 100.

12: 'flying is perhaps a little easier . . . on a lively horse': quoted in Paris, op. cit., p. 217.

12: the official historian . . . stately home: H. A. Jones, op. cit., vol. I, p. 192.

13: 'a crude but workable': Paris, op. cit., p. 163.

13: 'since Damocles . . . experiment': Morrow Jr, 'Expectation and Reality', p. 30.

14: 'various shifts and devices': Churchill, *1914–1918*, p. 265.

14: 'scrape and smuggle together': ibid.

14: 'promptly attacked . . . formidable hornets': *The Times*, 8 February 1916.

14: 'very reluctantly. . . almost hopeless task': *Hansard*, 17 May 1916.

14: 'what was possible . . . which were available': Churchill, *1914–1918*, p. 265.

14: 'the guidance of the police . . . with composure': Churchill, *The World Crisis 1911–1914*, pp. 327–44.

15: 'lit only enough to collect fares . . . dark curtains not drawn': Sylvia Pankhurst, *The Home Front*, p. 192.

15–16: In Sheffield . . . at 7.30 in the evening: H. A. Jones, op. cit., vol. V, p. 2.

16: 'complete exclusion of light . . . how dreary the winter world looked': IWM 97/3/1, Mrs A. Purbrook.

16: The fear . . . striking matches in the open: H. A. Jones, op. cit., vol. V, p. 3.

16: 'a lighted cigarette-end . . . a man a blow': Pankhurst, op. cit., p. 192.

16: The lake in St James's Park . . . to orient themselves: David Bilton, *The Home Front in the Great War*, p. 63.

16: 'passive defence . . . to be quite sure': *Hansard*, 17 March 1914.

16: 'an air blockade . . . a passive closing of the door?': Supf, op. cit., p. 284.

16: 'the great defence . . . point of departure': Churchill, *1911–1914*, pp. 327–44.
17: 'bigger than a battleship . . . Crystal Palace': quoted in Fredette, op. cit., p. 11.
17: 'going into a dark room to look for a black cat': Norman, op. cit., p. 54.
17: There they were assembled . . . air attack: Myron J. Smith, op. cit., p. 211.
17: The raid was planned . . . a day and a night: Norman, op. cit., pp. 55–6.
18: 'in a barbaric manner upon innocent civilians': ibid., p. 56.
18: 'go and milk their cows': Hyde, op. cit., p. 23.
18: Of 141 targets . . . three were hit: Fredette, op. cit., p. 12.

## Chapter 2: Zeppelins Overhead

21: 'necessity knows no law': Raymond H. Fredette, *The Sky on Fire*, p. 30.
21: 'historic buildings . . . as much as possible': ibid., p. 31.
22: 'apparently undefended places . . . particularly in America': Douglas H. Robinson, *The Zeppelin in Combat*, p. 65.
22: 'residential areas . . . royal palaces': Fredette, op. cit., p. 31.
23: In fact, no Zeppelin commander . . . 'silent raid': H. A. Jones, *The War in the Air*, vol. V, p. 93.
23: 'burned furiously . . . lurid glow': Frank Morison, *War on Great Cities*, pp. 43–4.
23: 'red with the reflection of many fires': ibid., p. 48.
23: 'Zeppelins are reported . . . the visit of airships': ibid., p. 33.
24: 'The City of London . . . sown with bombs': Kenneth Poolman, *Zeppelins Against London*, p. 36.
24: 'an army telegram . . . on the barrel-head': A. H. G. Fokker & Bruce Gould, *Flying Dutchman*, pp. 117–18.
24: 'open town . . . not in any way fortified': quoted in James M. Spaight, *Air Power and War Rights*, p. 200.
24–5: Bachmann then pointed out . . . the Tower of London: Otto Groos, *Der Krieg in der Nordsee*, Part IV, p. 263.
25: 'much more of a spray . . . the just and the unjust alike': L. E. O. Charlton, 'The New Factor in Warfare', pp. 48–50.
25: During the 8 September raid . . . the Great Fire of 1666: Morison, op. cit., pp. 29–30.
25: 'Several large blocks . . . all seriously damaged': *Weekly Dispatch*, 21 February 1926.
26: 'and of course . . . a dozen different points': Morison, op. cit., p. 32.
26: 'Having regard to . . . the rest of London': National Archives AIR1/2319.
26: 'to undertake to deal with all hostile aircraft . . . that reach these shores': ibid.
26: 'the two services . . . unnecessary duplication': ibid.
27: To prevent overlapping demands . . . the output of aircraft: National Archives AIR1/2312.

27: 'of a very minor character': ibid.

27: 'On no point . . . one service': ibid.

27: 'Fokker fodder': *Hansard,* 22 March 1916.

27–8: However, despite his expert knowledge . . . they were presented: Fredette, op. cit., pp. 26–7.

28: Asquith commissioned . . . 'unjustifiable': C. M. White, *The Gotha Summer,* p. 25.

28: 'The members of the Board . . . take his advice': *Hansard,* 17 May 1916.

29: The Hotel Cecil . . . the Allied cause: A. F. Hurley & R. C. Ehrhart, *Air Power and Warfare,* p. 26.

29: 'an invention of the devil': Fredette, op. cit., p. 4.

29: 'Had we caught . . . burning hydrogen': quoted in Guy Hartcup, *The War of Invention,* p. 160.

29: The Government . . . 'murder them': CAB 42/16; AIR 1/2296/209/77/18.

29: One officer noted . . . avoiding that fate: Captain A. C. Reid, *Planes and Personalities,* p. 132.

29: One pilot . . . an open grave: James Norman Hall & Charles Nordhoff, *The Lafayette Flying Corps,* vol. II, p. 123.

29: It was extraordinary . . . the exhausts of the engines: Hartcup, op. cit., p. 157.

29–30: There was no intelligence . . . to drop bombs on them: Quentin Reynolds, *They Fought for the Sky,* p. 153.

## Chapter 3: Turk's Cross

35: The Zeppelin menace . . . Germany was even now constructing: W. O. Horsnaill, *Air Navies of the Future,* pp. 1,056–63.

35: 'it was a [German] success of the first importance': H. A. Jones, *The War in the Air,* vol. II, p. 333.

36: 'one cobblestone . . . opposite No. 23': Raymond H. Fredette, *The Sky on Fire,* p. 4.

36: 'Between 11.50 and noon . . . above the haze': L. E. O. Charlton, *War Over England,* p. 134.

36: Injuries were reported . . . a cut on her right hand': John Hook, *They Come! They Come!,* p. 105.

36: 'England is no longer an island . . . old England': *Daily Mail,* 6 November 1906.

36–7: 'cheap and elusive . . . on an extended scale': *The Times,* 29 November 1916.

37: 'When the aeroplane raids start . . . his sacred city': *The Aeroplane,* 6 December 1916, pp. 1,079–81.

37: 'If I were asked . . . last November': *Flight,* vol. IX, no. 29, 19 July 1917.

37: 'the melt-pot room of the Danger Building': Hook, op. cit., p. 106.

37: 'a sordid district . . . the docks': Michael MacDonagh, *In London During the Great War,* p. 170.

37: 'tongue of crimson flame . . . the Royal Arsenal ablaze': ibid., p. 171.
37–8: 'saw in the sky . . . a vibrating tremor ran through London': ibid., p. 169.
38: 'A huge crater . . . razed to the ground': ibid., p. 170.
38: 'but by common report . . . War Office': ibid., pp. 170–1.
38: 'it must be an air-raid . . . terrifying kind': ibid., p. 169.
38: 'foul play . . . at the bottom of it': ibid., p. 170.
38: 'passionately devoted to the whole flying sector': Peter Supf, *Das Buch der Deutschen Fluggeschichte*, vol. 1, Berlin 1935, p. 284.
39: he owned his own balloon, 'Baby': ibid.
39: 'a true revolutionary to rise to the stars': *Der Frontsoldat*, 10, 1937, p. 305.
39: Those who impressed him . . . their recipients: Fredette, op. cit., p. 35.
39: 'all machines were to carry bombs on every war flight': Major Wilhelm Siegert, in Georg Paul Neumann, *The German Air Force in the Great War*, p. 157.
39: 'the best and most experienced pilots from every branch of the Air Force': ibid.
39: 'preserved as camouflage': Leutnant Andre Hug, *Cross & Cockade*, vol. 13, no. 4, 1972, p. 303.
40: 'an antediluvian machine . . . archaeopteryx': Major Wilhelm Siegert, 'The German Bomber Squadron Attack on Dunkirk', in *Nachrichtenblatt Fliegerring* no. 35, February 1926.
40: 'a bracket next to the observer . . . the firearms testing commission': ibid.
40: 'one for the pilot and one for the observer': Hug, op. cit., p. 290.
40: 'a carbine as my only weapon . . . its illusory calibre': Neumann, op. cit., p. 54.
40: 'to increase their mobility': Siegert, in Neumann, op. cit., p. 157.
40: 'to avoid bombing . . . returning after daybreak: Hug, op. cit., p. 304.
41: 'The moon illuminated . . . the countless searchlights': Siegert, 'The German Bomber Squadron Attack on Dunkirk'.
41: 'the only result . . . "women, children and old people" ': ibid.
41: 'To train the crews . . . Nieuport': Major Freiherr von Bulow, 'Die Angriffe des Bombengeschwader 3 auf England', p. 4.
41: 'its work being bombing . . . and line patrol duty': ibid., p. 5.
42: 'The increasing significance . . . in a single department': Walter Zuerl, *Pour le Mérite Flieger*, pp. 219–20.
43: 'the coherent restructuring . . . war resources': ibid.
43: 'What do an aerial bomb . . . land on innocents': Major Wilhelm Siegert, in *Nachrichtenblatt Fliegerring* no. 25, 1924.
43: 'Since an airship raid . . . practicable in the near future': von Bulow, op. cit., pp. 7–8.
44: 'a matter of urgent necessity . . . faith in ultimate victory': ibid., pp. 14–15.
44: 'war was . . . the source of supplies': ibid.
44: 'the crippling . . . the "solidarity of the enemy nations" be shaken': ibid., p. 15.

44: 'the Government buildings . . . Fleet Street': ibid., p. 16.

44: 'by dispatching eighteen aeroplanes . . . defeat our ends': ibid., pp. 7–8.

45: 'only battle-proven officers . . . are transferred there': Immanuel Braun, *Bombing Missions on Two Fronts*, pp. 47–8.

45: 'pretty soon . . . swim through the trenches': University of Texas at Dallas, Ferko Collection, Series 1, Aschoff, Walter, Box 4, Folder 7.

45: 'lay out in the sun . . . always envy them': ibid.

45: 'the hum of approaching aircraft . . . the German flew peacefully home': ibid.

45: 'a request . . . [Iron Cross, First Class]': ibid.

45: 'constant roaring. . . horrible there': ibid.

45: 'At first . . . horrible down there': ibid.

45: 'can be considered . . . not very many get to see': ibid.

46: The workmanship and construction . . . cheaper softwoods: AIR 1/2123/207/73/9.

47: 'examined captured enemy aircraft . . . aviation press': John H. Morrow, *German Air Power in World War I*, p. 77.

47: 'owing to the unsatisfactory performance . . . May 1917': von Bulow, op. cit., p. 9.

47: 'suffered from bad bearing metal . . . scrapped': ibid., pp. 10–11.

47: 'frequently impossible . . . badly designed': ibid.

47: He was also allocated . . . air-photography: Alex Imrie, *A Pictorial History of the German Air Service*, p. 39.

48: A chess player . . . soon won their affection too: W. von Eberhardt, *Unsere Luftstreitkräfte*, pp. 142–4.

48: He had already done . . . March 1911: ibid.

48: The England Squadron's losses . . . landing accidents: Jonathan Sutherland & Diane Canwell, *Battle of Britain 1917*, p. 46.

49: Even so . . . a 150kg bombload: Walter Aschoff, *Londonfluge*, p. 80.

49–50: On the early flights . . . hexanitrodiphenylamine: AIR 1/2123/207/73/9.

50: The latter . . . the roofs of buildings: ibid.

50: Although its climb rate . . . 8,000 to 11,500 feet: Aschoff, op. cit., p. 80.

50: All air-crew . . . hot water bottles: Andrew P. Hyde, *The First Blitz*, p. 42.

51: 'the strain . . . as a beginner': quoted in ibid., p. 40.

51: 'listened to the military concert . . . I shall take my honeymoon here!': University of Texas at Dallas, Ferko Collection, Series 1, Aschoff, Walter, Box 4, Folder 8.

52: 'inspected everything . . . able to meet him': ibid.

## Chapter 4: The Gotha Hum

57: Sir David Henderson . . . Home Defence duty: H. A. Jones, *The War in the Air*, vol. V, p. 7.

57: 'reduced to a dangerously low point . . . to be carried out': ibid., p. 12.

57–8: French recommended . . . the Western Front: ibid.

58: 'the presence of such apparatus . . . for repair': E. R. Calthrop, *Some Official Tests.*

58: 'Flying Corps headquarters . . . little short of murder': L. E. O. Charlton, *Charlton: An Autobiography*, p. 239.

58: 'our aviators . . . how to fight': Philip Gibbs, *Realities of War*, vol. II, p. 321.

58: 'had not even flown . . . his speed or mine': James McCudden, *Flying Fury*, pp. 135–6.

59: 'No aeroplanes or seaplanes . . . by day or night': H. A. Jones, op. cit., vol. V, p. 8.

59: 'ventured only a hundred yards . . . narrow escape': 'Kent Air-raid', undated newspaper clipping in diary of Lydia Peile, IWM 2589/94/2/1.

59: The ban on inland anti-aircraft . . . deadly new campaign: *The Times*, 8 May 1917.

60: 'the war ports . . . Ramsgate': Walter Aschoff, *Londonfluge*, pp. 58–64.

60: 'It was a rarely beautiful sight . . . into the sky': Major Wilhelm Siegert, in Georg Paul Neumann, *The German Air Force in the Great War*, p. 160.

60: 'Our aircraft . . . the Flanders coast': Aschoff, op. cit., pp. 58–64.

60: 'could not give the signal . . . its companions': Siegert, in Neumann, op. cit., p. 161.

60: 'a V-formation like a flight of ducks': Aschoff, op. cit., pp. 58–64.

60: 'a better target for the enemy A/A defences': Major Freiherr von Bulow, 'Die Angriffe des Bombengeschwader 3 auf England', p. 26.

61: 'saw at once . . . destroying enemy targets': Aschoff, op. cit., p. 58–64.

61: 'the passing minutes feeling like hours': ibid.

62: 'Our hopes rose again . . . a friendly welcome': ibid.

62: 'big white machines, making a loud noise': AIR 1/2123/207/73/9.

62: 'absolutely puerile': IWM, A. G. Burn, p. 76.

63: 'the texture . . . London blanketed beneath': L. E. O. Charlton, 'The New Factor in Warfare', p. 50.

63: 'Another thing . . . catch fire in the air': Captain C. B. Cooke, quoted in Andrew P. Hyde, *The First Blitz*, p. 76.

63: 'owing to . . . an air fight': Cole & Cheesman, op. cit., p. 235.

64: Although 'observation . . . very broken': AIR 1/2123/207/73/9.

64: 'a fleet of Zeppelins . . . a stink of paraffin': quoted in Cole & Cheesman, op. cit., p. 210.

64: 'the reply came they were engaged': PC A. S. Lyons, quoted in Hyde, op. cit., p. 78.

65: 'Bombs . . . the heavier bombs': Aschoff, op. cit., pp. 58–64.

65: 'anyone who spent any time . . . scan the sky': Alexander McKee, *The Friendless Sky*, p. 85.

66: 'the wasting of the food . . . the making of starch': Michael MacDonagh, *In London During the Great War*, p. 176.

66: 'shooting foxes . . . their hounds': ibid.

66: 'What a recognition . . . he so much enjoys!': ibid., p. 177.

66: 'Anyone . . . ease their aching backs': Mrs C. S. Peel, quoted in Martin Easdown & Thomas Genth, *A Glint in the Sky*, pp. 62–3.

67: 'emerging from the disc of the sun . . . danger': *New York Times*, 18 June 1917.

67: 'like seagulls'. . . 'like snowflakes': Cole & Cheesman, op. cit., p. 209.

67: 'about twenty aeroplanes . . . machines practising': Stanley W. Coxon, *Dover During the Dark Days*, pp. 194–5.

67: the town's Chief Constable . . . had contacted him: Jonathan Sutherland & Diana Canwell, *Battle of Britain 1917*, p. 52.

68: 'towards the hospital . . . covered in blood': Easdown & Genth, op. cit., p. 95.

68: 'a man's head . . . my parents': Richard Pinney, quoted in ibid., p. 100.

68: 'a thin coating of ice . . . under one's feet': Coxon, op. cit., pp. 194–5.

68–9: 'smoke and flames . . . swine in the sky': a Canadian sergeant, quoted in Sutherland & Canwell, op. cit., p. 53.

69: 'trying to find or recognize their lost ones': Mrs Gold, quoted in Easdown & Genth, op. cit., p. 96.

69: Three members . . . eight years of her life: ibid., pp. 74, 86.

## Chapter 5: Feverish Work

73: High above the shattered streets . . . homeward course: IWM K.89/801.

73: 'were startled . . . enemy aeroplanes': Stanley W. Coxon, *Dover During the Dark Days*, pp. 192–4.

73: 'The nearest bomb . . . for some time': A. Gathorne Hardy in the *Folkestone Herald*, 26 May 1917.

73: 'passing . . . in the air': ibid.

73: 'steep nose-dive, emitting smoke and steam': quoted in Raymond H. Fredette, *The Sky on Fire*, p. 23.

74: probably as a result . . . a heart attack: ibid., p. 24.

74: 'gone mad': AIR 1/2123/207/73/9.

74: 'never to be effaced from memory': J. C. Carlile, *Folkestone During the War*, p. 87.

74: 'There was a change . . . the even tenure of our way': Martin Easdown & Thomas Genth, *A Glint in the Sky*, p. 111.

74: 'The husbands . . . became so worried': ibid.

74: 'wholesale murder of women and children': Coxon, op. cit., pp. 192–4.

74: 'The official description . . . scorn and derision': Thomas Fegan, *The Baby Killers*, p. 42.

74: 'all Fleet Street knew the facts that same evening': Fredette, op. cit., p. 27.

75: 'a coastal town to the South-East': ibid., p. 28.

75: 'A large squadron . . . injuries came to light]': undated newspaper clipping in diary of Lydia Peile, IWM 2589/94/2/1.

75: 'childish and dangerous': *The Times*, 28 May 1917.

75: 'The public . . . official statements': Liddell Hart Archive, Montagu, IV/C/9.

76: 'You would not find . . . in war': Kenneth Poolman, *Zeppelins Against London*, p. 150.

76: 'wilful murder . . . the Crown Prince': Fredette, op. cit., p. 30.

76: 'a couple of hours . . . most of their time': H. W. Wilson & J. A. Hammerton, *The Great War*, quoted in Christopher Cole & E. F. Cheesman, *The Air Defence of Great Britain*, p. 307

76: 'essentially . . . carried out': *The Times*, 28 May 1917.

76: a captured German airman . . . intervened: AIR 1/2123/207/73/9.

76: 'it is absolute humbug . . . no military importance': Liddell Hart Archive, Montagu IV/C/10.

76: 'second Woolwich – one single arsenal': Edward Ashmore, *Air Defence*, p. 64.

76: 'may drop their bombs . . . bring the Government down': *The Aeroplane*, vol. XII, no. 14, 4 April 1917, p. 846.

76: for every civilian . . . should be shot: Winston Churchill, *The World Crisis 1915*, pp. 63–4.

77: 'the defence . . . by aeroplanes': Fredette, op. cit., p. 24.

77: 'such machines . . . disastrous results': H. A. Jones, *The War in the Air*, vol. V, pp. 24–5.

77: Yet, despite his criticisms . . . the Fleet: ibid., p. 23.

78: 'The visibility was particularly clear': Walter Aschoff, *Londonfluge*, pp. 58–64.

79: 'by several one-seaters . . . save the crew': ibid.

79: 'came across the water . . . imminent danger': undated newspaper clipping in diary of Lydia Peile, IWM 2589/94/2/1.

79: 'despite the flak . . . the target': Aschoff, op. cit., pp. 58–64.

79: 'on a huge building/arsenal . . . two large fires': University of Texas at Dallas, Ferko Collection, Series 1, Aschoff, Walter, Box 4, Folder 8.

79: 'which hit important targets, failed to explode': H. A. Jones, op. cit., vol. V, p. 25.

79: a group . . . alarmed onlookers: Andrew P. Hyde, *The First Blitz*, p. 107.

79: 'when the anti-aircraft guns . . . serious cases': undated newspaper clipping in diary of Lydia Peile, IWM 2589/94/2/1.

80: 'came home safe . . . made it home': University of Texas at Dallas, Ferko Collection, Series 1, Aschoff, Walter, Box 4, Folder 8.

80: 'England hopes such attacks will be repeated often': *Daily Express*, 7 June 1917.

80: 'well planned . . . the weather': Aschoff, op. cit., pp. 36–53.

81: 'a weather pattern . . . six to seven hours': ibid.

81: The squadron's weather officer . . . an airship squadron: Major Freiherr von Bulow, 'Die Angriffe des Bombengeschwader 3 auf England', p. 28.

81: 'All squadrons . . . raid on London': Aschoff, op. cit., pp. 36–53.

81: 'pilots and observers . . . memories': Major Wilhelm Siegert, in Georg Paul Neumann, *The German Air Force in the Great War*, p. 159.

81: 'We had envisaged . . . entrust our lives': Aschoff, op. cit., pp. 36–53.

82: 'tested the bomb release levers . . . just to check them': ibid.

82: 'The Gotha "G" aeroplanes . . . half an hour': von Bulow, op. cit., p. 32.

83: 'quickly have been remedied . . . after 1500 hours': ibid., p. 29.

83: Brandenburg . . . ten o'clock: Walter Zuerl, *Pour le Mérite Flieger*, pp. 102–5.

83: With the stimulus of war . . . night-photography: Neumann, op. cit., p. 54.

84: 'We dressed . . . our aircraft': Aschoff, op. cit., pp. 36–53.

84: 'You haven't left the rod behind?': ibid.

84: 'The propellers . . . "Come back in one piece"': ibid.

84: At exactly ten o'clock: nine o'clock in Britain.

85: Most carried . . . a heavier bomb-load: Zuerl, op. cit., pp. 102–5.

85: 'gave a quick look back . . . and off': Aschoff, op. cit., pp. 36–53.

85: 'We flew . . . the other squadrons': ibid.

85: 'like a flock . . . unknown territories': ibid., pp. 58–64.

86: 'Old towns . . . the North Sea': ibid., pp. 36–53.

86: 'it was always . . . were decisive': ibid., pp. 64–8.

86: 'out over the open . . . what lay before us': ibid., pp. 36–53.

87: 'today . . . a better target': ibid.

87: 'Suddenly . . . shell-bursts and blasts': ibid.

87: In any event . . . aimed too high: Zuerl, op. cit., pp. 102–5.

87: 'German bomber squadrons . . . our chests': Aschoff, op. cit., pp. 36–53.

88: 'Ostend . . . just north of London': von Bulow, op. cit., p. 27.

88: 'out of the green fields . . . London': Aschoff, op. cit., pp. 36–53.

88: 'all details could be made out with ease': Zuerl, op. cit., pp. 102–5.

88: 'We were flying . . . strength and resolve': Aschoff, op. cit., pp. 36–53.

88: 'wonderstruck' . . . 'like hawks over a dovecot': *John Bull*, 6 October 1917.

88–9: 'blue and gold and clear . . . unendurable suffering': *New York Times*, 14 June 1917.

89: 'a gorilla cracking a nut': Major Wilhelm Siegert, 'The German Bomber Squadron Attack on Dunkirk', in *Nachrichtenblatt Fliegerring* no. 35, February 1926.

89: 'Projectiles . . . rocking': *New York Times*, 2 July 1917.

89: 'The barrage . . . squadron formation': Aschoff, op. cit., pp. 36–53.

89: 'the sun was shining . . . running red': *Evening News*, 2 February 1935.

89–90: 'the drone . . . this district': John A. Stewart, in the *Evening News*, 2 February 1935.

90: 'what we like and the louder the better': John Hook, *They Come! They Come!*, p. 111.

90: 'Tongues of flame . . . claimed by death after all': John A. Stewart, in the *Evening News*, 2 February 1935.

90: 'had had four children and now had none': Hook, op. cit., p. 132.

90: 'With my telescope . . . the glaring sun': *New York Times*, 2 July 1917.

91: 'knee-deep in broken glass . . . with difficulty': *Weekly Dispatch*, 21 February 1926.

91: 'an explosion . . . flattened to the rails': *Evening News*, 7 February 1935.

91: 'stood wondering . . . groaning': Siegfried Sassoon, *Memoirs of an Infantry Officer*, p. 273.

91–2: 'standing in the road . . . scorched by the fire': *Evening News*, 4 February 1935.

92–3: 'a pram . . . the dead and dying': ibid., 2 February 1935.

93: 'everything changed . . . St Bartholomew's Hospital': ibid., 1 February 1935.

93: 'there came two deafening crashes . . . blown to pieces': ibid., 14 February 1935.

93: 'snatched the bag . . . not daring to move': ibid., 22 February 1935.

93–4: 'a crag of brickwork' / 'saw heads . . . on the pavement': ibid.

94: 'the cheers of a crowd in the street': ibid., 14 February 1935.

94: 'safes burst open . . . fur blown away': ibid.

94: 'something like a stick . . . in my life': Fredette, op. cit., p. 57.

94: 'as he was raising a cup of tea to his lips': ibid.

94: a caretaker's wife . . . the attic: AIR 1/2123/207/73/9.

94: 'Number 25 bus . . . already dead': Bill Goble, *Bill Goble: Lifelong Rebel*, p. 22.

94–5: 'had just given the sign . . . run to shelter': Mrs I. W. Edwards, in the *Evening News*, 31 January 1935.

95: 'all of a sudden . . . suffered shock': *Evening News*, 2 February 1935.

95: His sacrifice . . . ten shillings a week: Hook, op. cit., p. 113.

95: 'turned on its side . . . out of action': AIR 1/2123/207/73/9.

95: 'when a noise . . . some revived': *Evening News*, 2 February 1935.

96: 'directed my pilot . . . into my seat': Aschoff, op. cit., pp. 36–53.

96: Three men . . . steel shelving: AIR 1/2123/207/73/9.

96: 'still alive . . . broken': Mrs Murphy, in the *Evening News*, 5 March 1935.

96: 'the peculiar aptitude . . . massacre of innocents': L. E. O. Charlton, 'The New Factor in Warfare', p. 10.

97: 'the headmaster . . . come and gone': quoted in Hyde, op. cit., p. 136.

97: 'getting us to sing . . . shrill voices': Ivy Major, in the *Evening News*, 31 January 1935.

97: 'actually blasted . . . into the earth': Hyde, op. cit., p. 138.

97: 'The eleven other children . . . six weeks': Ivy Major, in the *Evening News*, 31 January 1935.

98: 'horrible vibration . . . doorstep: *Evening News*, 2 February 1935.

98: 'thinking only . . . in the mortuary': ibid.

98: 'Some mothers . . . looking for them': *New York Times*, 14 June 1917.

98: 'many of the little ones . . . as gently as we could': ibid.

98: 'The pathetic little bodies . . . on horse-drawn carts': 'Souvenir in Loving Memory . . .' IWM 92/1337.

98: 'the worst part . . . humanity': *New York Times*, 14 June 1917.

98: A child . . . in search of him: Albert Levy, quoted in Hook, op. cit., p. 124.

99: 'none too attractive . . . she sustained': Mr Monkhouse, quoted in ibid., p. 121.

99: 'As he stood there . . . crying': 'The First Blitz', *Timewatch*, BBC Television.

99: 'heard my mother . . . killed': Mrs F. Bush, in the *Evening News*, 1 March 1935.

100: 'With the last bomb gone . . . confirming it': Aschoff, op. cit., pp. 36–53.

100: 'with its left wing very much down, as if injured': AIR 1/2123/207/73/9.

100: his observer . . . killed instantly: AIR 1/2123/207/73/9.

100: 'the city's sea of houses . . . into the sky': Aschoff, op. cit., pp. 36–53.

100: 'dared to attack the squadron': Zuerl, op. cit., pp. 102–5.

100: 'over British airfields . . . lay below us once more': Aschoff, op. cit., pp. 36–53.

101: 'Aeroplanes . . . kept in sight': von Bulow, op. cit., p. 30.

101–2: 'At high altitude . . . "lucky day"': Aschoff, op. cit., pp. 36–53.

103: 'the size of pigeons' eggs' / 'the squadron might have come to grief': von Bulow, op. cit., p. 28.

103: 'went to our makeshift quarters . . . those who did not return': Aschoff, op. cit., pp. 36–53.

## Chapter 6: A City in Turmoil

107: On 20 June 1917 . . . the victims: John Hook, *They Come! They Come!*, p. 120.

107: 'If it were possible . . . he did it': *The Times*, 15 June 1917.

107: 'a) Giving a PUBLIC WARNING . . . air-raids on London': quoted in Hook, op. cit., p. 130.

107: The *Daily Mail* . . . Allied frontlines: *Daily Mail*, 15 June 1917.

107: 'amid great cheering': *The Times*, 18 June 1917.

107–8: 'Unaccustomed visitors . . . own door': Sylvia Pankhurst, *The Home Front*, p. 193.

108: 'it would be better . . . universal execration': *The Times*, 15 June 1917.

108: 'We have been steadily impressing . . . in the field': *Nation*, July 1917.

108: 'the English Government . . . London': *The Times*, 14 June 1917.

108–9: 'with comparative impunity . . . warning the public': ibid., 15 June 1917.

109: 'prophesied what was going to occur' / 'the authority of the Chair': *Hansard*, 15 June 1917.

109: 'I am afraid not . . . say for certain': *The Times*, 15 June 1917.

109: 'we are more interested . . . the banks': *Hansard*, 14 June 1917.

109–10: 'Before they can get up ... a nasty knock': Sir William Robertson to Douglas Haig, Liddell Hart Archive, 7/7/32.

110: 'for a week or two ... return to you': ibid.

110: 'a before-breakfast skirmish almost any morning on the Somme': *New York Times*, 26 June 1917.

110: 'the capture ... step of all': Andrew Boyle, *Trenchard*, pp. 221–2.

110: 'By bombing raids ... in the field': ibid., p. 223.

110: 'I have no reason ... its adoption': Haig, Liddell Hart Archive, 7/6/87.

110–11: 'Reprisals on open towns ... reprisals at all': Boyle, op. cit., p. 222.

111: 'the utmost damage ... the Western Front': ibid.

111: 'the double purpose ... England': ibid.

111: 'there is always the danger ... retaliation': Haig to Robertson, Liddell Hart Archive, 7/7/62.

111: 'twelve elated pilots ... our cockpits': Cecil Lewis, *Sagittarius Rising*, p. 152.

112: 'we walked off the playing fields into the lines': ibid., p. 11.

112 'to fight Hun bombers ... Lloyd George!': ibid., p. 154.

112: 'progressive increase ... 4,500 a month': H. A. Jones, *The War in the Air*, vol. V, p. 29.

112: 'the result ... into the street': letter to *The Times*, 19 June 1917.

112: 'Citizens ... distressing to hear': quoted in A. F. Hurley & R. C. Ehrhart, *Air Power and Warfare*, p. 26.

112: 'Order the Daily News ... minor claims': Liddell Hart Military Archive, LH 15/2/26.

112: 'charged one-sixth per cent ... £10,898,205': Edward Ashmore, *Air Defence*, p. 64.

113: 'the attacking squadrons ... dropped their bombs': Walter Aschoff, *Londonfluge*, pp. 56–8.

113: 'our defences ... continue the fight': ibid.

113: 'fortress London': ibid., pp. 36–53.

113: 'The Germans ... the process was': L. E. O. Charlton, 'The New Factor in Warfare', p. 48.

114: 'the docks ... the Thames': quoted in James M. Spaight, *Air Power and War Rights*, p. 222.

114: 'in the war reports ... "military establishments"': J. Mortane, *Histoire Illustrée de la Guerre Aérienne*, vol. II, p. 39.

114: 'As history had seen it ... "Brandenburg over London"!': Walter Zuerl, *Pour le Mérite Flieger*, pp. 102–5.

114: 'anything which could impede ... absolutely necessary': Erich von Ludendorff, *The General Staff and its Problems*, vol. 2, pp. 449–52.

114: 'acquaint me with the facts' / 'aroused the passions ... to a disastrous degree': ibid., pp. 453–8.

114: 'a hard race . . . forging weapons against us': ibid., pp. 449–52.
115: 'the effect must have been great' / 'among the docks . . . had been hit': Ernst von Höppner, *Deutschlands Krieg in der Luft*, pp. 111–12.
115: 'shatters Ghent . . . irreplaceable': Zuerl, op. cit., pp. 102–5.
115: 'knightly refinement . . . soldierly virtues': ibid., pp. 253–9.
115: 'an officer . . . weather conditions': Ashmore, op. cit., p. 44.
116: 'For us fliers . . . bad luck award' / 'almost all . . . the dead': Hermann Kohl (pilot), quoted in Peter Kilduff, *Germany's First Air Force*, p. 80.
117: 'Airships . . . turned on them': Otto Groos, *Der Krieg in der Nordsee*, in Liddell Hart Military Archive, LH15/2/26.
117: 'a considerable amount of cloud': AIR 1/2123/207/73/9.
118: Only one British aircraft . . . a DH4: ibid.
118: 'began to smoulder' / 'twisting and turning . . . rear-gunner's cockpit': Raymond H. Fredette, *The Sky on Fire*, p. 71.
118–19: A third of the sixty-five bombs . . . twenty-nine injured: Joseph Morris, *The German Air-raids on Great Britain*, p. 225.
119: 'Sometimes, . . . secret caves': Lewis, op. cit., p. 171.
119: 'lived supremely . . . to live': ibid., pp. 11–12.
119: 'I hope the gunner . . . he ended so': ibid., p. 172.
119: 'The defence of London . . . a grand war': ibid., p. 154.
120: 'wholly inadequate forces . . . disastrous': H. A. Jones, op. cit., vol. V, p. 40.
120: 'Dawn came up . . . turned south': Lewis, op. cit., p. 160.
121: 'I doubt . . . our planes': quoted in Christopher Cole & E. F. Cheesman, *The Air Defence of Great Britain*, p. 267.
121: 'Like the wind . . . the leader's machine': Major Wilhelm Siegert, in Georg Paul Neumann, *The German Air Force in the Great War*, pp. 161–2.
121: 'made a sudden dive . . . left-hand turn': AIR 1/2123/207/73/9.
121: 'until it again . . . exploded between them': ibid.
121: 'appear to have flown . . . 200 feet': ibid.
122: 'It was out of this haze . . . a score of swallows': *The Times*, 9 July 1917.
122: 'The height . . . preposterous': Michael MacDonagh, *In London During the Great War*, p. 198.
122: 'perfectly wonderful' / 'I'm glad . . . a flight of rooks': IWM Misc 223/3201.
122: Among . . . the Hotel Cecil: Aaron Norman, *The Great Air War*, p. 421.
122: 'As a spectacle . . . dispelled': *The Times*, 9 July 1917.
122: 'a young officer . . . hair in it': *Evening News*, 1 February 1935.
122–3: 'punctured . . . unbroken': *The Times*, 9 July 1917.
123: 'the too-familiar drone . . . legs blown off': *Evening News*, 1 February 1935.
123: 'the sound . . . "just one more chance"': ibid.
123: A bomb . . . women and children: AIR 1/2123/207/73/9.
123: 'send the Germans away . . . He was six': *Evening News*, 1 February 1935.

123: 'been blown to pieces . . . elm tree': ibid., 1 March 1935.

123–4: 'In the sidestreet . . . windows were broken': *The Times*, 9 July 1917.

124: 'wanton destruction . . . London': Fredette, op. cit., p. 76.

124: The Gothas . . . did not explode: *Evening News*, 2 March 1935.

124: 'There was no time . . . Aldersgate Street': A. F. King, Verger, St Giles, Cripplegate, quoted in Hook, op. cit., p. 141.

124: A car-woman's horse . . . Fleet Street: *Evening News*, 27 February 1935.

124: 'returning . . . timber and iron': William J. Baily, in ibid., 1 February 1935.

124–5: A portion . . . killed him: MacDonagh, op. cit., p. 201.

125: 'to take a last peep' / 'I remember . . . a firetrap': *Evening News*, 28 February 1935.

125: 'a blinding flash . . . three days': ibid.

125: 'three of our car-men . . . as long as I live': Mrs I. V. Van Colle, in ibid., 31 January 1935.

125–6: 'A crippled pavement artist . . . searchlight shafts' / 'shepherded . . . not a minute too soon': *The Times*, 9 July 1917.

126: 'Three little children . . . dust and soot': *Evening News*, 1 March 1935.

126: 'four racing pigeons . . . four days': ibid.

126: 'not a girl received so much as a scratch': *Sunday Pictorial*, 8 July 1917.

126: 'a large bomb . . . sixty lives': *Evening News*, 19 February 1935.

126: 'obtained a sack . . . the cells': ibid., 13 February 1935.

126: 'like a flock of huge birds . . . fifteen minutes': Reuters report, quoted in Zuerl, pp. 253–9.

126: 'puffs of black smoke . . . in the smoke': ibid.

126–7: 'when the raiders . . . fired at': *Sunday Pictorial*, 8 July 1917.

127: 'it seemed impossible . . . the invaders': *The Times*, 9 July 1917.

127: 'following in the track . . . overtake them"': MacDonagh, op. cit., p. 200.

127: 'disappeared . . . could be heard': Reuters report, quoted in Zuerl, op. cit., pp. 253–9.

127: 'an emergency force . . . working together': AIR 1/2123/207/73/9.

127: 'most gallant attacks . . . aircraft': ibid.

127–8: 'travelling faster . . . keep up with them': ibid.

128: 'because the Lewis . . . wage war': James McCudden, *Flying Fury*, p. 142.

128: 'in diving, . . . first dived': ibid., p. 148.

128: 'I flew abreast . . . consternation' / 'rather fed up with acting as ground-bait': ibid.

129: 'too awful . . . 400 rounds per minute': *The Aeroplane*, vol. XIII, no. 3, 18 July 1917, p. 190.

129: the CO's claim . . . British guns: cf Cole & Cheesman, op. cit., p. 272.

129: 'black smoke coming from the centre section': report of Second Lieutenant Frederick Grace, quoted in AIR 1/2123/207/73/9.

129: 'engaged forty miles . . . the Scheldt': *Sunday Pictorial*, 8 July 1917.

130–1: 'The fortified city, . . . returned home safely': German newspaper report, quoted in Zuerl, op. cit., pp. 253–9.

131: 'strangely enough, . . . a boy of seven': *The Times*, 9 July 1917.

131: Elsewhere . . . were injured: ibid.

131: 'The population . . . repel or avenge it': H. A. Jones, op. cit., vol. V, p. 38.

131: 'That London . . . country of origin': quoted in Neville Jones, *Origins of Strategic Bombing*, p. 134.

131: 'humiliating . . . in the air': *Graphic*, 9 July 1917.

131: 'deeply humiliated . . . London': *Flight*, vol. IX, no. 28, 12 July 1917.

131: 'there had not been . . . British men-of-war: *Daily Mail*, 9 July 1917.

132: 'caused no panic' / 'An extraordinary indication . . . splendid coolness': *The Times*, 9 July 1917.

132: 'during danger . . . the streets': R. Blair, LCC Education Officer, quoted in Hook, op. cit., p. 109.

132: Nonetheless . . . home with them: Beckton School log, 14 June 1917.

133: Such fury . . . was stoned: 'The First Blitz', *Timewatch*, BBC Television.

133: 'a regrettably large number of casualties': AIR 1/2123/207/73/9.

133: In the early stages . . . their families: David Bilton, *The Home Front in the Great War*, p. 220

133: 'a large body . . . German-sounding names': *Sunday Pictorial*, 8 July 1917.

133: 'ugly and menacing crowds': Joyce E. P. Muddock, *All Clear*, p. 21.

133: 'pay those German devils . . . we will': *New York Times*, 9 July 1917.

133–4: 'Down the street . . . can't you get on to *him*?"': Pankhurst, op. cit., pp. 194–5.

134: 'shouting . . . Dutch origin': *The Times*, 11 July 1917.

134–5: 'filled by the babble . . . the sack': Pankhurst, op. cit., p. 196.

135: 'got its window broken . . . the stock' / 'sent for him . . . scratch my face': ibid., p. 197.

135: One doubly unfortunate . . . enemy alien: Bilton, op. cit., pp. 46–8.

135: ' "The Unseen Hand" . . . 50,000 strong': ibid., p. 21.

135: 'Rumour raced . . . grew there': Pankhurst, op. cit., p. 194.

135–6: All 'foreigners' . . . a table plan: Bilton, op. cit., p. 21.

136: 'expressions . . . unscathed': *The Times*, 9 July 1917.

136: 'In the course . . . the coast': *East Kent Times*, 11 July 1917.

136: One police inspector . . . bombs fell: *Evening News*, 10 July 1917.

136: 'In many places . . . sought shelter': *The Times*, 9 July 1917.

136: 'On hearing . . . near at hand': HO45/10883/344919.

137: 'Unless a reasonably high proportion . . . offer protection': G. T. Garrett, 'Air-raid Precautions', pp. 132, 134.

137: 'the great mass . . . the slightest difference': ibid., p. 140.

137: 'would drag me . . . [the local pub]': James Fulljames, *The Time of Our Lives*, quoted in Hook, op. cit., p. 237.

137: 'take their chance . . . added protection': ibid.

137: 'supply of fine dry sand . . . pails or scuttles': HO45/10883/344919.

137: 'on no account . . . they should not be relied upon': ibid., p. 54.

137–8: 'congregated in the dining room . . . be put out': Mrs Byrne, in the *Evening News*, 11 March 1935.

138: 'it is dishonest . . . injury or death': Garrett, op. cit., p. 125.

138: 'There was an almighty bang . . . it saved our lives': Richard van Emden & Steve Humphries, *All Quiet on the Home Front*, p. 178.

138: 'these were often . . . a peculiarly horrible death': Garrett, op. cit., p. 125.

138: 'severely and adversely': H. A. Jones, op. cit., vol. V, p. 40.

138: 'much excitement . . . coming to an end': Robertson to Haig, Liddell Hart Archive, Robertson 7/7/35.

138: 'If anyone in this country . . . another Government': *The Times*, 14 July 1917.

139: 'withdrawal . . . may have to be abandoned': H. A. Jones, op. cit., vol. V, p. 39.

139: The squadron . . . within forty-five seconds: Cole & Cheesman, op. cit., p. 281.

139: 'an aircraft . . . make him fight': Peter Daybell, *Some Aspects of the Aircrew Experience During the Great War*, p. 3.

139: 'with the printed inscription . . . red ink': MacDonagh, op. cit., p. 217.

140: 'This fore and aft . . . the ridiculous': *Flight*, vol. IX, no. 29, 19 July 1917.

140: 'a fresh and able mind . . . prejudices': David Lloyd George, *War Memoirs*, vol. IV, p. 186.

140: 'the air-raids on London . . . exceptional measures': report of Lieutenant-General J. C. Smuts's Committee, July 1917.

140: 'trained to fight *in formation*': ibid. (italics in original).

141: three 'maroons': later amended to two.

142: The wreck . . . four hours later: Cole & Cheesman, op. cit., p. 276.

142: His fury . . . such incidents: Jonathan Sutherland & Diane Canwell, *Battle of Britain 1917*, p. 81.

142: 'Gunners . . . German': quoted in Cole & Cheesman, op. cit., p. 276.

143: 'In the early days . . . minimise the risk': letter to *The Times*, 19 June 1917.

143: 'east of Blackfriars Bridge . . . provided with parks': Garrett, op. cit., p. 136.

# Chapter 7: Home Defence

147: 'the comparative safety . . . the streets of London': Edward Ashmore, *Air Defence*, p. 40.

147: the *Daily Telegraph*'s proposal . . . artificial fog: *Daily Telegraph*, 5 February 1918.

147–8: Ashmore then added a refinement . . . priority: Ashmore, op. cit., p. 41.

148: 'fly to a flank' . . . attack him': ibid., pp. 41–2.

148: 'an ingenious arrangement of coloured lamps': ibid., p. 51.

148: divided into five hundred numbered squares . . . 'One, Two, Three and Four': Sir Alfred Rawlinson, *The Defence of London*, p. 175.

148: 'three minutes at best' . . . as long': Ashmore, op. cit., p. 76.

149: 'three large Klaxon horns . . . within a minute': Cecil Lewis, *Sagittarius Rising*, p. 166.

149: 'general searchlight . . . come down': Ashmore, op. cit., p. 75.

149: 'isolated attacks . . . a useless sacrifice': Lord French, quoted in H. A. Jones, *The War in the Air*, vol. V, p. 44.

149: 'the definite role . . . enemy formation': Lord French, quoted in ibid., p. 45.

149: 'it was often . . . a raid': quoted in Raymond H. Fredette, *The Sky on Fire*, p. 95.

150: 'a heap of torn and mangled humanity': ibid., p. 99.

150: 'killing a mother . . . 'watching the aeroplanes': newspaper clipping in diary of Lydia Peile, IWM 2589/94/2/1.

150: 'no system of warning in Southend': ibid.

150: 'the imbecility of the local authorities': Fredette, op. cit., p. 101.

150: 'on my buttons': Kurt Delang, 'Bomben über England', pp. 435–6.

151: 'bursting all its joints': ibid.

151: 'suffered a broken leg . . . burn up': ibid.

151: 'Although a strong wind . . . over the sea': Walter Aschoff, *Londonfluge*, pp. 58–64.

151: 'For a long time . . . the north-west': ibid.

151: 'suddenly . . . white wool': Immanuel Braun, *Bombing Missions on Two Fronts*, p. 49.

152: 'Now the flying . . . disappeared': ibid.

152: 'Within a few minutes . . . the winds': Aschoff, op. cit., pp. 58–64.

152: 'appearing and disappearing . . . home airfield': ibid.

152: 'the waves swiftly closed in over them': Kurt Küppers, quoted in Fredette, op. cit., p. 105.

152–3: 'Gale-force gusts . . . few to do so': Aschoff, op. cit., pp. 58–64.

153: 'We were back home . . . this altitude': Braun, op. cit., p. 49.

153: 'During my years . . . the squadron ever suffered': Aschoff, op. cit., pp. 58–64.

153: 'it would be the last . . . undertake': ibid., pp. 64–8.

153: 'our flock . . . the formation': ibid.

154: 'The picket ships . . . the air around us': ibid.

154: 'recently devised . . . excellent results': Ashmore, op. cit., p. 45.

154: three white star-shells . . . list of priorities): Major Freiherr von Bulow, 'Die Angriffe des Bombengeschwader 3 auf England', p. 27.

154: 'failed to understand . . . Margate to Dover': ibid.

154: 'morning visit of Hun machines' / 'While many persons . . . "It's hit"': *Isle of Thanet Gazette*, 25 August 1917.

154: 'The rear-gunner . . . plummeted from the sky': Aschoff, op. cit., pp. 64–8.

154: 'loud cheering . . . began to descend': *Isle of Thanet Gazette*, 25 August 1917.

155: 'all their clothes . . . unrecognisable': ibid.

155: '100 rounds . . . to make sure': *Morning Post*, 6 October 1917.

155: 'In the glorious sunlight . . . the sun's rays': *Flight*, vol. IX, no. 35, 30 August 1917.

155: 'a bullet . . . a single strand': Christopher Cole & E. F. Cheesman, *The Air Defence of Great Britain*, p. 293.

155: 'Both gunners . . . fired at': *Flight*, vol. IX, no. 35, 30 August 1917.

155: 'in close formation . . . bring to bear': Aschoff, op. cit., pp. 64–8.

156: 'The more we flew . . . altogether': ibid.

156: 'our people never could': *The Aeroplane*, vol. XIII, no. 9, 29 August 1917, p. 626.

156: 'The course of aerial combat . . . the warriors': diary of Major Wilhelm Siegert, vol. III, p. 17.

156: Among the legendary air aces . . . burn in mid-air': Michael Paris, *Winged Warfare*, p. 8.

156–7: 'souvenir matchboxes . . . other charities': Thomas Fegan, *The Baby Killers*, pp. 140–1; Fredette, op. cit., p. 109.

157: 'Those last daylight flights . . . we were sustaining': Aschoff, op. cit., pp. 64–8.

157: 'to carry out the raids solely at night': von Bulow, op. cit., p. 33.

157: 'the design . . . work by day': Major Wilhelm Siegert, in Georg Paul Neumann, *The German Air Force in the Great War*, p. 159.

157: 'fully appreciated' . . . rest and sleep': ibid., p. 178.

157–8: 'apart from the technical difficulties, . . . more difficult': von Bulow, op. cit., p. 33.

158: Ferdinand von Zeppelin . . . 1 August 1915: A. H. G. Fokker & Bruce Gould, *Flying Dutchman*, p. 141.

158: 'After tedious and expensive experiments': John H. Morrow, *German Air Power in World War I*, p. 39.

158: 'excellent results . . . island of Oesel': Siegert, in Neumann, op. cit., p. 190.

158: 'employed . . . strategic importance': Siegert, in ibid., p. 165.

158: 'the Giants had four, five or six engines': IWM K.89/801.

158–9: A five-engined Giant . . . (19,000 feet): www.rodenplant.com/HTML/055.htm

159: 'in flight . . . split apart': Oskar Kuppinger, *Bomber Observer*, Part II, p. 208.

159: Monoplanes . . . 1912: Paris, op. cit., p. 235.

159: 'flying level and in still air': AIR 1/2123/207/73/9.

160: and it doubled . . . May 1917: Morrow, op. cit., p. 83.

160: Each R-plane . . . radio technicians: www.rodenplant.com/HTML/055.htm

160: Many of the mechanics . . . proved valuable: G. W. Haddow & P. M. Grosz, *The German Giants*, p. 26.

160–1: 'large radius . . . night warfare alone': Siegert, in Neumann, op. cit., p. 189.

161: 'hung in long . . . folding doors': W. von Eberhardt, *Unsere Luftstreitkräfte*, Part II, pp. 442–4.

161: 'even if the bombs burst in the street or courtyard': von Bulow, op. cit., p. 22.

## Chapter 8: Night-time Excursions

165: 'rolling day and night raids': Walter Zuerl, *Pour le Mérite Flieger*, pp. 253–9.

165: '1) Simultaneous raids . . . carry on the war': Major Freiherr von Bulow, 'Die Angriffe des Bombengeschwader 3 auf England', p. 17.

165: 'The possibility . . . at night instead': ibid.

166: Trained electrical mechanics . . . janitors: John H. Morrow, *German Air Power in World War I*, p. 83.

166: Although Ludendorff . . . higher priority: Alex Imrie, *A Pictorial History of the German Air Service*, p. 46.

166: [which was in such short supply . . . billiard tables]: Holger H. Herwig, *First World War*, p. 354.

166: 'Inspection of our planes . . . began to cough': Hauptmann Hermann, *The Luftwaffe: Its Rise & Fall*, p. 6.

166–7: Fuel oil . . . 1,000 tons: John H. Morrow Jr, *The Defeat of the German and Austro-Hungarian Air Forces in the Great War, 1909–1918*, p. 121.

167: 'continuous day and night raids . . . came to naught': von Bulow, op. cit., pp. 33–4.

167: 'our reputation . . . romantic sheen' / 'not-so-expert fishing . . . five kilos': Walter Aschoff, *Londonfluge*, pp. 98–9.

167: 'beautiful . . . rhododendron bushes': University of Texas at Dallas, Ferko Collection, Series 1, Aschoff, Walter, Box 4, Folder 8.

167: 'French red wine . . . pheasants and hares': Aschoff, op. cit., pp. 98–9.

167: 'revolved around our airfields . . . welcome guests': ibid.

167: 'speedily . . . new machines': von Bulow, op. cit., p. 338.

168: 'in no way . . . Gotha G IV': ibid., p. 20.

168: 'raid targets of military importance': Kurt Küppers, quoted in Raymond H. Fredette, *The Sky on Fire*, p. 130.

168: 'Soon we knew . . . London': Aschoff, op. cit., pp. 64–8.

168: 'shooting . . . target types and tactics': ibid.

168: 'We preferred cloudless skies . . . unbroken cloud-bank': ibid.

168–9: 'a troublesome business . . . with accuracy': Major Wilhelm Siegert, in Georg Paul Neumann, *The German Air Force in the Great War*, pp. 166–7.

169: 'by systematic training . . . rain or snow': Siegert, in ibid., p. 167.

169: 'a heavy turnover . . . further training': Aschoff, op. cit., pp. 95–6.

169: 'Although two or three night-flights . . . identified and mastered': ibid., pp. 64–8.

169: 'placed at the end . . . take-off run': Oskar Kuppinger, *Bomber Observer*, Part I, p. 126.

169: 'Rocket batteries . . . sixty miles': Siegert, in Neumann, op. cit., p. 168.

169: 'that at X . . . a second shot': Siegert, in ibid., p. 169.

169–70: 'Anti-aircraft batteries . . . to be attacked': Siegert, in ibid., p. 177.

170: 'always flew over . . . a green flare': Kuppinger, op. cit., Part I, p. 126.

170: 'flying glass . . . did the damage': *New York Times*, 6 September 1917.

170: 'picking out bodies . . . the parade ground': E. Cronk, quoted in Martin Easdown & Thomas Genth, *A Glint in the Sky*, p. 134.

170–1: 'Everywhere . . . another raid such as this': Frederick W. Turpin, quoted in Thomas Fegan, *The Baby Killers*, p. 58.

171: 'any of the lost . . . in most cases': E. Cronk, quoted in Easdown & Genth, op. cit., p. 134.

171: 'an old order . . . the first night raid': Edward Ashmore, *Air Defence*, p. 51.

171: 'wave their beams . . . the attacking aircraft' / 'give away . . . another light': ibid., pp. 51–2.

171: 'tricky enough . . . at night': Cecil Lewis, *Sagittarius Rising*, p. 167.

171: 'by feel . . . forced down anywhere': ibid.

171–2: 'created . . . other pilots' / 'perhaps . . . air defence': Ashmore, op. cit., p. 53.

172: 'rushed off to Aircraft Depots': Lewis, op. cit., p. 167.

172: 'the Home Defence squadrons . . . night-fighters': ibid., p. 168.

172: 'the long arm . . . the third': ibid.

172: 'Instead of being able . . . worked out': ibid., p. 167.

172: 'each pilot . . . another machine': ibid.

173: Ballistics experts . . . the raider: Christopher Cole & E. F. Cheesman, *The Air Defence of Great Britain*, p. 312.

173–4: 'The night was clear . . . a perfect landing': Lewis, op. cit., pp. 168–70.

174: 'a keg of old ale': ibid., p. 173.

174: 'Down he came . . . brass hat off': ibid., pp. 174–6.

174: 'The result . . . angry General': ibid.

175: 'this time . . . at every stride': ibid.

175: 'Well, I bloody put the wind up him . . . Trouble!': quoted in Cole & Cheesman, op. cit., p. 304.

# Chapter 9: *Brandbomben*

179: 'owing to the difficulty . . . danger of collision': Major Wilhelm Siegert, in Georg Paul Neumann, *The German Air Force in the Great War*, p. 169.

179: 'collisions . . . unknown at the time': Major Wilhelm Siegert, 'The German Bomber Squadron Attack on Dunkirk', in *Nachrichtenblatt Fliegerring* no. 35, February 1926.

179: 'On these long-distance flights . . . hours on end': Walter Aschoff, *Londonfluge*, p. 80.

179: 'producing . . . the British public': Joseph Morris, *The German Air-raids on Great Britain*, pp. 247–8.

179: Additional bombs . . . daylight raids: Major Freiherr von Bulow, 'Die Angriffe des Bombengeschwader 3 auf England', p. 22.

180: 'The English . . . became lively': Walter Zuerl, *Pour le Mérite Flieger*, pp. 253–9.

181: 'They didn't shoot badly . . . targets': ibid.

181: 'It was curious . . . badly in others': von Bulow, op. cit., Part II, p. 3.

181: '"Look out . . . a feather on them': *Evening News*, 1 February 1935.

182: 'groping our way . . . only seventeen': ibid.

182: 'When the alarm . . . a trifle bored': ibid., 9 March 1935.

182: Cleopatra's Needle . . . struck by shrapnel: the marks are visible to this day.

182: 'stabbing the heavens . . . the woman': *Evening News*, 14 February 1935.

182: The two men . . . also killed: AIR 1/2123/207/73/9.

182–3: 'with the permission . . . a tailor's' / 'as the young men . . . a number of recruits': *Evening News*, 31 January 1935.

183: 'Either the Londoners . . . sort of panic': the Kogenluft, *Nachrichtenblatt der Luftstreitkräfte*, 20 September 1917.

183: 'from Rochester Bridge to Halling': AIR 1/2123/207/73/9.

183: 'with a view . . . special objective': von Bulow, op. cit., p. 34.

184: released by a lever marked *magazin*: AIR 1/2123/207/73/9.

184: '1) the intensive type . . . easily ignited materials': Augustin Prentiss, *Chemicals in War*, p. 248.

185: The *Brandbomben* . . . a carrying handle: Wolfgang Fleischer, *German Air-Dropped Weapons to 1945*, p. 15.

185: Despite this ingenious combination . . . substantial fires: J. Enrique Zanetti, *Fire from the Air*, p. 5.

185: One such bomb . . . the Blackwater river: Morris, op. cit., pp. 208–9.

185: The early aircraft incendiaries . . . extinguish them: Enrique Zanetti, op. cit., pp. 4, 13.

185: The greatest problems . . . extinguish them: ibid., pp. 16–17.

186: 'demoralising effect . . . casualties produced': Prentiss, op. cit., p. 252.

186: A larger . . . ease of extinction: Fleischer, op. cit., p. 15.

186: 'the construction of aerial bombs . . . to this end': General Giulio Douhet, *The Command of the Air*, quoted in Eugene Emme, *The Impact of Air Power*, p. 163.

186: 'Made of streamlined shape' / 'burst open . . . combustion': AIR 1/2123/207/73/9.

## Chapter 10: The Blitz of the Harvest Moon

189: 'the evening twilight . . . even deeper darkness behind': Walter Aschoff, *Londonfluge*, pp. 76–80.

189: 'it seemed to thrive . . . standard of living improved': Peter Ackroyd, *London: A Biography*, p. 722.

189: 'it was considered bad form': IWM 97/3/1, Mrs A. Purbrook.

190: 'one should not show . . . the trenches': Geoffrey Gorer, *Death, Grief & Mourning*, p. 6.

190: The striking . . . 10 p.m. and 7 a.m.: David Bilton, *The Home Front in the Great War*, p. 71.

190: 'local hazards . . . music halls were full': Ackroyd, op. cit., p. 722.

191: Even more stringent regulations . . . the war effort: Neil Hanson, *Walking Through Eden*, pp. 189–90.

191: 'strangely quiet . . . almost to zero': Cecil Lewis, *Sagittarius Rising*, p. 173.

191: 'street lights . . . expectancy of disaster': ibid.

192: 'special constables . . . electric lights': *Daily Mail*, 30 September 1917.

192: 'as they would . . . under cover': *Flight*, vol. IX, no. 34, 23 August 1917.

192: 'We Britishers . . . consideration of safety': *Southend Standard*, 17 May 1915.

193: 'difficult to alight . . . inside the station': Sir William Nott-Bower, Liddell Hart Military Archive 15/2/26.

193–4: 'The streets . . . the inquest on the dead': *Evening News*, 25 February 1935.

194: 'persons . . . in a storm': Michael MacDonagh, *In London During the Great War*, p. 218.

194: 'chiefly patronised . . . spectacular event': Frank Morison, *War on Great Cities*, p. 141.

194: 'invited disaster . . . at 8.55': *Daily Mail*, 30 September 1917.

195: 'damage to the building and some statuary': H. A. Jones, *The War in the Air*, vol. V, p. 78.

195: 'just swinging round . . . stop his tram': A. E. Green, in the *Evening News*, 1 March 1935.

195: A thirteen-year-old . . . the boy died: John Hook, *They Come! They Come!*, p. 165.

195: 'a specially heavy attack on Dover': AIR 1/2123/207/73/9.

196: 'the approach to the runway . . . cones of light': Aschoff, op. cit., pp. 76–80.

196: 'The last minutes . . . perilous flight': ibid.

196–7: 'suddenly . . . meet their end': ibid.

197: 'About 7.30 . . . shells screeching': IWM 15021 06/53/1, Mrs A. Purbrook.

197: 'As a moving . . . upset his plans completely': *Daily Mail*, 30 September 1917.

198: 'magnificent as was the work . . . "a piece of bomb"': ibid.

198: 'London is weary . . . German towns and cities': ibid.

198: 'composed of aged fathers . . . all-night vigils' / 'took the opportunity . . . happened out there': *Evening News*, 5 February 1935.

199: 'small front room . . . Poplar Patrol': *Evening News*, 12 March 1935.

199: 'At the Front . . . like / unlike a brick': *Punch*, October 1917.

199: 'We generally left at dusk . . . the engines': John H. Knauer, *Flying the AEG G IV*, quoted in Peter Kilduff, *Germany's First Air Force*, p. 79.

200: 'see the moon-glint . . . to the North': Edward Ashmore, *Air Defence*, p. 59.

200: 'always clearly visible . . . some districts': Christopher Cole & E. F. Cheesman, *The Air Defence of Great Britain*, p. 332.

200: 'on the silence . . . in the road': Sylvia Pankhurst, *The Home Front*, pp. 191–2.

200: 'a concourse of people estimated at 100,000': *Daily Telegraph*, 1 November 1935.

200: 'people began to flock . . . any warning': Joseph Morris, *The German Air-raids on Great Britain*, p. 244.

200: 'on its journey . . . deserted streets': MacDonagh, op. cit., pp. 252–3.

201: 'urged by fear . . . to the west': H. A. Jones, op. cit., vol. V, p. 135.

201: 'spontaneous . . . would not do': H. G. Castle, *Fire Over England*, p. 215.

201: The numbers . . . three hundred thousand: Edwin A. Pratt, *British Railways and the Great War*, Part V, pp. 183–4.

201: 'The majority . . . an alarm was given': Caroline Playne, *Britain Holds On*, p. 220.

201: 'People took up their places . . . to best advantage': *Daily Telegraph*, 1 November 1935.

201: 'The sights in the Tubes . . . "night nursery"': from *Untold Tales of Wartime London*, quoted in Hook, op. cit., p. 107.

202: 'the iron lattice door . . . "Full up; no more room"': MacDonagh, op. cit., p. 255.

202: 'wanted to get a picture of what we were doing': W. von Eberhardt, *Unsere Luftstreitkräfte*, pp. 222–4.

202: 'over a milk-white sea of clouds' / 'A full moon . . . the way': ibid.

202: 'Arcturus . . . London': ibid.

202: 'a big fork . . . in that fork': ibid.

203: 'from Dover . . . the white blanket beneath': ibid.

203: 'stars, compass and clock' / 'Their faint glow . . . through the clouds': ibid.

203: 'an impenetrable darkness . . . the fog and damp': ibid.

204: Lorenz felt the pressure . . . regain control: ibid.

204: Lorenz's compass . . . Ostend: ibid.

204: 'suffered heavily': Raymond H. Fredette, *The Sky on Fire*, p. 143.

204: 'landing with full fuel tanks . . . suicide': Kurt Delang, 'Bomben über England', pp. 435–6.

204: The raiders . . . never circulated: Cole & Cheesman, op. cit., p. 310.

205: 'on a still night . . . near at hand': Morris, op. cit., p. 251.

205: The human eye . . . a single Giant: Cole & Cheesman, op. cit., p. 310.

205: 'a determined . . . raiders': *The Times*, 30 September 1917.

205: 'picked up . . . Zeppelins': Major Freiherr von Bulow, 'Die Angriffe des Bombengeschwader 3 auf England', Part II, p. 4.

205: 'The floor of the saloon . . . into the street' / 'many seriously': Morison, op. cit., pp. 142–3.

205: The licensee, . . . killed instantly: Hook, op. cit., p. 175.

205–6: 'We had scored . . . we had played on': C. J. Creek, in the *Evening News*, 4 February 1935.

206: The All Clear . . . a lamp-post: *Evening News*, 14 February 1935.

206: 'There was a bright moon . . . air-raid warning': William Clarke, in the *Evening News*, 7 March 1935.

206: 'At that moment . . . across the road': *Evening News*, 14 February 1935.

206: 'nearly as much damage . . . by bombs': H. A. Jones, op. cit., vol. V, p. 84.

206–7: 'turned off . . . the final dive' / 'hit a row . . . the crash' / 'almost without injury . . . a tree' / 'found under the wreckage . . . concussion': Delang, op. cit., pp. 435–6.

207: '"Dugouts" . . . my aunt cried': *Evening News*, 7 February 1935.

207: 'It was pitiful . . . a bird in a cage': Mrs K. Sergeant, in ibid., 4 February 1935.

207: 'made a dash . . . "It's an awful life isn't it?"': Elisabeth Fagan, in ibid., 1 March 1935.

207: 'So vile . . . such shelter': IWM 97/3/1, Mrs A. Purbrook.

207: 'so noisome . . . the booking-office': Joyce E. P. Muddock, *All Clear,* p. 46.

208: 'people . . . outside' / 'there was a mad rush for re-entrance': ibid., p. 47.

208: 'the danger . . . hysterical': Mrs K. Sergeant, in the *Evening News*, 4 February 1935.

208: 'just in front . . . cut to pieces': Muddock, op. cit., pp. 47–8.

208: 'home on leave . . . home to bed': Baroness Hughwinkel, quoted in the *Evening News*, 25 February 1935.

208: 'in large or small quantities' / 'could cause . . . the Huns': *The Aeroplane*, vol. XIII, no. 17, 24 October 1917, p. 1,222.

208: At first sandbags . . . more affluent districts: Castle, op. cit., p. 215.

## Chapter 11: The Serpent Machine

211: 'Glorious moonlit nights . . . terrible experiences': Frank A. Lamb, in the *Evening News*, 4 February 1935.

211: 'midnight . . . the darkness: Walter Aschoff, *Londonfluge*, p. 80.

211–12: 'Our Serpent Machine's engine . . . the ferocious battle below us': ibid., pp. 81–4.

212–13: 'Before we crossed . . . towards London': ibid., pp. 85–92.

213: 'of every eighteen . . . the enemy': Edward Ashmore, *Air Defence*, p. 83.

213: 'supplied two rounds . . . the shell': Sir Alfred Rawlinson, *The Defence of London*, p. 241.

213–14: '*First* . . . to attack us': ibid., pp. 205–6.

214–17: 'searchlights . . . we had won back': Aschoff, op. cit., pp. 85–92.

217: 'Even when all the surviving aircraft . . . young lieutenants': ibid., pp. 76–80.

217: 'Last night . . . the impact': ibid., pp. 85–92.

217–18: 'a small aircraft . . . did not hit me': Immanuel Braun, *Bombing Missions on Two Fronts*, p. 50.

218: The barrage . . . in London alone: H. A. Jones, *The War in the Air*, vol. V, p. 85.

218: 'fired over 500 rounds . . . practically useless': Rawlinson, op. cit., p. 209.

218: 'instantly given . . . considerable': ibid., pp. 209–10.

218: When some of the gun-batteries . . . understandable smugness: ibid., pp. 210–11.

219: 'A three-inch shell . . . fourteen guns': Liddell Hart Military Archive, 15/2/26.

219: 'an infernal nuisance' . . . the moon': Michael MacDonagh, *In London During the Great War*, p. 228.

219: 'instruments of self-bombardment': Raymond H. Fredette, *The Sky on Fire*, p. 147.

219: 'this infernal Barrage . . . killed in bed thereby': ibid.

219: 'one of our own shells . . . Thomas Weight': H. Brown, in the *Evening News*, 14 February 1935.

219: 'Many lives were lost . . . the enemy': Rawlinson, op. cit., p. 201.

220: 'which was not . . . aeroplane attack': H. A. Jones, op. cit., vol. V, p. 91.

220: 'nicknames . . . "they flew right over"': John Twells Brex, *Adventures on the Home Front*, p. 35.

220: 'followed by . . . vast solitude': MacDonagh, op. cit., p. 219.

220: 'the raids of the Harvest Moon': Fredette, op. cit., p. 148.

220–1: 'two microphonic ears . . . a skilled listener' / 'the cadence . . . the aeroplane': Liddell Hart Archive 15/3/1-447, Anti-Aircraft Defences, pp. 8–9.

221: 'they would now hear . . . seen for them': Rawlinson, op. cit., p. 113.

221: '20 kilometres before Dover': Aschoff, op. cit., p. 4.

221: 'tenements . . . houses damaged: John Hook, *They Come! They Come!*, pp. 185–6.

221: A 50kg bomb . . . the fish: AIR 1/2123/207/73/9.

221–2: 'when a terrible flash . . . all killed': *Evening News*, 4 February 1935.

222: 'rescued alive . . . lunatic asylum': ibid., 8 March 1935.

222: 'climbing over the banisters . . . trampled to death: *East London Advertiser*, 6 October 1917.

# Chapter 12: Londoners Unnerved

225: 'the gun defences . . . ceased to exist': H. A. Jones, *The War in the Air*, vol. V, p. 89.

225: 'a tendency . . . to panic': ibid.

225: 'yielded excellent results ... London': Major Freiherr von Bulow, 'Die Angriffe des Bombengeschwader 3 auf England', p. 35.
225: Churchill ... the England Squadron: Jonathan Sutherland & Diane Canwell, *Battle of Britain 1917*, p. 144.
225: 'awoke in Britain ... the Grand Fleet': Malcolm Smith, *A Matter of Faith*, p. 428.
225–6: 'the September air-raids ... serious riots': von Bulow, op. cit., Part II, p. 15.
226: 'on Saturday ... suppress details': IWM 97/3/1, Mrs A. Purbrook.
226: 'full of nervous cases': quoted in von Bulow, op. cit., Part II, p. 16.
226: 'after an aerial attack ... to cure': AIR 1/2420/305/8/274721.
226: 'at the Coroner's Inquest ... the air-raids"': *Morning Post*, 11 September 1917.
226: 'in a collapsed condition' / 'Death ... consequent fear': *Evening News*, 10 July 1917.
226: The deaths ... attack on London: John Hook, *They Come! They Come!*, p. 149.
226: Gertrude Binstead ... nervous temperament indeed': ibid., pp. 151–2.
227: 'cowering in cellars': *Daily Mail*, 8 November 1917.
227: 'filled the Tubes ... Brighton': B. E. Sutton, *Journal of the RUSI, 1922*, p. 346.
227: 'after thorough and patient search ... possible to believe': IWM 97/3/1, Mrs A. Purbrook.
227: 'the moral effect ... the reverse is the case': Hugh Trenchard, in *Army Quarterly*, vol. II, no. 1, April 1921.
227: 'and I confess ... one is stranded': John E. Wrench, *Struggle 1914–1920*, p. 251.
227: 'in terror in the night ... sleep in school': *Evening News*, 28 February 1935.
227: 'crouching ... in school hours': Miss E. Broomfield, in ibid., 27 February 1935.
227–8: 'mainly wounded soldiers ... begin to realise': Mrs M. Atkins, in ibid., 25 February 1935.
228: 'poor mother' / 'lay trembling ... last hour had come': Miss E. Broomfield, in ibid., 27 February 1935.
228: 'On the Saturday night ... ghastly week': Frank A. Lamb, in ibid., 4 February 1935.
228: 'careful preparations' / 'remote villages ... they can take': G. T. Garrett, 'Air-raid Precautions', p. 130.
229: 'The noise of the guns ... through the window': IWM 84/52/1, W. A. Phillips.
229: 'his little son ... air attacks': H. Meyrick, in the *Evening News*, 5 February 1935.
229: 'The prevailing feeling ... the war would crumble': Scot Robertson, *The Development of Royal Air Force Strategic Bombing Doctrine Between the Wars*, p. 41.

229: 'to cracking the morale of London . . . maroons were exploded?': Sir Malcolm Campbell & James Wentworth Day, *Speed*, p. 42.

229: 'Whilst the scared people . . . grievous wickedness': IWM 97/3/1, Mrs A. Purbrook.

229: 'two chocolate sweetmeats' / 'might contain poison . . . hostile aircraft': HO45/10883/344919.

229–30: 'There appears . . . these things analysed': ibid.

230: 'liquorice lozenge' / 'seen to fall . . . in a bottle': ibid.

230: 'Some gelatine sweets . . . adherent to it' / 'presumed dropped . . . from a height': ibid.

230: 'pathological bacteria . . . no trace was found': ibid.

230: Two calves . . . ill effects: ibid.

230: 'resembling "Madeleines" . . . chemists are analysing': *The Times*, 8 September 1917.

230: 'poisoned soup powder' / 'Analysis . . . have died': *Daily Mail*, 17 December 1917.

230: 'killed by . . . aeroplanes': ibid.

230: 'I am trying . . . excluded': HO45/10883/344919/18.

231: 'that no poison of any sort was present': *The Times*, 8 September 1917.

231: 'a curious patter was heard' / 'about the size of sparrow eggs' / 'traces of arsenic': *Daily Express*, 20 February 1918.

231: 'reliable evidence': *Daily Graphic*, 21 February 1918.

231: 'arsenic-loaded sweets': *Daily Mirror*, 22 February 1918.

231: 'could not . . . aircraft' / 'small trace . . . without significance': *The Globe*, 22 February 1918.

231: 'These reports . . . once they have got hold': HO45/10883/344919.

231: 'from his statements . . . the whole story' / 'delinquent reporter . . . young man': ibid.

231: 'the latest production . . . searchlights': *The Times*, 17 May 1915.

232: 'who died . . . Nettlestead' / 'several bombs . . . building' / 'death . . . Shoreditch': HO45/10883/344919.

232: 'Had there been . . . the bombs': ibid.

232: Even though women workers . . . in 1916 alone: David Bilton, *The Home Front in the Great War*, p. 69.

232: 'The removal of the powder . . . should be consulted': HO45/10883/344919.

233: 'Attendance . . . last evening' / 'only thirty . . . the bell': Beckton School log, 1917.

233: 'compared with . . . in a war-factory': James M. Spaight, *Air Power and the Cities*, p. 160.

233: When Winston Churchill, . . . the normal rate: H. A. Jones, op. cit., vol. V, p. 87.

233: 'typical . . . a wide area': ibid., p. 86.

233: 'had reduced . . . fifty per cent': Admiral Mark Kerr, *Aviation in Peace and War*, pp. 91–2.

233–4: 'On receipt . . . the population': Joseph Morris, *German Air-raids on Great Britain*, p. 159.

234: 'the only damage . . . readily extinguished': HO45/10883/344919, quoted in Hook, op. cit., p. 307.

234: 'it would be practically impossible . . . immense': ibid.

234: 'or even of a warning . . . seriously affected' / 'work ceased . . . 5,000': H. M. Selby, quoted in Hook, op. cit., p. 314.

234: 'the position . . . explosion at times': Palmer's Shipbuilding & Iron Company, quoted in Hook, op. cit., p. 312.

235: 'punishable by fine . . . air-raid warning': HO45/10883/344919.

235: 'panic paid the newspapers': Admiral of the Fleet Hedworth Meux, quoted in Michael MacDonagh, *In London During the Great War*, p. 228.

235: He also summoned . . . air-raids: Christopher Cole & E. F. Cheesman, *The Air Defence of Great Britain*, p. 316.

236: 'the longer . . . from office': *Financial News*, 2 October 1917.

236: 'we appear to lie damn heavy on their stomachs': University of Texas at Dallas, Ferko Collection, Series 1, Aschoff, Walter, Box 4, Folder 8v.

236: 'a wild rush . . . on the ground': ibid.

236: 'so that . . . machine landing': Major Wilhelm Siegert, in Georg Paul Neumann, *The German Air Force in the Great War*, pp. 173–4.

236–7: 'There unfortunately . . . a whole army corps': newspaper clipping in diary of Lydia Peile, IWM 2589/94/2/1.

237: 'The only possible rejoinder . . . loud and resonant': L. E. O. Charlton, 'The New Factor in Warfare', p. 76.

237: 'Another very strong reason . . . modern buildings': ibid., p. 118.

237: 'Behind Germany's army . . . the war': *The Aeroplane*, vol. XII, no. 26, 27 June 1917, pp. 1,645–6.

237: 'the very word . . . sick': ibid., vol. XIII, no. 15, 10 October 1917.

238: 'the brutality . . . bloody rags': *The Times*, 18 June 1917.

238: 'initiate immediately . . . towns and cities': ibid.

238: 'paid for by the pennies of the people' / 'to instruct . . . towns and cities': ibid., 10 July 1917.

238: 'dissolve Parliament . . . their duty' / 'privateers of the air' / 'carry havoc . . . Germany': ibid.

238: 'fighting . . . "knuckledusters"': ibid., 24 July 1917.

238: 'Actually that raid . . . frightening scream': Cecil Lewis, *Sagittarius Rising*, p. 151.

238–9: 'indirectly . . . enemy country': Charlton, 'The New Factor in Warfare', p. 21.

239: 'fierce anger . . . at war': General Sir Ian Hamilton, Liddell Hart Military Archive, 16/456.

239: 'Go on improving arms . . . the first step': ibid.

239: 'a nation of lions . . . a revolution': *The Times*, 24 July 1917.

239: 'break strikes and suppress agitation': Tami Davis Biddle, *Rhetoric and Reality in Air Warfare*, p. 32.

239: 'We will give . . . compound interest': *New York Times*, 4 October 1917.

239: 'most harrowing description . . . proportion': Robertson to Haig, Liddell Hart Archive, Robertson 7/7/55.

239: 'Continuous aircraft raids . . . arrangements for them': H. A. Jones, op. cit., vol. V, p. 88.

240: 'took off . . . the English coast': Andrew Boyle, *Trenchard*, p. 235.

240: 'a violent barrage . . . its course': Raymond H. Fredette, *The Sky on Fire*, p. 155.

240: 'amazed . . . not reassuring': Boyle, op. cit., p. 235.

240: Lloyd George . . . arriving there: ibid.

240: 'loud grunting noises . . . 'The Camel': ibid., p. 34.

240: 'the long-range . . . winter': Charles a Court Repington, *The First World War*, vol. II, p. 64.

240: 'alter . . . suspended': ibid., p. 97.

240: Although the British attack . . . doing that: ibid., p. 64.

241: 'never thought that bombing alone' / 'it could have . . . shortened the war': Frederick Sykes, *From Many Angles*, p. 227.

241: 'complete harmony': Sir P. Joubert de la Ferte, *The Third Service*, p. 38.

241: 'at least 200 bombers in France': Boyle, op. cit., p. 204.

241: Trenchard had condemned . . . the front lines: ibid.

241: 'You prove . . . leave the bombing to me': ibid., p. 219.

241: 'had the foresight . . . other countries': Fredette, op. cit., p. 158.

241–2: 'The Germans . . . for which it was built': *The Aeroplane*, vol. XIII, no. 15, 10 October 1917, p. 1,007.

# Chapter 13: Air Defence Revisited

245: 'the squadron's performances . . . Pour le Mérite': Walter Zuerl, *Pour le Mérite Flieger*, pp. 253–9. Some sources cite 4 December as the date of Kleine's Pour le Mérite, but this was because of a confusion with the later award of the Pour le Mérite to Hans Klein, a fighter pilot.

245: 'great joy . . . Drory': Walter Aschoff, *Londonfluge*, p. 4.

245: 'neither the strength . . . devastating effect': Major Freiherr von Bulow, 'Die Angriffe des Bombengeschwader 3 auf England', p. 16.

246: 'three Caquot . . . in length': newspaper clipping, Liddell Hart Military Archive, 15/2/26.

246: 'in the pious hope . . . ludicrous.)': Cecil Lewis, *Sagittarius Rising*, p. 166.

246: Initial trials . . . Croydon: Edward Ashmore, *Air Defence*, p. 56.

246: 'deny . . . lower air' / 'induced to fly . . . their machines': ibid.

246: 'both guns . . . success': L. E. O. Charlton, 'The New Factor in Warfare', p. 58.

249–7: 'descending . . . effective': H. A. Jones, *The War in the Air*, vol. V, p. 112.

247: The key . . . the plotting room: see ibid., pp. 70–3.

247: 'it would have been cheaper to move London': Raymond H. Fredette, *The Sky on Fire*, p. 126.

247: 'to blow carborundum powder . . . the better it liked it': Ashmore, op. cit., p. 49.

248: Barrages . . . 17,500 feet: H. A. Jones, op. cit., vol. V, p. 76.

248: 'fancy names . . . 'Cold Feet': Sir Alfred Rawlinson, *The Defence of London*, p. 189.

248: 'who blew bugles . . . motor-cars': H. A. Jones, op. cit., vol. V, p. 51.

248: 'to selected points . . . 2/6d': Enfield Archaeological Society, 'Enfield at War', quoted in John Hook, *They Come! They Come!*, p. 161.

248: a businessman . . . his bugle: *Flight*, vol. IX, no. 45, 8 November 1917.

249: 'a fierce . . . London': Fredette, op. cit., p. 164.

249: 'owing to the prompt action . . . the flaming bomb': St Mary & St Edward's School log, quoted in Hook, op. cit., p. 213.

250: 'Up till this time . . . 4.45 a.m.': E. J. Page, in the *Evening News*, 7 February 1935.

250: 'storms and rain': Aschoff, op. cit., p. 96–7.

250: 'not well suited for the winter season': Fredette, op. cit., p. 150.

251: The Government . . . if it arose: see B. Millman, 'British Home Defence Planning and Civil Dissent', pp. 204–32.

251: 'mainly civil servants . . . departments' / 'the strikers . . . "blackleg"' / 'thirteen shillings . . . pay': Michael MacDonagh, *In London During the Great War*, p. 316.

251: 'contempt of the British Empire': quoted in Fredette, op. cit., p. 167.

251–2: 'get precious . . . disgraceful work': *The Aeroplane*, vol. XIII, no. 23, 5 December 1917, pp. 1,637–8.

252: 'clear moonlight . . . attempted': AIR 1/2123/207/73/9.

252: 'last week . . . German airplane': G. W. Haddow & P. M. Grosz, *The German Giants*, p. 30.

252: 'burn down . . . population': Joseph Morris, *The German Air-raids on Great Britain*, p. 248.

252: 'now made . . . incendiary material': Hook, op. cit., p. 218.

252: 'half-moon, ringed with haze' / 'covered with rime': Frank Morison, *War on Great Cities*, p. 151.

253: '"If," . . . "Drinks all round"': Lewis, op. cit., pp. 184–5.

253: 'There was nothing to do . . . a raid': ibid., p. 185.

253: 'the feeling . . . pell-mell': ibid.

254: 'twenty . . . forty-five': ibid., pp. 186–7.

254: 'if the Huns . . . a stupid stunt': ibid.

254: '"Switch off . . . away she went': ibid.

254: 'rose . . . patrol height' / 'the night . . . night' / 'like coals . . . about them': ibid.

254: 'cut off the engine . . . a dive' / 'tail up . . . a large aerodrome': ibid.

255: 'the charred ironwork . . . the wires': ibid.

255: 'very quiet . . . themselves' / 'raiders . . . the sheds': ibid., p. 189.

256: 'somehow the news . . . lynched' / 'I suppose . . . an internment camp': ibid.

256: 'most formidable effort . . . the War': Morison, op. cit., p. 152.

256: 'four of them serious': Ashmore, op. cit., p. 72.

256: 'afforded . . . effective': Rawlinson, op. cit., p. 230.

256–7: 'futility . . . demonstrated': Morison, op. cit., p. 152.

257: 'One incendiary . . . did no damage': *The Times*, 8 December 1917.

257: 'the ignition . . . the H.E. bombs': von Bulow, op. cit., p. 23.

257: 'a great deal . . . materials employed': ibid., pp. 22–3.

257: 'although fires . . . every one' / 'in only six . . . fires caused': Report of the Chief Officer of the London Fire Brigade, 1919.

257: 'to trick . . . demolition bombs': von Bulow, op. cit., p. 34.

258: 'so organised . . . semicircles' / 'caught and held . . . after another': ibid., Part II, p. 4.

258: 'far to the north and south of the Thames' / 'many enemy fighters': ibid.

258: 'the ground anti-aircraft defence . . . effective': ibid., Part II, p. 5.

258: 'a dispersal . . . in the future': ibid., p. 36.

258–9: 'The loss . . . flying crews': Aschoff, op. cit., pp. 96–7.

259: 'The brave . . . fallen comrades': quoted in Zuerl, op. cit., pp. 253–9.

259: 'five separate divisions . . . the river': quoted in Rawlinson, op. cit., p. 231.

259: 'It had not been thought probable . . . to attack': Hook, op. cit., p. 219.

259–60: 'hurrying to find shelter . . . the windows': Mrs D. Cambray, in the *Evening News*, 28 February 1935.

260: 'Very few . . . blood': Mrs Gibson, in ibid., 8 March 1935.

260: possibly the blaze . . . this raid: Morison, op. cit., p. 154.

261: 'if you stop . . . the bells': Hook, op. cit., p. 183.

262: 'risking their necks for pitifully small results': Ashmore, op. cit., p. 76.

262: On 22 December . . . the crime: Jonathan Sutherland & Diane Canwell, *Battle of Britain 1917*, p. 118.

# Chapter 14: A Failure of Strategy

265: 'all they found . . . disappeared': Immanuel Braun, *Bombing Missions on Two Fronts*, p. 53.

265: 'silencers and cut-outs': Sir Alfred Rawlinson, *The Defence of London*, p. 239.

265: 'so much damage . . . so insanitary': Frank Morison, *War on Great Cities*, p. 156.
265: 'a new precaution . . . first time': Miss L. Kutcher, quoted in John Hook, *They Come! They Come!*, p. 234.
266: 'On this night . . . second house': *Evening News*, 12 February 1935.
266: 'begging to be let in': Miss L. Kutcher, quoted in Hook, op. cit., p. 234.
266: 'forced . . . behind' / 'mad rush . . . narrow opening': *Evening News*, 5 March 1935.
266: 'Someone must have . . . fallen' / 'Women and children . . . the pressure': *Evening News*, 12 February 1935.
266: 'someone seems . . . behind': Morison, op. cit., p. 157.
266: 'A woman . . . the mortuary': Morison, op. cit., p. 157.
266: 'struggled hard . . . the bank': *Evening News*, 12 February 1935.
266: 'mostly aliens . . . miserable skins': *Weekly Dispatch*, 21 February 1926.
266–7: 'the behaviour . . . hold of them' / 'entirely unworthy . . . animals': quoted in Hook, op. cit., p. 235.
267: 'the wounded soldiers . . . keep still': T. W. H. Wood, in the *Evening News*, 14 February 1935.
267: 'a man . . . were found': George Bentley, in the *Evening News*, 5 February 1935.
267: 'stood by . . . to town': Cecil Lewis, *Sagittarius Rising*, pp. 172–3.
267–8: 'thirty feet . . . swept over everyone': ibid.
268: 'Pictures . . . by the cords': quoted in Morison, op. cit., p. 158.
268: 'A mighty disturbance . . . House of Commons]': Michael MacDonagh, *In London During the Great War*, p. 252.
268: 'when the "take cover" . . . our shelter': J. Sullivan, in the *Evening News*, 5 February 1935.
268: The basement . . . the basement: H. A. Jones, *The War in the Air*, vol. V, p. 115.
268: The blast . . . nine inches thick: HO45/10883/344919, p. 17.
268: 'grossly overloaded with rolls of paper': AIR 1/2123/207/73/9.
268: 'The outbreak . . . the debris': H. A. Jones, op. cit., vol. V, p. 115.
268: 'the terrified refugees . . . bearings' / 'made frantic efforts . . . machine room': Morison, op. cit., p. 159.
269: 'had just got settled . . . my little baby': Mrs McCluskey, in the *Evening News*, 4 March 1935.
269: 'playing on a big roll of paper' / 'everything seemed . . . safety': J. Sullivan, in ibid., 5 February 1935.
269: 'deluging . . . several feet': Morison, op. cit., p. 160.
270: 'In order to gain access . . . save another': ibid.
270: 'it seemed . . . during the night': *Evening News*, 31 January 1935.
270: 'Right around the building . . . never found': Mrs Mary Hart, in ibid., 25 February 1935.

270: 'Everyone . . . all night': Charles Conroy, in ibid., 2 March 1935.

270: 'sat shivering' / '"Look . . . a drink of water"': Mrs Francis Livingstone Toft, in ibid., 7 February 1935.

270–1: 'lay in a dead hush . . . disappeared': MacDonagh, op. cit., p. 253.

271: Margate . . . 311 houses: H. A. Jones, op. cit., vol. V, p. 114.

271: Both men . . . (£1.75) each: Christopher Cole & E. F. Cheesman, *The Air Defence of Great Britain*, p. 374.

271: He had just returned . . . hospitalised: Edward Ashmore, *Air Defence*, p. 32.

272: 'railway hubs . . . dumps': Walter Zuerl, *Pour le Mérite Flieger*, pp. 102–5.

272: 'a "V" . . . group of seven': Cole & Cheesman, op. cit., p. 393.

274: The Giant . . . fifty-eight miles per hour: Jonathan Sutherland & Diane Canwell, *Battle of Britain 1917*, Appendix III.

274: 'paralysed by fright' / 'within an ace . . . would have done so': AIR 1/2123/207/73/9.

274: 'not usually . . . concerted attack': ibid.

275: 'by demolishing . . . the flames expired': Tacitus, *Annals*, XV, p. 40.

275: 'to counteract . . . the Front' / 'lay in not concentrating . . . objective': Major Freiherr von Bulow, 'Die Angriffe des Bombengeschwader 3 auf England', pp. 16–17.

275: 'the point . . . *in toto*': F. W. Lanchester, *Aircraft in Warfare*, pp. 191–2.

275: 'Had the German commanders . . . difficult to control': Morison, op. cit., p. 172.

275–6: 'His chief concern . . . conflagration': ibid.

276: 'a poor residential character': ibid., p. 173.

276: 'the old-fashioned roof . . . incendiary': HO45/10883/344919, p. 13.

276: 'great fire': *Illustrated London News*, 11 December 1897.

276: 'a heartening target . . . the bomber': quoted in James M. Spaight, *Air Power and the Cities*, p. 157.

277: 'In over three and a half years . . . reaching it': Joseph Morris, *The German Air-raids on Great Britain*, p. 72.

277: 'a lodge of all combustibles': Neil Hanson, *The Dreadful Judgement*, p. 107.

## Chapter 15: Giants in the Night Sky

281: News . . . Washington DC: *New York Times*, 31 January 1918.

281: If the USA . . . Germany: Aaron Norman, *The Great Air War*, pp. 405–9.

282: 'so severe . . . his hands' / 'first pulled . . . the port side': report of Oberleutnant von Seydlitz-Gerstenberg, quoted in G. W. Haddow & P. M. Grosz, *The German Giants*, p. 32.

282: 'alive': *Weekly Dispatch*, 21 February 1926.

282: 'a fine piece . . . responsible': AIR 1/2123/207/73/9.

283: 'knocked out the side-wall almost entirely': ibid.

283: 'All the surrounding glass . . . much damaged': HO45/10883/344919, p. 47.

283: 'the conductorette . . . had been killed': George Jellicoe, in the *Evening News*, 31 January 1935.

283–4: 'My mother . . . the sky': Mrs Edith Gooday, in ibid., 27 February 1935.

284: 'Crowds . . . King's Cross' / 'brought their beds . . . all night': Lilah Morrison-Bell, quoted in Thomas Fegan, *The Baby Killers*, p. 59.

284–5: 'never properly undressed . . . Glasgow': Mrs R. Kane, in the *Evening News*, 1 February 1935.

285: 'carried out . . . unforgettable picture': Frank Morison, *War on Great Cities*, p. 164.

285: 'the whole . . . England' / 'an enormous amount . . . wasted' / 'apparently from nervousness' / 'not only . . . thirty kilometres away': Major Freiherr von Bulow, 'Die Angriffe des Bombengeschwader 3 auf England', Part II, p. 11.

285: 'two Bristols sounded like one Gotha': Christopher Cole & E. F. Cheesman, *The Air Defence of Great Britain*, p. 402.

285–6: 'These alarms . . . had become': H. A. Jones, *The War in the Air*, vol. V, p. 119.

286: 'who was having a warm bath' / 'inadequately clad . . . a few days later' / 'a physical wreck' / 'splinters . . . lying' / 'the shock . . . a few days later': Thomas W. Parkin, quoted in John Hook, *They Come! They Come!*, p. 244.

286: 'rolled out . . . assigned task': W. von Eberhardt, *Unsere Luftstreitkräfte*, Part II, pp. 442–4.

287: 'a frugal supper . . . dark night': ibid.

287: 'pin-marked course . . . the darkness': ibid.

287–8: 'saw the beacon . . . the earth below': ibid.

288: 'of the type . . . materials': HO45/10883/344919, p. 52.

288: 'a very large number . . . pulled down': ibid.

288: 'The whole area . . . passed over it': Morison, op. cit., p. 165.

288–9: 'very excited and happy'. . . 'The next day . . . a sunset': Mrs D. Sevenson, in the *Evening News*, 12 February 1935.

289: 'high up . . . her hands': Charles Conroy, in ibid., 5 March 1935.

289: 'the barking . . . the basement': Rev. William Kilshaw, in ibid., 4 February 1935.

290: 'reduced . . . shaken homes': Morison, op. cit., pp. 165–6.

290: 'peeled off . . . flying past us' / 'Beneath us . . . danger': W. von Eberhardt, *Unsere Luftstreitkräfte*, Part II, pp. 442–4.

291: 'its familiar signals . . . artillery fire': ibid.

291–2: 'more than 23,000 kilograms . . . 'open towns': Ernst von Höppner, *Deutschlands Krieg in der Luft*, p. 145.

292: 'gave expression . . . bombing raids': ibid.

292: 'The opposing views . . . further attacks': ibid., pp. 145–6.

292: On 11 March . . . anti-aircraft guns: Arthur M. Soltan & James Davilla, *The Bombardment of Paris*, p. 254.

292: 'With our backs to the wall . . . fight to the end': IWM S81/24, Field Marshal Sir Douglas Haig.

## Chapter 16: The Whit Sunday Raid

297: 'Land at Ghistelles . . . parachutes': G. W. Haddow & P. M. Grosz, *The German Giants*, p. 45.

298: 'actively efficient': Liddell Hart Military Archive, 15/2/26.

298: 'an effective system . . . the police': L. E. O. Charlton, 'The New Factor in Warfare', p. 43.

299: 'magnificent aerodrome almost a mile square': Cecil Lewis, *Sagittarius Rising*, p. 181.

300: 'which also enveloped my own machine for an instant': C. J. Quinton Brand, quoted in Edward Ashmore, *Air Defence*, p. 87.

300: By then . . . his moustache: Jonathan Sutherland & Diane Canwell, *Battle of Britain 1917*, p. 135.

300: 'over the south-east side of the Isle of Sheppey': Ashmore, op. cit., p. 87.

300: A second Gotha . . . 'Devil in the Dusk': Thomas Fegan, *The Baby Killers*, p. 70.

300: 'the lights . . . machine' / 'I dived . . . 150 yards behind': IWM 97/22/1, Lieutenant A. J. Arkell.

300: who was flying with him for the first time: ibid.

300–1: 'saw sparks . . . several times' / 'in a sheet of flame'/ '200 yards . . . the Thames': ibid.

301: 'Sirens . . . victory': *The Times*, 21 May 1918.

301: 'electrified . . . crash to earth': *Kentish Express & Ashford News*, 8 June 1918.

301: 'a long and satisfied roll of cheering': *The Times*, 21 May 1918.

301: 'first meeting with the Hun': *Kentish Express & Ashford News*, 8 June 1918.

301: 'I couldn't help . . . hostile country': IWM 97/22/1, Lieutenant A. J. Arkell.

301: 'displayed . . . all round us': Christopher Cole & E. F. Cheesman, *The Air Defence of Great Britain*, p. 430.

301: 'presumed . . . engines' / 'a bit of charred wood . . . souvenirs' / 'a three-ply box . . . slightly charred' / 'compact heap . . . a dozen yards square': *New York Times*, 21 May 1918.

302: Several other Gothas . . . was killed: Peter Kilduff, *Over the Battlefronts*, pp. 126–7.

302: 'followed the crowd . . . apprehension': *Evening News*, 22 February 1935.

302–3: 'An air-raid . . . expectant mothers': Rev. Vernon Jones, in ibid., 5 February 1935.

302: 'fairly good class houses' / 'reduced . . . wreckage' / 'flapping in the air' /

'suspended as if in mid-air': Michael MacDonagh, *In London During the Great War*, p. 296.

303: 'the landlord . . . wife' / 'two eight-roomed houses' / 'had apparently retired . . . their house': *Kentish Mercury*, 23 May 1918.

303: 'still suffers from fits': Mrs Chater, in the *Evening News*, 5 March 1935.

303: A woman . . . Hither Green: Mrs Brown, in ibid., 6 March 1935.

303: 'made for St Bartholomew's . . . the Salvation Army': ibid., 25 February 1935.

303: 'round the road . . . survivors': ibid., 1 March 1935.

303: 'four small coffins . . . the day before': Miss S. Lansdowne, in ibid., 12 March 1935.

304: 'admiration . . . the enemy's attack': Graham Wallace, *RAF Biggin Hill*, p. 51.

304: 'most of the fire . . . often wild': H. A. Jones, *The War in the Air*, vol. V, p. 128.

## Chapter 17: The Elektron Fire Bomb

307: It was a job . . . arrayed against them: Charles a Court Repington, *The First World War*, p. 336.

307: 'a war of engineers . . . soldiers': J. A. Henry, *Science: The War and After*, pp. 150–4.

307–8: 'rendered indispensable services . . . of all kinds': Hermann Raschen & Peter Hoffmann, *75 Jahre Chemische Fabrik Griesheim-Elektron*, p. 49.

308: 'exceedingly important for warfare' / 'chemical products for ammunition': ibid., p. 33.

308: '1. Burn . . . transportation or use': Augustin Prentiss, *Chemicals in War*, pp. 259–60.

308: 'Since 1914, . . . incendiary bomb': diary of Major Wilhelm Siegert, vol. VI, p. 155, after Sept. 7, 1918, possibly Sept. 14 or 15.

308–9: 92.5 per cent . . . manganese: Renato Ravalli, 'Elektron, light alloys and their use in aeronautical techniques', *Rivista Aeronautica*, January 1929.

309: An alloy . . . magnesium: J. Enrique Zanetti, *Fire from the Air*, pp. 25–6.

309: 'melts . . . the fuse': Lieutenant-Colonel Vauthier, *Le Danger Aérien et L'Avenir du Pays*, pp. 23–5.

309: First, magnesium . . . previous bombs: Enrique Zanetti, op. cit., pp. 25–6.

309: This vapour . . . 1,800°C: ibid., pp. 26–8.

309: 'a furnace . . . fuels': ibid., pp. 33–4.

309–10: In the Elektron . . . reaction was complete: ibid., pp. 34, 36.

310: The burning thermite's . . . savage effect: ibid., pp. 28, 30.

310: 'Their enormous combustible temperature . . . within reach': Vauthier, op. cit., pp. 23–5.

310: 'once the fuse . . . the rest': ibid.

310: 'fires caused . . . worked': HO45/10883/344919, p. 54.

310–11: The only way . . . oxygen: Enrique Zanetti, op. cit., pp. 30–1.

311: The cylindrical Elektron bombs ... one kilogram: Wolfgang Fleischer, *German Air-Dropped Weapons to 1945*, p. 15.

311: 'a 200 gram bomb would have sufficed': Vauthier, op. cit., pp. 23–5.

311: 'residents ... cellars' / 'would often not ... on fire': Darius Paul Bloch, *La Guerre Chimique*, p. 97.

311: Even if the occupants ... and streets: Enrique Zanetti, op. cit., pp. 41–3.

311: 'The operational orders ... firestorm': Fleischer, op. cit., p. 15.

311: Elektron bombs ... burned out: Arthur M. Soltan & James Davilla, *The Bombardment of Paris*, p. 255.

312: 'engulf the capital ... 250 years earlier': H. G. Castle, *Fire Over England*, p. 223.

312: 'the nerve centre ... the Entente': Hilmar von Bülow, *Geschichte der Luftwaffe*, pp. 108–9.

312: 'at the time ... an explosion': Marshal von Hindenburg, *Out of My Life*, p. 358.

312: The statistics ... were shot down: Jules Poirier, *Les Bombardements de Paris*, quoted in H. A. Jones, *The War in the Air*, vol. V, pp. 157–8.

312: '*Nein*': Aaron Norman, *The Great Air War*, pp. 405–9.

313: 'the area of towns ... a not inconsiderable number': Vauthier, op. cit., pp. 23–5.

313–14: 'Even supposing ... supplies and resources': ibid.

314: One very conservative estimate ... the first raid alone: *Die Luftwacht*, no. 6, June 1927, pp. 332–9.

314: 'England shall be destroyed by fire': Raymond H. Fredette, *The Sky on Fire*, p. 31.

314: 'one of the gravest perils ... the capital': Frank Morison, *War on Great Cities*, p. 172.

314–15: Since 21 March 1918 ... the whole city: Henry W. Miller, *The Paris Gun*, p. 160.

315: 'drawn forward to the area of Ham': von Bülow, op. cit., pp. 108–9.

315: 'fire circus': Hauptmann Hermann, *The Luftwaffe: Its Rise & Fall*, pp. 3–4.

316–17: 'the half-circle ... we had created': ibid.

317 'other German bombers ... put all of them out': ibid.


# Chapter 18: Ludendorff's Intervention

321: 'information ... dropped simultaneously': AIR 1/2420/305/8/274721.

321: 'according to ... being prepared': AIR 1/1975/204/273/25.

321: '*Der schwartze Tag des Deutschen Heeres in der Geschichte dieses Krieges*': Erich von Ludendorff, *My War Memories*, quoted in Harold Nicolson, *King George V*, p. 323.

322: 'an alarmist report of German air strength': David Edgerton, *England and the Aeroplane*, p. 32.

322: 'the Bombshell Memorandum' . . . 'as a minimum': Mark Kerr, *Land, Sea and Air*, pp. 290–1.

322: A civic group . . . charity: *The Aeroplane*, vol. XIII, no. 17, 24 October 1917, p. 1,226.

322: 'carrying bombs . . . the ground' / 'absolutely wipe out . . . German towns': Sir Almeric Fitzroy, *Memoirs*, vol. II, p. 667.

323: 'easier to bomb Berlin in headlines': Andrew Boyle, *Trenchard*, p. 254.

323: 'Two of our bombing squadrons . . . right and proper': diary of Major Wilhelm Siegert, vol. V, p. 170.

323: 'the "Frogs" . . . the night': ibid., pp. 194–5.

324: 'How hoity-toity!' . . . somewhat different': ibid.

324: 'have him shot': Boyle, op. cit., p. 288.

324: 'would ten thousand times . . . be done': quoted in *Flight*, vol. IX, no. 26, 28 June 1917.

324–5: 'a) Do military and vital damage . . . the working class': quoted in A. F. Hurley & R. C. Ehrhart, *Air Power and Warfare*, p. 32.

325: 'was obvious . . . bombs landed': Eric Ash, *Sir Frederick Sykes and the Air Revolution*, p. 167.

325: 'if houses . . . production': memo from Admiral Mark Kerr, AIR 1/461/15/312/107.

325: An officer . . . at night: Major Lord Tiverton, quoted in Tami Davis Biddle, *Rhetoric and Reality in Air Warfare*, p. 39.

325: 'If I were you . . . inaccuracy': Boyle, op. cit., p. 312.

325: 'In an incendiary system . . . campaign: 'Incendiary Operations as a Means of Aerial Warfare', AIR 1/461/15/312/11.

325: 'start up . . . German towns': John H. Morrow Jr, 'Expectation and Reality: The Great War in the Air', p. 33.

326: 'the enemy . . . bombs' / 'We could hear . . . the explosion': AIR 1/1975/204/273/25.

326: 'some incendiary fuses . . . necessary': ibid.

326: 'relentless offensive' . . . 'a lack of ginger': S. F. Wise, *Canadian Airmen*, p. 326, quoted in Biddle, op. cit., p. 318.

326: In one period . . . establishment: Biddle, op. cit., p. 44.

326: 'the expense . . . Germany': James S. Corum, *The Luftwaffe*, p. 40.

326: 'looked as if they had been slaughtering animals': AIR 1/1975/204/273/25.

326: 'one walked . . . great': ibid.

326: 'completely wrecked by an air-raid': ibid.

326: 'the people . . . anything about it': ibid.

326: 'The uproar . . . day or night': ibid.

326: 'a permanent and mighty thunder fills the air': ibid.

326: 'Who knows . . . uneasiness here': ibid.

326: 'the excellent moral effect' / 'The panic . . . expectations': AIR 1/460/15/312/99.

326–7: 'No one saw the machines . . . day by day': AIR 1/1975/204/273/25.

327: 'At Herstal . . . the factory again': ibid.

327: Out of 107 . . . actually followed: *Evening Standard*, 12 October 1918.

327: the alarm . . . never bombed at all: James M. Spaight, *Air Power and the Cities*, p. 155.

327: 'expressed the opinion . . . all the way through': AIR 1/1975/204/273/25.

327: 'the bombs . . . the middle classes lived]': ibid.

327–8: 'a terrible panic . . . danger is passed': ibid.

328: 'interned in hotels near the factories': ibid.

328: 'ample opportunity . . . waging war': ibid.

328: 'so as not to frighten . . . Imperial Palace: ibid.

328: 'less threatened locales . . . to the utmost': AIR 1/460/15/312/99.

328: 'One is deprived . . . wooden soles': AIR1/1975/204/273/25.

328: 'One is suffering . . . little fat': ibid.

328–9: 'My eyes . . . prepared for the worst': ibid.

329: 'There are times when one doesn't wish to live': ibid.

329: 'the authorities . . . quiet' / 'scenes of disorder' / 'lasted most of the day . . . a number of wounded': ibid.

329: 'to protest violently . . . a great deal of trouble': ibid.

329: A German prisoner of war . . . intensified: ibid.

329: Ludendorff . . . in Cologne alone: Holger H. Herwig, *First World War*, p. 325.

329: Trains . . . the front lines: ibid., p. 420.

330: an estimated . . . American troops: John Ellis, *Eye Deep in Hell*, p. 181.

330: '36 planes . . . Elektron bombs': Lieutenant-Colonel Robert Eyb of the Austrian Air Force, 'Protection of towns against air attack', quoted in Vauthier, op. cit., pp. 23–5; see also Major Freiherr von Bulow, 'Die Angriffe des Bombengeschwader 3 auf England', p. 24.

330: 'Bombing Squadron 3': an error by Major Wilhelm Siegert. Bogohls 1, 2 and 4 were to target Paris; Bogohl 3, the England Squadron, was to bomb London.

330: '45 heavy bombers . . . Paris': diary of Major Wilhelm Siegert, vol. VI, p. 155, after Sept. 7, 1918, possibly Sept. 14 or 15.

330: The pilots . . . engines: Hauptmann Hermann, *The Luftwaffe: Its Rise & Fall*, pp. 3–4.

331: 'In the near impenetrable blackness . . . crews': Walter Aschoff, *Londonfluge*, pp. 76–80.

331: runners: the literal translation from German is 'strikers'; there is no direct English equivalent. 'Dogsbodies' probably comes closest.

331: 'We took our seats . . . a car came racing': Hermann, op. cit., pp. 3–6.

331: 'a staff officer . . . a severe shock to us': ibid.

331: 'the supreme commander . . . the attack': Lieutenant-Colonel Robert Eyb of the Austrian Air Force, 'Protection of towns against air attack', quoted in Vauthier, op. cit., pp. 23–5; see also Major Freiherr von Bulow, 'Die Angriffe des Bomben-geschwader 3 auf England', p. 24.

331: 'Then came . . . win the war': Hermann, op. cit., pp. 3–6.

332: 'which had decided . . . already lost': ibid., pp. 4–7.

332: 'that day . . . ten days later': ibid., pp. 3–6.

332: 'as Ludendorff . . . allowed ourselves': diary of Major Wilhelm Siegert, vol. VI, p. 155.

332: folly: the German word Siegert used was 'Michelei' (foolery), a derogatory anti-German expression deriving from 'Michel', a figure representing the mythic citizen of the country, like the French equivalent 'Marianne'.

332–3: 'Something is going on . . . But we will see': ibid., p. 15.

333: 'Because of the gravity . . . its own sake': Erich von Ludendorff, *Kriegs-erinnerungen*, p. 565.

333: '"begged the Supreme Command . . . that decision': ibid.

334: 'the Supreme Army Command . . . soon fall': diary of Colonel von Thaer, 1 October 1918.

334: 'contaminated . . . ideas' / 'Any day now . . . American troops' / 'This catas-trophe must be averted by all means': ibid.

334: 'demanded . . . "14 Points"': ibid.

334: 'An old man . . . ceasefire': ibid.

334–5: 'pale and lined . . . held high' / 'terrible and appalling' / 'involuntary tears . . .cheeks' / 'bring those circles . . . lie in it!': ibid.

335: 'lowered his head . . . adjoining room': ibid.

335: 'ordinary raids' / 'to keep . . . our strength': von Ludendorff, *Kriegs-erinnerungen*, p. 566.

335: 'Paris was bombed . . . 1, 2 and 4': *Nachrichtenblatt der Luftstreitkräfte*, 31, Year 2, 26 September 1918.

335: 'strongest resistance . . . great fortress': Hilmar von Bülow, *Geschichte der Luftwaffe*, pp. 108–9.

335: 'volcano in eruption': Maurice Thiery, *Paris Bombardé*, pp. 277–80.

335: 'only three airplanes . . . the city': Major Thomas R. Phillips, 'In Defense of Antiaircraft', in *Army Ordnance*, XIX, no. 113, p. 282.

335: 'concentric air-raids on Paris': von Bülow, op. cit., pp. 108–9.

335: 'undisturbed in the interior of the circle of fire': Leutnant Jaeschue, *Die Fliegerbuch*, p. 67.

335: 'more elevated part . . . perimeter': *Journal*, 17 September 1918.

335–6: 'fires broke out . . . subsequently sank': *Éclair*, 17 September 1918.

336: 'the most damaging . . . police': *Nachrichtenblatt der Luftstreitkräfte*, 35, Year 2, 24 October 1918.

336: 'powerful attacks . . . starvation blockade': von Bülow, op. cit., pp. 108–9.

336: 'It had never occurred to us . . . the enemy': Aschoff, op. cit., p. 131.

337: 'We flew low . . . in the mist': ibid., pp. 134–5.

337: 'From that night . . . was crumbling?': Hermann, op. cit., pp. 4–7.

337: 'all rendered . . . weapons': Oskar Kuppinger, *Bomber Observer*, Part II, pp. 222–3.

337: 'in huge bonfires': John H. Knauer, quoted in Peter Kilduff, *Germany's First Air Force*, p. 85.

337: 'Outwardly . . . those machines': Aschoff, op. cit., p. 138.

338: 'Even if our time . . . warriors for Germany': ibid., pp. 99–101.

338: As the retreat . . . the River Scheldt: Major Freiherr von Bulow, 'Die Angriffe des Bombengeschwader 3 auf England', p. 24.

338: 'be placing a noose . . . future wars': quoted in Sven Lindqvist, *A History of Bombing*, p. 96.

338: 'to weaken . . . the whole town' / 'defeat the very purpose of bombardment': quoted in ibid.

339: 'The Bloody Paralysers': Thomas Fegan, *The Baby Killers*, p. 78.

339: When Austria-Hungary . . . 12 November: Myron J. Smith, *World War I in the Air*, p. 249.

# Epilogue

341: The Turkencreuz . . . £70 million a year: Robin Higham, *Air Power*, p. 52.

341: The pilots . . . machines required: H. A. Jones, *The War in the Air*, vol. V, pp. 153–4.

342: 'aspired to cause . . . their number': L. E. O. Charlton, 'The New Factor in Warfare', p. 24.

342: 'It is perhaps no exaggeration . . . nervousness and unrest': Major Freiherr von Bulow, 'Die Angriffe des Bombengeschwader 3 auf England', p. 24.

343–4: 'The acceptance conditions . . . 4,100 metres': ibid., p. 19.

344: By the time . . . 1,700 metres: ibid., p. 21.

345: 'I sat overlooking the map . . . half a minute': Edward Ashmore, *Air Defence*, p. 93.

345: 'Captain Brandenburg . . . future war': *The Aeroplane*, vol. XIII, no. 1, 4 July 1917, p. 9.

345: 'the moral effect . . . towns and cities]': *London Gazette*, 1 January 1919.

346: 'It is clear . . . decisive': quoted in Sir Frederick Sykes, 'Air Defence', p. 220.

346: 'to make the enemy burn and bleed in every way': Jonathan Sutherland & Diane Canwell, *Battle of Britain 1917*, p. 147.

346: 'occasionally . . . damaged garden': Alexander McKee, *The Friendless Sky*, p. 166.

346: 'can hardly be overestimated': quoted in Tami Davis Biddle, *Rhetoric and Reality in Air Warfare*, p. 61.

346: 'the progress in air science' / 'a powerful . . . victory': AIR 1/2115/207/56/1.

346: 'there is no doubt . . . defend his record': Biddle, op. cit., p. 62.

346–7: 'I think it well . . . save yourselves': *The Times*, 11 November 1932.

347: 'An army . . . *objectives*': Cecil Lewis, *Sagittarius Rising*, p. 153 (italics in original).

347: 258 incendiaries: 267, according to Britain's official air historian H. A. Jones.

347: 'under the modern system . . . square mile': Frank Morison, *War on Great Cities*, p. 196.

347: 'the dreadful act of power and terror' / 'at least . . . sanitation': Winston Churchill, *While England Slept*, pp. 142–3.

347: 'Whitehall and Westminster were wiped out': quoted in Raymond H. Fredette, *The Sky on Fire*, p. 236.

347–8: 'We cannot expose . . . air bombing': Lord Ironside, *Time Unguarded*, pp. 61–2.

348: 'terrified . . . Great Britain': ibid., pp. 42–3.

348: 'the authorities . . . air-raids': ibid., pp. 61–2.

348: 'the Fuhrer . . . how many there are': Derek Wood & Derek Dempster, *The Narrow Margin*, p. 45.

348: 'the only defence . . . the enemy': H. A. Jones, op. cit., vol. V, p. 159.

348: 'to produce . . . war industry': Hanson W. Baldwin, introduction to Fredette, op. cit., xviii.

348: 'never resort . . . terrorism': J. F. C. Fuller, *The Conduct of War*, p. 303.

349: 'a bombing raid . . . this country': Constantine Fitzgibbon, *The Winter of the Bombs*, p. 40.

349: 'the Hun raiders' bombs . . . disgraceful work': *The Aeroplane*, vol. XIII, no. 23, 5 December 1917, pp. 1,637–8.

349: 'to capture the imagination of the British people': Sir Robert H. M. S. Saundby, *Air Bombardment*, p. 128.

# BIBLIOGRAPHY

## Brigham Young University, Utah
World War I Document Archive
Diary of Colonel von Thaer
(http://net.lib.byu.edu/~rdh7/wwi/1918/thaereng.html)

## British Library
**Unpublished Theses**
Ferris, J., 'The Evolution of British Strategic Policy 1919–1926', Ph.D., University of London, 1986
Sweetman, J., 'Strategic Bombing and the Origins of the Royal Air Force', Ph.D., University of London, 1983
Williams, George Kent, 'Statistics and Strategic Bombardment', Oxford University, 1987

## Guildhall Library, London
**Manuscripts Section**
Ms 36616 Correspondence and related papers concerning precautions taken against air-raids, 1915
Ms 02462 Record of proceedings taken by the Library Committee of the Corporation of the City of London to protect the City's records and the Library's treasures from damage by enemy air-raids during the Great War of 1914–18, 1923
Ms 17810 Air-raid map of the Metropolitan area and Central London (Anon.), c. 1918
Pr. L75.5 Monson, Major E. C. P., & Marsland, Ellis, British Fire Prevention Committee, Air-raid Damage in London – being a record of the effect of aircraft attack on certain public and private buildings, with map showing where bombs fell on the cities of Paris and Venice
Ms 14206 Great Britain, Army, Inns of Court and City Yeomanry
Inns of Court Officers Training Corps
Orders relating to hostile aircraft, 1916–18
Ms 17697 Instructions relating to action to be taken in the event of an air-raid or fallen enemy aircraft
C 75.5 fifty-seven photographs of damage caused by German aircraft in the City of London, September and October 1915 (photographs by Miles and Kaye), 1915

# BIBLIOGRAPHY

## Imperial War Museum, London
**Documents**
22062/2 Home Forces GHQ Air Raids 1914–16
63999 97/3/1 Memoir of Mrs A. Purbrook
15021 06/53/1 Diary of Mrs A. Purbrook
2589 94/2/1 Diary of Mrs L. Peile
2448 92/49/1 Dayrell-Browning
4066 84/52/1 Phillips
1807 91/5/1 Bawtree
11793 Misc 223 (3201)
P76 Lieutenant Colonel A. G. Burn
6706 97/22/1 Lieutenant A. J. Arkell
12053 71/11/2 & DS/MISC/17 P. M. Yearsley
06/49/1 E. S. Oak-Rhind
S81/24, Field Marshal Sir Douglas Haig
Misc 215 (3116) Rear Admiral Sir Murray Sueter

**Printed Books**
K.89/801 Report on Gotha bomber, with notes on Giant Aeroplanes
15771 Bülow, Hilmer von, *Geschichte der Luftwaffe: eine kurze Darstellung der Entwicklung der fünften Waffe*, Frankfurt, 1934
Bülow, Hilmer von, *Geschichte der Luftwaffe: eine kurze Darstellung der Entwicklung der fünften Waffe*, Frankfurt, 1937
19101 'Hermann, Hauptmann' (pseud.), *The Luftwaffe: Its Rise & Fall*, New York, 1943 (London, 1944)
15316 Langsdorff, Werner von, *Flieger Am Feind*, Berlin, 1934
12250 Ludendorff, Erich von, *The General Staff and its Problems* (repub. 1988)
7028 Ludendorff, Erich von, *My War Memories* (2 vols), 1919
41818 Ludendorff, Erich von (tr. A. S. Rappoport), *The Nation at War*, n.d.
90/2208 Air-raid over Southend
92/1337 Souvenir in loving memory of the men, women and children killed in the London air-raid on Wednesday, June 13th, 1917
94/2447 Höppner, Ernst Wilhelm von, *Germany's War in the Air: the development and operations of German military aviation in the World War*. General of Cavalry, Commanding General of the Air Force. Tr. from the German by J. Hawley Lamed, Nashville, Tennessee, Battery Press, 1994

**Sound**
8778 Bineham, Lilian Mary
506 Lees, Mary

## Liddell Hart Centre for Military Archives, King's College London
Aston 4/10 1904 Jan 2 – 1929 Apr 11
Brooke Popham 8/5 1920 Jan
Douglas Scott-Montagu 3/9 1916 May 31
Douglas Scott-Montagu 4/9 1917 Jun 26
Douglas Scott-Montagu 4/10 1917 Jun 28
Douglas Scott-Montagu 4/15 [1917]
Douglas Scott-Montagu 4/17 1917 Nov 13
Douglas Scott-Montagu 6/1 1916
Fuller 4/3/174 1915 Dec 29
Hamilton 16/456 1934 Jun 10
Hamilton 20/3/12 1917 May 13 – 1917 Aug 15
Liddell 15/2/26 1916–1961
Robertson 7/7/61 1917 Oct 18
Robertson 7/7/62 1917 Oct 21
Robertson 7/6/77 1916 Sep 28
Robertson 7/6/87 1916 Nov 2
Robertson 7/7/35 1917 Jul 9
Robertson 7/7/36 1917 Jul 10
Robertson 7/7/48 1917 Aug 29
Robertson 7/7/56 1917 Oct 3

## Liddle Collection, University of Leeds
AIR 213A Item R6: Robson, J., Letter to P. H. Liddle
Air Misc. Transcripts of recorded interviews: Taff, Miss C. (1890–) (Tape 720); MBE; Ward Sister UCH; Zeppelins and bi-planes; Opinions of Suffragettes; Patriotism of the wounded; Attitude of Doctors and Nurses; Air raids
AIR 254 Ranken, Frances

## London Metropolitan Archives
40 Northampton Road, Clerkenwell, London, EC1R 0HB
Court of Common Council: Streets Committee
committee papers – ref. COL/CC/STS/02
Report of the Chief Officer of the London Fire Brigade, 1919

## McDermott Library, University of Texas at Dallas
The Ferko/Williams World War I Collection
A. E. Ferko History of Aviation Collection
Box 2.14 Lt Adolf Eduard von Marcard Xerox photo albums Kagohl 4/22 FFL ABT 12 and FL ABT 12
Box 61.3 Die Kgl. Wurtbg. Flieger-Abteilung (war diary)

Box 61.4 *Gotha! Death from the Sky*, by Peter Grosz
Box 61.6 Der Kommandierende General der Luftstreitkräfte, Various Photographs of Pilots, 1916
Box 510.6 German Giants
Box 513.12 Fliegertruppe Brieftaubenabteilung O, Lt Leberecht von Viebahn, March–July 1915. The formation of groups and plans to bomb England.
**Kerr Collection**
Box 65.3 Major Wilhelm Siegert (tr. Ursula E. Wolff), 'The German Bomber Squadron Attack on Dunkirk', in *Nachrichtenblatt Fliegerring*, no. 35, February 1926

## National Archives, London
HO45/17577 Civil Defence: Air-raid warning system
HO45/10883/344919 Air-raid damage
CAB37/122/93 (microfilm) Protection of London against air-raid
CAB27/9 Air-raids
MT6/2466/4 Railways under the Thames: danger in air-raids
MT10/1889 Lights – memorandum issued to harbour authorities relating to extinction etc. of certain lights during air-raids
MT23/440 Transport Department Staff – Instructions in the event of air-raids
MT23/770 Proposal concerning lights on the River Thames to give warning of air-raids
AIR 1/564/16/15/82 Precautions to be taken in air-raids; lighting in towns and movement of vehicles
AIR 1/512/16/3/62 Defence of London against air-raids
AIR 1/876/204/5/573 Note on air-raid over London Dec 18/19 1917
AIR 1/654/17/122/498 Restriction on flying by RNAQS when enemy air-raids are imminent
AIR 1/654/17/122/509 Notification to Postmaster General: cessation of enemy air-raids over London
AIR 1/657/17/122/566 Enemy air-raid on Venice
AIR 1/622/17/1222/669 Home Defence: Reorganisation of London air-raid defence
AIR 1/621/16/15/367 Proposed scheme by Mr G. E. Hoskins for defence against air-raid
HO45/10883/344919
HO45/10884/346450 WAR Air-raids: precautions to be taken by the public
AIR 1/460/15/312/99 Morale effect of air-raids on German industrial centres
AIR 1/461/15/312/107
AIR 1/461/15/312/11 Incendiary Operations as a Means of Aerial Warfare
AIR 1/1975/204/273/25 Reported results through various channels of air-raids on German towns

AIR 1/2115/207/56/1

AIR 1/2123/207/73/9 Air-raids on Britain

AIR 1/2123/207/73/14–28 Air-raids on Britain

AIR 1/2126/207/79/23 Höppner translation

AIR 1/2126/207/79/48 German extracts on air-raids on Britain (Bulow, Major Freiherr von, 'Die Angriffe des Bombengeschwader 3 auf England' – articles in *Die Luftwacht* May–August 1927)

AIR 1/2255/209/58/3 Intelligence report on German Service aviation, also proposed air-raids on London

AIR 1/2296/209/77/18

AIR 1/2312

AIR 1/2319

AIR 1/2405/303/4/10 Cuttings on air-raids

AIR/2417/303/42 Cuttings on air-raids

AIR 1/2420/305/8 Reports on air-raids on Great Britain

ADM1/8464 GHQHF (General Headquarters Home Forces) Air-raids 1917–18, vol. I

AIR 1/177

AIR 1/258

AIR 1/588

AIR 1/589

AIR 1/614

AIR 1/668

AIR 1/691

AIR 1/2123/207/73/9 GHQHF Air-raids 1917–18, vol. IA, prepared under the direction of Lieutenant Colonel H. G. de Watteville

AIR 1/2312

AIR 1/2319

AIR 2

CAB 17

CAB 37

CAB 38

CAB 42/16

CAB 38/22/32

CO535

WO32

WO106

CAB/23/2

CAB/23/3

CAB/24

CAB/24/20

## Newham Local Studies Library, London
Beckton School log 1917–1918

## Royal Air Force Museum, Hendon
Miscellaneous Air Documents
Marshal of the RAF Viscount Trenchard Papers
Sykes papers MFC 77/13/12
Air Publications, RAFM
Air Pub 38 'Notes on Aerial Flying'
Air Pub 242 'Notes on Aerial Bombing Parts II and III'
Air Pub 381 'Offence Versus Defence in the Air'

## Royal Aeronautical Society, London
Miscellaneous Air Documents

## Deutsches Technikmuseum, Berlin
Major Wilhelm Siegert, diaries, vol. 6, p. 15, 13 or 14 September 1918

## Bundesarchiv-Militärarchiv, Kriegsgeschichtliche Forchungsanstalt des Heeres, Freiburg
General Oskar von Hutier diary (Tagebuch v. Hutier, W-10/50640)
General Herrmann von Kuhl diary (Tagebuch v. Kuhl, W-10/50652)
*Nachrichtenblatt der Luftstreitkräfte*, Kogenluft, Chef des Feldflugwesens Berichte, Berlin, 1916
Kogenluft, *Nachrichtenblatt der Luftstreitkräfte*, vol. I, Berlin, 1917; vol. II, Berlin, 1918 (Official German History of the Air War)

## Newspapers, Periodicals
*Aeronautics* XLIII, November 1960, pp. 27–9
*The Aeroplane*, vol. XI, no. 23, 6 December 1916, pp. 1,079–81; vol. XII, no. 14, 4 April 1917, p. 846
*Air Classics* XI, May 1975, pp. 20–4
*Air Force Law Review* XVII, Summer 1975, pp. 39–60
*Air Power Historian* VII, July, October 1960, pp. 165–77, 205–15; VIII, October 1961, pp. 194–206; III, April 1956, pp. 134–7; IV, July 1957, pp. 141–9
*Air Power Journal* – Winter 1996
'Air Raids', in *Independent* XCIII, 23 March 1918, p. 480
'Air Raids', in *Living Age*, CCXCV, 10 November 1917, pp. 376–7
'Air Raids', in *Spectator*, CXIX, 6 October 1917, pp. 348–9
*Air University Quarterly Review* VII, Spring 1955, pp. 37–49; VIII, no. 3, Summer 1956, pp. 24–5; VIII, Summer 1955, pp. 88–137

'Air War', in *Life*, LVI, 20 March 1964, pp. 62–78

*Albion*, vol. 13, no. 1, Summer 1981, pp. 43–57

'Alfred Fleischer', in *Cross & Cockade* VI, Winter 1965, pp. 358–61

*American Journal of International Law* IX, January 1915, pp. 93–101

Anderson, Orvil A., 'How Air Power Grew', in *Air Power Historian* III, April 1956, pp. 134–7

*Army Ordnance* XV, 1934, pp. 71–4

Atkinson, J. L. B., 'The Italian Influence on the Origins of the American Concept of Strategic Bombardment', in *Air Power Historian* IV, July 1957, pp. 141–9

'Avion', 'The Evolution of Air Power', in *Army Quarterly*, vol. IX, no.1, October 1924, pp. 328–41

Bahn, Heinrich, 'In a German Airship over England', in *Journal of the Royal United Services Institute*, vol. LXXI, 1926

Baldwin, Mary, 'The Home Front: Victim of the Night Raiders', in *Treasury*, February 1920, pp. 398–9

Barr, M., 'All Clear: How the Pomeroy Incendiary Bullet Saved London', in *Collier's* LXXXIV, 27 July 1929, p. 16

Bentivegni, Richard von, 'Riesenflugzeuge', in *Illustrierte Flug-Welt*, 1920

Bewsher, Paul, 'The First Raid', in *Blackwoods* CCV, February 1919, pp. 257–73

*Blackwoods Magazine* CCV, February 1919, pp. 257–73

'Bombardment from Above', in *Independent* LXXXIII, 20 September 1915, pp. 380–1

'Bomber Tactics of World War I', in *Popular Flying* III, February, June 1934, p. 596ff, p. 135ff

'Bombing Planes and their Targets', in *Scientific American* CXIX, 3 August 1918, p. 86ff

Braun, Immanuel, 'Bombing Missions on Two Fronts', in *Cross & Cockade*, 1982

Breithaupt, Joachim, 'I Bombed London', in *RAF Flying Review* XII, December 1956, pp. 49–50

Bright, Charles D., 'Air Power in World War I: Sideshow or Decisive Factor?', in *Aerospace Historian* XVIII, June 1971, pp. 58–62

—— 'Imperial Air Policy in World War I', in *Quarterly Review* CCXL, July 1923, pp. 74–93

*British History Illustrated* II, June 1975, pp. 40–51

Bulow, Major Freiherr von, 'Die Angriffe des Bombengeschwader 3 auf England', in *Die Luftwacht*, no. 5, May 1927; no. 6, June 1927; no. 7, July 1927

*Business History Review*, XLIII, no. 4, Winter 1969, pp. 476–95

Caldwell, Cyril C., 'I Was a Night Bomber', in *Flying* LVII, September 1955, pp. 36–7ff

Carnahan, Burrus M., 'The Law of Air Bombardment in its Historical Context', in *Air Force Law Review* XVII, Summer 1975, pp. 39–60

Chant, C., 'The History of Aviation to 1917', in *Wings*, vol. II, no. 154, 1980, pp. 61–80

Charlton, L. E. O., 'German Air Power since 1914', in *Fortnightly* CLX, July 1943, pp. 35–40

Clark, V. E., 'Types of Military Aeroplanes: The Possibilities of the Bomber', in *Scientific American Supplement* LXXXV, 25 May 1918, p. 322

Clarke, I. F., 'The Shape of Wars to Come', in *History Today* XV, no. 2, February 1965, pp. 1,108–16

*Collier's* LXXXIV, 27 July 1929, p. 16

Cooper, Malcolm, 'Blueprint for Confusion: The Administrative Background to the Creation of the Royal Air Force, 1912–1919', in *Cross & Cockade*, vol. 22, no. 3, July 1987, pp. 437–53

—— 'A House Divided: Policy Rivalry and Administration in Britain's Military Command 1914–1918', in *Journal of Strategic Studies* 3, September 1980, pp. 178–201

*Cross & Cockade*, vol. 22, no. 3, July 1987, pp. 437–53

Crossmann, Edward C., 'Shotguns for our Aviators', *Scientific American* CXVIII, 2 February 1918, p. 107

*Current History* VI, July 1917, pp. 76–8; VI, May 1917, pp. 333–8; X, April 1919, pp. 151–6; VII, December 1917, pp. 458–60; VI, September 1917, pp. 521–3

*Daily Express*, 7 June 1917

*Daily Mail*, 8 July 1917

*Daily Pictorial*, 8 July 1917

Davidson, Robert, 'The New York Bomber', in *Air Classics* XI, May 1975, pp. 20–4 (how the Germans hoped to employ their Mannesmann [Poll] giant Triplane in 1919)

'Day Bomber Formations 1918', in *RAF Quarterly* II, January, April 1931, pp. 70–5, 253–7

Delang, Kurt, 'Bomben über England', in *Der Frontsoldat*, no. 14, 1937, pp. 435–6

'Dodging Searchlights and Shrapnel in the Old Air Raid Days', in *Literary Digest* LXIII, 6 November 1920, pp. 61–6

*Edinburgh Review* no. 235 (482), 1922, pp. 209–27; no. 239 (487), 1924, pp. 13–26; no. 242 (493), 1925, pp. 380–94

Edwards, Frederick A., 'The Air Raids on London', in *Quarterly Review*, October 1921, pp. 270–91

Emme, Eugene M., 'Technical Change and Western Military Thought 1914–1945', in *Military Affairs*, vol. 24, no. 1 (Spring 1960), pp. 6–19

*Engineer* CXX, 17 September 1915, pp. 265–6; CXXV, 21 June 1918, pp. 537–8

*English Review* XXII, May 1916, pp. 481–6

*Evening News*, various, 1914–21, 1935

*Everybody's* XXXVIII, February 1918, p. 84

Eyb, Robert, 'Protection of towns against air attack', in *Luftflotten* (special edition of Militarwissenschaftliche and Technische Mitteilungen), July–October 1929, Vienna

Fearon, P., 'The Formative Years of the British Aircraft Industry, 1913–24', in *Business History Review* XLIII, no. 4, Winter 1969, pp. 476–95

*Flight* LXVIII, 28 October 1955, pp. 673–6; IX, 12 July 1917

*Flying* LVII, September 1955, pp. 36–7

*Fortnightly* CLX, July 1943, pp. 35–40

Fredette, Raymond H., 'Bombers of the Black Cross: German Bombardment Aviation in World War I', in *Air Power Historian* VII, July, October 1960, pp. 165–77, 205–15

—— 'First Gothas over London: The Story of a Daring Raid and its Aftermath', in *Air Power Historian* VIII, October 1961, pp. 194–206 (the raid of 13 June 1917)

French, William F., 'Dreadnoughts of the Air', in *Illustrated World* XXIX, May 1918, pp. 406–11

*Der Frontsoldat*, no. 10, 1937

Garner, J. W., 'The Aerial Bombardment of Undefended Towns', in *American Journal of International Law* IX, January 1915, pp. 93–101

'A German Airman's Story of a Raid on London', in *Current History* VI, September 1917, pp. 521–3

'Germany's Gotha Battleplane and its Machine Gun Tunnel', in *Scientific American* CXVII, 22 September 1917, p. 201

'Giant Aeroplanes', in *Engineer* CXXV, 21 June 1918, pp. 537–8

Gollin, Alfred, 'England is no Longer an Island: The Phantom Airship Scare of 1909', in *Albion*, vol. 13, no. 1, Summer 1981, pp. 43–57

*Graphic*, 8 & 9 July 1917

Grey, Charles G., 'The Defence of London', in *London Magazine* XXXIX, 1918, pp. 451–8

'Hans Waldhausen', in *Cross & Cockade* VIII, Summer 1967, pp. 103–16

*Hansard*: Churchill, Winston S., speech in the House of Commons, 17 May 1916; Pemberton-Billing, Noel, speech in the House of Commons, March 1917

Henry, J. A., 'Science: The War and After', in *Nature*, 96, 14 October 1915, pp. 150–4

*History Today* XV, no. 2, February 1965, pp. 1,108–16

Horsnaill, W. O., 'Air Navies of the Future', in *Fortnightly Review* XCIX, June 1916, pp. 1,056–63

Hug, A. (ed. N. Shirley), 'Carrier Pigeon Flieger: The World War I Experiences of A. Hug', in *Cross & Cockade*, XIII, no. 4, 1972

*Illustrated World* XXX, September 1918, pp. 54–7; XXIX, May 1918, pp. 406–11

*Illustrierte Flug-Welt*, 1920

*Independent* XCIII, 23 March 1918, p. 480; LXXXIII, 20 September 1915, pp. 380–1

*Journal of Contemporary History*, vol. 15, no. 3, July 1980, pp. 423–42

*Journal of the Royal United Services Institute* LXXI, 1926

Kilduff, Peter, 'Bogohl 3 Combat Log', in *Cross & Cockade* XXIII, no. 1, 1982

—— 'Combat Fliers of Baden', in *Over the Front*, 1989

Kuppinger, O. (tr. Peter Kilduff), 'Bomber Observer: The Reminiscences of O. Kuppinger, Parts I and II', in *Cross & Cockade* XIX, no. 2, 1978

Kuster, K. (ed. E. Swearingen), 'Kuster und der Drachen', in *Cross & Cockade*, 1964

'The Last Flight of Walter Gottsch', in *Cross & Cockade* VI, Autumn 1965, pp. 237–41

Lees, C. H., 'The Aeroplane Bomber's Problem', in *Nature* XCIX, 2 August 1917, pp. 449–50

Lefranc, J. A., 'Dropping Bombs from Aeroplanes', in *Scientific American Supplement* LXXXIV, 18 August 1917, pp. 108–9

Liddle, Peter, 'Aspects of the Employment of the British Air Arm, 1914–1918', in *JRUSI*, vol. 131, no. 4, December 1986, pp. 65–73

'Lieutenant Rudolf Matthaei', in *Cross & Cockade* XI, Spring 1970, pp. 36–43

*Life* LVI, 20 March 1964, pp. 62–78

*Literary Digest* LXIII, 6 November 1920, pp. 61–6; LVII, 8 June 1918, pp. 41–4

*Living Age* CCXCV, 10 November 1917, pp. 376–7

*London Magazine* XXXIX, 1918, pp. 451–8

Lufbery, Raoul, 'A Bombing Expedition', in *Everybody's* XXXVIII, February 1918, p. 84

'Lufbery Vanquished in a Battle with a Huge German Plane', in *Literary Digest* LVII, 8 June 1918, pp. 41–4

MacMillan, Norman, 'A History of the Aerial Bomb', in *Aeronautics* XLIII, November 1960, pp. 27–9

Manton, Grenville, 'Duel in the Dark', in *RAF Flying Review* XII, April 1957, pp. 21–2

'The Method of Bombing from the Air', in *Motor Age* XXXI, 5 September 1918, pp. 28–9

Miller, T. (ed.), 'The Hornets of Zeebrugge', in *Cross & Cockade*, 1970

Millman, B., 'British Home Defence Planning and Civil Dissent', in *War in History* V, no. 2, April 1998, pp. 204–32

Mills, George H., 'Bomber Command of the Royal Air Force', in *Air University Quarterly Review* VII, Spring 1955, pp. 37–49

Morrow Jr, John H., 'Expectation and Reality: The Great War in the Air', in *Air Power Journal*, Winter 1996

*Motor Age* XXXI, 5 September 1918, pp. 28–9

*National Geographic*, Special Issue devoted to World War I, January 1918

*Nature* CXXVII, 3 October 1928, p. 318; XCIX, 2 August 1917, pp. 449–50

'The New Phase of Air Raids on England', in *Current History* VI, July 1917, pp. 76–8

Nickerson, Hoffman, 'Munition Makers and Common Sense; With an Account of War-Time Bombing in the Briery District', in *Army Ordnance* XV, 1934, pp. 71–4

*Nineteenth Century* LXXXII, July 1917, pp. 31–8; LXXXIII, May 1918, pp. 905–12

'Number 100 Squadron Receives its Standard: A Brief History of a Notable Bomber Unit Born in World War I', in Flight LXVIII, 28 October 1955, pp. 673–6

*Outlook* CXVII, 7 November 1917, pp. 371–2; CXIV, 25 October 1916, pp. 445–54

Pankhurst, Estelle Sylvia, *Women's Dreadnought,* 17 July 1917, vol. IV, no. 16, pp. 800–1

Paris, Michael, 'Air Power and Imperial Defence, 1880–1919', in *Journal of Contemporary History*, vol. 24, no. 2, April 1919, pp. 209–25

Pemberton-Billing, Noel, 'Myopia Britannica', in *English Review* XXII, May 1916, pp. 481–6

*Popular Aviation* IX, October 1931, pp. 8–10, 58

*Quarterly Review* CCXL, July 1923, pp. 74–93; CCXXXVI, October 1921, pp. 270–91

Rader, P. D., 'Zeppelin Strafing: Hazards of the Night Sky Over Darkened London', in *Sunset* XL, April 1918, pp. 29–31

Raesch, Josef, 'The Diary of Josef Raesch', in *Cross & Cockade* VIII, Winter 1967, pp. 307–35

*RAF Flying Review* XII, December 1956, pp. 49–50; XIII, April 1957, pp. 21–2

*RAF Quarterly* I, July 1949, pp. 3–7

Ransom, H. H., 'Lord Trenchard: Architect of Air Power', in *Air University Quarterly Review*, vol. VIII, no. 3, Summer 1956, pp. 24–5

Ravalli, Renato, 'Elektron, light alloys and their use in aeronautical techniques', in *Rivista Aeronautica* (the magazine of the Italian Air Force), January 1929

Ray, Arthur B., 'Incendiaries in Modern Warfare', in *Journal of Industrial and Engineering Chemistry*, vol. XIII, nos. 7 & 8, July and August 1921

Richardson, James M., 'The Wartime Diary of Clifford Allsopp, Bomber Pilot', in *Popular Aviation* IX, October 1931, pp. 8–10, 58

Robertson, Scot, 'The Development of Royal Air Force Strategic Bombing Doctrine Between the Wars', in *Air Power Journal*, Spring 1988

Saundby, Sir Robert H. M. S., 'The Development of Bombing', in *RAF Quarterly* I, July 1949, pp. 3–7

*Scientific American* CXIX, 3 August 1918, pp. 86–90; CXVIII, 2 February 1918, p. 107; CXVII, 22 September 1917, p. 201

*Scientific American Supplement* LXXXV, 25 May 1918, p. 322; LXXXIV, 18 August 1917, pp. 108–9

Simonson, L., 'Bombing London', in *Nature* CXXVII, 3 October 1928, p. 318

Smith, Malcolm, 'A Matter of Faith: British Strategic Air Doctrine Before 1939', in *Journal of Contemporary History*, vol. 15, no. 3, July 1980, p. 423–42

Soltan, Arthur M. & Davilla, Dr James, 'The Bombardment of Paris', in *Over the Front,* vol. 4, no. 3, 1989

*Spectator* CXIV, 5 June 1915, pp. 769–71; CXIX, 6 October 1917, pp. 348–9

Speranza, G. C., 'Venice and the Invaders', in *Outlook* CXVII, 7 November 1917, pp. 371–2

'Spotter' (pseud.), 'Bird Up: A Tale of a Wartime Archie: Absorbing Incidents in the Trail of the Anti-Aircraft Forces', 1918

'The Staaken R Giant', in *Cross & Cockade* IV, Summer 1963, pp. 169ff

Stevenson, William C., 'Raiding England from the Sky', in *Outlook* CXIV, 25 October 1916, pp. 445–54

Stienon, Charles, 'Zeppelin Raids and their Effects on England', in *Current History* VI, May 1917, pp. 333–8

'The Strategic Bomber', in *Air University Quarterly Review* VIII, Summer 1955, pp. 88–137

*Sunset* XL, April 1918, pp. 29–31

Sutton, B. E., *Journal of the RUSI*, 1922, p. 346

Sweetman, J., 'The Smuts Report of 1917: Merely Political Window Dressing?', in *Journal of Strategic Studies*, vol. 4, no. 2, Summer 1981, pp. 152–74

Sykes, Sir Frederick, 'Air Defence', in *Edinburgh Review*, no. 235 (482), 1922, pp. 209–27

—— 'Air Power and Policy', in *Edinburgh Review*, no. 242 (493), 1925, pp. 380–94

—— 'Some Reflections on Air Warfare', in *Edinburgh Review*, no. 239 (487), 1924, pp. 13–26

*Treasury*, February 1920, pp. 398–9

Trenchard, General Hugh M., 'Bombing Germany: General Trenchard's Report of Operations of British Airmen Against German Cities', in *Current History* X, April 1919, pp. 151–6

Trenchard, Sir Hugh, 'Aspects of Service Aviation', in *Army Quarterly* II, no. 1, April 1921, pp. 10–21

*US Artillery*, September 1919, pp. 330–42

Vuillaret, E., 'The Defense of Paris Against Aeroplanes During the War', in *US Artillery*, September 1919, pp. 330–42

Wales, David, 'Surprises in German Aviation', in *Illustrated World* XXX, September 1918, pp. 54–7

*Wings* II, no. 154, 1980, pp. 61–80

*Women's Dreadnought*, 17 July 1917, vol. IV, no. 16, pp. 800–1

Woodward, David R., 'Zeppelins over London', in *British History Illustated* II, June 1975, pp. 40–51

Wyatt, Harold F., 'Air Raids and the New War', in *Nineteenth Century* LXXXII, July 1917, pp. 31–8

—— 'The German Creed and the Aeroplane', in *Nineteenth Century* LXXXIII, May 1918, pp. 905–12

'Zeppelin and Aeroplane Raids', in *Engineer* CXX, 17 September 1915, pp. 265–6

'The Zeppelin Raid on London, May 1915', in *Spectator* CXIV, 5 June 1915, pp. 769–71

'Zeppelins in a New Raid Meet Disaster', in *Current History* VII, December 1917, pp. 458–60


## Books

Adam, H. Pearl, *Paris Sees It Through: A Diary, 1914–1919*, 1919

Addison, Paul, *Churchill on the Home Front, 1900–1955*, Cape, 1992

Aerial Defence Fund, *The Aerial Danger and How to Fight It*, Surbiton, 1915

Air Ministry, *Results of Air Raids on Germany Carried Out by British Aircraft, January 1st – September 30th, 1918*, Imperial War Museum; *Results of Air Raids on Germany – October 1918 and August 1919*; *A Short History of the Royal Air Force*, Air Publication 125, 1929

*The Air Raids on England – The Times History of the War*, 1918

Alderson, A. G. D., *The First War in the Air 1914–1918: by a fighter pilot No. 3 Squadron Royal Flying Corps*, 1990

Allen, Hubert Raymond, *The Legacy of Lord Trenchard*, Cassell, 1972

Andler, C., *Frightfulness in Theory and Practice*, 1916

Armstrong, H. C., *Grey Steel: J. C. Smuts, A Study in Arrogance*, 1937

Armstrong, William, *Pioneer Pilot*, Blandford Press, 1952

Aschoff, Walter, *Londonfluge 1917*, Potsdam, Ludwig Voggenreiter Verlag, 1940

Ash, Eric, *Sir Frederick Sykes and the Air Revolution, 1912–1918*, Cass, 1999

Ashmore, Edward B., *Air Defence*, 1929

Ayling, Keith, *Bombardment Aviation*, Harrisburg, Pa, 1944

Balfour, Harold, *Wings over Westminster*, Hutchinson, 1973

Baring, Maurice, *Flying Corps Headquarters, 1914–1918*, W. Heinemann, 1930

Barnett, Correlli, *The Swordbearers: Studies in Supreme Command in the First World War*, Eyre & Spottiswoode, 1963

Bartlett, Charles Philip Oldfield (ed. Chaz Bowyer), *Bomber Pilot, 1916–1918*, Allan, 1974

Beaverbrook, Lord (Max Aitken), *Men and Power 1917–18*, Hutchinson, 1956

Bernhardi, F., *Germany and the Next War*, 1914

Best, Geoffrey, *Humanity in Warfare: The Modern History of the International Law of Armed Conflicts*, Columbia University Press, New York, 1980

Bialer, Uri, *The Shadow of the Bomber: The Fear of Air Attack and British Politics*, 1980

Bickers, Richard Townshend, *The First Great Air War*, Hodder & Stoughton, 1988

Biddle, Tami Davis, *Rhetoric and Reality in Air Warfare: the evolution of British and American ideas about strategic bombing*, Princeton, NJ; Chichester: Princeton University Press, 2002

Bidwell, S., & Graham, D., *Fire Power: British Army Weapons and Theories of War, 1904–1945*, 1982

Bilton, David, *The Home Front in the Great War*, Pen & Sword, 2003

Bishop, J., *The Illustrated London News Social History of the First World War*, Sidgwick & Jackson, 1993

Bishop, William, *Winged Warfare*, 1918

Blake, R. (ed.), *The Private Papers of Douglas Haig 1914–1919*, 1952

Bloch, Darius Paul, *La Guerre Chimique*, Paris, 1927

Blunden, Edmund, *Undertones of War*, 1928

Bond, Alexander Russell, *Inventions of the Great War*, New York, 1919

Boraston, J. H. (ed.), *Sir Douglas Haig's Despatches, Dec 1915 – Apr 1919*, 1919

Boyle, Andrew, *Trenchard: Man of Vision*, Collins, 1962

Boyne, Walter J., *The Influence of Air Power upon History*, Pelican, 2003

Brex, John Twells, *Adventures on the Home Front* (reprinted from the *Daily Mail*), 1918

British Museum (London), *The British Museum*. A selection from the numerous signed letters and leading articles; printed for Sir John Sandys at the Cambridge University Press, Cambridge, 1918

Brooks, Stephen, *Bomber: Strategic Air Power in Twentieth Century Conflict*, 1983

Budingen (ed.), *Entwicklung und Einsatz der Deutschen Flakwaffen und des Luftschutzes im Weltkriege*, Berlin, 1938

Bülow, Hilmer von, *Geschichte der Luftwaffe: eine kurze Darstellung der Entwicklung der fünften Waffe*, Frankfurt, 1934

—— *Geschichte der Luftwaffe: eine kurze Darstellung der Entwicklung des dritten Wehrmachtteils / von Oberst (E). Frhr. v. Bülow; mit einem Geleitwort des Reichsluftfahrtministers Generaloberst Göring*, Frankfurt, 1937

—— *Die Luftwacht*, Berlin, 1927

Burge, C. Gordon, *The Annals of 100 Squadron*, 1919

Burney, Sir Charles Dennistoun, *The World, the Air and the Future*, 1929

Burns, Edson L. M., *Megamurder*, Clarke Irwin, 1966

Bushby, John R., *The Air Defence of Britain*, Ian Allan, 1973

Buttlar-Brandefels, T. von, *Airship Attacks on England: A Lecture Read before the Marine Institute of the University of Berlin*, 1919

—— (tr. Huntley Peterson), *Zeppelins over England*, New York, 1932

Calthrop, E. R., *Some Official Tests of E. R. Calthrop's Patent Safety 'Guardian Angel' Parachute, Type A, from Aeroplanes, at the Experimental Station of the Royal Flying Corps, at Orfordness, in January, 1917*, privately published, London, 1920

Campbell, Sir Malcolm, *The Peril from the Air*, 1937

—— & James Wentworth Day, *Speed: The Authentic Life of Sir Malcolm Campbell*, 1931

Carlile, J. C., *Folkestone During the War*, Folkestone, 1920

Castle, H. G. (Harold George), *Fire Over England: The German Air Raids of World War I*, Secker & Warburg, 1982

Chandler, Malcolm, *The Home Front, 1914–18*, Oxford: Heinemann Educational, 2001

Charlton, L. E. O., *Charlton: An Autobiography*, 1931

—— 'The New Factor in Warfare', in John R. Bushby, *The Air Defence of Britain*, 1938

—— *War from the Air, Past, Present and Future*, 1935

—— *War Over England*, 1936

Chaumier, J. A., *The Birth of the Royal Air Force*, 1943

Chitto, Walter Raleigh, *The War in the Air*, 1922

Churchill, Winston S., *While England Slept*, New York, 1938

—— *The World Crisis 1911–18*, 1938

Clark, Alan, *Aces High*, Cassell, 1999

Clarke, Reverend Andrew, *Echoes of the Great War*, Oxford UP, 1985

Cole, Christopher, & Cheesman, E. F., *The Air Defence of Britain 1914–1918*, Putnam, 1984

Cole, Christopher & Donovan, Tom (eds), *Great Britain: Royal Air Force, Royal Air Force Communiqués, 1918*, c. 1990

Cole, G. D. H. (George Douglas Howard), *The War on the Home Front*, Fabian Society, n.d.

Collier, Basil, *A History of Air Power*, Weidenfeld & Nicolson, 1974

Condell, D. & Liddiard, J., *Working for Victory?*, RKP, 1987

Cooksley, Peter G., *The RFC/RNAS Handbook 1914–18*, Stroud: Sutton, 2000

—— *Skystrike*, 1980

Cooper, Malcolm, *The Birth of Independent Air Power: British Air Policy in the First World War*, Allen & Unwin, 1986

Corum, James S., *The Luftwaffe: Creating the Operational Air War, 1918–1940*, Lawrence, Kansas, University Press of Kansas, c. 1997

—— *The Roots of Blitzkrieg: Hans von Seeckt and German Military Reform*, Lawrence, Kansas, University of Kansas Press, 1992

Coxon, Stanley W., *Dover During the Dark Days*, 1919

Cuneo, John, *Winged Mars*, vols 1 & 2, Harrisburg, Pa, 1942, 1947

Dallas-Brett, R., *The History of British Aviation 1908–1914*, 1933

Darrow, Margaret H., *French Women and the First World War: War Stories of the Home Front*, Oxford, Berg, 2000

Dean, Maurice, *The Royal Air Force and Two World Wars*, Cassell, 1979

Delbrück, Hans (tr. Walter J. Renfroe), *History of the Art of War*, 4 vols, University of Nebraska Press; reprint edition, 1990

Delve, Ken, *World War One in the Air: A Pictorial History*, Marlborough: Crowood Press, 1997

Dickhuth-Harrach, G. (ed.), *Im Felde Unbesiegt*, vol. I, Munich, 1921

*Die Deutschen Lufstreitkräfte von ihrer Entsehung bis zum Ende des Weltkrieges 1918*, 7 vols, Mittler, Berlin, 1941–43

Divine, D., *The Broken Wing: A Study in the British Exercise of Air Power*, 1966

Doerflinger, Joseph, *Stepchild Pilot*, Longo, Tyler, Texas, 1959

Dommett, William E., *Aeroplanes and Airships, including Steering, Propelling and Navigating Apparatus, Bombs, Flechettes, Anti-Aircraft Guns and Search-lights . . .*, 1915

Douhet, Giulio, *The Command of the Air*, Arno Press, New York, 1972

Doyle, Paul A., *Fields of the First: a history of aircraft landing grounds in Essex used during the First World War*, North Weald Bassett: Forward Airfield Research, 1997

Dudley, E., *Monsters of the Purple Twilight*, 1960

Duval, G. R., *War in the Air, 1914–1918: A Pictorial Survey*, Truro: Barton, 1975

Easdown, Martin & Genth, Thomas, *A Glint in the Sky*, Pen & Sword, 2004

Eberhardt, W. von, *Unsere Luftstreitkräfte 1914–18*, Vaterlandischer Verlagweller, 1930

Edgerton, David, *England and the Aeroplane*, Macmillan, 1991

Emme, Eugene M., *The Impact of Air Power*, D. Van Nostrand, Princeton, NJ, 1959

Faber, Henry, *Military Pyrotechnics*, 3 vols, Government Printing Office, Washington, 1919

Fegan, Thomas, *The Baby Killers: German Air Raids on Britain in the First World War*, Barnsley: Leo Cooper, 2002

Ferko, A., *Fliegertruppe 1914–1918*, Salem, Ohio, 1980

Fischer, F., *Germany's Aims in the First World War* (revised edition, 1967)

Fitzgibbon, Constantine, *The Blitz*, Wingate, 1957

—— *The Winter of the Bombs*, Norton, New York, 1957

Fitzroy, Sir Almeric, *Memoirs*, 2 vols, 1925

Fleischer, Wolfgang, *German Air-dropped Weapons to 1945*, 2004

Fokker, Anthony, *Flying Dutchman*, 1931

Franks, Norman L. R., *Above the Lines*, Grub Street, 1993

—— *Casualties of the German Air Service 1914–20: as complete a list as possible arranged alphabetically*, Grub Street, 1999

Fredette, Raymond H., *The Sky on Fire: The First Battle of Britain 1917–1918*, Smithsonian, 1991

French, Major G., *Some War Diaries, Addresses and Correspondence of the Earl of Ypres*, 1937

Fridenson, Patrick (ed.), *The French Home Front, 1914–1918*, Berg, Providence, RI, 1992

Fries, Amos A. & West, Clarence J., *Chemical Warfare*, New York, 1921

Fritzsche, Peter, *A Nation of Flyers: German Aviation and the Popular Imagination*,

Harvard UP, Cambridge, Mass., 1992

Fuller, J. F. C., *The Conduct of War*, 1961

Fyfe, G., *From Box-Kites to Bombers*, 1928

Gamble, Charles Frederick Snowden, *The Air Weapon*, vol. 1, 1931/1947

—— *The Story of a North Sea Air Station: being some account of the early days of the Royal Flying Corps*, 1928

Garner, James Wilford, *International Law and the World War*, 1920

Garrett, G. T., 'Air Raid Precautions', in John R. Bushby, *The Air Defence of Britain*, 1938

Genthe, Charles V., *American War Narratives, 1917–1918: A Study and Bibliography*, David Lewis, New York, 1969

Gilbert, Martin, *Winston S. Churchill*, vols 3 & 4, Heinemann 1975 & 1977

Giles, Joseph, *Crisis 1918: The Leading Actors, Strategies and Events in the German Gamble for Total Victory on the Western Front*, W. W. Norton & Company, New York, 1974

Goble, Bill, *Bill Goble: Lifelong Rebel*, Shepherd's Bush Local History Society, 1984

Gollin, Alfred, *The Impact of Air Power on the British People and Their Government, 1909–14*, Macmillan, 1989

—— *No Longer an Island: Britain and the Wright Brothers 1902–1909*, 1984

Goodspeed, D. J., *The German Wars 1914–1945*, Houghton Mifflin, Boston, 1977

—— *Ludendorff: Genius of World War I*, Houghton Mifflin, Boston, 1966

Grey, Charles G., *Bombers*, 1941

Groos, Otto, *Der Krieg in der Nordsee*, Munich, 1922

Grosz, P., *Gotha!*, Windsock Datafile 83, Albatros Productions, 2000

Groves, P. R. C., *Behind the Smoke Screen*, 1934

Guinn, P., *British Strategy and Politics, 1914–1918*, 1965

Gunston, B., *Fighters, 1914–1918*, 1978

Haddow, G. W. & Grosz, P. M., *The German Giants: The Story of the R-planes, 1914–1919*, Putnam, New York, 1963

Hall, James Norman & Nordhoff, Charles, *The Lafayette Flying Corps*, 2 vols, 1920

Hallion, Richard P., *Rise of the Fighter Aircraft 1914–1918*, Ian Allan, 1971

*Handbook of German Military and Naval Aviation (War), 1914–1918*, issued by the Air Ministry (A.1.2), Imperial War Museum, Department of Printed Books in association with Battery Press and Arti, 1995

*Hansard*, 1914–1918

Harper, H., *The Aeroplane in War*, 1942

Hart, B. L., *Paris: Or, The Future of War*, 1925

Hartcup, Guy, *The War of Invention*, Brassey's Defence, 1988

Hartley, Arthur B., *Unexploded Bomb: A History of Bomb Disposal*, Cassell, 1958

Havard, Cyril, *The Trenchard Touch*, Chichester, Countrywise Press, c. 2000

Hawton, Hector, *Night Bombing*, 1944

Hayward, James, *Myths and Legends of the First World War*, Stroud: Sutton, 2002

Hearne, R. P., *Aerial Warfare*, 1919

Henshaw, Trevor, *The Sky their Battlefield*, Grub Street, 1995

Herlin, Hans, *Udet: A Man's Life*, Macdonald, 1960

Hermann, Hauptmann, *The Luftwaffe: Its Rise & Fall*, New York, 1943 (London, 1944)

Higham, Robin, *Air Power: A Concise History*, Macdonald, 1972

—— 'Air Power in World War I', in *The War in the Air, 1914–1994*, ed. Alan Stephens, RAAF Air Power Studies Centre, Canberra, 1994

—— & Harris, Stephen J. (eds), *Why Air Forces Fail: the anatomy of defeat*, Lexington, Kentucky, University Press of Kentucky, 2006

Hindenburg, Marshal von, *Out of My Life*, 1920

Hogben, Arthur, *Designed to Kill: Bomb Disposal from World War I to the Falklands*, Patrick Stephens, 1987

Hogg, I. V., *Anti-Aircraft: A History of Air Defence*, Macdonald & Jane's, 1978

Hook, Alex, *World War I Day by Day*, Grange Books, 2004

Hook, John, *The Air Raids on London During the 1914–1918 War . . . The Raids on the City of London*, privately published, 1989

—— *Even Such is Time: the air raids on London, 1915–1918*, privately published, 1996

—— *London Air Raid Incidents (1915–1918)*, privately published, 1990

—— *They Come! They Come! The Air Raids on London During the 1914–18 War*, privately published, 1986

Höppner, Ernst von, *Deutschlands Krieg in der Luft*, Berlin 1920/Leipzig, von Hase & Kohler, 1921

—— (tr. J. Hawley Lamed), *Germany's War in the Air: the development and operations of German military aviation in the World War*, Battery Press, Nashville, Tennessee, 1994

Hurley, A. F. & Ehrhart, R. C. (eds), *Air Power and Warfare: The Proceedings of the 8th Military History Symposium, United States Air Force Academy, 18–20 October 1978*, Princeton, New Jersey, 1979

Hyde, Andrew, *The First Blitz: The German Bomber Campaign against Britain in the First World War*, Barnsley: Leo Cooper, 2002

Hyde, Harford Montgomery, *British Air Policy Between the Wars*, Heinemann, 1976

—— *Solitary in the Ranks: Lawrence of Arabia as airman and private soldier*, Constable, 1977

Immelmann, F. (ed.), *Immelmann der Adler von Lille*, Leipzig, 1934

Imperial War Museum (Great Britain), Dept of Sound Records, *Military and Naval Aviation 1914–18*, 1982

—— *The Royal Air Force and the Development of Air Power, 1918–1939*, 1982

Imrie, Alex, *Pictorial History of the German Army Air Service 1914–1918*, Ian Allan, 1971

*Incendiary Bombs and Fire Precautions*, HMSO, c. 1938

Ironside, Lord, *Time Unguarded*, New York, 1962

Jackson, Robert, *Fighter Pilots of World War I*, A. Barker, 1977

Jaeschue, Leutnant, *Die Fliegerbuch*, Berlin, 1918

Johnson, J. E. (James Edgar), *Full Circle: the story of air fighting*, Chatto & Windus, 1964

Jones, H. A. (and Walter Raleigh, vol. 1), *War in the Air: being the story of the part played in the Great War by the Royal Air Force* (7 vols, 1922–37), Naval & Military Press, 2002

Jones, Ira, *Tiger Squadron: The Story of 74 Squadron, R.A.F., in two world wars*, W. H. Allen, 1954

Jones, Neville, *Origins of Strategic Bombing: A Study of the Development of British Air Strategic Thought and Practice up to 1918*, William Kimber, 1973

Joubert de la Ferte, Sir P., *The Third Service: The Story behind the Royal Air Force*, 1954

Joynson-Hicks, William, *The Command of the Air*, 1916

*Keep the Home Fires Burning: documents from the British home front 1914–1918*, Imperial War Museum, c. 1991

Kennedy, Capt J. R., *Modern War Defence Reconstruction*, 1936

Kennett, Lee, *The First Air War, 1914–1918*, New York: Free Press, c. 1991

—— *A History of Strategic Bombing*, New York: Scribners, 1982

Kerr, Mark, *Land, Sea and Air*, 1927

Kilduff, Peter, *Germany's First Air Force 1914–1918*, Arms & Armour, 1991

—— *Over the Battlefronts: amazing air action of World War One*, Arms & Armour, c. 1996

Killen, John, *The Luftwaffe: A History*, Pen & Sword, 1969

Kingston-McCloughry, E. J. (Edgar James), *War in Three Dimensions: the impact of air-power upon the classical principles of war*, Cape, 1949

Kitchen, Martin, *The Silent Dictatorship: The Politics of the German High Command under Hindenburg and Ludendorff, 1916–1918*, London, 1976

*Kriegsbrauche im Landkriege*, Berlin, 1902

Lanchester, F. W., *Aircraft in Warfare: The Dawn of the Fourth Arm*, 1916

Langsdorff, Werner von, *Flieger am Feind*, Gutersloh, 1934

—— *Kriegserlebnisse Deutscher Flieger*, Gutersloh, date n/k

Lawson, Eric, *The First Air Campaign, August 1914–November 1918*, Conshohocken, Pa: Combined Books, c. 1996

Lee, A., *No Parachute*, 1968

—— *Open Cockpit*, 1969

Lee, A. G., *The Flying Cathedral*, 1965

Lefebvre, Victor, *The Riddle of the Rhine: Chemical Strategy in Peace and War*, 1921

Lehmann, Ernst August (tr. Jay Dratler), *Zeppelin: the story of lighter-than-air craft*, Longmans Green, 1937

Lewis, Bruce, *A Few of the First: the true stories of the men who flew in and before the First World War*, Leo Cooper, 1997

Lewis, Cecil, *Farewell to Wings*, Temple Press, 1964

—— *Sagittarius Rising*, Penguin, 1977

Lewis, Gwilym H. (ed. Chaz Bowyer), *Wings over the Somme, 1916–1918*, Kimber, 1976

Lewis, P., *The British Bomber since 1914*, 1980

—— *The British Fighter since 1912*, 1979

Lewis, Wyndham, *Blasting and Bombardiering*, 1937

Liddell Hart, B. H., *Paris, or the Future of War*, 1925

—— *The Real War 1914 to 1918*, Little Brown, Boston, 1930

—— *The Revolution in Warfare*, Faber, 1946

—— *When Britain Goes to War*, 1935

Liddle, Peter, *The Airman's War 1914–1918*, Poole: Blandford, 1987

—— *Voices of War: front line and home front*, Leo Cooper in association with Channel Four Television and Tyne Tees Television, 1988

—— *The Worst Ordeal*, Leo Cooper, 1994

Lindqvist, Sven (tr. Linda Haverty Rugg), *A History of Bombing*, Granta Books, 2001

Lloyd George, David, *War Memoirs*, vol. IV, 1933–6

Longstreet, S., *The Canvas Falcons*, New York, 1970

Lowenstern, E. von, *Der Frontflieger*, Berlin, 1937

Lucas, J., *The Big Umbrella*, 1973

Ludendorff, Erich von, *The General Staff and its Problems* (repub. 1988)

—— *Kriegserinnerungen*, Berlin, n.d.

—— *Ludendorff's Own Story*, 2 vols, New York, 1919

—— *My War Memories*, 2 vols, 1919

—— (tr. A. S. Rappoport), *The Nation at War*, n.d.

—— *Der Totale Krieg*, Munich, 1935

Ludwig, Emil, *Kaiser Wilhelm II*, 1926

McCudden, Captain James, VC, *Fighting and the SE5a*, 1918

—— *Flying Fury: Five Years in the Royal Flying Corps*, Greenhill Books, 2000

MacDonagh, Michael, *In London During the Great War*, 1935

McKee, Alexander, *The Friendless Sky: the story of air combat in World War 1*, Mayflower, 1968

Macmillan, Norman, *The Chosen Instrument*, 1938

—— *Into the Blue*, 1929

Maddow, G. W. & Grosz, Peter, *The German R-Planes 1914–1918*, Putnam, 1988

Marben, Rolf (tr. Claud W. Greenhill), *English Zeppelin Adventures*, 1986

# BIBLIOGRAPHY

Martin, C., *English Life in the First World War*, Wayland, 1974

Marwick, A., *The Deluge*, Bodley Head, 1965

Mason, Francis Kenneth, *Battle over Britain: A History of the German air assaults on Great Britain, 1917–18 and July–December 1940; and of the development of Britain's air defences between the World Wars*, McWhirter Twins Ltd, 1969

Miller, Henry W., *The Paris Gun: The Bombardment of Paris by the German Long Range Guns and the Great German Offensive of 1918*, New York, 1930

Miller, L., *The Chronicles of 55 Squadron RFC & RAF*, 1919

Mitchell, W., *Winged Defense*, New York, 1925

Mohr, Eike, *Heeres- und Truppengeschichte des Deutschen Reiches und seiner Lander 1806 bis 1918*, Osnabruck, 1989

Monson, E. C. P. & Marsland, Ellis, *Air Raid Damage in London: Being a Record of the Effect of Aircraft Attack on Certain Public and Private Buildings*, 1923

Montane, J., *Histoire Illustrée de la Guerre Aérienne*, n.d.

Morison, Frank (pseud. for Albert H. Ross), *War on Great Cities: A Study of the Facts*, 1937

Morris, Alan, *First of the Many*, Jarrold, 1968

Morris, Captain Joseph, *Distribution of Propaganda by Air, 1914–1918*, Lee Richards, 2001

—— *The German Air Raids on Great Britain 1914–1918*, 1925

Morrow Jr, John Howard, *Building German Air Power 1909–1914*, University of Tennessee Press, Knoxville, 1976

—— 'The Defeat of the German and Austro-Hungarian Air Forces in the Great War, 1909–1918', in Robin Higham & Stephen J. Harris (eds), *Why Air Forces Fail*, University of Kentucky, 2006

—— *German Air Power in World War I*, University of Nebraska Press, Lincoln, 1982

—— *The Great War in the Air: military aviation from 1909 to 1921*, Washington: Smithsonian Institution Press, c. 1993

Moynihan, M., *People at War 1914–1918*, David & Charles, Newton Abbot, 1973

Muddock, Joyce Emmerson Preston (Dick Donovan), *'All Clear': a brief record of the work of the London Special Constabulary, 1914–1919*, 1920

Munson, Kenneth, *Bombers 1914–1919*, Blandford Press, 1968

—— *Fighters 1914–1918*, Blandford Press, 1968

Murray, Williamson, *War in the Air, 1914–45*, Cassell, 1999

Musciano, Walter A., *Lieutenant Werner Voss*, Hobby Helpers, New York, 1962

'Neon', *The Great Delusion*, 1927

Neumann, Georg Paul, *Die Deutschen Luftstreitkräfte in Weltkriege*, Berlin, 1920

—— *The German Air Force in the Great War*, Cedric Chivers Ltd, 1969

—— (ed.), *In der Luft Unbesiegt*, Munich, 1923

Night-Hawk, *Rovers of the Night Sky*, Greenhill, 1984

Noffsinger, James P., *World War I Aviation Books in English: An Annotated Bibliography*, Scarecrow Press, Metuchen, NJ, 1987

Norman, Aaron, *The Great Air War*, New York: Macmillan, 1968

Norris, G., *The Royal Flying Corps: A History*, 1965

Norton, Graham, *London before the Blitz, 1906–40: from the coming of the motor-car to the outbreak of war*, Macdonald, 1970

Nowarra, Heinz J., *Eisernes Kreuz und Balankreuz*, Mainz, 1968

—— *A Pictorial History of the Luftwaffe*, 3 vols, Berlin, 1961–7

O'Connor, Neal W., *Aviation Awards of Imperial Germany in World War I and the Men Who Earned Them: Aviation Awards of Eight German States and the Three Free Cities*, Schiffer Publishing, 2002

Odhams, W. J. B., *The Story of the Bomb*, privately published, London, 1918

Offermann, Erich, *Riesenflugzeuge*, Schmidt, Berlin, 1927

—— *Die Technischen Grandlagen des Riesenflugzeuges fur den Luftverkehr*, Berlin, 1919

Ormes, I. & R., *Clipped Wings*, 1973

Paget, Henry L., *Record of the Raids*, 1918

Pankhurst, Estelle Sylvia, *The Home Front: a mirror to life in England during the World War*, Hutchinson, 1932

Paris, Michael, *Winged Warfare: the literature and theory of aerial warfare in Britain, 1859–1917*, Manchester: Manchester University Press, c. 1992

Pattinson, L. A., *History of 99 Squadron Independent Force*, 1920

Pemberton-Billing, Noel, *Air War: How to Wage It*, 1916

—— *Defence Against the Night Bomber*, 1941

—— *PB: The Story of his Life*, 1917

Penrose, H., *British Aviation: The Great War and Armistice, 1915–1919*, 1969

Philpott, Bryan, *History of the German Airforce*, Gallery, 1986

Pisano, Dominick A., Dietz, Thomas J., Gernstein, Joanne M., & Schneide, Karl S., *Memory and the Great War in the Air*, University of Washington Press for the National Air and Space Museum, Seattle, Washington, 1992

Playne, Caroline Elisabeth, *Britain Holds On*, 1933

Pletschacher, P., *Die Koniglichen Bayerischen Fliegertruppen 1912–1919*, Stuttgart, 1978

Poolman, Kenneth, *Zeppelins Against London*, John Day, New York, 1961

—— *Zeppelins Over London*, Evans Bros, 1960

Popham, H., *Into Wind*, Hamish Hamilton, 1969

Pound, Reginald & Harmsworth, Geoffrey, *Northcliffe*, Cassell, 1959

Powers, B. D., *Strategy Without Slide-Rule: British Air Strategy, 1914–1918*, 1976

Prentiss, Augustin, *Chemicals in War*, New York, 1937

Price, Alfred, *Sky Warriors: Classic Air War Battles*, Arms & Armour, 1994

Raschen, Hermann & Hoffmann, Peter, *75 Jahre Chemische Fabrik Griesheim-Elektron (1863–1938)*, Griesheim am Main, 1938

Rawlinson, Sir Alfred, *The Defence of London 1915–1918*, 1923

Reid, Captain A. C., *Planes and Personalities*, 1920

Rennles, Keith, *Independent Force: The War Diary of the Daylight Bomber Squadrons of the Independent Air Force*, Grub Street, 2002

Repington, Charles a Court, *The First World War*, 1920

Reynolds, Quentin James, *They Fought for the Sky: The Story of the First War in the Air*, Cassell, c. 1958

Rimell, Raymond Laurence, *Air War over Great Britain, 1914–1918*, Arms & Armour, 1987

—— *The German Army Air Service in World War One*, Arms & Armour, 1985

—— *The Royal Flying Corps in World War One*, Arms & Armour, 1985

—— *Zeppelin: a battle for air supremacy in World War I*, Conway Maritime Press, 1984

Robertson, General Sir William, *Soldiers & Statesmen*, vol. 2, 1926

Robinson, Douglas Hill, 'The Bombing War' and 'Strategic Bombing', in Bernard Fitzsimons (ed.), *Warplanes and Air Battles of World War I*, Beekman House, New York, 1973

—— *The Zeppelin in Combat: A History of the German Naval Airship Division, 1912–1918*, Seattle, University of Washington Press, 1971

Ropp, Theodore, *War in the Modern World*, CUP, London, 1960

Roskill, S. W. (ed.), *Documents Relating to the Naval Air Service, 1908–1918*, 1969

Royal Air Force, *Synopsis of British Air Effort During the War, Air Ministry*, 1919

Royse, M. W., *Aerial Bombardment and the International Regulation of Warfare*, New York, 1928

Sassoon, Siegfried, *Memoirs of an Infantry Officer*, 1930

Saundby, Sir Robert H. M. S., *Air Bombardment: the story of its development*, Chatto & Windus, 1961

*Schlachten des Weltkrieges in Einzeldarstellungen*, Ed Reichsarchiv, 37 vols, Oldenburg, Berlin: Stalling, 1921–30

Schneider, Eric F., *What Britons Were Told about the War in the Trenches 1914–1918*, University of Oxford, 1997

Schröder, Hans (tr. Claud W. Sykes), *A German Airman Remembers*, Greenhill, 1986.

Seesselberg, Friedrich, *Der Stellungskrieg 1914–1918 auf Grund amtlicher Quellen und unter Mitwirkung namhafter Fachmänner technisch, taktisch und staatswissenschaftlich dargestellt*, 1926

Shanks, Edward, *People of the Ruins*, London, 1920

Sherry, Michael S., *The Rise of American Air Power: The Creation of Armageddon*, Yale UP, New Haven, 1987

Showalter, Dennis E., *German Military History 1648–1982: A Critical Bibliography*, Garland Publishing, New York, 1984

Simkins, P., *Air Fighting, 1914–1918*, 1978

Simms, E., *Fighter Tactics and Strategy, 1914–1970*, 1972

Slessor, J. C., *Air Power and Armies*, 1936

Slessor, Sir John, *The Central Blue*, 1956

Smith, Malcolm, *British Air Strategy Between the Wars*, Clarendon Press, Oxford, 1984

Smith, Myron J., *World War I in the Air: a bibliography and chronology*, Scarecrow Press, Metuchen, NJ, 1977

Spaight, James M., *Air Power and the Cities*, 1930

—— *Air Power in the Next War*, 1938

—— *Air Power and War Rights*, Longmans Green, 1947

—— *Aircraft in War*, 1914

—— *The Beginnings of Organised Air Power*, 1927

'Squadron Leader', *The Basic Principles of Air Warfare*, 1927

Stark, Rudolf, *Wings of War*, Arms & Armour, 1973

Steel, Nigel & Hart, Peter, *Tumult in the Clouds*, Hodder & Stoughton, 1997

Stevenson, John, *British Society 1914–45*, Pelican, 1984

Stewart, O., *The Strategy and Tactics of Air Fighting*, 1925

Stone, Norman, 'Ludendorff', in Michael Carver (ed.), *The War Lords: Military Commanders of the Twentieth Century*, Weidenfeld & Nicolson, 1976

Strange, Louis A., *Recollections of an Airman*, Greenhill, 1989

Sueter, Sir Murray, *Airmen or Noahs*, 1928

Supf, P., *Das Buch der Deutschen Fluggeschichte*, vol. II, Stuttgart, 1958

Sutherland, Jonathan & Canwell, Diane, *Battle of Britain 1917*, Pen & Sword, 2006

Sutton, H. T., *Raiders Approach!*, Gale & Polden, Aldershot, 1956

Sykes, Sir Frederick, *Aviation in Peace and War*, 1922

—— *From Many Angles: An Autobiography*, 1942

Taylor, J. W. R., *A History of Aerial Warfare*, 1974

Taylor, John, CFS, *Birthplace of Air Power*, Jane's Publishing, 1987

Terraine, John, *White Heat: The New Warfare 1914–18*, Sidgwick & Jackson, 1982

Thiery, Maurice, *Paris Bombardé*, Paris, 1921

*The Times History of the War (1914–1918)*, 32 vols, 1914–1919

Tirpitz, Alfred von, *My Memoirs*, 1919

Townshend, Charles, ' "Civilization and Frightfulness": Air Control in the Middle East Between the Wars', in Chris Wrigley (ed.), *Warfare, Diplomacy and Politics, Essays in Honour of A. J. P. Taylor*, 1986

Travers, T. H. E., *The Killing Ground: The British Army, the Western Front and the Emergence of Modern Warfare, 1900–1918*, 1987

Treadwell, Terry C., *The First Air: a pictorial history, 1914–1919*, Brassey's, 1996

—— *German Knights of the Air, 1914–1918: the holders of the Orden Pour le Mérite*, Brassey's, 1997

Turner, E. S., *Dear Old Blighty*, Michael Joseph, 1980

Turner, John, *Britain and the First World War*, Hymen, 1988

Ulanoff, Stanley M. (ed.), *Bombs Away: True Stories of Strategic Air Power from World War I to the Present*, Doubleday, Garden City, NY, 1971

Van Emden, Richard, *All Quiet on the Home Front*, Headline, 2004

Vauthier, Paul, *Le Danger Aérien et L'Avenir du Pays*, Paris, 1930

Verrier, Anthony, *The Bomber Offensive*, 1968

Wade, W. L., *The Aeroplane in the Great War*, 1920

Wallace, Graham, *RAF Biggin Hill*, Putnam, 1957

Webster, Sir C. & Frankland, N., *The Strategic Air Offensive against Germany 1939–45: Vol. I, Preparation*, 1961

Weir, Brigadier-General J. G., *Report on Gotha bomber: with notes on Giant aeroplanes*, 1918

Welkoborsky, N., *Vom Fliegen, Siegen und Sterben einer Feldflieger Abteilung*, Berlin, 1939

Werner, J. (ed.), *Briefe eines Deutschen Kampffliegers an ein junges Mädchen*, Leipzig, 1930

White, C. M., *The Gotha Summer: the German daytime air raids on England, May to August 1917*, Robert Hale, 1986

Whitehouse, Arthur G. J., *Bombers in the Sky*, New York, 1960

Williams, Ian (ed.), *Dateline World War I: Facsimile Reproductions of Major Stories from Newspapers of the Day*, Taplinger, New York, 1970

Williamson, R., *The Politics of Grand Strategy*, Cambridge, Mass., 1969

Wilson, H. W. & Hammerton, J. A. (eds), *The Great War*, 13 vols, 1914–1919

Winter, Denis, *The First of the Few: fighter pilots of the First World War*, Allen Lane, 1982

Winter, J. M., *The Experience of World War I*, Macmillan, 1988

Winter, Jay & Robert, Jean-Louis (eds), *Capital Cities at War: Paris, London, Berlin, 1914–1919*, 1977

Wintringham, T., *Weapons and Tactics*, 1943

Wolff'schen Telegr.-Bureaus, *Amtliche kriegs-Depeschen nach Berichten des*, vol. 6, Berlin

Wood, Derek & Dempster, Derek, *The Narrow Margin*, Hutchinson, 1961

Woodhouse, Jack and Embleton, G. A., *The War in the Air, 1914–1918*, Almark Publishing, 1974

Woodman, H., *Early Aircraft Armament – The Aeroplanes and the Gun up to 1918*, 1989

Woolven, Robin, *First in the Country: Dr. Richard Tee and air raid precautions*, Hackney History, vol. 6

Worne, John, *Unrest on the Home Front*, 1930

Wortley, R. S., *Letters from a Flying Officer*, 1982

Wrench, John E., *Struggle 1914–1920*, 1935

Wrigley, Chris (ed.), *Warfare, Diplomacy and Politics, Essays in Honour of A. J. P. Taylor*, 1986

Wyatt, R. J. (Robert John), *Death from the Skies: the Zeppelin raids over Norfolk, 19 January 1915*, Norwich: Gliddon, 1990

Wykeham, Peter, *Fighter Command: a study of air defence 1914–1960*, Putnam, 1960

Zanetti, J. Enrique, *Fire from the Air: the ABC of Incendiaries*, Columbia University Press, New York, 1941

Zuerl, Walter, *Pour le Mérite Flieger*, Munich, Curt Pechstein Verlag, 1938

# PICTURE ACKNOWLEDGEMENTS

IWM = Imperial War Museum, London

**Endpapers:** detail of a map of the positions where Zeppelin and aeroplane bombs landed on London, *Daily Mail*, 1919. Guildhall Library Print Room © City of London

**In the text**
vi–vii Artist's impression of a Gotha bomber floodlit whilst on a mission. IWM/HU97043
viii Handley-Page bomber being tuned up before going on a raid. IWM/Q12037.
x Townspeople posing in front of a bomb crater. Dover Museum
1 German propaganda postcard celebrating Flieger Leutnant Caspar's fictitious first bombing of England, Dover, 1914. Dover Museum
19 'The Raider', British postcard, 1916. Guildhall Library Print Room © City of London
33 German airmen posing in front of 1,000kg bomb. Thomas Genth
55 German officers, men and Gotha behind a crater caused by an Allied bomb, Gontrode, 1917. IWM/HU 63634.
71 A Gotha gunner/observer sucking on an oxygen tube. IWM/ Q73550.
105 Attack on a German-owned shop, London, August 1914. ullstein bild.
145 Anti-aircraft gun and crew in action, Dover, 1917. Dover Museum.
163 Flying officers of the England Squadron with some female company on the terrace of the Château Drory, spring 1917. IWM/Q109948.
177 Diagram of a German incendiary bomb. IWM/Q35390.
187 Pedestrian air-raid warning, 14 July 1917. Getty Images
209 Quadruple-trumpet sound locator. IWM/Q35879
223 London air-raid victims, *Illustrazione Italiana*, 1917. Mary Evans Picture Library
243 Balloon apron set up for the defence of London, 1915–18. IWM/Q61156.
263 Recruitment poster, 1914–18. © Museum of London/Bridgeman Art Library
279 Air-raid damage to the Royal Hospital, Chelsea, 16 February 1918. IWM/HO 33.
295 Leutnant Walter Georgi, the England Squadron's weather officer, prepares to release a pilot balloon from the rooftop of the University of Ghent to measure the wind before a raid on England. IWM/Q73546.
305 Paris gun firing, 1918. © Topham Picturepoint/Topfoto.co.uk.
319 Poster advertising the Ludendorff-Spende, 1918. Funded by war veterans, the Ludendorff-Spende gave aid to those injured in the war. ullstein bild.

340 Map showing British air-raid deaths and casualties and Gotha bomber losses during the First World War.

**Picture sections**

*Section One*

'Macht uns frei': akg-images

General view of Gontrode, 1917: IWM/HN97036; the Kaiser, von Hindenburg and General Ludendorff: © ullstein bild/TopFoto; Captain Brandenburg: IWM/Q108840; Major Siegert: IWM/HN97035; Captain Strasser: IWM/Q58493; Captain Kleine: IWM/Q108841

Gotha in flight: IWM/Q108846; loading bombs: IWM/Q108844; dropping a bomb, 1917: ullstein bild; pouring liquid oxygen into containers: IWM/Q73543; dressing the pilots, 1917: ullstein bild

Aerial view of an air-raid, 7 July 1917: IWM/Q108954; air-raid damage, the Eaglet, London, 30 September 1917: IWM/HO 108; air-raid damage, Odhams Printing Works, London, 28/29 January 1918: IWM/HO122A; air-raid damage, Warrington Crescent, 7/8 March 1918: IWM/HO123C

Upper North Street School, photo by William Whiffin, 1917: courtesy Tower Hamlets Local History Library and Archives; Upper North Street School, funeral: mirrorpix

*Section Two*

Cockpit view of a Giant: ullstein bild; Siemens-Schuckert R 8 Giant Aircraft, from Major Georg Paul Neumann, *The German Air Force in the Great War*, 1921

Area control room: IWM/HU765564; technical diagram: IWM/Q67830; Major General Hugh Trenchard and Queen Mary, 5 July 1917: IWM/Q2536; the men who brought down the Gotha: IWM/HU97329; General Viscount French: mirrorpix

Air-raid shelter, Paris, February 1918: Getty Images; 'British means Pluck', from *The Graphic*, 5 February 1916: Mary Evans/Mary Evans ILN Pictures; London lawyer's office: © Topham Picturepoint/TopFoto.co.uk; air-raid shelter, London, October 1917: Getty Images; sheltering in caves, Dover: Dover Museum; 'L'Heure des Gothas' illustration by R. Vion for *Fantasio*, 1 April 1918: Mary Evans Picture Library

Remains of an incendiary bomb, 1917: IWM/Q54102; Chief Constable Hunt examines an unexploded incendiary bomb: IWM/Q53584; fire-fighters, London, 1917: IWM/HO77; incendiary bomb damage, Messrs G. Briggs & Co., 8/9 September, 1915: IWM/LC47

Dresden after allied bombing, 1944: Getty Images; air-raid damage, Joseph Barber warehouse, Cooper's Row, Trinity Square, London, 7/8 September 1915: © City of London/Guildhall Library, Prints and Drawings

# INDEX